Engaging Campus and Community

The Practice of Public Scholarship in the State and Land-Grant University System

Scott J. Peters, Nicholas R. Jordan,
Margaret Adamek, and Theodore R. Alter

This book draws on research that was supported by the Charles F. Kettering Foundation, the W. K. Kellogg Foundation, and the Cornell University Agricultural Experiment Station federal formula funds, Project No. NYC-137403, received from the Cooperative State Research, Education, and Extension Service, U.S. Department of Agriculture. Any opinions, findings, conclusions, or recommendations expressed in this book are those of the authors and do not necessarily reflect the view of the U.S. Department of Agriculture.

This book is printed on acid-free paper.
First edition, 2005
Manufactured in the United States of America

> ISBN-13: 978-0-923993-15-3
> ISBN-10: 0-923993-15-0

Library of Congress Control Number: 2005938795

In memory of Ron Prokopy (1935-2004)
and Dick Broeker (1942-2004)

Contents

Acknowledgments

This book was made possible by the support and encouragement of many people. We want to acknowledge, first, the support we received from the staff at the Charles F. Kettering Foundation, especially John Dedrick, David Mathews, and Deborah Witte. The value of their steady enthusiasm for, and commitment to, our research would be impossible to over stress. We thank them heartily. We also wish to thank Gail Imig for securing support for our work from the W. K. Kellogg Foundation. Gail's commitment to the engagement ideal in American higher education served as an ongoing inspiration. Dan Decker, professor in the Department of Natural Resources at Cornell University and former director of the Cornell University Agricultural Experiment Station, served as a crucial inspiration for our work as well. Dan's life work exemplifies the civic and academic possibilities of public scholarship. In both his faculty and administrative roles, he has been steadfast in his commitment to the land-grant mission. We offer him our thanks.

As crucial mentors, John Forester and Susan Damme also deserve special thanks. John's innovative use of practitioner profiles as tools for illuminating and interpreting the deliberative dimensions of practice in the urban planning field inspired our own inquiry into the practice of public scholarship. We drew on Susan's relational approach to organizational and professional development as we worked to create a space for scholars to join us in reflecting on the civic dimensions of their practice.

We owe a great deal to the members of our research project team, our case study authors, and all those who offered their reviews, criticisms, and suggestions for improving this book at various points in its development. Included among them are Don Wyse, Okey Ukaga, Paul Schultz, Harry Boyte, Naomi Scheman, David Pelletier, David Campbell, Gail Feenstra, Karen Lehman, Dan Cooley, Bill Coli, Steve Simmons, Susan White, Jeffrey Gunsolus, Roger Becker, Hana Niemi-Blissett, Frank Clancy, Bob Williamson, Ellen Smoak, Margo Hittleman,

Marianne Krasny, Victor Bloomfield, Neil Schwartzbach, Steve Hamilton, Francille Firebaugh, Peg Michels, Karl Lorenz, Craig Hassel, Alton Thompson, Robert Zabawa, John Gerber, Katherine Asher, Katherine Barrett, Jeffrey Bridger, Jennifer Wilkins, Frank Fear, Gerry Campbell, George McDowell, Richard Lerner, Mel Hill, Noëlle McAfee, Maria Farland, David Brown, Claire Snyder, Anna Sims Bartel, Estus Smith, Julie Fisher, and Derrick Barker. Our families and friends also provided us with support and inspiration in ways beyond counting. For everything, thanks. Maggi would like to extend her special gratitude to the elders at the White Earth Reservation, who taught her to think and know very differently about what relationship means in its fullest definition.

For many reasons, this was not an easy book to edit. Ilse Tebbetts, our skilled and insightful editor, deserves a huge thanks for the time she spent working with our manuscript. In numerous ways, the book is much better because of her efforts.

Finally, we wish to acknowledge our profound sorrow over the loss of Ron Prokopy and Dick Broeker, two extraordinary people you will meet in this book who unfortunately died before it was published. For nearly 30 years, Ron served as a professor of entomology at the University of Massachusetts at Amherst. The internationally recognized program of integrated pest management in apple production that he established and led demonstrates the promise of public scholarship in the natural sciences. Dick was a highly skilled and savvy organizer and a lifelong civic leader in his home state of Minnesota. In his work as executive director of a community-university partnership in southeast Minnesota, he demonstrated how indispensable the craft of organizing is in pursuing the challenge of engaging campus and community in respectful and productive ways. We are honored to have had the chance to learn from Ron and Dick, and we dedicate this book to their memory.

-The Editors

Preface

M y admiration for what Scott Peters and the other authors in this book are attempting knows no bounds. But more may be afoot here than they modestly claim. I see *Engaging Campus and Community* as pushing far ahead on the issues raised in the Kellogg Commission Report. I think it points to more than institutions of higher education engaging communities, as important as that is. "Putting the scholar in the world" takes on a more precise and richer meaning in these chapters.

This book may be the harbinger of a public-scholarship movement that will prove to be as profound as the one Christopher Jencks and David Riesman wrote about in 1968 in *The Academic Revolution.* Although talk today speaks of "engaged universities," most of the initiatives I have seen when invited to campus meetings have been faculty initiated and faculty led. Their initiatives could become counter to the trends that Jencks and Riesman wrote about. Public scholarship doesn't reflect the meritocratic politics that Jencks and Riesman found dominating higher education in the late 1960s and 1970s.

This book is evidence that scholars are reconsidering both what it means to know as well as what knowledge contributes to society. The epistemological issues raised by public scholarship push much farther into the terrain that Ernest Boyer explored when he raised questions about research. And, as the authors recognize, public scholarship has significant implications for democracy. Although at this point in time, no one can say where this movement will go, like democracy itself, it may be more a journey than a destination.

Certainly this is a book that other public scholars will find useful. Yet it deserves a much wider audience. Because the book takes higher education outside the confines of institutions, it has a great deal to say to those who stand at the intersection of society and academe—particularly trustees and alumni associations. It even has implications for institutional governance. Although there isn't a chapter on governance, how could "engaging communities" not have implications for those who make decisions about the role of colleges and universities? Furthermore, shouldn't the communities to be engaged have something to say about those decisions? If so, what forum should be available to them?

Having made claims for this book that may be, on some points, more than the authors intend, I should say a bit more about the potential I see in these pages. For instance, the public that public scholars come to see as they go about their research is critical. Perhaps the book's greatest contribution will come from raising questions about exactly what kind of public American higher education is supposed to serve. Juxtaposing *public* and *scholarship*, two words not usually seen together, begs for clarification of both, particularly today. *Engaging Campus and Community* has been published at a time when citizens feel pushed out of the political system. People aren't sure whom they can depend on. The government? Their fellow citizens? Most want to be able to make a difference in combating the problems that endanger them, but they aren't sure they can. What does public scholarship have to say to them?

"The public" can mean anything from just everyone to an aggregation of interest groups. And there is a tendency to think of citizens as consumers of services or the constituency of institutions like colleges and universities. Citizens are the served, not the producers. The obvious problem with these concepts is that American democracy is based on a different notion of citizenship. Collectively, the people are sovereign in our political system. And "sovereignty" is defined by the strength or power to act—to decide, to judge, and to institute change—the actions that make it possible to rule. It follows, then, that as the sovereign, the public must do the kinds of things that monarchs once did— make decisions and act on them. This is why the public is more than an audience to be addressed, a market to be enticed, or a constituency to be served. Sovereign citizens have work to do, which Harry Boyte calls public work.

The authors recognize the issues that are implicit in this concept of the public: If the public is a citizenry-at-work, what does academic research contribute to that work? One answer— and a defensible one—is that academics are not responsible for contributing anything. Should the worth of theoretical physics be measured by what it contributes to citizens doing public work? Surely not. A more acceptable answer is that scholars provide the public with useful expert knowledge. But while essential, that kind of knowledge may not be sufficient for public work to go forward. Here is where the epistemological issues come in. Expert knowledge describes *what is,* but public work requires still anoth- er type of knowledge—"practical wisdom" about *what should be.* That is, the central question in public work is What *should* we do to solve a problem? It is a normative question, and there are no expert answers.

Practical wisdom is sound judgment about what should be done, and it isn't the same as local knowledge. It is socially constructed in a type of dialogue called "deliberative." The ancient Greeks considered this the talk we use to teach ourselves before we act. Public deliberation is weighing possible courses of action to solve a problem against what people consider deeply important to their collective well-being. Perhaps the ultimate challenge for public scholarship is to find ways to contribute to the formation of practical wisdom.

The potential of the public-scholarship movement off campus is as great as the potential on campus. Since public scholarship takes the academy outside its institutional boundaries, it has implications for how colleges and universities deal with the communities that are being engaged. Some would probably argue that trustees are citizens who represent their communities, so there is no problem. Others might advocate public hearings or the other ways official bodies open themselves to citizens. Public scholarship calls for something different, and that is a way of relating to communities so that public work—the work of citizens —flourishes. The usual board meetings and public hearings are not well-suited to building these kinds of relationships. Citizens have to do more than present needs, and institutions have to do more than provide information. Institutions and communities need to create more space for public work to be done, both on and off campus.

Some of this space could be created in the governance structures of colleges and universities. I have met trustees who want a relationship with the public, based on a two-way exchange to identify points at which community organizations and academic institutions have interdependent interests. Trustees need an environment that is conducive to making these connections. One way to create such a setting would be to add a special kind of town-gown forum to the panoply of board committees. I am not suggesting unstructured, open meetings; I have in mind the original meaning of *forums* as "marketplaces." Communities and institutions both have things to trade, which have been identified in this book's discussions of mutual benefits and meshing self-interests.

I am reminded of a proposal for a town-gown exchange once made by one of the American Association of University Professors' (AAUP) founders, Professor James McKeen Cattell. He proposed something more legalistic than a forum, but the purpose was similar to what I have in mind. Cattell advocated combining internal and external constituencies in a unified governance system, an arrangement I always thought had considerable merit. He favored an inclusive corporation of professors, administrators, alumni, and even "members of the community who wished to pay dues to belong." I don't consider such a

"United Nations" as an alternative to separate student, faculty, alumni, and other associations, but as useful public space. Cattell's colleagues in the AAUP rejected his plan, but I cite it now as an example of the governance restructuring that might be done if advancing public scholarship is embraced as a way for a university to engage communities.

My speculations on how far and where the journey into public scholarship may take higher education aren't made to lobby for any particular direction, although I have my own biases. I only want to make the point that the journey is far from complete. Fundamental change in institutions takes decades, and the public-scholarship movement is relatively new. Nonetheless, it has strong traditions to draw on, as well as the energy generated by restless faculty members seeking what the Greeks called "public happiness" (these are scholars who want to validate their public identity in their professional careers). The movement might also make common cause with efforts at civic renewal. Today, we know a great deal more about how the democratic world needs to work and why it fails to live up to its promise. So the public-scholarship movement can go well beyond what was possible during the last decades of the twentieth century. These case studies demonstrate what can happen when scholarly inquisitiveness is joined with democratic commitment. They also show how much more waits to be done.

—*David Mathews, President*
Kettering Foundation

Chapter One:
Introduction and Overview
by Scott Peters

T he clichéd image of scholars as detached ivory-tower
intellectuals who are unwilling or unable to contribute in
direct ways to the so-called "real" world beyond the campus is
widely recognized. While this cliché is in some ways a relic of the
past, it also captures a continuing reality about the minimal extent
to which scholars, especially but not only in research universities,
participate in what are sometimes referred to as "public service"
activities. As James Fairweather (1996, pp. xii-xiii) found in his
examination of survey data of thousands of faculty from hundreds of colleges and universities, "for most faculty public
service, including direct involvement in economic development,
continues to represent such a small percentage of their job that it
hardly registers."

While the image of ivory-tower detachment represents a
familiar, and, if Fairweather's study is to be trusted, dominant
reality about the contemporary scholar, there is a less familiar
counter image that represents another reality. The counter image
is one of *engagement*, of scholars as active, contributing participants in economic, social, cultural, and political affairs. Far from
being new, this counter image is at least a century old. It emerged
as an ideal during the academic revolution that took place in
American higher education in the late nineteenth and early
twentieth centuries (Flexner 1930; Conference of Universities
1933; Coffman 1934; Butts 1939; Hofstadter 1963; Veysey 1965;
Jencks and Riesman 1968; Bender 1993; Fink 1997).

During the past three decades, the ideal of engagement has re-emerged as a key theme in two different but related literatures. First, it is a central theme in the new literature about the nature and meaning of higher education's public-service mission—what it is and who performs it, its actual and potential value for the academy and the public, and its current status. In this literature, new ways of conceptualizing and naming the service mission have been proposed, including "civic mission," "professional service," "service learning," and "outreach" (Martin 1977; Crosson 1983; Elman and Smock 1985; Boyer 1990, 1996; Lynton 1995; Lerner and Simon 1998; Kellogg Commission 1999; Campus Compact 1999; Ehrlich 2000; Checkoway 2001; Braxton, Luckey, and Helland 2002; Jacoby and Associates 1996, 2003; Ward 2003; Kezar et al. 2005).

Second, the engagement ideal is a central theme in a new literature about the problems with and limits of prevailing academic research methodologies, and with the assumptions, aims, politics, and practices of professional scholars (e.g., Lindblom and Cohen 1979; Carr and Kemmis 1986; Lindblom 1990; Harding 1991; Lather 1991; Gitlin 1994; Hammersley 1995). In this literature, more civically engaged and explicitly political forms of scholarship are being proposed and critiqued. These include action research (e.g., Greenwood and Levin 1998; Reason and Bradbury 2001), participatory inquiry and research (e.g., Maguire 1987; Fischer 2000), community-based participatory research (e.g., Strand et al. 2003; Minkler and Wallerstein 2003; Israel et al. 2005), citizen science (Irwin 1995), and contextualized science (Gibbons et al. 1994; Nowotny, Scott, and Gibbons 2001).

As they have developed in the academic literature and in some institutional reform and community-university engagement efforts, conversations about higher education's public-service mission and the problems with conventional research models and practices reflect a general, but not universal, agreement on four related points:

- First, through the work of engagement, higher education's public-service mission directly links the academy with external partners in both the public sphere and the private sector. Ideally, engagement is a *scholarly* activity that draws upon both academic *and* local knowledge and expertise in ways that facilitate and/or produce significant learning and discovery aimed at addressing a wide range of "real-world" problems and issues (Walshok 1995). It should, therefore, not be viewed as being separate from, or unrelated to, the academy's teaching and research missions, but rather as a particular way of pursuing them in collaboration with external partners.

- Ideally, engagement is a two-way activity. It is *mutually beneficial* in that it helps to advance the interests of specific external partners and the general public while it also advances and enhances the interests and work of the academy (Kellogg Commission 1999; Holland 2001). According to the authors of a 1993 report to the provost of Michigan State University, as a result of engagement, "on-campus research and teaching become more vital, more alive, and the intellectual life of the whole university is more stimulating" (quoted in Lynton 1995, p. 11).

- Third, engagement has for various reasons declined in the post-World War II era in both status and frequency (Boyer 1990; Lynton 1995; Bender 1997; Sullivan 2000). The conversation, therefore, has focused on the need for *renewal*.

- Finally, despite widespread rhetoric about the importance of engagement, there are significant barriers and disincentives blocking scholars from pursuing it. In general, engagement is not sufficiently appreciated, valued, documented, assessed, or rewarded, especially with respect to faculty who hold tenured or tenure-track positions (Glassick, Huber, and Maeroff 1997; Driscoll and Lynton 1999; O'Meara 2002; Ward 2003).

There is an additional point, about which there has been
relatively little discussion and agreement, particularly with
regard to proposals for more civically engaged forms of academic
research: *Renewing the academy's civic mission by engaging campus
and community holds promise of contributing to the larger task of
renewing democracy.* This book examines why and how one
group of scholars has pursued this promise.

Democracy, Politics, and Scholarship

The study that led to the publication of this book grew out
of a concern about the lack of direct attention to the democratic
purposes, practices, and contributions of academic professionals,
both as an explicit topic of inquiry in the study of American higher education and as a guiding theme in faculty and organizational
development efforts. An awareness of the neglect of what might
be termed the democracy question—not only in the academy but
in K-12 and adult education as well—has recently emerged in
educational literature (Boggs 1991; Quigley 2000; McDonnell 2000;
Wellman 2000; Schneider 2000; Hartley and Hollander 2005). Such
awareness has been inspired in large measure by heightened concerns about the apparent erosion of the overall quality and vitality of American civic life, and even of democracy itself (National
Commission on Civic Renewal 1998; Eliasoph 1998; Beem 1999;
Putnam 2000; Crenson and Ginsberg 2002; Skocpol 2003).

Democracy is a deeply contested term (Hanson 1985; Held
1996; Wiebe 1995; Crick 2002; Cunningham 2002). Generally
speaking, it describes a political system of elected representatives,
free, fair, and frequent elections, freedom of expression and
association, access to independent sources of information, and
inclusive citizenship (Crick 2002). More expansively cast by
theorists such as John Dewey (Caspary 2000), democracy is a
way of life: not something we have, but something we do.

As David Mathews (1999) and Harry Boyte (2004) have
argued, a broad view of democracy as a way of life—an ongoing

practice that is located in everyday affairs and not just in periodic elections—suggests expansive conceptions of politics and of citizenship. Politics becomes more than just what politicians do. It is also what ordinary citizens do when they come together to pursue and negotiate their self-interests in relation to larger common interests. As Mathews (1999, p. 122) puts it, politics includes "a wide range of formal and informal efforts to solve common problems and advance the common well-being. Politics is acting publicly to foster the well-being of a polity." In Boyte's (2004, p. 5) words, citizenship can be understood as public work: "sustained effort by a mix of people who solve public problems or create goods, material or cultural, of general benefit."

Drawing on these relatively moderate and populist views, we can view the contemporary renewal of the academy's public or civic mission as holding promise for contributing to the renewal of democracy, where citizenship is conceived as public work that is grounded in everyday politics. I acknowledge that in most of the literature on American higher education, the theory and practice of service/engagement is not explicitly conceptualized and discussed in political terms. Yet, the way it has been framed in recent years suggests that engagement is in fact a political activity—not defined by narrow, partisan, activities but by the expansive conception of "everyday politics" embraced by Mathews and Boyte. However it is named—as public or professional service, as outreach, or as engagement—the discussion about the academy's civic mission is focused on the question of how academic professionals and students might more actively and effectively use their knowledge and expertise to address issues of broad public significance.

Ernest Boyer placed this question at the center of his influential and widely read book *Scholarship Reconsidered* (1990). In the book's preface, Boyer (1990, p. xii) proclaimed: "At no time in our history has the need been greater for connecting the work of the academy to the social and environmental challenges beyond the campus." To address this need, Boyer called for the development and adoption of a new and more expansive vision of the meaning of scholarship, one that encourages and rewards scholars who seek to "relate the work of the academy more directly to the realities of contemporary life" (p. 13).

Boyer's book can be read as a call for scholars to engage with their fellow citizens in public work. Such a call raises several practical and theoretical questions:

- First, how and why might scholars choose to become engaged in public work beyond the campus?
- Second, what roles would scholars play, and what contributions would they make, as active participants in public work? How might such engagement enable them to enrich and enliven their research and teaching? In what specific ways might their engagement contribute to the renewal of democracy? As professionals with specialized forms of expertise and knowledge, how might scholars work out what political theorist Mary Parker Follett (1924, p. 4) once termed a "legitimate" relationship with the non-expert public—that is, legitimate with respect to its implications for democracy?
- Third, what kinds of challenges and barriers would scholars encounter in their efforts to become engaged in public work, and how should they respond to them?

Eight Case Studies from State and Land-Grant Universities

These are large and complex questions. In this book, we attend to them by presenting and interpreting a set of eight contemporary case studies of scholars who are actively and directly engaged in public work with their fellow citizens beyond the campus. Our broad purpose is to contribute to the emerging discussion about the theory and practice of academic engagement by illuminating and interpreting its civic dimensions. Following our own experiences and interests, we pursue this purpose within the context of the state and land-grant university system.

While the ideal of mutually beneficial engagement as a means for pursuing the academy's public service or civic mission has been embraced across the whole of American higher education, it holds a particular significance in state and land-grant universities (Lerner and Simon 1998; McDowell 2001). This was demonstrated in 1999 when the Kellogg Commission on the Future of State and Land-Grant Universities issued a call for the renewal of the "land-grant ideal of public university service to community and nation" through a broad-based, institution-wide commitment to engagement (Kellogg Commission 1999, p. 9). The Commission explicitly emphasized that the kind of engagement it had in mind was not a "one-way process of transferring knowledge and technology from the university (as the source of expertise) to its key constituents" (p. 27). Rather, it called for a "profoundly different" approach, tied to a conception of engagement that is grounded in a "commitment to sharing and reciprocity":

> By engagement the Commission envisions partnerships, two-way streets defined by mutual respect among the partners for what each brings to the table. Such partnerships are likely to be characterized by problems defined together, goals and agendas that are shared in common, definitions of success that are meaningful to both university and community and developed together, and some pooling or leveraging of university and public and private funds. The collaboration arising out of this process is likely to be mutually beneficial and to build the competence and capacity of all parties (p. 27).

The Commission's call for mutually beneficial engagement reflects a strong, historically grounded sense of civic identity and mission in the state and land-grant system. This is reflected in historians' use of terms such as *democracy's college* (Ross 1942) and *people's colleges* (Smith 1949) in the titles of their studies on the origins and development of this system. These titles reflect one of the major reasons the land-grant system was established during the second half of the nineteenth century: to bring the academy into close relation with the common people in the so-called "industrial classes" (Eddy 1956/57).

To make good on this aim, a new kind of scholar was needed, one that would be directly and deeply engaged in the nation's life. Henry Clay White, a professor of chemistry from the University of Georgia, prophesied the coming of such a scholar in his 1898 address as president of the Association of American Agricultural Colleges and Experiment Stations, delivered in Washington, D.C., before an audience gathered at the Association's twelfth annual convention. White drew inspiration for his prophecy from "The American Scholar," Ralph Waldo Emerson's Phi Beta Kappa oration delivered in 1837 at Harvard University.

In his oration, Emerson (1837) criticized the received wisdom that "the scholar should be a recluse" and a "bookworm," that scholars are a remote and isolated "book-learned class, who value books, as such; not as related to nature and the human constitution, but as making a sort of Third Estate with the world and the soul." White picked up on Emerson's theme in his 1898 address. But he took it a step further. "The future scholar," White (1899, p. 37) proclaimed,

> particularly he [sic] who should come to illustrate the great Republic, might not be a recluse, a bookworm, a solitary dreamer; he should be filled with the vigor of the young and lusty nation, in intimate touch with and a part of the abounding activities of the nation's life. But Emerson did not clearly foresee that the scholar might be contributory to these activities as well as inspired by them.

Even as White spoke, "future" scholars, such as Perry Greeley Holden, were already at work in the state and land-grant system. Born and raised on a Minnesota farm, Holden earned two degrees from Michigan Agricultural College before taking up a post in 1896 as the first professor of agronomy at the University of Illinois (Moores 1970). In 1902, four years after White delivered his address, Holden was offered a position as professor of agronomy at Iowa State College. In accepting this position, he said the following:

> Take the college to the people. Go to the people and help them where they are, as they are, under their own conditions, with their own problems. See that knowledge is translated into actual life, and living, by the people of the state (Holden quoted in Lord 1939, p. 50).

A generation of men and women joined Holden in establishing a tradition of engaged scholarship in the state and land-grant system. By 1909, Liberty Hyde Bailey (1909, p. 192), a pioneering horticultural scientist who served as dean of Cornell University's College of Agriculture from 1903-1913, could report that the "whole trend of education is to put the scholar into the actual work of the world."

With the establishment of the national Cooperative Extension System through the passage of the Smith-Lever Act, signed into law by President Woodrow Wilson on May 8, 1914, a mechanism was created that enabled scholars in land-grant institutions to expand and sustain their engagement in the "actual work of the world" (Rasmussen 1989). While extension in its early years was focused on addressing technical problems in farming and homemaking (referred to at the time as "home economics"), by the late 1920s, its focus had enlarged considerably to include attention to cultural and civic matters. This was vividly articulated in 1930 in a book entitled *The Cooperative Extension System,* authored by two national extension leaders, C. B. Smith and M. C. Wilson. Smith and Wilson (1930, p.1) opened their book with the following paragraph:

> There is a new leaven at work in rural America. It is stimulating to better endeavor in farming and home making, bringing rural people together in groups for social intercourse and study, solving community and neighborhood problems, fostering better relations and common endeavor between town

and country, bringing recreation, debate, pageantry, the drama and art into the rural community, developing cooperation and enriching the life and broadening the vision of rural men and women. This new leaven is the cooperative Extension work of the state agricultural colleges and the federal Department of Agriculture, which is being carried on in cooperation with the counties and rural people throughout the United States.

In 1940, the director of the national Cooperative Extension System, M.L. Wilson, declared that extension's central purpose was civic organizing and leadership development. "Extension workers and others who are charged with assisting in the development of programs to meet not only current needs, but also the changed needs of the world, are vitally concerned with questions of leadership," Wilson (1940, p. 4) wrote. "Their primary job is to help the community analyze its problems in the light of all available information and so to organize itself that the necessary action can be taken."

Articulating the same basic view in greater detail in 1945, USDA sociologist Douglas Ensminger and University of Kentucky sociologist Irwin T. Sanders wrote:

> One of the really great contributions of extension education is that it develops people as individuals, leaders, and cooperative members of the local community and the world society. Through participation in extension activities farmers gain a new vision. They are brought face to face with their neighbors' problems and thus aided in seeing the interdependence of their welfare and the welfare of their neighbors, their community, and indeed, the entire nation. Problems are thus recognized as being group problems requiring group consideration and action. Working within the democratic framework which exists in most communities around the world, extension can help farm people not only in the solution of their individual problems but also aid them in the solution of their common problems. Extension then becomes education

for action, action on the individual farm as well as group and community action (Ensminger and Sanders 1945, p, 6).

Importantly, extension work was not only viewed as being valuable or beneficial for the development of individuals and communities; it was also viewed as being valuable for the development of better colleges. Ruby Green Smith articulated this view in her history of Cornell University's extension work, published in 1949 under the title *The People's Colleges.* According to Smith, who held an extension faculty position for nearly thirty years in Cornell's College of Home Economics,

> There is vigorous reciprocity in the Extension Service because it is *with* the people, as well as "of the people, by the people, and for the people." It not only carries knowledge from the State Colleges to the people, but it also works in reverse: it carries from the people to their State Colleges practical knowledge whose workability has been tested on farms, in industry, in homes, and in communities. In ideal extension work, science and art meet life and practice. Mutual benefits result for the people and for the educational institutions they support. Thus the Extension Service develops not only better agriculture, industries, homes, and communities, but better colleges (Smith 1949, p. ix).

In its 1999 report, published 50 years after Ruby Green Smith wrote these words, the Kellogg Commission observed that the tradition of mutually beneficial engagement in the state and land-grant university system, a tradition that embodies Smith's notion of "vigorous reciprocity," had eroded and was in need of renewal.

Despite its apparent decline, however, the contemporary case studies included in this book show that this tradition has not disappeared. Nor have its democratic leadership development and organizing dimensions been lost. This is evident in the following summary descriptions of three of these cases:

- A natural scientist from the University of Massachusetts at Amherst spends 25 years out in the fields working closely with apple growers, helping them produce apples in a way that is more responsible and sustainable in environmental, economic, and social terms. He also facilitates discussions among a diverse group of growers, distributors, scientists, environmentalists, consumers, and others about how they might work together to advance their self-interests in relation to the larger public interest. Drawing from research conducted both in the field and on campus, he publishes more than 400 academic papers. He views his work with apple growers as an expression of the mission of his university, which he says is to "create a responsible and socially conscious citizenry."

- On the other side of the country, two social scientists from the University of California at Davis work with citizens to promote, support, and evaluate efforts to build "community food systems." As one of them puts it, their work as scholars is focused on developing "ideas about how people in community settings can create forms of economic development that have a greater degree of democracy and community control and a higher environmental sensibility to them." Through their collaborative work with one community that pursued these ideas in practice, the two scholars publish several papers and book chapters. They see their work as an expression of the mission of their university, which one of them describes as being "about supporting local people, in all their variety, in developing a sense of efficacy, pride, standing, and problem-solving capability that is at the heart of the democratic capability of citizens."

- A professor in the department of agronomy and plant genetics at the University of Minnesota organizes and leads a diverse "knowledge network" devoted to helping farmers in Minnesota learn how to manage weeds in a more sustainable manner. The network involves regular conversations between farmers and university scientists, held at participating members' farms. The lead professor, an ecologist and evolutionary biologist by training, is motivated to organize and participate in the network because he sees it as a means of pursuing "interesting questions about how farming in partnership with nature is really organized." He publishes several papers on these questions in academic journals and books. His scholarly work with the knowledge network embodies his view of the University of Minnesota's mission: to be a "center of learning that is working, above all, to look after the welfare and well being of the democratic society."

In these case studies and five others, we see academic professionals and students in the land-grant system who have chosen to directly relate their academic work to the social and environmental challenges beyond the campus.

In developing and interpreting the cases in this study, our focus of attention was on understanding the nature and significance of scholars' academic and civic purposes and practices rather than on determining and evaluating the actual results of their work. Drawing mainly from scholars' own subjective accounts of their motivations and experiences, our goal was to understand why they choose to become engaged in public work, what roles they play and what contributions they seek to make. Because we are aware that it is not easy to undertake and sustain public engagement, especially for scholars working out of academic cultures that do not always support it, we also sought to identify the kinds of difficulties and challenges scholars who are engaged in public work encounter.

Civic engagement is a relatively new topic of inquiry in the research literature on the academic profession. Despite a long history of public work in the land-grant system (and beyond), there is little research specifically focused on identifying and examining the civic purposes, roles, and contributions of scholars who are employed by this system—or any other system, for that matter

(Wellman 2000). Our research is therefore exploratory, setting the stage for a new line of inquiry rather than building upon an established one.

Public Scholarship

In the conversation that has developed in recent years about American higher education's civic mission, engagement is viewed as a scholarly activity. In this book, we call the scholarly practice of engagement in public work *public scholarship*. As we define it, public scholarship is a particular variety of action research (Greenwood and Levin 1998) and community-based research (Strand et al. 2003). It is creative intellectual work that is conducted in public, with and for particular groups of citizens. Its results are communicated to, and validated by, peers, including but not limited to peers in scholars' academic fields. Scholars who practice public scholarship seek to advance the academy's teaching and research missions in ways that hold both academic and public value.

It is important to note at the outset that we view public scholarship as distinctly different from the public intellectual tradition under which scholars aim to influence public opinion by speaking to, and writing for, popular audiences. The central difference is that public scholars work *with* specific publics, whereas public intellectuals work on behalf of the general public, typically by engaging in social criticism (Jacoby 1987; Fink 1997; Walzer 2002; Melzer, Weinberger, and Zinman 2003). This does not make public scholars inherently "better" than public intellectuals. Each offers something of academic and public value. And it should be noted that scholars might choose to work both as public intellectuals and public scholars. While different, these are not mutually exclusive approaches.

As a new way of naming an old but generally overlooked tradition that dates at least as far back as the Progressive Era, the term *public scholarship* holds a special value as a conceptual tool that can be used to analyze and stimulate discussion and debate about scholars' public identities, roles, and contributions. Introducing the concept of public scholarship into the conversation about the academy's public-service mission serves as an invitation for scholars to view their work through a civic lens. It invites scholars to think critically and imaginatively about how they can make both the methods and aims of their scholarship more public. It also invites scholars to explore how engagement in public work might improve and advance their scholarship.

Public scholarship, as we view it, is an expression of what William Sullivan (1995, 1999, 2003) refers to as "civic professionalism"—a concept that points to the public functions and social responsibilities of the professions. As Steven Brint (1994) notes, professionalism has two aspects: a technical aspect having to do with the competent performance of skilled work and a social aspect that grounds and guides professionals in an appreciation of the larger public ends they serve. According to William Sullivan (2003, p. 10), civic professionals attend in equal ways to both of these aspects by making a "public pledge to deploy technical expertise and judgment not only skillfully but also for public-regarding ends and in a public-regarding way." Accordingly, what makes professionalism more or less "civic" is not just the degree to which professionals' intentions can be shown to be public-regarding, but the degree to which their practices can be shown to be so as well.

The academic professionals and students featured in this book all seek to enact the civic professional's public pledge as they become actively engaged in public work at the local community level. Their engagement brings them into close, working relationship with their fellow citizens beyond the campus. Whether this relationship is legitimate in terms of public and academic goals is a key question; I attend to it in Chapter Eleven in my discussion of the findings of our research.

It is important to acknowledge that almost everything a scholar does—from classroom teaching to the most basic forms of research—can be argued to be public-regarding with respect to its intended purpose of contributing in some way to the general public, however indirect or distant such contributions may be. What is distinctive about public scholarship is its direct and immediate connection to the democratic work of specific publics in specific contexts. Public scholarship is practiced when academic professionals participate *as scholars* in the public work of democratic politics.

There are two audiences we hope to reach with this book. Because our cases are all drawn from the national system of land-grant colleges and universities, our primary audience includes students, academic professionals, and stakeholders in the land-grant system who have a particular interest in learning about how the practice of public scholarship can be an effective means for pursuing the system's civic mission. We also hope to reach a broader audience that includes all those who have an interest in gaining a deeper understanding of how academic professionals and students might contribute to democracy through a public scholarship that puts academic experts in respectful and productive relationships with their fellow citizens. We hope both audiences will find this book to be informative, provocative, and inspiring.

I wish to be clear at this juncture that the purpose of this book is not to argue or imply that all academic professionals should be actively and directly engaged in public work as public scholars. All of us who participated in the research that led to the publication of this book are pluralists who believe that there are many ways to configure an academic career in pursuit of many different ends. Our purpose is to contribute to the emerging conversation about the academy's civic mission. In doing so, we open a line of inquiry into a distinct way of viewing and interpreting the nature and significance of the civic roles public scholars play and the contributions they seek to make as they connect their scholarly work to the social and environmental challenges beyond the campus.

Project Origins

The research project that led to the publication of this book was inspired in part by discussions about public scholarship convened and published by the Kettering Foundation. It was also inspired by the aforementioned 1999 report by the Kellogg Commission on the future of state and land-grant universities, titled *Returning to Our Roots: The Engaged Institution.* We wrote a proposal to the Kettering Foundation for a research initiative that aimed to advance the theory and practice of public scholarship as a means for realizing the Kellogg Commission's vision of "mutually beneficial" engagement. In pursuit of the same aim, two additional proposals were written and submitted to the Cornell University Agricultural Experiment Station and the W. K. Kellogg Foundation.

After successfully receiving funding from all of these sources, we recruited a project team of academic professionals and interested stakeholders with affiliations to several different land-grant universities. Team members were selected on the basis of their personal interest and involvement in the kind of engagement the Kellogg Commission called for in its report, as determined through an informal process of querying key contacts in the land-grant system. In recruiting the project team, we also sought to achieve a measure of diversity in terms of geographic region, academic discipline, gender, race, and stage of career.

Briefly, our approach in this study was to identify, develop, and interpret cases of public scholarship that closely embody the Kellogg Commission's conception of mutually beneficial engagement. In doing so, we followed a collaborative model of inquiry that involved practitioners of public scholarship both in writing or telling stories from their experiences and practices, and in interpreting their meaning and significance (Heron and Reason 2001; Lyons and LaBoskey 2002; Bray et al. 2000).

Following a shared interest, we decided to identify and commission cases of public scholarship that relate to the pressing challenge of facilitating a shift to agriculture and food-system sustainability. Land-grant institutions became committed to placing sustainability at the center of their domestic agriculture and food systems work as a matter of official policy through a memorandum issued in 1996 by the U.S. Secretary of Agriculture. The memorandum committed USDA and the Cooperative State, Research, Education, and Extension Service (CSREES)—which channels federal funding to the land-grant system—to work "toward the economic, environmental, and social sustainability of diverse food, fiber, agriculture, forest, and range systems" by balancing "goals of improved production and profitability, stewardship of the natural resource base and ecological systems, and enhancement of the vitality of rural communities" (Glickman 1996).

Achievement of these goals may appear on its surface to be a relatively straightforward technical challenge that mainly—or even only—requires the production and one-way diffusion of scientific knowledge and technologies. However, as individuals and organizations have pursued the aim of sustainability, they have discovered that the challenges are not solely technical in nature. Working toward sustainability in practice raises a broad and highly complex set of technical, economic, political, ecological, cultural, moral, and even spiritual challenges (NRC 1989, 1991, 1999, 2003; Hamlin and Shepard 1993; McIsaac and Edwards 1994; Pretty 1995; Bird, Bultena, and Gardner 1995; Röling and Wagemakers 1998; Berry 2000; Shiva and Bedi 2002). Farmers, consumers, communities, states, and nations face tough choices about the way food is produced, processed, priced, distributed, marketed, and consumed. The choices that are made about these matters—and *how* they are made—have implications for a variety of interests and livelihoods, the economic, social, and cultural well-being of rural and urban communities, the health and integrity of the natural environment, and even for democracy itself.

Given these implications, the task of facilitating sustainability should be viewed as an educational task that has many dimensions: technical, political, economic, cultural, etc. This positions it as a prime focus for the academy's engagement mission. It points to the need to complement or integrate scientific research that is conducted in on-campus labs with public scholarship that is conducted in the context of specific communities and regions.

It is important to emphasize what is at stake in pursuing the challenge of facilitating sustainability. It is not just the economic interests of consumers or particular commodity groups (e.g., corn producers). Nor is it just the level of agricultural productivity (measured in bushels per acre, for example). It is also the integrity of the environment, the vitality of rural communities and cultures, and the protection and advancement of the larger public interest. Scientific knowledge and technical rationality are important but insufficient resources for citizens to draw upon in discerning and pursuing the public interest. As Fischer (2000) and Flyvbjerg (2001) have shown, other kinds of knowledge and rationalities are of crucial importance in informing and improving the deliberations and decision-making ability of the public.

A brief anecdote from writer and farmer Wendell Berry helps to highlight what can be contributed to the deliberation of publics from what Fischer (2000) calls "cultural rationality." In the preface of his book, *The Unsettling of America: Culture and Agriculture,* Berry (1986, p. viii) writes:

> I recently attended a meeting at which an agricultural econo-
> mist argued that there is no essential difference between
> owning and renting a farm. A farmer stood up in the audience
> and replied: "Professor, I don't think our ancestors came to
> America in order to rent a farm."

What we see here is an expert agricultural economist bringing a form of technical rationality to bear upon the issue of farm ownership. Data, presumably from empirical studies of farmers' incomes, lead the economist to conclude that there is no difference between owning and renting a farm. But the cultural rationality that guides the farmer's perspective leads to quite a different judgment. For the farmer, there is a huge difference between owning and renting, which cannot be captured in measurements of income. These different judgments reflect the differences between the two forms of rationality. As Fischer (2000) puts it, while technical rationality is a mind-set that puts its faith in empirical evidence and the scientific method, relying on experts to make judgments about what ought to be done, cultural rationality puts faith in and takes account of cultural values and ideals, including the cultural ideal of owning one's own farm.

The point of this anecdote is not to imply that one form of rationality is better than the other, but that both are needed if deliberations are to help advance democratic and cultural ideals as well as economic goals and technical problem solving. This has implications for how scholars work out a legitimate relationship with their fellow citizens. It means that scholars who become engaged in the public work of facilitating a shift to sustainability must be open to integrating their technical rationality with cultural rationality.

Selecting the Case Studies

Cases of public scholarship that seek to integrate multiple forms of rationality and ways of knowing in problem setting and solving can be found both at the local community level and at state, national, and international levels. Because they are more common and accessible for study, we chose to focus only on local, community-based cases. Using an informal process of querying colleagues across the country, we searched for cases from land-grant universities that involve academic professionals in active and mutually beneficial engagement with local publics on some aspect of agriculture and food system sustainability. Eight cases were selected for development, and authors were commissioned to write them. Each author was asked to write her or his case in a way that would include attention to the following questions:

- What are the public issues or problems the case addresses, how were they identified, and who was involved in identifying them?

- What are the self-interests and motivations of the scholars and the publics in the case, and how were they identified, negotiated, and/or transformed? How have scholars' backgrounds and life experiences led them to become interested in civic engagement in relation to sustainability?

- In what ways did the case involve scholarly engagement in line with the Kellogg Commission's call? What specifically were the roles of the academic professionals in organizing and facilitating the engagement?

- How were the academic professionals in the case pursuing the academy's teaching and research missions in a way that can be judged to be valid scholarship? Who learned or discovered what from the project described in the case, how was the learning communicated, and who reviewed and validated it for its quality and legitimacy?

- What "habits of mind," politics, relevant skills, routines, and standards for measuring quality were used by the academic professionals in the case? How are these especially or uniquely related to the practice of public scholarship?

- What kinds of public products and/or outcomes were produced?

- What barriers and frustrations did scholars encounter in their work, and how did they deal with those issues? What were the main supports that enabled scholars to pursue the work? What specific roles did money and power play?

- How might the work of the academic professionals in the case have been made more public and more scholarly? What are the next steps in terms of working towards change in relevant institutions and publics that will promote and support civic engagement and public scholarship?

We asked members of the project team and other colleagues to write critical reviews of the case studies at two points in their development. In response to these reviews, each case was redrafted at least twice. The drafts and reviews sparked a good deal of discussion among the project team at three face-to-face meetings and in numerous e-mail exchanges and telephone conversations. Detailed notes were kept during these meetings and exchanges. In addition, project team meetings were tape recorded, transcribed, and shared with team members and authors.

To complement the case studies and expand the study's data, I developed a set of "practitioner profiles" based on the edited transcripts of tape-recorded interviews with 17 of the academic professionals and students involved in the cases. In my interviews, I followed Forester's (1999) approach of drawing out detailed accounts of specific practice stories that are meant to shed light on what practitioners do and experience in specific examples of their work. In response to a series of open-ended questions, the scholars I interviewed provided accounts of three things: (1) their personal and professional backgrounds, which helped to illuminate their motivations and interests, (2) their work and experience in the particular community-based project they were involved in, and (3) their reflections on the meaning and significance of their work and experiences.

While the data generated in this research provide insight into many issues, we chose to focus our attention on three main themes: (1) the motivations, purposes, and interests that compel scholars to become engaged in public work; (2) the roles they seek to play and the contributions they seek to make; and (3) the nature of the difficulties and challenges they face. In line with our theoretical conception of public scholarship, we also looked to our data for evidence that public scholarship can, in actual practice, serve as a means for improving and enhancing both the public work of democracy and the teaching and research missions of the academy.

Overview

Our case studies are presented in Chapters Two through Nine. We begin with a pair of cases that show academic professionals at work with citizens in projects aimed at developing and strengthening community food systems, local efforts to produce, process, and distribute food in a manner that enhances the economic, environmental, and social well-being of particular places. The first case involves the work of two scholars from the University of California at Davis: David Campbell, a cooperative extension specialist in community studies in the Department of Human and Community Development, and Gail Feenstra, food systems coordinator for the University of California's Sustainable Agriculture Research and Education Program (SAREP). The authors describe one example of their work as catalysts, mentors, and chroniclers of community food systems initiatives. They discuss how they connected their academic work to the public work of developing a collaborative agricultural marketing program in Placer County, California.

The second case focuses on a specific example of public scholarship developed through the Experiment in Rural Cooperation (ERC). The ERC is an innovative community-university partnership devoted to establishing and supporting collaborative projects with the University of Minnesota in support of the ERC's mission of fostering a sustainable, "homegrown" economy in southeast Minnesota. The authors explore Judy Brienza's master's thesis, which was devoted to helping Farming with Nature, a cooperative composed of several small-scale pork and beef producers from southeast Minnesota, determine whether and how they might brand and market their products in the region.

The third case study is presented in Chapter Four in the form of a practitioner profile of David Pelletier, an associate professor of nutrition policy in the Division of Nutritional Sciences at Cornell University. It focuses on an ambitious action research project Pelletier conducted in six counties in northern New York. The project was initiated in late 1996, when Pelletier, then an untenured associate professor, received a grant from the Centers for Disease Control (CDC) and USDA to develop and test a model for involving citizens in community-based food and nutrition-related planning and policymaking. The idea for the project emerged from a series of intellectual and professional transformations Pelletier moved through during his graduate studies and 12 years of working as a research and extension associate on nutritional surveillance and community-based nutrition monitoring. Critical reflection on his experience in a series of unsuccessful attempts to influence nutrition policy through standard data collection and dissemination approaches led him to consider experimenting with a more civically engaged approach that would directly involve ordinary citizens in deliberation and action planning on nutrition and food-systems-related policies.

The next two cases, presented in Chapters Five and Six, provide insight into why and how natural scientists have become engaged with citizens and agricultural producers in addressing the issue of sustainability. Chapter Five explores the work of a team of natural scientists from the University of Massachusetts at Amherst (UMass). The chapter is written by two members of the team: Dan Cooley, an associate professor in the Department of Plant, Soil, and Insect Sciences at UMass, and Bill Coli, statewide coordinator of the UMass Extension Integrated Pest Management (IPM) Program. The story focuses on entomologist Ron Prokopy's work in establishing and leading UMass's internationally recognized IPM program in apple production. The authors discuss how the program has evolved over the years, and how the research and outreach efforts it has involved were designed to serve the public interest. Chapter Six features the work of Nick Jordan, a professor in the Department of Agronomy and Plant Genetics from the University of Minnesota. The chapter, which Jordan wrote with several of his colleagues, provides an account of the development and implementation of an experiment in collaborative learning and public scholarship with Minnesota farmers aimed at pursuing the ideal of "farming in partnership with nature."

The sixth case study, presented in Chapter Seven, explores the public scholarship involved in developing and conducting an innovative undergraduate honors course at the University of Minnesota. The course engaged students, university faculty and staff, and Native American elders in examining and responding to an emerging public conflict between the university and the Minnesota Native American community involving the university's research on the wild rice plant. The chapter offers a background on the issue and a discussion of how learning experiences were designed to engage undergraduate students and community members in action-oriented public inquiry.

The last two cases illuminate the work of public scholars engaged with communities on aspects of the sustainability challenge that involve youth. The first, presented in Chapter Eight, involves the work of Robert Williamson and Ellen Smoak, both of whom work as cooperative extension specialists at North Carolina A&T University (NCA&T). Their case focuses on a community-university partnership they built between NCA&T and the Smithfield Middle School in Johnston County, North Carolina. The partnership involved the development and implementation of a youth science curriculum called *Down-to-Earth: Enriching Learning through Gardening* (DTE). DTE encourages youngsters in Grades 6 to 8 to work with classmates, parents, and community volunteers to research a food or fiber production problem of their choice. The authors discuss why and how DTE was developed, the public issues it was intended to address, and the challenges and barriers that were encountered along the way.

The case study presented in Chapter Nine features the work of Marianne Krasny, a professor in the Department of Natural Resources at Cornell University. Krasny discusses her efforts to integrate and balance the interests of faculty colleagues and youth-development educators with her own research and

scholarly interests. It explores this theme through a discussion
of the evolution of her youth program and her research over the
years she has been at Cornell, followed by an in-depth discussion
of *Garden Mosaics*, a program that uses a participatory approach
to engaging youth and community members in research and to
engaging educators in designing educational programs.

The last section of the book contains three chapters. In Chapter
Ten, Victor Bloomfield, Vice Provost for Research and Dean of the
Graduate School at the University of Minnesota, offers an administrator's perspective on the place and value of public scholarship
in the research university. Chapter Eleven presents and supports
the main findings of our research, drawing on case studies, interviews, and other supporting data. In the final chapter of the book,
Ted Alter offers his perspective on what must be done to more
fully achieve the promise of public scholarship and engagement
as a means for pursuing the academy's civic mission.

It is our hope that readers will find this book helpful in
enriching their understanding of how scholars can become
engaged in mutually beneficial ways with their fellow citizens
beyond the campus. In specific terms, we hope that it will help
to strengthen the administrative and political support for public
scholarship in the land-grant system, while motivating and
inspiring its practitioners to improve their practice. And, we
hope that this book will encourage scholars to closely attend—
in a critically reflective manner—to the civic dimensions and
possibilities of their work. Our research became a means for
encouraging such reflection among members of our project team
even as it was conducted. Most of this book's chapters were
written in the first-person, by academic professionals who played
central roles in the cases they describe, and many of the authors
served as members of the project team.

As a product of exploratory research, this book represents
the opening of a door to an expansive new horizon of inquiry. In
this respect, it marks a beginning, not an ending. It also marks a

"returning to our roots," as the Kellogg Commission aptly titled its report on engagement in the state and land-grant system. A democratic-minded, community-oriented mission expressed through the practice of public scholarship does indeed have roots in the history of land-grant institutions. But does it have a future? The answer to this question will depend in part on how the value of public scholarship—for both the academy and the public—is perceived and assessed. We hope this book proves helpful in informing this task.

References

Bailey, L. H. 1909. *The Training of Farmers.* New York, NY: The Century Company.

Beem, C. 1999. *The Necessity of Politics: Reclaiming American Public Life.* Chicago, IL: University of Chicago Press.

Bender, T. 1993. *Intellect and Public Life.* Baltimore, MD: The Johns Hopkins University Press.

Bender, T. 1997. "Politics, Intellect, and the American University." *In American Academic Culture in Transformation,* ed. T. Bender and S. R. Graubard. Princeton, NJ: Princeton University Press.

Berry, W. 1986. *The Unsettling of America: Culture and Agriculture.* San Francisco, CA: Sierra Club Books.

———. 2000. *Life is a Miracle: An Essay Against Modern Superstition.* Washington, DC: Counterpoint.

Bird, E. A. R., G. L. Bultena, and J. C. Gardner. 1995. *Planting the Future: Developing an Agriculture that Sustains Land and Community.* Ames, IA: Iowa State University Press.

Boggs, D. L. 1991. *Adult Civic Education.* Springfield, IL: Thomas Books.

Boyer, E. L. 1990. *Scholarship Reconsidered: Priorities of the Professoriate.* San Francisco, CA: Jossey-Bass.

———. 1996. The Scholarship of Engagement. *Journal of Public Service and Outreach* 1(1): 11-20.

Boyte, H. C. 2004. *Everyday Politics: Reconnecting Citizens and Public Life.* Philadelphia, PA: University of Pennsylvania Press.

Braxton, J.M., W. Luckey, and P. Helland. 2002. *Institutionalizing a Broader View of Scholarship Through Boyer's Four Domains.* ASHE-ERIC Higher Education Report, vol. 29, no. 2. San Francisco, CA: Jossey-Bass.

Bray, J.N., Lee, J., Smith, L.L., and Yorks, L. 2000. *Collaborative Inquiry in Practice: Action, Reflection, and Making Meaning.* Thousand Oaks, CA: Sage Publications.

Brint, S. 1994. *In an Age of Experts: The Changing Role of Professionals in Politics and Public Life.* Princeton, NJ: Princeton University Press.

Butts, R. F. 1939. *The College Charts Its Course: Historical Conceptions and Current Proposals.* New York, NY: McGraw-Hill.

Campus Compact. 1999. "Presidents' Fourth of July Declaration on the Civic Responsibility of Higher Education." *Campus Compact and the Presidents' Leadership Colloquium Committee.* http://www.compact.org/presidential/plc/plc-declaration.html.

Carr, W. and S. Kemmis. 1986. *Becoming Critical: Education, Knowledge and Action Research.* New York, NY: Routledge.

Caspary, W. R. 2000. *Dewey on Democracy.* Ithaca, NY: Cornell University Press.

Checkoway, B. 2001. Renewing the Civic Mission of the American Research University. *Journal of Higher Education* 72(2): 125-127.

Coffman, L.D. 1934. *The State University: Its Work and Problems.* Minneapolis, MN: University of Minnesota Press.

Conference of Universities. 1933. *The Obligation of Universities to the Social Order.* New York, NY: New York University Press.

Crenson, M. A. and B. Ginsberg. 2002. *Downsizing Democracy: How America Sidelined Its Citizens and Privatized Its Public.* Baltimore, MD: The Johns Hopkins University Press.

Crick, B. 2002. *Democracy: A Very Short Introduction.* New York, NY: Oxford University Press.

Crosson, P. H. 1983. *Public Service in Higher Education: Practices and Priorities.* ASHE-ERIC Higher Education Research Report, vol. 83 no.7. Washington, DC: Association for the Study of Higher Education.

Cunningham, F. 2002. *Theories of Democracy: A Critical Introduction.* New York, NY: Routledge.

Driscoll, A. and E. A. Lynton. 1999. *Making Outreach Visible: A Guide to Documenting Professional Service and Outreach.* Washington, DC: American Association for Higher Education.

Eddy, E. D., Jr., 1957. *Colleges for Our Land and Time: The Land-Grant Idea in American Education.* New York, NY: Harper and Brothers.

Ehrlich, T., ed. 2000. *Civic Responsibility and Higher Education.* Westport, CT: Oryx Press.

Eliasoph, N. 1998. *Avoiding Politics: How Americans Produce Apathy in Everyday Life.* Cambridge, UK: Cambridge University Press.

Elman, S. E. and E. M. Smock. 1985. *Professional Service and Faculty Rewards: Toward an Integrated Structure.* Washington, DC: National Association of State Universities and Land-Grant Colleges.

Emerson, R. W. 1837. *The American Scholar.* http://www.vcu.edu/engweb/transcendentalism/authors/emerson/essays/amscholar.html.

Ensminger, D. and I. T. Sanders. 1945. "What Extension Is." In *Farmers of the World: The Development of Agricultural Extension,* ed. E. Brunner, I. T. Sanders, and D. Ensminger. New York, NY: Columbia University Press.

Fairweather, J. S. 1996. *Faculty Work and Public Trust: Restoring the Value of Teaching and Public Service in American Academic Life.* Boston, MA: Allyn and Bacon.

Fink, L. 1997. *Progressive Intellectuals and the Dilemmas of Democratic Commitment.* Cambridge, MA: Harvard University Press.

Fischer, F. 2000. *Citizens, Experts, and the Environment: The Politics of Local Knowledge.* Durham, NC: Duke University Press.

Flexner, A. 1930. *Universities: American, English, German.* New York, NY: Oxford University Press.

Flyvbjerg, B. 2001. *Making Social Science Matter: Why Social Inquiry Fails and How It Can Succeed Again.* Cambridge, UK: Cambridge University Press.

Follett, M. P. 1924. *Creative Experience.* New York, NY: Longmans, Green and Co.

Forester, J. 1999. *The Deliberative Practitioner: Encouraging Participatory Planning Processes.* Cambridge, MA: MIT Press.

Gibbons, M., C. Limoges, H. Nowotny, S. Schwartzman, P. Scott, and M. Trow. 1994. *The New Production of Knowledge: The Dynamics of Science and Research in Contemporary Societies.* Thousand Oaks, CA: Sage Publications.

Gitlin, A., ed. 1994. *Power and Method: Political Activism and Educational Research.* New York, NY: Routledge.

Glassick, C. E., M. T. Huber, and G. I. Maeroff. 1997. *Scholarship Assessed.* San Francisco, CA: Jossey-Bass.

Glickman, D. 1996. *USDA's Secretary of Agriculture's Memorandum 9500-6: Sustainable Development.* http://www.usda.gov/agency/oce/oce/sustainable-development/secmemo.htm.

Greenwood, D.J. and M. Levin. 1998. *Introduction to Action Research: Social Research for Social Change.* Thousand Oaks, CA: Sage Publications.

Hamlin, C. and P. T. Shepard. 1993. *Deep Disagreement in U.S. Agriculture: Making Sense of Policy Conflict.* Boulder, CO: Westview Press.

Hammersley, M. 1995. *The Politics of Social Research.* Thousand Oaks, CA: Sage Publications.

Hanson, R. L. 1985. *The Democratic Imagination in America: Conversations with Our Past.* Princeton, NJ: Princeton University Press.

Harding, S. 1991. *Whose Science? Whose Knowledge? Thinking from Women's Lives.* Ithaca, NY: Cornell University Press.

Hartley, M. and E. L. Hollander. 2005. "The Elusive Ideal: Civic Learning and Higher Education." In *The Public Schools,* ed. S. Fuhrman and M. Lazerson. New York, NY: Oxford University Press.

Held, D. 1996. *Models of Democracy.* 2nd ed. Stanford, CA: Stanford University Press.

Heron, J. and P. Reason. 2001. "The Practice of Co-operative Inquiry: Research 'With' Rather than 'On' People." In *The Handbook of Action Research: Participative Inquiry and Practice,* ed. P. Reason and H. Bradbury, 179-188. Thousand Oaks, CA: Sage Publications.

Hofstadter, R. 1963. "The Revolution in Higher Education." In *Paths of American Thought,* ed. A. M. Schlesinger, Jr. and M. White. Boston, MA: Houghton Mifflin Company.

Holland, B. 2001. *Exploring the Challenge of Documenting and Measuring Civic Engagement Endeavors of Colleges and Universities.* Paper present ed at the Campus Compact Advanced Institute on Classifications for Civic Engagement, March 23, 2001. http://www.compact.org/advancedtoolkit/measuring.html.

Irwin, A. 1995. *Citizen Science: A Study of People, Expertise and Sustainable Development.* New York, NY: Routledge.

Israel, B.A., Eng, E., Schulz, A.J., and Parker, E.A. eds. 2005. *Methods in Community-Based Participatory Research for Health.* San Francisco: Jossey-Bass.

Jacoby, B. and Associates. 1996. *Service-Learning in Higher Education: Concepts and Practices.* San Francisco, CA: Jossey-Bass.

Jacoby, B. et al. 2003. *Building Partnerships for Service-Learning.* San Francisco, CA: Jossey-Bass.

Jacoby, R. 1987. *The Last Intellectuals: American Culture in the Age of Academe.* New York, NY: The Noonday Press.

Jencks, C. and D. Riesman. 1968. *The Academic Revolution.* Garden City, NY: Doubleday.

Kezar, A.J., Chambers, T.C., and Burkhardt, J.C. eds. 2005. *Higher Education for the Public Good: Emerging Voices from a National Movement.* San Francisco: Jossey-Bass.

Kellogg Commission on the Future of State and Land-Grant Institutions. 1999. *Returning to Our Roots: The Engaged Institution*. Washington, DC: National Association of State Universities and Land-Grant Colleges.

Lather, P. 1991. *Getting Smart: Feminist Research and Pedagogy With/In the Postmodern*. New York, NY: Routledge.

Lerner, R. M. and L. A. K. Simon. 1998. *University-Community Collaborations for the Twenty-First Century: Outreach Scholarship for Youth and Families*. New York, NY: Garland Publishing, Inc.

Lindblom, C.E. 1990. *Inquiry and Change: The Troubled Attempt to Understand and Shape Society*. New Haven, CT: Yale University Press.

Lindblom, C. E. and D. K. Cohen. 1979. *Usable Knowledge: Social Science and Social Problem Solving*. New Haven, CT: Yale University Press.

Lord, R. 1939. *The Agrarian Revival: A Study of Agricultural Extension*. New York, NY: American Association for Adult Education.

Lynton, E. A. 1995. *Making the Case for Professional Service*. Washington, DC: American Association for Higher Education.

Lyons, N. and V. K. LaBoskey, ed. 2002. *Narrative Inquiry in Practice: Advancing the Knowledge of Teaching*. New York, NY: Teachers College Press.

McDonnell, L. M. 2000. "Defining Democratic Purposes." In *Rediscovering the Democratic Purposes of Education*, ed. L. M. McDonnell, P. M. Timpane, and R. Benjamin. Lawrence, KS: University Press of Kansas.

McDowell, G. R. 2001. *Land-Grant Universities and Extension into the 21st Century: Renegotiating or Abandoning a Social Contract*. Ames, IA: Iowa State University Press.

McIsaac, G. and W. R. Edwards, ed. 1994. *Sustainable Agriculture in the American Midwest: Lessons from the Past, Prospects for the Future*. Urbana, IL: University of Illinois Press.

Maguire, P. 1987. *Doing Participatory Research: A Feminist Approach*. Amherst, MA: University of Massachusetts, Center for International Education.

Martin, W. B., ed. 1977. *Redefining Service, Research, and Teaching.* San Francisco, CA: Jossey-Bass.

Mathews, D. 1999. *Politics for People: Finding a Responsible Public Voice.* 2nd ed. Urbana, IL: University of Illinois Press.

Melzer, A.M., J. Weinberger, and M. R. Zinman. 2003. *The Public Intellectual: Between Philosophy and Politics.* Lanham, MD: Rowan & Littlefield.

Minkler, M. and N. Wallerstein, ed. 2003. *Community-Based Participatory Research for Health.* San Francisco, CA: Jossey-Bass.

Moores, R. G. 1970. *Fields of Rich Toil: The Development of the University of Illinois College of Agriculture.* Urbana, IL: University of Illinois Press.

National Commission on Civic Renewal. 1998. *A Nation of Spectators: How Civic Disengagement Weakens America and What We Can Do About It.* College Park, MD: National Commission on Civic Renewal.

National Research Council (NRC). 1989. *Alternative Agriculture.* Washington, DC: National Academy Press.

———. 1991. *Sustainable Agriculture Research and Education in the Field.* Washington, DC: National Academy Press.

———. 1999. *Our Common Journey: A Transition toward Sustainability.* Washington, DC: National Academy Press.

———. 2003. *Frontiers in Agricultural Research: Food, Health, Environment, and Communities.* Washington, DC: National Academy Press.

Nowotny, H., P. Scott, and M. Gibbons. 2001. *Re-Thinking Science: Knowledge and the Public in an Age of Uncertainty.* Malden, MA: Polity Press.

O'Meara, K. 2002. *Scholarship Unbound: Assessing Service as Scholarship for Promotion and Tenure.* New York, NY: RoutledgeFalmer.

Pretty, J. N. 1995. *Regenerating Agriculture: Policies and Practice for Sustainability and Self-reliance.* Washington, DC: Joseph Henry Press.

Putnam, Robert D. 2000. *Bowling Alone: The Collapse and Revival of American Community.* New York, NY: Simon and Schuster.

Quigley, B. A. 2000. "Adult Education and Democracy: Reclaiming Our Voice Through Social Policy." In *Handbook of Adult and Continuing Education,* ed. Arthur L. Wilson and Elisabeth R. Hayes. San Francisco, CA: Jossey-Bass.

Rasmussen, W. D. 1989. *Taking the University to the People: Seventy-Five Years of Cooperative Extension.* Ames, IA: Iowa State University Press.

Reason, P. and H. Bradbury, ed. 2001. *The Handbook of Action Research: Participative Inquiry and Practice,* 179-188. Thousand Oaks, CA: Sage Publications.

Röling, N. G. and M. A. E. Wagemakers, ed.1998. *Facilitating Sustainable Agriculture: Participatory Learning and Adaptive Management in Times of Environmental Uncertainty.* Cambridge, UK: Cambridge University Press.

Ross, E. D. 1942. *Democracy's College: The Land-Grant Movement in the Formative Stage.* Ames, IA: Iowa State College Press.

Schneider, C. G. 2000. "Educational Missions and Civic Responsibility: Toward the Engaged Academy." In *Civic Responsibility and Higher Education,* ed. T. Ehrlich, 323-344. Westport, CT: Oryx Press.

Shiva, V. and G. Bedi, ed. 2002. *Sustainable Agriculture and Food Security: The Impact of Globalization.* Thousand Oaks, CA: Sage Publications.

Skocpol, T. 2003. *Diminished Democracy: From Membership to Management in American Civic Life.* Norman, OK: University of Oklahoma Press.

Smith, C. B. and M. C. Wilson. 1930. *The Agricultural Extension System of the United States.* New York, NY: John Wiley & Sons.

Smith, R. G. 1949. *The People's Colleges.* Ithaca, NY: Cornell University Press.

Strand, K., S. Marullo, N. Cutforth, R. Stoecker, and P. Donohue. 2003. *Community-Based Research and Higher Education: Principles and Practices.* San Francisco, CA: Jossey-Bass.

Sullivan, W. M. 1995. *Work and Integrity: The Crisis and Promise of Professionalism in America.* New York, NY: HarperBusiness.

————. 1999. What is Left of Professionalism after Managed Care? *Hastings Center Report* 29(2): 7-13.

————. 2000. "Institutional Identity and Social Responsibility in Higher Education." In *Civic Responsibility and Higher Education,* ed. T. Ehrlich. Westport, CT: Oryx Press.

————. 2003. Engaging the Civic Option: A New Academic Professionalism? *Campus Compact Reader* (summer): 10-17.

Veysey, L. R. 1965. *The Emergence of the American University.* Chicago, IL: University of Chicago Press.

Walshok, M. L. 1995. *Knowledge Without Boundaries: What America's Research Universities Can Do for the Economy, the Workplace, and the Community.* San Francisco, CA: Jossey-Bass.

Walzer, M. 2002. *The Company of Critics: Social Criticism and Political Commitment in the Twentieth Century.* New York, NY: Basic Books.

Ward, K. 2003. *Faculty Service Roles and the Scholarship of Engagement.* ASHE-ERIC Higher Education Report vol. 29 no. 5. San Francisco, CA: Jossey-Bass.

Wellman, J. V. 2000. "Accounting for the Civic Role: Assessment and Accountability Strategies for Civic Education and Institutional Service." In *Civic Responsibility and Higher Education,* ed. T. Ehrlich, 323-344. Westport, CT: Oryx Press.

White, H. C. 1899. "President's Address." In *Proceedings of the Twelfth Annual Convention of the Association of American Agricultural Colleges and Experiment Stations.* Washington, DC: USDA.

Wiebe, R. H. 1995. *Self-Rule: A Cultural History of American Democracy.* Chicago, IL: University of Chicago Press.

Wilson, M. L. 1940. "Foreword." In D. Sanderson, *Leadership for Rural Life.* New York, NY: Association Press.

Chapter Two:

Community Food Systems and the Work of Public Scholarship

by David Campbell and Gail Feenstra

W hen politicians want to hear from the agricultural public, they seek input from organized constituencies, such as the farm lobby or agrochemical companies, or gather advice from opinion polls. When marketing executives map the food-buying public they see shifting market niches and mutable consumer preferences that can be exploited for private gain. These conceptions of "the public"—as a previously organized constituency, an aggregation of individual opinions, or changeable consumer segments—differ markedly from a democratic vision in which publics emerge through active citizenship. From the democratic standpoint, the quality of being public is tied to a particular kind of civic relationship, in which a broad array of citizens engage in collective deliberation, public judgment, and community problem solving, guided by widely held values.

For the past decade, the authors have been engaged in public scholarship that has sought to envision and catalyze food and agricultural publics that embody these democratic features. Two premises ground our work. The first is that democratic publics do exist, but mostly in latent form. Unlike well-defined political con-stituencies or consumer niches, these publics must be patiently nurtured into being before their civic energy can be tapped. The second premise is that scholars working in land-grant universities have a special responsibility to take on this work of creating and engaging democratic publics, since this work is at the heart of the historic land-grant mission. This is particularly true in the realm of food and agricultural issues.

In this chapter we seek to illuminate some of the scholarly roles, relationships, and routines that have marked our imperfect but determined efforts to pursue public scholarship on these terms. The examples we cite come from a decade-long engagement with *community food system* initiatives in California—local efforts to produce, process, and distribute food in a manner that enhances the economic, environmental, and social well-being of particular places. Our purpose is threefold: 1) to describe our roles and activities as public scholars—specifically, how we went about framing the community food systems concept, supporting local implementation, and evaluating the results; 2) to assess the public and professional outcomes of the work; and 3) to use this case history to reflect on the meaning of public scholarship and the nature of the scholarly activities and challenges that accompany this approach to generating and sharing knowledge.

To ground our reflections as concretely as possible, we will focus on the relationship with one of the more noteworthy community initiatives—a collaborative agricultural marketing program known as PlacerGROWN. The PlacerGROWN case harkens back to a tradition of land-grant education that took root at the beginning of the past century. This approach to scholarship places central importance on "helping people help themselves" by developing a vibrant and democratic public life. The university role is as a partner in public work by which the common good is promoted or defended (Boyte and Kari 1996; Peters 1996). At issue is whether and how this understanding of "education for democratic citizenship" is relevant to the land-grant university in the twenty-first century, and to the society it exists to serve (Sullivan 2000; Campus Compact 1998).

The Context

Public scholarship implies a relationship between campus-based academics and some identifiable community. In the case of PlacerGROWN, university and community actors brought distinct but complementary motivations, interests, and goals to the table, as well as somewhat different understandings of the public issues that were at stake. These starting points reflected the campus and community contexts that gave shape to the common work. What follows describes these contexts, focusing first on the professional commitments of the authors and the institutional space that enabled us to link our commitments to those of the community—in this case provided by the University of California Sustainable Agriculture Research and Education Program (SAREP). We then describe the community setting and the nature and goals of the PlacerGROWN organization.

The Academic Perspective

Community voice played a strong role in the creation of SAREP, a statewide cooperative extension program of the University of California. Community organizers put concerns about university research priorities on the legislative agenda, and this advocacy led to 1986 legislation (SB 872) that created an institutional home in the university for research and education work oriented toward agricultural sustainability. Many early SAREP supporters shared concerns about the public-interest role of the land-grant university, and the legislation articulated a broad, integrated systems definition of agriculture that included social and political issues of farm labor and public health. The wording of the legislation defined the parameters of the program in a way that created unique institutional space for a UC-administered program and an unusual degree of community engagement. For example, SAREP's program advisory committee includes public members who join academics in reviewing proposals to its competitive grants program.

While the initial focus of SAREP's grants program was on developing viable alternatives to pesticides for farmers, the founding legislation speaks to a broader set of concerns regarding sustainability. SAREP's purpose is defined in Article 8, section 552 b:

> This article is intended to foster economically and ecologically beneficial means of soil improvement, pest management, irrigation, cultivation, harvesting, *transportation, and marketing for California agriculture* based on methods designed to accomplish all of the following: Produce, *process, and distribute food and fiber* in ways that consider the interactions among soil, plant, water, air, animals, tillage, machinery, *labor, energy, and transportation* to enhance agricultural efficiency, *public health,* and resource conservation. (Emphasis added.)

To consider how to address a broader range of sustainability concerns, especially those directly affecting community quality of life, SAREP convened an economic and public policy advisory committee (EPPAC) in October 1989. EPPAC included representatives from the university's Division of Agriculture and Natural Resources, Cooperative Extension, and grassroots farm policy and environmental organizations. Over a six-month period, EPPAC met three times at different locations in the state. EPPAC recommended that SAREP award one-third of its competitive grant money to action-oriented research in three areas: farm labor, rural community development, and economic and policy issues related to sustainable production practices.

The authors were the SAREP staff with responsibility for implementing these recommendations. Gail Feenstra has worked at SAREP since 1987, where her title is now Food Systems Analyst. David Campbell was hired in 1991 to develop SAREP's social and policy-related work and then continued to work with Feenstra on community food system initiatives after leaving SAREP in 1996 to become director of the UC Davis-based California Communities

Program. Since April 2000, he has been a cooperative extension specialist in community studies in the Department of Human and Community Development at UC Davis.

At the time we worked together at SAREP, neither of us were in tenure-track positions, though both of us held terminal degrees. As a nutritionist, Feenstra is particularly interested in promoting direct connections between producers and consumers and providing fresh, locally grown food to consumers in all income spectrums. Through several professional organizations, she is linked to nutritionists, sociologists, and others who are spearheading concepts such as local food systems, seasonal eating, and increased local self-reliance (Gussow and Clancy 1986; Wilkins and Bokaer-Smith 1996). As a political scientist, Campbell is following the revived interest in the concepts of civil society and social capital among academic writers and environmental activists (Berry 1987; Kemmis 1990; Putnam 1993; Strange 1988), as well as the growing literature on the kinds of scholarship needed to connect universities with community issues and problems (Boyer 1990).

As we came to envision it, a *community food system* is not a new, university-conceived and designed technical assistance program to be disseminated and implemented at the local level. Rather, it is an attempt to articulate and give conceptual shape to nascent practical developments in California communities. When we began discussing these ideas in the early 1990s, we were aware of the growing appeal of "community-supported agriculture" (i.e. subscription farms) and the resurgence of interest in local farmers' markets. Guided by these community experiments and by SAREP's institutional philosophy, our idea was to capture a new way to think about and respond to food and agricultural issues, marked by a *systems approach* that identifies the complex inter-relationships between various food system components. By definition, this mode of thinking precluded a "cookie-cutter" approach; the benefits of systems thinking require an open-ended process in which local citizens exercise their own intellects as they marshal assets, make normative judgments, and forge context-specific strategies.

Our interest in doing research and educational outreach that was connected to communities was not coincidental. During our graduate training, each of us was privileged to work with academic mentors who modeled engaged scholarship as they struggled to realize their strong commitments to democracy, equity, and sustainability. Their approach went beyond typical notions of applied research to embody community-based praxis, in which reciprocal engagement and influence between theory and experience is ongoing. Equally important, these mentors have given us hope that it is possible to have respectable and respectworthy academic careers while simultaneously contributing to community problem solving and social justice.

For both authors, religious faith is a source of values and commitment. Within our faith traditions is the idea of being called to promote a sense of community and to work for social and environmental justice. We also embrace the idea of the equality of all people and the necessity of living with hope and patience amidst a prevailing culture in which cynicism and the quick-fix mentality are rampant. We cannot profess to practice these religious values perfectly; nor do we frequently make them explicit in carrying out our work. Nonetheless, these values are an important common denominator that helped to motivate and sustain us as the community food systems initiative slowly unfolded.

Even with these strong commitments, we would never have moved forward without the valuable and nurturing support from SAREP's director and associate director. The director's style was to encourage staff members to use their strengths for the program's benefit. Both authors were encouraged to "go for it" with the full knowledge that they would be backed up in a crunch. Having such a champion in place was critical to our ability to work creatively, taking advantage of the distinctive values, skills, and proclivities each of us brought to the work. Behind the desire to defend community food systems experimentation, SAREP director, William Liebhardt, held consistent philosophy and values. As he put it:

> I'm a firm believer in the land grant concept and philosophy. We do the state's business—what the people want, not some other grandiose concept or philosophy. Growing up in Wisconsin there was a significant rural community and it was fairly vibrant and healthy. The concept of a rural community was where small and medium-sized farms interacted around a town center. We've lost a lot of that in the Midwest, but that was the experience that shaped my vision.

The Community Context

PlacerGROWN started as an outgrowth of a citizen's forum in 1994, organized in response to growing concerns about rapid population growth and the loss of a rural quality of life. Participants shared a sense that the county had reached a critical juncture in which the future of agriculture was in serious jeopardy. Farmland acreage in Placer County had dropped 35 percent since 1978, as the population increased by 4.6 percent per year (Campbell and Feenstra 2001, p. 208). Located along the I-80 corridor between the rapidly growing Sacramento region on the west, and the booming resort areas of the high Sierra and Lake Tahoe on the east, Placer faced the prospect of becoming another California region, like Silicon Valley and Los Angeles before it, in which agriculture gradually disappeared.

Seeking to avoid this fate and exercise control over their future, a group of citizens assembled to articulate a vision of a win-win arrangement rooted in a partnership between local residents and farmers. The idea was to develop local markets and nurture more direct farmer-consumer connections in order to keep small and medium-scale agriculture viable in Placer County. Consumers would benefit from fresh, high quality produce; farmers would get help maintaining economic viability; and the community would be able to preserve working open space and maintain the environmental qualities that attracted both old and new residents to the community. With extensive help from the cooperative extension office, this vision was promoted in a newspaper tabloid insert that was distributed to over 70,000 community residents.

With a start-up grant of $97,000 from the Placer County Board of Supervisors in 1994-95, a diverse planning group made up of farmers, ranchers, consumers, farmers' market managers, and representatives from local government came together to form a nonprofit membership organization that promoted Placer County agricultural products. PlacerGROWN accomplishments during the late 1990s made an impressive list: over 150 paid member-ships; a promotional campaign including a logo, slogan, point of purchase cards, posters, signs and stickers; a farm trail map and harvest calendar featuring agricultural (ag) producers, restaurants, caterers, bed and breakfasts, and other outlets for PlacerGROWN products; educational packets geared to media, consumers, the general public, growers, and restaurants and caterers; a bimonthly newsletter for 1,800 ag producers in the county; an annual farm conference; educational workshops on water and value-added marketing, and a short course on agricultural marketing; a youth educational curriculum; 15 community volunteers trained as food educators; and contacts with local restaurants, grocers, institutions, and other users of fresh produce.

Interviews we conducted with community leaders made it abundantly clear that PlacerGROWN would not have been possi-ble without the staff resources, technical support, and political legitimacy provided by the local cooperative extension office. The three local extension advisors involved with the project (Sharon Junge, the county director; Roger Ingram, livestock; Garth Veerkamp, cropping systems) demonstrated how cooperative exten-sion can spark, nurture, and complement citizen-led initiatives. Despite their location within a university organization that rewards narrowly defined expertise, these local advisors saw themselves not solely as providers of technical knowledge, but as community developers with a broader mandate to ensure that the resources of the university serve ends defined by the local community.

Citizen initiatives are inherently fragile, particularly those that are attempting to counter current trends backed by powerful institutions. The work requires a long-term commitment, but most initiatives lack basic organizational elements needed to sustain themselves over time (Goldrich and Cooper 1984). One could make a strong case that PlacerGROWN would not exist today if not for the county cooperative extension office with the staff and resources to support local action related to the food and agricultural system. For example, extension staff ensured that the ideas generated at the 1994 citizen's forum were not simply recorded but were carried forward and shaped into a proposal to the Board of Supervisors for funding. The local extension office provided space for PlacerGROWN staff, and the three advisors performed essential tasks to complement and extend what would have been possible by relying solely on the minimal staff, consultants, and volunteer board members.

Most of the tasks performed by the university advisors involved activities that are quite common in extension work. For example, the local advisors gathered data from surveys of consumers, producers, and bulk food buyers to determine their awareness of local agriculture, the potential for expanding local agriculture, and the most promising marketing methods. Results of the consumer survey showed that a majority of consumers were interested in more access to local, seasonal produce and other local food products such as beef, lamb, and rice. Furthermore, they were willing, and many could afford, to pay a little more for local products. The cooperative extension office followed up with "A Reason for the Season," a consumer education campaign and local food guide. Master food preservers and other volunteers were trained to educate consumers about how to purchase, cook, and eat local, seasonal foods. These materials plus information about local agriculture have also been incorporated into curricula for Grades One through Three and Four through Six, as well as for households that use food stamps.

Our Roles and Challenges

Since 1994, the authors have played a variety of roles in support of the PlacerGROWN initiative—providing funding, information, resource connections, moral support, and evaluation. In return, we have had opportunities to enhance and deepen our own scholarship. On the front end this occurred as we read and analyzed the growing literature on the consequences for local communities of concentration of power in the food system, and developed our own literature synthesis as we articulated the community food systems concept. On the back end, this occurred as we reflected and wrote about PlacerGROWN and other community food system projects SAREP had funded, gaining insight from their practical experiences. In between, we provided support for local actors, implementing their project ideas.

Articulating the Concept of a Community Food System

After seeing the fairly traditional research projects funded in SAREP's first solicitation of proposals dealing with social, economic, and public policy concerns, the authors began discussing how to better frame and support more holistic projects. Beginning in 1992, we amended the SAREP Request for Proposals (RFP) slightly to seek projects in the area of "consumers and the food system." Responding to this language in our subsequent 1994 funding cycle, the three Placer County cooperative extension advisors proposed a project they called "Impacts of Local Food Systems on Communities and Agriculture/A Reason for the Season: Increasing Sustainable Practices among Consumers." SAREP funded the three-year project (1994-1997) for a total of $30,000.

Inspired by what we saw in PlacerGROWN and other local food system projects, we made a major shift in our next yearly

RFP, adding "community food systems" and "community food security" as topical areas of focus, and renaming the economics and public policy area "Community Development and Public Policy." The new RFP wording, which has since resulted in a growing number of funded projects around California, articulated the concept of community food systems as:

> ... collaborative efforts in particular places (e.g., a city, county, region, or bioregion) that take a holistic approach to developing a sustainable community food system. SAREP funding could support new collaborations or augment existing ones. The projects should work toward several of the following goals and should be consistent with all of them:

- access by all community members to an adequate, affordable diet of high nutritional value;

- a stable base of family farms using production practices that are less chemical and energy-intensive;

- marketing practices that create more direct and beneficial links between farmers and consumers and, to the extent possible, reduce the resources used to move food between production and consumption;

- development of ag-related businesses that create jobs, reduce leakage of dollars from the community or in other ways contribute to the community's economic development;

- improved working and living conditions of farm labor such that farmers and farm workers can be fully contributing members of the community;

- public policies to encourage a community's transition to sustainable agriculture by protecting farmland, developing necessary infrastructure and providing research and technical assistance.

In articulating the community food systems concept, we were practicing what Boyer (1990) calls the scholarship of integration, providing an account of what we saw happening in the world and how that might be changed to support sustainable development. One typical rationale put forth by the university is that "advances in technology equal advances in agriculture equal advances in community." We tried to be more sensitive to the reality that advances from the perspective of certain interests could be detrimental to other parties or values. In particular, we saw the story of technological advance as one that was not sufficiently cognizant of what was happening to the human and natural ecology of particular places. The community food system vision offered a way of thinking about how people in those places were organizing themselves to defend their connections to their natural setting, food shed, and heritage, while exercising their problem-solving capacities as citizens.

One measure of the success of our role as catalysts of this type of public work is the quantity and quality of responses to our yearly request for proposals. SAREP routinely receives 5 to 20 community food system proposals from which to choose. There is significant diversity and variety in the more than 20 such projects SAREP has funded in the past 10 years. A few focus on developing traditional research data, but most exist to build links among members of the community or to implement a community education or development program. One of the most notable features of this collection of projects is the inclusion of nontraditional extension audiences, including many marginal or disenfranchised groups such as farm workers, organic producers, low-income community residents, and limited resource farmers. All the projects are shaped by a specific geographic or institutional context, as opposed to generic research or extension work that seeks generalizations applicable anywhere. Project leaders work with local conditions in mind, fitting projects to the situation at hand, rather than imposing an abstract concept on reality.

As SAREP staff, we faced some resistance. Some of the university misgivings arose because funds often went directly to grassroots community organizations, including those with little if any previous track record with university grants. This created a different power relationship than the traditional mode in which extension dollars fund outreach or research by cooperative-extension professionals.

Many of the projects had minimal involvement of UC researchers, and some had none at all. In part this was due to the dearth of academics with expertise or interest in pursuing this type of work with such meager resources (typical grants were in the range of $15,000-$25,000). This is understandable in light of the difficulty a university faculty member or an extension specialist would have in reconciling the holistic, collaborative and often slow-moving nature of community food systems work with the time-sensitive requirements of publishing, specialization, and tenure. It is also true that our proclivity was to use the process not so much to organize faculty interest, but to validate local knowledge and community development activity as a viable mode of research and extension work, supported but not controlled by the university. Much of the marketing of the ideas was done through personal conversations, on the phone, at conferences and meetings, and through word-of-mouth networks. Given the limited faculty interest in the ideas, indeed the paucity of UC social scientists doing any community work related to agriculture, we put more energy into making connections outside of the university.

A particular challenge we faced as staff of the community food systems initiative was overcoming the concerns of some members of SAREP's Program and Technical Advisory committees. As one member recalls, the arrival of the proposals put new demands on the committees:

> There was genuine confusion about the different kinds of criteria required to judge some of the education projects versus

the agriculture projects in which you had a much more clear-cut standard for accepting both project performance and project results. I think that was one of the things that was a little bit more challenging in the community development arena. There is just not as clear a set of guidelines. That made some of the straight technical folks somewhat uncomfortable.

Part of what we learned is that the experimental "institutional space" SAREP had carved out was inherently fragile, and continual staff energy had to be expended to prevent its erosion. For example, many members of our review committees wondered why the research component was relatively small in most projects, raising questions such as "I don't know why we're doing this. What are we going to learn? How is it going to help anyone else? What's the replicable knowledge here?" These concerns point to legitimate and difficult questions about how to promote learning of general applicability when dealing with such context-specific projects. In defending our approach, we noted that our primary initial goal was to catalyze the creation of new community work that could provide a basis for analytical reflection as it began to reach a critical mass. Our strategy was similar to that articulated by one scholar in describing "institution-forming sociology": "You have to create the institutions first, then you can study them" (Etzkowitz 1970).

Supporting PlacerGROWN

The initial link with PlacerGROWN came when Feenstra met two of the Placer County cooperative extension advisors at a planning meeting for the 1993 California Farm Conference. When they told her what they were beginning to work on, she eagerly informed them of the SAREP Request for Proposals and answered questions about the proposal process. After PlacerGROWN received SAREP funding, we stayed in close connection, with Feenstra serving as the primary liaison with the project. For example, she worked with the advisors to develop a consumer survey that was funded by another university source. She also attended several meetings at the Placer extension office, listening, offering advice, and putting them in touch with resource people she knew. This networking gradually led them into greater involvement with PlacerGROWN leaders and other local citizens. We took part in an agricultural bus tour, for example, and spoke at the annual PlacerGROWN farm conference. While some of the information we imparted was technical—such as advice on survey design— much of our relationship involved deepening our understanding of the local situation, and connecting local actors to grant resources and to ideas gleaned from other community food system projects.

Equally important, we sought to provide moral support and inspiration by reminding local leaders of the broader importance of what they were trying to accomplish. The meanings they attached to their work were understandably parochial, while our tendency was to view the local activity within a bigger frame of reference. Both perspectives are critical. For example, until we understood more clearly how PlacerGROWN fit in the context of previous organizing efforts in the county, we did not fully under-stand the meaning it held for local activists. Similarly, community members were often unaware of how their local efforts to protect farmland might be better supported by developing alliances at the regional or state levels. In general, we found the work of "meaning making" to be enriched and made more useful when reciprocal engagement took place.

In relating to PlacerGROWN, both of us realized that connect-ing the resources of the university to the local community requires getting out and meeting people and understanding their needs and their desires for the community. We spent a good deal of time in Placer County, becoming familiar with the landscape, meeting farmers, restaurateurs and others who were involved with various parts of the PlacerGROWN effort. We saw the technical and organizational difficulties facing an organic grower and what it meant for him to sell products at 10 to 12 farmers' markets per week. We took part in a working session with a local farmer seeking ideas on how to expand agri-tourism within the scope of his operation. We got a glimpse of what is really required to make this kind of effort succeed and how difficult that can be.

The most basic challenge in this phase of our engagement was to be good learners. To do this, we needed to set aside our preconceived notions of what a community food system project should look like, and understand the meanings and motivations of PlacerGROWN from the local perspective. This required a willingness to spend time listening carefully, bringing our experience and faculties to bear on a conversation about the real challenges and difficulties Placer County leaders were facing. Though we were helped by our geographic proximity to Placer County (about an hour's drive from Davis) and by fairly regular occasions to interact with the local cooperative extension advisors at meetings and conferences, we found it consistently difficult to carve out this kind of time. Moreover, as we made our first efforts to "tell the story" of PlacerGROWN to an academic audience, we learned how important it was to test our version of the story with local actors.

Reflecting on Results

A major hurdle we faced in all the community food system projects was ensuring that a reflective and analytic component was included—both within each project and across the range of SAREP-funded projects. The idea was to promote community-based inquiry and not simply community action. What we found was that time demands on us and on community leaders typically prohibited ample reflection time, at least in an organized or systematic way. This was one reason we decided on our own, in 1999, to develop a case study describing the development and achievements of PlacerGROWN.

The case study turned out to be more complicated than we thought. For one thing, getting good data on project results was difficult, even in the areas where it seemed the project had managed to put a good program in place. We had pushed the advisors to collect outcome data as a condition of their grant, but quickly learned how long it can take to see results from this kind of project and how difficult it can be to know where to look for results.

In reporting on PlacerGROWN, we were initially preoccupied with the limitations of existing data sources for tracking the impact of a local marketing collaborative on farm viability or on the effort to plug leaks in the local economy. Later, we realized that the most important impact of PlacerGROWN was the continuity it provided with past organizing efforts in the community (e.g. the creation of farmers' markets in the late 1980s) and the impetus it gave to new initiatives. Rather than considering PlacerGROWN simply as a discrete project, we came to see the wisdom of viewing it in the evolutionary context of local history and politics.

The initial drafts of our case study focused a good deal of attention on the failure to achieve many of the original objectives of PlacerGROWN, such as supporting itself primarily through member dues, or expanding the use of the PlacerGROWN marketing label. Local reviewers were not shy about taking exception to what they saw as our partial and shortsighted analysis. Their objection was not so much to the accuracy of our remarks as to their tone and their failure to address positive developments that were less visible to our eyes as outsiders. In hindsight, the "flaws" we focused on in the original drafts of our PlacerGROWN case study needed to be viewed in a broader perspective, one which incorporated a fuller understanding of local history and people. It was also true that we had not yet built up a sufficient degree of trust with key local actors to have their unreserved buy-in to engage in a mutual process of critical reflection—one that might reveal the limitations in their own perspectives.

Personal, Civic, and Intellectual Outcomes

As the community food systems vision went from the stage of hypothetical conjecture to real-world experiment we found ourselves reacting in distinct and personal ways. For Feenstra, the community engagement represented a significant new step in a journey she had been on for some time, away from her early training in dietetics and narrowly conceived public health courses, and toward a focus on community health and local empowerment. Extroverted by nature, she found the work energizing and was caught up in a sense of optimism.

For Campbell, the experience raised ambivalent feelings. As an academic who had spent most of his career teaching political theory and public policy in the classroom, he was used to stimulating student thinking by contrasting *what is* with *what ought to be*. It felt quite different to be influencing real-world projects in which the primary risks were borne by community people who were investing their own time, money, and energy, without knowing where this would lead. What if we were encouraging people down the wrong path or into adverse consequences? On the other hand, the community food systems initiative represented an important way to put into practice ideas that he had articulated in his dissertation, which was concerned with how to support grassroots community organizers so that they can sustain their political commitments over the long haul. In this regard the community food systems work provided an important sense of professional fulfillment and continuity.

One of the most immediate, and far from trivial, results of our engagement with PlacerGROWN stakeholders was mutual recognition. Community leaders saw themselves in our RFP language, and we saw in their experiment a way of expanding and enriching our concept of a community food system. As William Sullivan (2000, p. 36) notes:

> A common horizon of democratic values enables individuals to recognize each other, and themselves, as potential civic

partners. This experience of mutual recognition draws individuals beyond themselves, sometimes in quite remarkable
ways. It is, as Dewey saw in a different philosophical idiom,
the ignition point of genuine democratic life, the catalytic
moment in the development of the democratic character.

From the local perspective, not only was it important to
secure funds to advance the local work, but also to gain implicit
university validation for the direction PlacerGROWN was heading.
From our perspective, it was tremendously exciting to read a
proposal aimed at putting into practice many of the concepts
and ideas we were seeking to promote.

We can point to a number of ways in which our ongoing
communication with the project mobilized tangible resources that
supported the local effort. One example is support for the survey
of local consumers and producers that the advisors conducted.
We put them in touch with people across the country working
on local food system issues, including a Cornell researcher whose
own survey became a model for Placer County (Wilkins and
Bokaer-Smith 1996). We also provided detailed feedback about
the survey design. The survey work helped the advisors make
the case for exploring changes with local farmers; just doing the
survey provided a first step in organizing the farmers around
the PlacerGROWN ideas. In addition, talks we gave at conferences and meetings stimulated interest in PlacerGROWN's work
from others around the country. This increased the networks on
which local leaders could draw and put them in touch with new
ideas and sources of funding.

Tracing the civic outcomes associated with the PlacerGROWN
initiative is difficult; more difficult still is any attempt to ascertain
the influence of our roles as public scholars on those outcomes.
A few developments in the community are noteworthy, however.
While the PlacerGROWN initiative cannot claim sole credit, it was
nevertheless instrumental in influencing broader policy developments in the county. For example, PlacerGROWN provided

support for the new Placer Legacy program to preserve farmland and open space using conservation easements and other strategies. It also was instrumental in securing a new agricultural marketing position within the County Agricultural Commissioner's office. The job description for this position supports the goals originally articulated by PlacerGROWN, and the first person hired was a veteran member of the PlacerGROWN organization. These developments suggest that PlacerGROWN has been at least partially successful in meeting two implicit goals of the local marketing strategy: 1) to broaden and solidify the political constituency in support of farmland protection, and 2) to develop a compelling rationale to convince economic development planners how an investment in agriculture will pay off.

PlacerGROWN has not resolved all the challenges rapid development poses for Placer County. On the other hand, its existence has helped to catalyze a unique set of political dynamics around development issues. In most California communities, development issues are the province of a handful of powerful insiders, particularly land developers who have disproportionate influence over decisions. If citizen politics exists at all it takes the form of "ballot-box planning" that is often unsatisfying and seldom very deliberative. By contrast, PlacerGROWN has helped catalyze forums for debate and public judgment that bring together diverse community sectors and has promoted cooperative practices through which different segments of the community can work together to realize public goods (e.g., preservation of working open spaces and scenic vistas) and shared values (e.g., local autonomy).

In terms of our own research, the existence of PlacerGROWN and other SAREP-funded local experiments created a valuable laboratory for research and learning, enriching our understanding of the community food system concept, and deepening our ability to create an evolving synthesis of the associated opportunities and challenges. We have already noted how the PlacerGROWN proposal helped solidify our initial concept of a community food system. As PlacerGROWN developed, the extension staff connected the authors with local leaders to interview for our case study. More generally, they have used the insights gained from studying the community projects to add to the sustainable agriculture and community development knowledge base. Our work has included staff publications and peer-reviewed journal articles (Feenstra 1997; Campbell 1997; Campbell and Feenstra 2001), a high profile SAREP-sponsored conference on community food systems, participation in a national research project on local food systems (NE-185), and various public and professional presentations.

Various parties within our own institution and elsewhere in academia have reviewed this body of work for quality and legitimacy. For the most part, the reception has been positive, and both authors have used this work as part of successful academic merit packages and career advancement. On the other hand, criticism from within the university has never been absent, coming primarily from administrators who would like to see SAREP pursue a narrower agenda focused on reducing pesticide use.

From our perspective, the most important measure of the value of the work is its utility to community actors. While community members have not found all of our academic work immediately useful, we are encouraged that SAREP staff and publications have become a recognized source of practical expertise and support for community leaders. Most satisfying is that the community food system ideas have continued to spark local interest, and the resulting projects are better grounded due to what is being learned from experience and continue to gain political credibility and legitimacy. For example, the food systems concept is now an explicit part of how USDA defines community food security.

The Meaning of Public Scholarship

In preparing this case study, the authors have been asked to reflect on how our particular experience might inform a practical theory of public scholarship. Four scholarly routines or practices have been integral to our effort to catalyze democratic publics, including 1) community networking and "scoping"; 2) community forums, submitting academic products for the review and reflection of local citizens; 3) community organizing to create space for public scholarship within the university; and 4) integrating technical, relational, and political forms of knowledge. These four features of public scholarship appear worthy of more reflection and experimentation.

Community Scoping

A responsible academic does not dare venture into a new research project without conducting a literature review. The public scholarship equivalent of this process is to engage in community networking and scoping. In our case, monitoring ongoing developments in California communities enriched our initial vision of community food systems and ensured that our Request for Proposals resonated with local leaders. Spending time in Placer County and seeing the world from the perspective of diverse local actors made it possible to tell the story of the project in a way that made sense to Placer citizens and better informed similar efforts elsewhere. Community scoping produced benefits similar to what a good literature review produces, enabling us to build on past work (rather than to repeat the obvious) and to benefit from the perspectives of others who were thinking seriously about the issues that mattered to us.

Modern technology has made it relatively easy to conduct a literature review from the confines of an academic office, but even so, academics find it useful and necessary to venture out to conferences and other events to stay abreast of the latest developments in the field. Similarly, effective use of the telephone, Internet, and listservs can contribute to a useful community scan, but are no substitute for visiting particular communities and seeing firsthand the challenges they are facing.

Community Forums

Our experience suggests the reciprocal benefits of creating forums in which the products of academic reflection can be shared with community actors. For the community, these forums create space in which citizens can reflect on the meaning of what is happening and can better assess what ought to be done. This type of reflective space is in short supply in most communities and organizations. We found that conducting reflective interviews with key PlacerGROWN leaders gave them a welcome opportunity to consider the meaning of what the organization had already done and to frame issues for the future. A more public space for reflection occurred when we shared some of our interview findings with the PlacerGROWN board of directors. That presentation helped inform decisions facing the board, many of whom welcomed the big-picture perspective we brought to the table. We do not wish to paint too rosy a picture of this reflective process, which included many times at which we felt frustrated that community members did not address issues we felt were important.

Despite some frustration, the process of submitting our work for community review and discussion helped strengthen its validity. We would argue that in public scholarship, academic rigor is enhanced not primarily through methodological correctness but by aggressively seeking multiple perspectives on the accuracy, meaning, and utility of the work. We have noted how vital local knowledge was to ensure that our PlacerGROWN case reflected the way the organization's activities fit in a larger history of community initiatives. More basically, the entire body of academic work we have produced related to community food systems would not have been possible without the sustained conversations we have had with community leaders across the state.

Community Organizing

Community organizing is essential to creating the institutional space—within the community and the university—in which the work of public scholarship can occur. In Placer, a diverse group of citizens organized themselves to defend agriculture and the rural quality of life against the threats of rapid growth. This citizen organizing, marked by a moderate mainstream appeal, stood in sharp contrast to the progressive activism that contributed to the creation of the SAREP program within the University of California. Both organizing efforts, however, articulated *community voice* with sufficient clarity and power to carve out space that expanded community influence on the research agenda of a public university.

Making this space productive, and sustaining it in the face of obstacles, became our basic challenge as academics. We found ourselves building bridges and connections between university and community cultures. While this work required significant intellectual effort—such as that needed to synthesize the literature to articulate the community food systems concept—at its root it required an organizer's frame of mind, attentive both to the internal politics of the university and to community voices.

While the research we have done has helped somewhat to define and legitimize this work within the university, we cannot claim to have created much of an impact on the university itself. Few faculty members have been attracted to participate in community food system projects or related research. The projects themselves have been devoted to local goals rather than making a concerted effort to affect university research policies. The limited SAREP funding has been more successful in leveraging funds from local governments or foundations than in securing research funds from the university.

Our experience suggests the need for community organizing within the university itself, aimed at creating both space and rewards for increasing faculty engagement with civic concerns (Boyte and Kari 1996). Without such an effort, public scholarship will likely remain on the periphery of most universities, primarily carried out by a handful of committed faculty or by academic staff in university-based outreach programs similar to SAREP. A key question is whether it will remain there, a token nod to critics, or become a catalyst for broader changes in how faculty members work, graduate students are trained, and scarce resources are allocated.

Integrating Forms of Knowledge

Public scholarship involves intentional efforts to support civic education by integrating and applying different forms of knowledge— technical, relational, and political. The modern university prides itself as a source of reliable technical knowledge, and extension advisors are typically hired and rewarded based on their technical competence. But the land-grant ideal, as reflected in the early history of cooperative extension, was to develop and disseminate technical knowledge while building common values (relational) and fostering active citizenship (participation in power). Political knowledge alone does not fit common definitions of scholarship. Technical knowledge alone might not be "engaged" or "public." As illustrated by the PlacerGROWN case and by other SAREP-funded community food system projects, public scholarship is research and extension activity that rejoins these disparate but interconnected forms of knowledge.

Drawing on the pioneering work of Habermas (1971), Mezirow (2000) has described three domains of adult learning: *instrumental* (a technical understanding of cause-and-effect relationships in order to solve problems), *communicative* (understanding what others mean and how to make ourselves understood), and *emancipatory* (becoming free from forces that limit our options or that seemed beyond human control). What seems important in the Placer case is that the search for technical knowledge (e.g. what alternative crops could be grown in the local soils and climate; what products consumers could be expected to buy if farmers produced them) was part of a larger inquiry. The community was learning what norms and values could garner widespread support (e.g. the vision of an agriculture-community partnership promoted by PlacerGROWN), and what tangible leverage an understanding of these values could give them in altering the seemingly inevitable path of population growth and urban development. Without the technical knowledge the achievement of an efficacious political response would remain a dream; without the shared vision and political will the technical knowledge would be fruitless or would serve only private ends.

We have witnessed this same integration of the three types of knowledge in other community food system initiatives. Many project leaders report learning practical lessons that were technical (how to), relational (local players, local beliefs), and political (organizing, lobbying, and community action skills). In describing the results of his study on the feasibility of locally marketing grass-fed beef, one cooperative extension advisor described project participants learning about producing grass-fed beef (technical), but went on to comment, "I think all parties were somewhat amazed with what we learned about the laws and regulations." Many project leaders report that the knowledge they gained about the structure of local institutions—how they work, and where to find the leverage points for change—was critical to their efforts. What they learned over time was an ability to "read" the structure of local networks, seizing opportunities and avoiding unnecessary detours or roadblocks.

The importance of the different types of knowledge is reflected also in how local project leaders described the outcomes of their activities. Many involved policy changes that resulted from providing decision makers with new information about the local food system. For example, one project integrated a county's physical and habitat data with area vineyard maps to produce GIS maps to assess patterns of vineyard development. The maps could then be used to evaluate proposed and adopted regulations about land use. Another community changed its general plan to include a working urban farm, after seeing the benefits of a farm at which university and middle-school students could receive technical training in agricultural subjects and farming techniques.

Still another community project demonstrated that, when given a choice, school children prefer fresh, local produce in their school lunches. This led to the development of a districtwide school food policy encouraging procurement of local, organic foods. While they involved the creation or dissemination of some technical knowledge, none of these projects would have succeeded without the time taken to build relationships and develop trust through an open-ended process of listening and through tireless networking.

Conclusion

Kettering Foundation President David Mathews describes the goal of public scholarship as producing and communicating the forms of knowledge that a democratic citizenry needs to govern itself. Learning how to do this well entails heeding the lessons forged in particular cases. As Harry Boyte and Nancy Kari (1996) put it:

> Democratic theory of any use is never created in a vacuum. It needs grounding in experience, practical experiment, and real-world settings that reflect the diverse challenges and possibilities of the public world. It evolves as it is constantly tested. Traditions of thinking about public topics over the centuries and contemporary university-based research are of use in this process. But practical experiences and experiments are the touchstones of effective theory that guides practical action.

This case history offers both comfort and concern for those interested in the task of "realizing the engaged institution." On the one hand, it is not necessary to comprehensively reinvent the skills and capacities of most research and extension personnel in order to pursue this type of democratic engagement. On the other hand, the key element is not the skills themselves but the way in which they are harnessed by a vision that subsumes scholarship to the broader civic mission of the land-grant university.

SAREP's community food systems work shows that it is possible, though not straightforward or simple, to take democratic aspirations seriously within the context of mainstream research and extension work in a modern land-grant university. Among other things, this means sharing the university's resources and making them truly responsive to the research agenda advanced by community leaders. It also means adopting higher expectations of local citizen capacity to organize relevant and useful inquiry, bringing together technical and local forms of knowledge in creative ways.

Acknowledgments

Background information used in this analysis was gathered during a two-month period (October through November 2000) by Dr. Robert Pence, who conducted a thorough document review and 22 open-ended interviews with current and former SAREP staff members, SAREP grant recipients both inside and outside the University of California, and former members of SAREP advisory committees. We are grateful to him for contributing significantly to our thinking, particularly in the sections referring to the Habermas and Mezirow theories of knowledge. Both authors are grateful to the many exemplary community leaders with whom we have worked and whose insights and spirit have shaped our own reflections.

References

Berry, W. 1987. *Home Economics.* San Francisco, CA: North Point Press.

Boyer. E. L. 1990. *Scholarship Reconsidered: The Priorities of the Professoriate.* Princeton, NJ: Carnegie Foundation for the Advancement of Teaching.

Boyte, H. C. and N. N. Kari. 1996. *Building America: The Democratic Promise of Public Work.* Philadelphia, PA: Temple University Press.

Campbell, D. 1997. Community-controlled Economic Development as a Strategic Vision for the Sustainable Agriculture Movement. *American Journal of Alternative Agriculture* 12(1): 37-44.

Campbell, D. and G. Feenstra. 2001. "A Local Partnership for Food and Agriculture: The Case of PlacerGROWN." In *Creating Sustainable Community Programs,* ed. M. R. Daniels. Westport, CT: Praeger Press.

Campus Compact. 1998. *Establishing Universities as Citizens: Toward the Scholarship of Engagement.* Indiana Campus Compact.

Etzkowitz, H. 1970. Institution-formation Sociology. *American Sociologist* (May): 120-124.

Feenstra, G. 1997. Local Food Systems and Sustainable Communities. *American Journal of Alternative Agriculture* 12(1): 28-36.

Goldrich, D. and T. Cooper. 1984. *The Challenge of Internal Development for a Public Interest Coalition.* Report to Participants in the Northwest Conservation Act Coalition, November 10-11.

Gussow, J. D. and K. L. Clancy. 1986. Dietary Guidelines for Sustainability. *Journal of Nutrition Education* 18(1): 1-5.

Habermas, J. 1971. *Knowledge and Human Interests.* Boston, MA: Beacon Press.

Kemmis, D. 1990. *Community and the Politics of Place.* Norman, OK: University of Oklahoma Press.

Mezirow, J. et al. 2000. *Learning as Transformation: Critical Perspectives on a Theory in Progress.* San Francisco, CA: Jossey-Bass.

Peters, S. 1996. *Cooperative Extension and the Democratic Promise of the Land-grant Idea.* Minneapolis, MN: Minnesota Extension Service and the Hubert H. Humphrey Institute of Public Affairs, University of Minnesota.

Putnam, R. D. 1993. *Making Democracy Work: Civic Traditions in Modern Italy.* Princeton, NJ: Princeton University Press.

Strange, M. 1988. *Family Farming: A New Economic Vision.* Lincoln, NE: University of Nebraska Press.

Sullivan, W. 2000. Higher Education and Civic Deliberation. *Kettering Review* 18:23-38.

Wilkins, J. and J. Bokaer-Smith. 1996. *The Northeast Regional Food Guide.* Ithaca, NY: Cornell University.

Chapter Three:
Organizing for Public Scholarship in Southeast Minnesota
by Scott Peters and Karen Lehman

Late on a Monday evening, members of the board and staff of the Experiment in Rural Cooperation (ERC), a formal partnership established in 1997 between the people of southeast Minnesota and the University of Minnesota, sit together to discuss the progress and status of the projects they're supporting to advance sustainable development in the region. Seated around the table is an interesting mix of folks: there's a dairy farmer, a few extension educators, a small-town banker, an adult educator, a philosopher, an entomologist, a watershed specialist, a hog farmer, a former deputy mayor of St. Paul, and a goat farmer, among others. What ties these people together is a shared concern about the tough economic, environmental, and social problems the rural communities of southeast Minnesota are facing and a strong belief that the state's land-grant institution at the University of Minnesota can and should help address them.

While the ERC board and staff are meeting, an hour and a half away on the University of Minnesota's St. Paul campus, graduate student Judy Brienza works on her master's thesis, which also happens to be an ERC-supported project. Her project is devoted to helping Farming with Nature, a cooperative composed of several small-scale pork and beef producers from southeast Minnesota, determine whether and how they might brand and market their products in the region. As Brienza sits at her computer, plugging number after number into a spreadsheet, she's not only thinking about her thesis, she's worried about whether she's asked Farming with Nature the right questions. She's concerned that she might have pushed them too hard—or not enough—as she asked questions about what they'd be willing to do to market their high quality, sustainably produced meats in local grocery stores and restaurants.

To get her degree in applied economics, Brienza could have chosen any number of topics that would have produced fewer personal worries and dilemmas. For example, she could have developed a theoretical model for analyzing the dynamics of globalization on some sector of the national economy. But Brienza wanted to work on something "real." She wanted her graduate work to actually matter to someone in a direct and immediate way. She wanted to make a difference in the lives of real people.

In this chapter, we tell the story of how the Experiment in Rural Cooperation is building the community-university partnerships that make it possible for Judy Brienza and others to do scholarly public work that is real for the people of southeast Minnesota. The story sheds light on the nature and challenges of *public scholarship* in land-grant education, where scholars engage with community members in research, deliberation, and problem solving to address pressing public problems in specific contexts. It reveals the essential role of *organizing* in supporting and maintaining community-university partnerships as vehicles for public scholarship. It teaches us that serious partnerships cannot be willed or even legislated into existence. They are the hard-won products of ongoing efforts, strategically expended by skilled organizers working with committed groups of people.

The story of the first few years of the ERC's work is a story of strategic, aggressive organizing aimed at revitalizing the land-grant mission in order to pursue and support public scholarship for sustainable development. While, on balance, we believe it is a hopeful story, it's impossible to hide or ignore the discouraging things that have happened (or not happened) that cast doubts on the ability of the ERC to deepen and sustain its partnership with the university. We consider both the hopeful and discouraging aspects of the story.

We begin with a brief background account of how and why the ERC was established, followed by a broad overview of the eight-county section of southeast Minnesota that serves as the ERC's operating base. We then turn to an account of how the ERC has developed and pursued its vision and goals and what has been learned and accomplished along the way. We provide a concrete grounding for our discussion by focusing on Judy Brienza's public scholarship work with Farming with Nature. Brienza's scholarship made a direct contribution in a small but significant way to the ERC's core public goal: the fostering of "a homegrown economy in southeast Minnesota that will support self-reliant communities and a healthy natural environment" (Experiment 1999a). We conclude with a set of lessons that we think are broadly relevant to those who have an interest in advancing public scholarship efforts in land-grant education.

The data we draw on in writing this chapter come from two main sources. First, each of us has significant experiential knowledge of the ERC gained from direct, personal involvement in and observations of the ERC's work and from numerous informal conversations we had with people who have been engaged in it. The story we construct draws heavily on the insights we gleaned from these experiences. Second, we draw from transcriptions of tape-recorded interviews we conducted with six of the key players in the ERC's work. These interviews helped us understand the experiences of those who have been involved in the ERC, and the kinds of challenges that will need to be addressed for it to succeed. They gave us perspectives not only on the "what" and "how" questions in the ERC story but also on the "why" and "so what" questions. In other words, they helped us understand the significance of the ERC story—its larger value and meaning to the people of southeast Minnesota, the University of Minnesota, and the national land-grant education system.

Background

The ERC is part of a larger statewide initiative, established in 1997, called the Regional Sustainable Development Partnerships (RSDP). The broad purpose of the initiative is to address a set of problems related to sustainable development by creating close partnerships between the University of Minnesota and the citizens of five ecologically distinct regions of the state. Its specific goals are:

- to build and strengthen effective relationships between citizens, communities, and the University of Minnesota;

- to promote active citizen leadership in strengthening the long-term social, economic, and environmental health of greater Minnesota; and

- to invest in research, education, and outreach projects that advance the understanding and achievement of regional sustainability (www.regionalpartnerships.umn.edu).

To support the initiative, the Minnesota Legislature provides $2.4 million biannually to the College of Agricultural, Food and Environmental Sciences (COAFES), the College of Natural Resources (CNR), and the University of Minnesota Extension Service. Each of the five regions involved in the initiative receives $200,000 a year, to be spent on projects related to sustainable development. The projects in each region are identified, developed, and implemented by an active board of directors composed of local citizens and a few university faculty and staff. Each region employs a full-time executive director who helps facilitate the process of program planning and development, oversees the progress of funded projects, and develops relationships between the region and the university.

Three main factors motivated the development of the RSDP initiative. First, in the 1980s and early 1990s, many rural communities and farmers across Minnesota (and the rest of the Midwest) experienced hard times due to the effects of a complex set of economic, political, environmental, and cultural forces. Second, during the same time period, the concept of sustainable development emerged as a promising tool for understanding and dealing with these forces. Interest in this concept was reflected in a statute adopted by the Minnesota Legislature in 1996 that committed the state to follow a sustainable development path that "maintains or enhances economic opportunity and community well-being while protecting and restoring the natural environment upon which people and economies depend" (Minnesota Statutes 1996).

A third and especially important motivating factor was the re-emergence of a "civic" understanding of the land-grant mission to work not only for ordinary people, but also with them by involving them as full participants in shaping and conducting educational work. The land-grant mission, under this conception, is devoted to engaging people of many different backgrounds and interests especially, but not exclusively, people in rural communities with an interest in agriculture in scholarly public work that advances the well-being of people and communities. Such a mission calls for direct engagement with people and their problems and goals. Its success is dependent on skilled organizers who know how to bring people from inside and outside universities together to identify, learn about, deliberate, and act on pressing public issues and problems.

In 1993, all these factors were brought together and shaped into the idea for the RSDP by the Minnesota Institute for Sustainable Agriculture (MISA), a partnership established in 1990 between the University of Minnesota's College of Agricultural, Food and Environmental Sciences and the Sustainers' Coalition, a group of individuals and nonprofit organizations devoted to advancing and supporting sustainable agriculture. The idea was developed and refined into a specific proposal to the Minnesota Legislature by MISA staff and board members over a four-year period (1993-1997), drawing on the input and suggestions of farmers, rural citizens, and legislators as well as university students, faculty, staff, and administrators.

Implementation

When the RSDP initiative received its first appropriation from the Minnesota Legislature in 1997, a statewide task force composed of community and university members was created to develop the operating guidelines and principles for the partnerships, refine the geographic boundaries of each of the three regions that had received initial funding (a second appropriation was passed in 1999 that created funding for two additional partnerships), and determine how the partnerships would be staffed. The statewide task force was also charged with identifying a small group of people in each region who would serve as the nominating committee for that region's board of directors. Once the boards were set up, the task force was to help them understand the partnerships' mission and objectives and support them as they began their work.

While overall there was a high degree of enthusiasm and shared vision among task force members for the partnerships, discussions were, at times, quite tense, especially over questions about the nature and degree of power sharing between the university and the regions. Task force members were concerned about how much power and control the regional boards would have over the partnerships' work, and how much power and influence the university would have, particularly the deans of COAFES, CNR, and Extension. Discussion of this question concluded with the understanding that the regional boards would drive the work, and thus hold the balance of the power and influence, but that because the partnerships were to be *partnerships,* there would have to be an ongoing way to share and negotiate power and interests between the regions and the university.

As the task force began to form the nominating committees for the boards of directors that were to be established in each region, another contentious issue emerged. Because the idea for the regional partnerships did not emerge from coordinated grassroots efforts in each of the three regions where they were to be initially established but was rather the product of MISA's efforts and the lobbying of university personnel, the idea of the partnerships had to be sold to people in the regions who were sometimes suspicious or cynical about the university's motives. There was no pre-existing group in any of the regions that had been directly involved in organizing and fighting for the partnerships, which meant that there was little understanding of the partnerships idea and little, if any, initial buy-in.

While questions about where the power should be lodged and whose agenda the partnerships would pursue reflected underlying tensions and skepticism among task force members there was nevertheless, a strong sense that something good and important was being born—that the partnerships offered a promising opportunity to engage the university with the regions in pursuing sustainable development. The process the task force used for selecting the nominating committees and boards in each of the regions facilitated trust and hope. Task force members started with their personal and professional networks and expanded the list of candidates through ensuing contacts. MISA was influential in this process as a uniquely positioned community-university partnership with a strong network of community and university people who were already involved in sustainable development work. The task force developed criteria for selecting regional board members that called for careful selection among people with specific characteristics. The list ranged from "ability to work with a diverse group" to "ability to bring an ethical dimension" or "ability to function in a risk environment" (Guidelines 1998).

Ironically, as the statewide task force was going about its work establishing the regional partnerships, the Minnesota Round Table on Sustainable Development issued its report to the governor. Apparently unaware of the regional partnerships initiative, the Round Table's report concluded with a recommendation that a new institution be established to facilitate sustainable development in the state. "Sometimes, new concepts need new institutions to support them," the report said. "While we are committed to change within existing institutions—and consider such change essential—we also believe that a new institution may be needed to help people and organizations understand and pursue opportunities for sustainable development" (Minnesota Round Table 1998).

The three RSDPs, as they were established in 1997, were to be the first large-scale experiment in creating such a new institution. The partnerships would also function as an experiment in engaging and ultimately changing an existing institution: the University of Minnesota. The regional partnerships were specifically designed to be an innovative mechanism for strengthening the role of the citizens of Minnesota in the work of their land-grant university.

Establishing the Experiment in Cooperation

Whether the theory behind the regional partnerships initiative would actually work in practice could only be discovered by trying to implement it. Of the three regions that were initially funded, southeast Minnesota looked to be the most promising place to establish a successful community-university partnership devoted to advancing sustainable development. No other region of Minnesota has the agricultural diversity, innovation in food-related enterprises, and daring food-marketing initiatives to promote organic and sustainable products than does this eight-county region. Unlike other parts of the state, southeast Minnesota still boasts a strong family-farm-based livestock sector that supports a range of custom, state-inspected, and USDA-inspected meat processing plants. There are more than 1,000 dairy farms with herds under 100 cows. The region is an abundant source of vegetables, fruits, meats, mushrooms, and herbs, many of them produced in ways that protect watersheds and preserve habitat. Organic grain miller operate there, as do a variety of frozen vegetable processors, including Sno-Pac, a family-owned company with

national and international markets that has produced organic
frozen vegetables since the 1940s. Inspired by all this dynamic
activity, a local county commissioner predicted in January 1999
that the region was poised to become the "Sonoma Valley of
the Midwest."

The geography of the region partly explains its strong sense
of place and its dynamism and diversity of enterprises. Unlike
the expansive plains of western Minnesota, southeast Minnesota
is defined by the many small watersheds that funnel into the
Mississippi River, by the Mississippi itself, and by the plains
on top of the bluffs. Farmers, bankers, livestock processors, and
vegetable processors define their service areas in terms of 25- to
45- mile radii. When asked to describe their region, people who
live in specific communities refer to their proximity to the hub
cities of Rochester and Lacrosse—neither of which is more than
60 miles away from the community in question.

As important as its distinctive landscape features are,
southeast Minnesota's greatest resource is its people. The
region is home to hundreds of innovative initiatives. The Benike
family in Dover opened a farmstead cheese plant to bring back
the cheeses that disappeared from the region when the local
creamery stopped making cheese. The founders of Paradise
Prairie Products plan to use the bounty of sweet corn and dairy
products from the prairie surrounding Plainview, a town of 3,000
people, to create a line of processed foods to be sold in the region
and beyond. Rebekah's Restaurant in Plainview purchases all of
its dairy products, vegetables, and meats directly from local
farmers and processors. Badgersett Research Farm is developing
a woody agricultural system centered on hazelnuts, which hold
tremendous promise for their food value. The Apple Crisp Cooperative is developing new value-added uses for #2 Harrelson
apples that could help member growers weather the difficulties
of the international market, while offering a new product to
commercial bakers.

The Founding Board

The ERC's founding board was representative of the diversity in the region and the desire to balance university and community. Farmers like Mary Doerr, a goat farmer, Donna Christison, a hog farmer, and Carolyn Dingfelder, who operates a small business specializing in field-grown perennials, embodied the broad range of agricultural enterprises in the region and the different views on sustainability they imply. As president of the Cannon River Sustainable Farming Association, Doerr was deeply involved in developing an alternative agriculture model that included farm-based tourism, while Christison chaired the Animal Processing Task Force and articulated the interests of "traditional" farmers—the medium-sized family farms that concentrate on grains and livestock for commodity markets. These different experiences and perspectives generated substantive debates, not without tension, about the balance between environmental and economic sustainability the ERC should promote. Other board members such as Dean Harrington, president of a family-owned bank; Kathryn Gilje, organizer of a nonprofit organization centered on migrant worker issues; John Torgrimson, publisher of the *Fillmore County Journal*; and Gary Holthaus, a writer on the topics of sustainability and culture; brought additional community perspectives and innovative ideas to the board.

University board participants included Toni Smith, an extension educator recognized for her work developing tourism along the Mississippi River; Roger Moon, a livestock entomologist; and Tim Wagar, a crops and soils specialist with the University of Minnesota Extension Service who managed the River Friendly Farmer Program. As people working for the university but living in the community, they were important in bridging the existing mission of the university with the new mission of the ERC. Again, this was not without tension. Extension representatives, especially, were concerned that the ERC, with its mission to engage in research, education, and outreach, would duplicate what extension was already doing in the region.

Jeff Gorfine, an adult educator with a background in mental health, corrections, and poverty work, was nominated to serve as the ERC's first board chair. Gorfine told us that he sees his role as one of a facilitator for an activist board that will work to reveal and develop local leadership for the ERC's work. As he describes it:

> We need to stay honest to these bedrock principles of partnership, active citizenship, and sustainable development. And on the active citizenship side, let's not think that we now know what southeast Minnesota needs. That really will be known by projects that we work with and partner with and develop with folks who bring those ideas in. Really, the true leadership lies in the region, not around the board table. I feel that I'm good on process and I've always beat it to death that we need to have an open, fair, and consistent process. We need to relish and keep sacred the minority view. We must ensure that that's always spoken, that everyone feels comfortable in doing that.

The Staff

As part of its work in helping to establish the initial regional partnerships, the statewide task force wrote a broad job description for the executive director position to be created in each region. The description is full of action verbs, such as *facilitate, guide, motivate,* and *direct.* It also contains an explicit mandate to the executive directors, referred to in the document as *educators,* to "work from an organizing framework and philosophy" (Partnership Task Force 1997).

Clearly, the ERC's board of directors took this seriously in the hiring of its first executive director, Dick Broeker. Broeker, self-described as "an at-bats guy who'll swing at anything and as often as possible," had recently moved to the Southeast and was ready to retire from a remarkable career as an organizer. His track record included a stint as deputy mayor of St. Paul. In that role, he organized and directed a series of high-profile projects, including the St. Paul Farmers' market, the Energy Park development, and the Summit Brewery. Less well known was his long commitment to, and involvement with, the University of Minnesota. Broeker had two graduate degrees from the university. He had served as an associate graduate dean for a period of time in the early 1970s, and had taught and worked in a number of colleges and departments.

During his tenure at the university, Broeker devoted considerable time to linking the university with communities. For example, he developed and promoted the concept of the "applied university" in the late 1960s when he was the director of a program that placed over 3,000 students in the community during a time of urban upheaval. His experience with this kind of work was not altogether positive, however. He left the university in the mid-1970s because, in his judgment, "it was clear that the university had good intentions in developing community relations, but by and large they were not willing to put the resources into the system or build the incentives internally, within the university, that were reflective of the aspirations they articulated."

The new regional partnerships initiative gave Broeker a sense of hope that things might be different this time, so when he saw the position announcement, he submitted an application. He talked about his reasons in a 2000 interview with the authors:

> I was attracted to the position by the people who are running the project, the citizen board of directors. They called me in and I had a wonderful set of conversations with them. And they were totally committed to doing it. There was a real strong sense of localism, as opposed to university organization surrounding the project. All of those were features that in my experience suggested that this one could be done differently.
>
> I think the distinction in this case is that the university set up a program, but the shots were being called by the citizen leaders. And I think that's a big change from almost all of the

initiatives the university sponsors out in the community. So the interesting aspect of this position was the effort to reformulate the linkage, the connection between community and university, by putting the authority and the power with the citizen groups. I didn't feel as if I was hired by the university this time. I actually was hired by a group of citizens, and it didn't feel like university at all, even though technically I'm a university employee, and even though technically and legally, they are simply using referred authority, starting with the Board of Regents on down through the deans.

The board liked what it saw and heard when it interviewed Broeker, so they hired him. As executive director, Broeker's central responsibility was to help the board develop a process for identifying potential projects related to sustainability, and then organize relationships between the university and southeast Minnesota communities to make the projects happen. Broeker's organizing philosophy and practice fit well with the activist stance the ERC board wanted to take toward its work. As board chair Gorfine observed:

I've never seen anyone like him in my life, in terms of both quality and substance. He's thorough and tenacious, and he's also a team player. He's not pursuing his own agenda. I feel very strongly he's been doing what we wanted.

We came together as a board very much wanting to be an activist board, especially the citizen folks around the table, and Dick has followed through with that. I think that's one of the aspects of our board that really attracted Dick to us and has kept him with us. He has great credibility in terms of his credentials, his experience in government, and his experience with the university. He's hard nosed but I think he's extremely diplomatic. We definitely made the right hire, there's no question. We would not be where we are if it were not for Dick Broeker.

Hitching Up the Projects

After Broeker came on board as executive director in November of 1998, the ERC engaged in a process of naming and refining its vision and goals. The overall goal the ERC settled on was "to foster a homegrown economy in southeast Minnesota that will support self-reliant communities and a healthy natural environment" (Experiment 1999a). The board envisioned the ERC as "a farmer tending the fields of sustainable development."

> The crops are community self-reliance and a healthy environ-ment. The tractors that work the fields are home-grown businesses or enterprises—the ones that the Experiment wishes to support and that comprise the homegrown economy. The equipment or implements that make it feasible for the tractor to do its work are University of Minnesota resources.... Hitching up the projects to the University of Minnesota is a daunting task in need of an innovative strategy (Experiment 1999a).

The ERC board hoped that hitching its projects to the university would bring about a number of changes: redirecting the university's teaching, extension, and research agendas to meet identified needs in the region, increasing community input and access to University of Minnesota resources, and fostering the development of agricultural and natural resources systems that would increase profitability, protect environmental quality, and enhance community vitality (Southeast Minnesota Partnership 1998).

Reaching Out to the Community

In establishing a relationship with the university, the ERC's activist board did not intend to anoint itself as the voice for southeast Minnesota citizens. Rather, they were determined to make the ERC a participatory community initiative. To make it so, they undertook a painstaking process of soliciting input and ideas from the region.

First, the board set about "beating the bushes," talking with people in the region about the ERC's goals and soliciting ideas for potential projects. At the same time, they embarked on a more formal resource-mapping survey to collect information on issues, assets, and priorities in the region. The survey included a direct call for citizen engagement:

> The Experiment, to succeed, must be shaped by a strong citizen voice. The purpose of the Resource Mapping questionnaire is to obtain a citizen voice as well as initiate further communication between the Experiment in Rural Cooperation and the citizens of the region. It is anticipated that partnerships in areas of sustainable development, specifically agriculture and natural resources, including farming, tourism and forestry, will be formed in this process to address the priorities of southeast Minnesota (Experiment 1999b).

Second, they took outreach a step farther by visiting face-to-face with interested individuals, businesses, and nonprofit organizations. This step was a crucial one and has characterized the ERC's direct relationship approach, so different from conventional, more distanced and bureaucratic outreach approaches.

Third, the board moved these conversations from the individual level to a community level when they organized a round of community forums to engage others in the themes that were beginning to emerge. The forums were conducted and led by board members and staff and were held in different locations. Together, they attracted well over 150 people.

Citizens who participated in report-back sessions to the ERC noted that they wanted to drive the process through community discussion to establish a "problem-solving relationship with the University of Minnesota." They wanted to "harness the university's resources based on a citizen agenda," such that the work would have "everyday meaning to the citizens of rural Minnesota." One participant reflected that the work must incorporate an "ethic toward the land; every inch is precious. Will is the issue in the face of diminished profit [from agriculture]."

At a meeting to discuss the potential of a cooperative grocery store in Houston, Minnesota, participants reflected on the importance of "flying under the radar. We don't want to play by the rules of those who have written off rural Minnesota, who say that the days of family farms and small communities are over. It doesn't fit what people think here." Participants felt that money from the ERC should be dedicated to those who are "comfortable with not fitting." In the end, one participant said, "the university should be used as effectively by citizens as it is by Monsanto," a large multinational corporation that develops and sells agricultural products.

Finally, the board issued a request for proposals (RFP). Rather than simply acting as a conduit for funding, however, the ERC, like other the regional partnerships, is based on "the concept of active partnership, which calls on us each to think first and foremost as citizens with a commitment to working through issues and exploring opportunities democratically" (Experiment 1999a). While the directive of "dispersing funds for local and regional research, education, and outreach programs" (Guidelines 1998) is clear, the opportunity to establish criteria and a process for "funding at the local level to target needs" is left open to regional interpretation. The ERC board decided that local citizens should take active roles in the establishment of both the criteria and the process. The role of faculty from the university would be to help people think through problems, linking the university back into the community in a practical way.

The ERC board decided to fund those projects that came out of local deliberations with a high degree of support and promise. Such projects would likely be small in scale, at least in comparison to the multimillion dollar initiatives in genomics and biotechnology that universities increasingly focus on these days. The small size of the ERC's projects was a matter of concern to the board and staff. Would they be taken seriously in a university that is increasingly dominated by big-time, big-money science? Dick Broeker predicted that ERC-supported projects "would succeed if the [university's] system was not rigged against small projects."

The ERC board received 45 proposals in response to the forums and its on-the-ground outreach efforts, demonstrating a remarkable outpouring of interest. The decision-making process about which projects to select for community-university partnerships was the first real test of board members' ability to facilitate the relationship between the community and the university. Were they the community's link to the university, the university's link to citizens, or both? From where did their power derive, and how would they use it?

In the decision-making process, board members function as citizen leaders as well as listeners and translators who learn what citizens in the region want from the regional partnership and then transform that set of desires into concrete projects and action with the university. They are advocates both for the community and the university. This is a difficult role to play. "People expect us to help leverage university resources," lamented one board member, "but how can we do that when we don't understand how the university works?"

In developing its review process for proposals, ERC board members wanted to be open to making mistakes and learning from them. They didn't want to make arm's-length judgments, using a single standard, about the worth and viability of projects in the region. Rather, they wanted to discuss how the projects could contribute to sustainable development in southeast Minnesota on a case-by-case basis. Should they emphasize projects with a stronger public purpose or focus on those that propose to utilize university resources to a greater degree? Should they attach more weight to projects with applicability beyond the region?

In their first decision about how to spend their appropriation, the ERC board funded 17 projects, with allocations totaling nearly $350,000. It approved some projects with the proviso that they flesh out their rather vague ideas for how they would engage university faculty, staff, and students. The board also decided to encourage projects in similar issue areas to find points of commonality that could be presented as part of a larger package to the university.

Bringing the University and Community Together

The ERC had established a solid board with members from both the region and the university. It had sought input from citizens, defined an agenda, found people in the region who wanted to enter into partnership with the university, and allocated resources for an initial set of projects. In short, southeast Minnesota was ready to engage the University of Minnesota. Was the university ready to engage southeast Minnesota?

The university is peopled with brilliant researchers and educators who have looked deeply into critical issues and questions related to the pursuit of sustainable development. Food safety issues, processing and marketing questions, finance strategies, business planning, cooperative development, greenhouse technology—all of these are areas of expertise sorely needed by citizens to build their local economies without sacrificing the environment. Yet people from the community were baffled about the points of entry into the university. Despite the fact that it is an institution, it functions like a region of small towns. Faculty use the word *fiefdom* in jest to describe university departments, but the political relationships it conjures are real. "Faculty are all individual entrepreneurs," remarked one faculty member. "Incentives for cross-disciplinary work are almost non-existent. In fact, there may even be disincentives. For university faculty to engage community members around their multidisciplinary questions is a new way of engaging for many."

The ERC's early efforts to gain university support for research on issues of concern to the whole region were disappointing. No faculty member showed interest in participating. It became apparent very quickly that research agendas were full. "The university metabolism was not in sync with the projects whose time frames were much more about the rhythm and necessity of their work," reflected Broeker.

The ERC board concluded that it needed a critical mass to interest the university in what it was doing. A set of food-related projects the board was supporting emerged as the best candidates. A meeting was called for people involved in the projects to learn more about each other's work, discover points of commonality, and consider how best to present their needs and interests to the university. They decided to form a "Southeast Foods Work Group," and developed a statement of identity and mission to submit to the university, as well as a matrix of projects categorized under marketing, product development, business planning, and organizational development. They developed a list of over 30 research, technical assistance, and marketing questions to present to university colleges that might have an interest in collaboration. These ranged from studies of regional marketing efforts in other areas of the country to business planning for sustainably produced beef and pork, to biodiversity studies for new woody agriculture systems. The long-term vision of the group was well expressed by a farmer with a fruit and vegetable business who asserted that "I don't just want to go to the university, get support for my project and leave it at that. I want to know that this will add up to something for the region over the long term."

The ERC supported work on two issues of particular importance to the Southeast Foods Work Group: the flow of food dollars in the region, and consumers' interest in purchasing local and sustainably produced foods. Unfortunately, project coordinators were unable to secure faculty assistance to conduct research on either of these issues. Instead, they engaged a graduate student to work with an outside consultant on a study of one of the issues, and a market research firm to work on the other.

The findings from the two commissioned studies detailed the stark realities of southeast Minnesota in a global food economy. In southeast Minnesota, 8,436 farms sold $866 million of farm products in 1997, but they spent $947 million for the privilege of doing so. The net loss was $80 million. Meanwhile, the 303,256 residents of southeast Minnesota spent $506 million on food, almost all of it from producers outside the state. Farm families spent $400 million per year purchasing inputs and credit from distant suppliers. "This means," say the authors of the report, "as much as $800 million each year flows out of our agricultural region as local families grow and buy food.... This represents an amount equivalent to $1 of every $9 of income earned by the region's 303,000 residents, and constitutes a tremendously significant—and brutally weakening—loss" (Meter and Rosales 2001).

The studies showed that southeast Minnesota consumers are putting a lot of food dollars into the economy—but not necessarily the local economy. The 120,000 households in the region earn $7.6 billion per year and spend 7 percent on food—$506 million. They spend $300 million for home consumption, and the rest is spent on meals away from home. Low-income people receive $8 million in food stamps. More than one-third of the region's retail sales are devoted to food-related purchases. The region's schools spend $15 million a year providing school lunches. Research also confirmed that people in the region would be willing to pay more for sustainably produced food.

The studies reinforced the Southeast Foods Work Group's views that there is potential in southeast Minnesota to reclaim the value in sustainable food production and sale that is being lost, thus creating the "homegrown economy" the ERC called for when it set its overall goal. The trick would be to achieve it in the face of global dynamics and trends. "We're taking folks in farming who are very diverse in terms of the products they produce," explained Jeff Gorfine. "And we're trying to say, 'How can we stay around the table and create a homegrown economy that will be able to provide you a livelihood but will also help us see that there are a lot of others we need to try to help establish and sustain their own businesses?' And I think if we can keep people around the table and figure out an infrastructure and an approach to regional marketing, regional processing, storage, and transportation, then we will be able to garner some of the 504 million dollars that goes out of this region and keep that money circulating here."

The Organizing Question

The ambitious goal of bringing local citizens and university faculty, staff, and students to the table—and keeping them there— in order to figure out how to develop a homegrown economy in southeast Minnesota raises a host of questions and challenges. For example, it raises the question of whether a homegrown economy is technically possible. It strikes us, however, that the central challenge in pursuing the ERC's goal is a political one involving public judgments about what the problems and opportunities of the region are, and developing the will, ideas, relationships, and resources to address them. Therefore, the most urgent and important question the ERC faces is what we refer to as the "organizing" question, in which organizing is understood as the craft of building public relationships and power, facilitating deliberation that leads to public judgment, and identifying and negotiating interests and roles. The question is what *kind* of organizing or what *approach* to organizing will work best in establishing and maintaining a partnership with the university that will allow the ERC to succeed in pursuing its central goal?

From the beginning, the ERC board and staff opted for an organizing rather than a "networking" approach to their work with the university. They made a decision not to go for the "low hanging fruit" by selecting projects that would be easy fits for existing university programs. Instead, they developed an ambitious agenda that called for new relationships. Rather than simply linking up individual projects to get support from specific faculty and students, the ERC wanted to elicit an ongoing commitment from the university to the region as a whole. ERC board and staff believed strongly that the region's relationships with the university should be formal, and that commitments should be explicit to ensure that people in the region would be able to use university resources most effectively. They were working out of an "active citizenship" mode, defined as "the means for developing the intentional public relationships, among individuals and across institutions, required to establish a base of citizen leaders powerful enough to create ideas, wealth, and justice" (Guidelines 1998).

The ERC's initial attempts to forge an ongoing commitment from the university to the region as a whole had produced disappointing results. This failure, the ERC board and staff concluded, revealed a flawed assumption in the operating theory of the regional partnerships initiative: the assumption that only the community outside the university needed to be organized, because the university was there ready and waiting to be engaged. When the leadership of the ERC realized that this assumption was in fact false, it began to undertake the painstaking work of organizing university staff and faculty so that the organized citizens in southeast Minnesota would have a group to relate to.

Don Wyse, the former executive director of MISA, thinks that lack of experience with organizing processes was a factor in the university's inability to engage. "I'm a weed guy, a weed scientist. What do I know about organizing?" The ERC's executive director, however, did have experience as an organizer. His organizing skills and his hardworking persistence are what enabled the ERC to advance as it has.

In his position as a university staff person reporting to a community-based board, Broeker was the person directly responsible for testing out project ideas, organizing and maintaining relationships, and negotiating the flow of information and resources. No matter how "activist" the ERC board wanted to be, they relied heavily on Broeker as their lead organizer. He was the one who did most of the work required to establish and maintain a hitch with the university.

As an organizer, Dick Broeker was tough, street-smart, savvy, logical, intensely practical, and above all, relentlessly persistent.

All of these qualities can be gleaned from his general description of how he approached his work:

> You hear of someone who's got an idea. You go over and visit with them, or have them fill out a very simple form. I usually bounce it off a couple board members. Have a committee meeting on it. Maybe make a site visit.
>
> We work up a set of questions and issues. They submit a more formal proposal to my board. My board gives either a thumbs-up or a thumbs-down, or an in-between thing: let's look at it more.
>
> And I usually trot up to the university campus and have some meetings, nab some people in the hallways, talk about whether they'd be interested, develop enough of a relationship so I can bring the project people up from southeast Minnesota to meet with the faculty or even, in some cases, although it's rare, bring the faculty down here at that point. And then formulate it into a project with a budget and have the board support it.
>
> And then go to work on it. Set up a schedule that essentially identifies what we want to get done when, who's going to be involved from the university side.
>
> And then I service that project. Usually the way these things go, people don't always follow through on what the original plan is, or there's good reason to change the original plan. So you do a lot of mid-course corrections. They're by and large pretty high maintenance things. I mean, there's only one of me. I don't have any support staff or secretarial help, so it's a matter of essentially me touching base with a project person to see how it's going. And if there's been some communication problems between the project and the faculty members or the students working on it, trying to repair that.
>
> I try to develop relationships between projects, like the food projects, when it makes sense to work with them as a group,

and look for areas of linkages with the other regional partnerships, if it makes sense, like we've done with the energy
project. But you're doing a lot of connections work, a lot
of trying to get people to work together, a lot of trying
to develop harmony between community interests and
university interests, or across the regional partnerships. So
it's not complicated. You just keep doing what would be
logical if you believed in the notion of these cooperative
relationships between community priorities and the university, as defined by the community.

Looking closely at Broeker's description of his organizing
approach, we can see that there are more than a dozen different
steps involved just in getting projects established, linked with
university resources, and funded. Beyond that, Broeker took
responsibility for making sure that the projects were running
smoothly. He discovered, in the process, that even when a relationship develops between a faculty member and a community
project, university protocols and incentives aren't necessarily in
place to support it and keep it going.

Broeker's account of what happened when he attempted to
implement one of the ERC's project ideas helps us get a closer
look at the kinds of challenges his organizing work involved:

So let me just take one project. It came through as the Apple
Crisp Cooperative. These are six orchard owners in southeast
Minnesota who are looking for ways of being more competitive, to keep orchard property in agricultural production—
orchard property that was largely stimulated through the
University of Minnesota at the turn of the century when they
introduced the apple crops into the Southeast.

They're being basically put out of business by the surplus of
apples coming out of Washington State or coming from overseas. They know that with the shortened season in Minnesota,
even though they produce a superior quality product, they
can't be competitive on the commodity market. So they want

to move more and more toward value-added products. One of their strategies has been to pull the #2 apples out of the production stream, as opposed to those apples coming and suppressing the price as well as lowering the quality of the overall product. They'd like to process those apples, particularly the Harrelson apples as the prime baking apple, by slicing them and freezing them and developing a secondary market to get those #2's out of the pipeline as well as to increase the revenue stream from another source, through the bakers in Minnesota.

So they came to us, and they had some ideas. They'd done some preliminary research. Although they had some university relationships, because one of them went to school there in the College of Agriculture, I basically started from scratch.

They ended up in the university's Carlson School of Management. So we threw $10,000 in there not knowing what it would cost. That's always a problem, because you don't know what these things cost in advance, which doesn't sit very well with a lot of the university protocols. You're doing estimates and then you have to sign this contract that doesn't work at all. It's a vendor's contract, but it makes no sense.

There's no such thing as a partnership agreement at the university. There's no legal grounds to spend the money unless you set up a vendor's contract. So what we did is hire them as a vendor. This is one of the institutional barriers to doing this work. You don't have facilitative stuff that causes the activity to happen. You basically have to find ways around existing structures that are put in place for an entirely different reason. So you do it. We signed a contract with them, and put $10,000 in their account number.

And then I found a faculty member at the Carlson School, just through a series of eliminations. I just started making a lot of telephone calls. I suppose I made five or six different contacts and I finally found Professor Johns. I think I contacted her on the phone first and she wasn't really interested. So I sent her some stuff. And then I went up to see her, and dropped in on her a couple of times. I got her on the phone with one of the project people, and pretty soon she decided to use this as a class project. It turned out she had a graduate course that was doing marketing research and she took this on as a class project. So she divided the graduate class into four or five teams of students that went out and researched the market opportunities for this frozen apple product.

The experiences of Apple Crisp and other food-related projects led the ERC to undertake a process for hammering out a comprehensive, long-term collaboration with the university. The board directed Broeker to spend most of his time at the university during the winter months of 2000 to find people interested in partnering with southeast Minnesota. As Broeker recalled:

I realized that I wouldn't get anywhere just making phone calls. I took to hanging out behind potted plants in the halls to catch faculty as they went into their offices. The partnerships weren't on anybody's agenda—in fact everybody was confused at first when I started talking with them—but now it only takes about five minutes for them to get that this really is a crucial piece of work in the context of the land-grant mission. I never had a conversation with someone who ended up saying, "Gee, I'm not interested in helping the people of southeast Minnesota." Most were open to thinking about things we could do together.

MISA and the departments in the College of Agriculture, Food, and Environmental Sciences were natural partners for the ERC. But Broeker recognized that if the tough problems related to sustainability were to be addressed effectively, the ERC and the other regional partnerships needed the participation of other colleges and institutes such as the Carlson School of Management, the Humphrey Institute of Public Affairs, and the Institute of Technology.

Over the winter of 1999-2000, Broeker and the ERC board organized a carefully planned series of parallel meetings in southeast Minnesota and at the university. The approach Broeker used to set up the meetings was guided largely by the practical organizing philosophy he had developed over the course of his long career in the public sector. It was a gritty, no-nonsense approach that focused on creating an open but disciplined space for the discovery of mutual self-interests both within and between the university and the citizens of southeast Minnesota and the negotiation of roles and expectations. "The energies once married and harmonized will work because people believe in sustainability," Broeker said. "We have to open enough space and believe they will do the right thing." Broeker also predicted that the organized momentum coming from the southeast region would create a "citizen back-pressure" that would lead the way in bringing the two communities together.

In southeast Minnesota, the Southeast Foods Work Group met regularly to build relationships among the group's members, identify their points of commonality, prepare an initial list of requests for university assistance, and decide how best to present their work to potential university collaborators. Part of the work they did together was to write a clear statement of the future they wanted to see in their region. "Our work has two passions," they wrote, "both of which will determine our destiny. One is the establishment of an environmentally sound, sustainable economy. The other is the revitalization of the critically important culture of small communities that were, and still are, the pillars of democratic society" (Southeast Minnesota Foods Work Group 2001). They articulated a fundamental shared vision of community. "We used to all know each other. Now people come and go. Our children are scattered all around the country.... It is this uncertainty of the future of our communities and of our relationships with each other and the land that has brought the Foods Work Group together."

In the university, Dick Broeker assembled a diverse group of faculty and staff to see whether, collectively, they could arrive at a shared definition of interest in pursuing further conversations with the Southeast Foods Work Group. Department heads, faculty, and staff from the College of Agriculture, Food, and Environmental Sciences, the Carlson School of Management, the Institute of Technology, the Humphrey Institute of Public Affairs, and centers like the Center for Alternative Plant and Animal Products and the Food Retail Marketing Center met to discuss potential areas of collaboration. One of the faculty members who attended the meeting was Rob King, a professor in applied economics. Before attending the meeting, King recalls, "I didn't really know much about the regional partnerships. And then one day Dick Broeker just gave me a call and said that he'd like to meet me and talk to me a little bit. So I heard what he was doing and he began to invite me to some of the meetings they were having on campus."

After the meeting, Broeker circulated an idea for a Southeast Minnesota Lab, modeled on the 3M Lab that operated for several years out of the Carlson School of Management. The 3M Lab was a collaboration between the 3M Corporation and the Carlson School, in which students were assigned to work on real problems identified by 3M. The program was very successful, but has since been discontinued. Why not do the same thing, Broeker reasoned, for the farms and businesses of southeast Minnesota?

King thought that was a good idea. "At the time, I was doing work on supply-chain management issues. Basically, how can farmers get their products in the markets, how can they retain identity of those as they move through the system, and how can we design food systems that give a more equitable share to the farmers? I think in the whole food system there's a desire to have more coordination between producers and processors and retailers. But figuring out how to do that can be a real challenge."

Several attempts to advance the laboratory concept ran into dead ends. But out of the process, King saw an opportunity to link Judy Brienza, one of his graduate students, with the ERC:

At one of those meetings, it really became clear that one of the issues was that if these products are going to go, in order for people to buy them, they have to be available some place where people shop. Within the southeast regional group, there are some who very firmly believe that products should stay in the southeast, and others want to export them to the Twin Cities and beyond. But regardless of where you sell them, you need to get them into the stores or other places where people can buy them.

It's very expensive to do direct marketing for large quantities of stuff. So I was thinking about that and at the same time working on retail food issues. And it became clear that there might be some opportunities to fund a student, and right about that time, one of our master's students just came in to see me about possible research topics. That was Judy Brienza. She had been a buyer for Pillsbury. She had worked for IATP [Institute for Agriculture and Trade Policy] as a writer and researcher. And she was very much interested in the food industry and had a lot of good skills. So I saw this as an opportunity to do some research that would help people in the southeast and to give Judy a good research project for a master's thesis.

Regional Supply Chains

We turn now to a discussion of the regional supply chains work the ERC has supported. The cornerstone of the work is Judy Brienza's master's thesis. Her thesis provides an inspiring example of how public scholarship can contribute to the ERC's goal of developing a homegrown, sustainable economy in southeast Minnesota. We view Brienza's work as public scholarship because it engaged, and was shaped by, the interests of both university and community members, and it included a collaborative, real-time process of inquiry into a pressing, context-bound problem with strong public dimensions.

Background

Judy Brienza grew up in suburban New Jersey. She first developed an interest in agriculture and food systems work when she was a student at Montana State University, where a course she took opened her eyes to the field. She eventually completed an undergraduate degree in applied economics at the University of Minnesota, and then took a job as a buyer for the Pillsbury Corporation, which is located in the Minneapolis-St. Paul metropolitan area. While working at Pillsbury, she took a side job writing a newsletter on trade and sustainable development issues with an action-oriented nonprofit organization called the Institute for Agriculture and Trade Policy (IATP). Her work with IATP interested her more than her work with Pillsbury. She decided to go back to the University of Minnesota to pursue a master's degree in applied economics in order to prepare herself for a career working on agricultural trade and development issues.

Brienza's search for a "practical" project for her master's thesis led her to Rob King, who in turn connected her with the ERC. Judy describes why she was looking for a practical project:

> You take a year of course work and then you do a thesis and the thesis generally lasts about a semester or two semesters. I had been looking for a thesis topic and looking at things that were a little more theoretical at first, but nothing was really clicking for me. It just didn't seem right.
>
> I wanted to do something very practical and solution-oriented because I just think there has always been a gap there. I didn't want to do something that was very theoretical. What's the value? I'm not a great economist. I'm only doing a master's, and so my interest was to do something that really used my business experience and skills to advance something real, modest as it might be.
>
> Someone mentioned that Rob [King] did things that were a little more practical, especially along agribusiness capacity

development. And so I just started talking to him and we just explored a few ideas and he suggested that there might be something from the southeast area that might be of interest to me.

Following King's suggestion, Brienza approached Dick Broeker to ask whether he had any ideas of who she might work with. Dick told her about a project Jody Dansingburg, a farmer and staff member of a nonprofit organization called the Land Stewardship Project (LSP), was working on. LSP had been approached by an environmental group called Clean Water Action about the possibility of offering locally raised pork as a benefit to its members who were interested in supporting Minnesota's sustainable farmers. Dansingburg had taken the idea to a small group of producers who raise hogs and beef in line with sustainability principles set out by the Midwest Food Alliance to see whether they might be able to respond to the request. The group decided to go for it. They formed a cooperative they called Farming with Nature and began working with Dansingburg to figure out how to respond to Clean Water Action's request. Soon they started thinking bigger, hoping that they might figure out how to develop a brand for their products and get them into local markets in Minnesota.

Brienza went down to talk with Dansingburg to see what they were up to, and to assess whether she might collaborate with them on a project that could become the focus of her master's thesis. As Brienza recalls:

> I went down to [Jody's] office in Lewiston, and I spent about two hours with her as she described what they were trying to do, how this particular grouping had come together. They were trying to respond to a need or a request from Clean Water Action. Clean Water Action wanted to be able to offer locally raised pork to its members from small, sustainable farmers. And she was telling me about where they were with that, and that out of that they wanted to maybe have their own label.

It was very disjointed. They had to find people who wanted to do it, but they had no real business plan and they had no real information about what they have to do to get into local supply chains. They had been selling in their e-retail chain maybe four pounds or five pounds a month of pork chops through something called Simon Delivers in the metro area. That's an e-retailer.

And it was sort of like, "Okay, what do we do now? Do we get more serious with each other and try to make this a real brand, or what are we doing? Is this something we really want to do?" They were all separately selling hogs to various hog buyers or at farmers' markets. So they were at a decision point when I encountered them about what to do next, if anything.

After her initial meeting with Dansingburg, Brienza spoke to several other people in the region before deciding that the connection with the Farming with Nature group looked like a good place to ground her master's thesis work. As she told us,

I had had that conversation, and then I had five other conversations, and my response to it was, "Well, this is where I could do the most good." The reason I settled on them was because I saw the greatest need and they were the most willing to participate. I had been reading about the "Label Rouge" in France, about forging your own brand and doing cooperative marketing. I thought it sounded a lot like what they were trying to do in the southeast. I thought, "Let's see if there's an application here."

It started out being a little grander than it ended up being, simply because their needs were greater at the tactical level. For example, I first started thinking, "Well, I'll look at the region as a whole and whether they can forge this whole new quality label," and then I realized there is more to be done at a supply chain level. So I asked Jody if I could put together a proposal to work with the group towards identifying requirements that they would need to meet in order to succeed or to participate at all in more formalized supply chains, meaning other than a farmers' market.

Dansingburg and the Farming with Nature group expressed a strong interest in working with Brienza. Brienza recalls:

> They were eager to have me do something because they're very busy and they didn't have time. These were things that they had been thinking of but had had no time to address themselves. There was interest in selling value-added pork products so that they could get more money. And we knew theoretically or anecdotally that there was interest in the consumer side for these products because people want to buy from smaller farms—people want to preserve the family farmer and buy sustainable products. I wasn't looking at the demand per se, but I knew there was a demand.

The Thesis Project

Working with Rob King as her advisor, Brienza developed a proposal that would simultaneously attempt to make a contribution to Farming with Nature's work, while also serving as her master's thesis. The proposal's focus, in Brienza's words, was on "building the capacity of smaller regional producers to supply or to sell value-added food products into various supply chains." She presented the proposal to Farming with Nature. They liked it and encouraged her to go ahead. She presented it to the ERC, which agreed to fund it by paying for a graduate research assistantship for Brienza while she worked on the project.

Brienza began to work on the project during the fall semester of 2000. Her research focus was to get "tactical and strategic requirements" from suppliers about how small producers in southeast Minnesota could enter supply chains in the region. The university's Retail Food and Industry Center gave her the names of suppliers to grocery stores, restaurants, nursing homes, food service distributors, and e-retailers. She developed a questionnaire to determine the requirements for entry into each market, including details about UPC coding, slotting fees, packaging, transportation, and other requirements. She did a literature review, developed the questionnaire, and gave it to several people to critique. She subsequently called and visited 15 people representing the full range of food distribution to which Farming with Nature might want access. Most important, Brienza took pains to ensure that Farming with Nature had input into the focus and direction of the research. "I met with the Farming with Nature group whenever they had their meetings," she told us. "I talked about possible supply opportunities or just talked about things in general. I tried to understand as much as possible about where they were going, what their concerns were, what their needs were."

Brienza finished her work in March of 2001. The findings from her research indicated that e-retail and retail formats were most suited to Farming with Nature's goals. The volume requirements of larger distributors couldn't be met because the Farming with Nature members weren't interested in expanding the scale of their operations. Promotional costs were prohibitive as well. Whereas Farming with Nature had high hopes of selling to regional restaurants, Judy discovered that the restaurants are strongly committed to their distributors, who find it difficult to incorporate local products in their offerings. Moreover, the difference between what the distributors were willing to pay and the farmers wanted to earn was too great.

Far from being disappointed by the results of Brienza's research, the producers involved in Farming with Nature felt as though they had moved closer to their goals. According to Brienza:

> They were really excited about it because it was the first time they had ever put in place what they had to do to participate if they wanted to be a brand. And it also was the first time they

looked at the costs in a comprehensive manner. I think it really opened their eyes. [It] facilitated some decision making on their part which they had been putting off because they would only have one bit of information here or there and they never had a comprehensive look at selling to these supply chains. So they were really excited. They told me they were pleased, so I hope they were.

Brienza's advisor, Rob King, had a similar view of the impact of Brienza's research:

I felt it was really positive. What we felt good about is that Judy really laid out the options and the pros and cons. I don't know if they'll change their mind, and whatever they choose is the right thing. But it was a good experience. Maybe our conclusions as to what one might do might have been different, but we're not in their shoes.

Whatever the success of Brienza's work, it was also both difficult and frustrating. According to Brienza, the difficulties centered on communication and organizing issues:

Well number one, it's hard because the group I worked with —and I think this is maybe true for most of the groups in the area—they're loose associations. So there's not a master plan and there's not necessarily uniform agreement amongst the participants about what direction they want to go in. So it was hard in the sense of, sometimes, I didn't understand the needs that well because they wanted different things. Or I didn't understand what their ultimate goal was because they didn't know.

They're not organized very well in that region, and that's, I think, the nature of rural producers. That was a little difficult. Feeling a little bit like I'm presuming what needs to be answered. And so it was trying to ask the right questions but not knowing exactly the question that definitely needed to be answered. So some of it was my own decision about what needed to be answered, and that's why I was a little bit nervous when I was done. Did I answer the right questions? It seems like I did.

We asked Brienza to tell us what kinds of skills scholars need to be able to successfully engage in public scholarship under the conditions she encountered in southeast Minnesota. "Mostly just people skills," she told us.

> Really being able to work with people. Be very persistent because they're multi-tasking in terms of farm, family, and off-farm jobs, and you have to understand that you're not their highest priority. Even though this was my highest priority, it was not theirs. You have to be very patient. They're not working for you, and so you have to be very persistent, but in a pleasant manner, and you have to understand their constraints.

> It's also important to understand just what they're bringing to the table and being very aware of where you come from. If you don't understand the workings of a farm from growing up, just be aware of that, and the suspicions that go along with that from the farmers' standpoint. But also understand that the knowledge you bring is different, but no greater than, the knowledge they bring and that we need each other. Not being pretentious about that.

It's interesting to note that, while Brienza began her answer to our question by mentioning "people skills," she went on to stress the importance of respect, understanding, and humility, which are not really skills, but rather attitudes and principles.

Spin-Offs

Inspired by Brienza's work with Farming with Nature, Dick Broeker saw an opportunity to engage other faculty in the southeast who have an interest in supply chains. Fred Beier, a professor emeritus at the Carlson School of Management, was one of the faculty members Broeker most wanted to engage. Beier was developing a supply-chain curriculum at the graduate and undergraduate levels, and he was viewed by his colleagues as having something important to contribute. Beier's response to Broeker's approach follows a familiar pattern that we saw in our research: first, skepticism about getting involved, but due to Broeker's persistence and his ability to tap others' self-interests, finally "succumbing" to the invitation. Beier told us:

> Dick Broeker came over to the school and talked to a variety of faculty here, including the associate dean of academic programs. And he explained to these people that he was interested in trying to improve the efficiency of flow of southeastern Minnesota products to market. And people generally said, "Yeah, we do a little bit of that, but you have to talk to Fred Beier."

> Eventually he caught up with me and I tried to get some explanations as to what the project was. I sat with Dick for about an hour, hour and a half, and he made some sense, but it was a very idealistic kind of project. I view these projects as being very difficult because they depend so much on cooperation and varied interests. They certainly need somebody like Dick to be the rallying cry.

> I describe Dick as sort of a piece of gum that gets on your shoe and you just can't get rid of him. You finally succumb to cooperating with him, and you find out it's worthwhile. But I mean these are extraordinarily difficult things to do because these people that he's trying to serve are fiercely independent and they've got their own ideas and it's like herding cats.

> At any rate, we started talking and he said, "Well, are you interested in helping?" And it turns out that I have an interest in southeast Minnesota. I spend a lot of my time down in Fillmore County. So I agreed to cooperate.

Beier, King, and Brienza collaborated in two workshops with southeast Minnesota food producers to share the results of Brienza's study and to explore how others in the region could incorporate supply-chain thinking into their work to improve the potential of the region's food businesses. Fifty farmers, food processors, and retailers from the region attended. Brienza presented her research, and Beier and King conducted exercises with the group to engage them in thinking about supply chains.

Beier, who had been least involved in the process and was essentially coming to the meeting without any pre-existing relationships, viewed the workshop as an event at which "a number of issues were put before the audience, in terms of opportunities for them to exploit their market position and get organized so that they could make some gains in efficiency." More accustomed to consulting with corporate clients, such as Archer Daniels Midland, than with broader community groups, he was skeptical of his impact on the group. "When I was trying to lead the discussion, I just couldn't get it to go anywhere. There were just an extraordinary number of divergent views, all relevant, making it very difficult." Beier's assessment was that he was trying to provide the information they needed to get into conventional retail markets, and he was surprised to discover that they were resistant to that:

> After I was done with my section of the presentations, I wasn't at all sure that I had contributed any value, and then after I observed the discussion, I thought, "Well, maybe I had superimposed a dose of reality and provided some kind of education." But it wasn't that obvious. It was too mainstream for them.

> My sense is that one of the motivations of many producers down in that part of the state is that they want to try to follow an independent path. They don't want to follow conventional wisdom, they want to try to do things themselves in their own way that satisfies not only economics, but their sense of right and moral responsibility.

I don't want to make light of it. If you take a professor who has been looking at business models for a long time and say, "Well, we're not interested in profit," which is what some of the people told me, then I really don't have very good models. I was not prepared for the different motivation that the producers themselves in southeastern Minnesota have.

Interestingly, whereas some vocal members of the group did challenge Beier's conception of scale, others found the analyses he did of the supply chains for specific businesses represented in the room extremely useful. The workshop led to subsequent workshops in which participants developed working groups to look at transportation and storage infrastructure, the potential for developing retail markets in the region, and business planning. Another university faculty member from the Carlson School conducted a workshop on business planning. The workshops served the purpose of putting common questions on the table for the members of the Southeast Foods Work Group, thus enabling them to take the next steps in developing an action plan. A core group of those who attended are in the planning stages of developing a cooperative that will market farmers' products in the region.

The supply-chain work raises questions about the role of scholars (both students and faculty) in addressing public problems, and what it is they have to bring to the table. In Rob King's view, "I think for someone, let's say from applied economics, which is what I'm in, I think we bring training in how to look at a particular problem and how to ask questions, not just about the dollars and cents, but about what other costs and benefits that are non-monetary there might be with a particular alternative." King helped us understand how Judy Brienza's work revealed the limits of university scholars' roles, while also demonstrating how such work could actually provide key knowledge that enriches and enhances a faculty member's knowledge and work. King told us:

One thing we probably don't have as often as people think we do, is the immediate answer to a very specific question. In other words, I did not know in advance of this exactly what it takes to get into a regular food distributor's warehouse to be able to sell to lots of stores. I think we don't always carry around a lot of real practical immediate knowledge that would answer every question. I think sometimes there's an expectation that we do have that kind of knowledge. But this is the way we get it, too, if we're going to have it.

So, now, from having worked on this with and through Judy, I know a lot more about the particular costs of getting these products to market. And in addition to a framework for how to analyze it, I know a few more specific facts about what's required. And so it's through those experiences of just doing some applied research in a project that you turn around quickly and is not necessarily path-breaking, but is important to somebody, that you can get some good knowledge.

The Practice of Public Scholarship

Our study of how the ERC is building community-university partnerships has provided us with evidence to support four key assertions about the practice of public scholarship in the land-grant system. We present them below with the caveat that our assertions must be treated as suggestive rather than conclusive, given the limits of our study and the need to compare what we learned with evidence generated from further research.

First, public scholarship is relatively rare in land-grant education. Informed by personal experience and by our understanding of why the Regional Sustainable Development Partnerships were created in the first place, we approached this study with a hunch that public scholarship is not a common occurrence in land-grant education. Our study has provided us with evidence to support this assertion. While the evidence is not overwhelming, based as it is on the experiences of a small study sample, we nevertheless view it as sufficiently trustworthy to put it on the table as our first assertion.

From Judy Brienza's experience, we learned that it is relatively rare for graduate students to approach their research as public scholarship, and conduct it in the context of community-university partnerships. "It just happens to be my personality, but most people don't do things that have a practical application," Brienza told us. "They're mostly more theoretical or looking at an economic problem in general, maybe examining research that's already been done. There aren't a lot of students who are doing practical applications of something that will have a real lasting value."

We also learned that public scholarship is rare for faculty, even faculty who have significant public interests and concerns. For example, Rob King has a strong commitment to the public interest that motivates his academic work. He's a member of MISA's joint seminar, a committee made up of university and community participants that advises MISA. He has developed educational materials for MISA and written a publication on collaborative marketing to serve co-ops and other groups of farmers. He's worked on crop insurance and commodity marketing strategies. Despite this history, however, he found the close collaboration with the ERC unusual. "I've had those experiences before in some cases," King told us, "but it's maybe a once-in-five- or-ten-years type of thing."

King gave us three reasons why he hasn't been more engaged in public scholarship: there's been a lack of opportunity to meet people in the state; he's already too busy with other things; and he is shy. In his words:

> I've been here for a long time, for 18 years, and I know very few people out in counties. I have very few opportunities to meet them. I'm sort of a shy person, too. A lot of times they're

going to have to come to me, rather than me going to them, because my plate is always overfull and I'm not a good socializer, I guess.

For Fred Beier, the experience of deep partnerships with communities is just as rare. Beier told us that in his 34-year career, he has had the opportunity to help community initiatives "four or five, half a dozen times." Beier thinks that a key reason why public scholarship is rare is because the university's reward structure doesn't value activities with entities like the ERC.

> To a certain extent, particularly for junior faculty or younger faculty, it's very difficult to justify involvement in this kind of thing. The academic payoffs just may not be there in terms of ability to publish in a scholarly journal. You have to identify where the payoff for this kind of participation is going to be. Rob King apparently has been able to identify that in terms of leveraging it with graduate students in his own work. But for a lot of faculty, it's difficult to see where this is going to turn out.

Second, making public scholarship less rare requires official, well-funded structures. If public scholarship is rare in land-grant education, what can be done to make it less so? We believe the ERC story shows that an official ongoing platform supported by significant financial resources can facilitate public scholarship, even against the kind of internal university barriers that Fred Beier noted above. Certainly Judy Brienza's supply chain work provides supportive evidence of this assertion. Without the ERC as a platform, and without the financial support it provided, Brienza's work with Farming with Nature would probably not have been done.

An official, ongoing platform has a great deal of value in opening two-way communication and creating continuing relationships for public scholarship, as Rob King helped us understand when we asked him how and why the ERC and the other RSDPs were valuable to him as a scholar.

Well, first of all they provide very good, effective, two-way communication. People feel like we, on the Twin Cities campus, are a little distant, and we might feel a little distant from the people out in the state. But the regional partnerships have gotten communication going. It's nice to see the same people and to know them and know where they're coming from and kind of watch their problems and activities evolve over time. I think that's been a really good thing about it. It's a continuing relationship, rather than working on just one thing and then not seeing the people again. So I think it's been good in that way.

Our assertion about the value of an official platform and dedicated resources in facilitating public scholarship encourages us to question the role of the formal cooperative extension system in this case, the University of Minnesota Extension Service—in facilitating public scholarship. One of the main reasons why the national cooperative extension system was created in 1914 was to provide dedicated resources and a platform for linking land-grant universities with rural communities in order to advance their economic, civic, and cultural well-being. For a wide variety of reasons that are beyond the scope of this chapter, the formal extension system's ties with faculty and students at land-grant institutions have weakened. One of the things we uncovered in our research was the hope that the ERC and the other regional partnerships might help extension rebuild these ties. Conversely, we also found that the reason some people feel the regional partnerships are needed is because the formal extension system is no longer able or willing to place the facilitation of public scholarship at the center of its mission and work. What we may be witnessing in Minnesota with the RSDP initiative, then, is either the renewal of cooperative extension's role in facilitating public scholarship, or the birth of a whole new system that will take this role on.

Third, skilled organizing is essential to public scholarship.
As important as an official platform and dedicated resources are
in facilitating public scholarship, they are not enough, by themselves, to do the job. The key ingredient in facilitating public
scholarship is skilled, aggressive, strategic organizing, both inside
and outside the university. This is so because getting a land-grant
university to work respectfully and effectively with citizens and
communities is akin to getting the government to support civil
rights or making sure banks invest in inner-city neighborhoods.
In each case, the mission of the institution would seem to support
the outcome. But the incentives, culture, and governing pressures
that influence the daily workings of such institutions are often
oriented to other priorities. Sustained organizing by grassroots
constituencies and civic-minded professionals proves necessary
to bring actions in line with institutional missions.

Skilled organizers build relationships and power to pursue
public ends. They help people identify their self-interests in relation to larger public interests. This is not something that faculty
can always do on their own. As Rob King told us, "I think we as a
university and as individuals within it, are often just concerned
with the things that we're interested in. Sometimes we don't see
an opportunity to apply our skills and our interests in a way that
can both help us learn a lot and help some people out." Working
with Dick Broeker, Rob King was able to take advantage of an
opportunity to apply his skills and interests in supply chains in a
way that both helped him learn and helped people in southeast
Minnesota move a step closer to their goal of establishing a
sustainable homegrown economy.

Over and over again, people involved with the ERC mentioned
Dick Broeker's tenacity, energy, and enthusiasm as being essential
for the ERC's success, and for their own involvement. We asked
Rob King to tell us what he found valuable in Broeker's work:

> I think first of all, just his energy in terms of coming up here
> and talking to people has been remarkable, and that's what

got us into this project. Second, he knows everybody and he was very helpful in giving names to Judy as to who she should contact, and maybe in what order she should contact them. He would talk to people in advance also so that they would know that she was coming. He has a very good sense of how to make things happen. I think he was not deeply involved or wanting to find out what Judy was doing at every minute, but when he was hearing about what she was doing, he was very comfortable in terms of asking questions and also very supportive. And he gave us a lot of trust, too.

Here is Fred Beier's view:

Dick Broeker is just a tiger. He gets a hold of you and he doesn't let go. Without Dick there's no question in my mind that I wouldn't have become involved with this. And, you know, his tenacity. First of all, he talks faster than virtually anybody in the world. And he's just full of ideas and optimism and energy.

Fourth, civic interpretations of the land-grant mission provide a powerful means for inspiring and justifying public scholarship. We saw this in Jeff Gorfine, who told us that he became involved in the ERC because he saw it as something that could help revitalize the land-grant mission:

For a long time, at least the last 15, maybe 20, years but certainly after the major crisis of farming in the late 80s, I had felt that our country was losing some of its national soul by the way farmers are being dealt with. I saw an opportunity, in terms of what the sustainable development partnerships were about, of trying to bring the University of Minnesota back into play in a more vigorous way than they had been playing in the past. I think they've become more corporate, especially the extension service. I thought this was an opportunity that would provide us a way to revitalize the land-grant mission, but also try to help folks in southeast Minnesota revitalize their own small town communities as well as farming natural resources. That was the attraction.

Judy Brienza demonstrated an exceptional commitment to making sure her research was of value to the members of the Farming with Nature cooperative. She traces her commitment to the land-grant mission, to lessons her parents taught her when she was growing up.

> Both my parents went to Rutgers, which is a land-grant university, and my dad was on the Board of Regents there. He instilled in me the land-grant philosophy in terms of the responsibilities of the land-grant university toward educating people, but also the responsibility of students that are educated by that system. If I'm going to be educated in a subsidized manner, then I have a responsibility to use the education towards something greater than myself, as much as you can say this work was greater than myself. I was subsidized by the taxpayer and the Experiment in Rural Cooperation. I think it contributed at least to the knowledge of the region, and that that was part of my responsibility benefiting from the education of the university.

We found that, while faculty tend to have a rather vague understanding of what the land-grant mission is, what they do understand about it provides authority for public scholarship. Rob King's view focuses on a connection with place:

> I guess I would say the land-grant mission is to provide research, both applied and basic research, and then also education, which is on campus and through extension to the people of the state and the nation. I think out of that, the things that make a land-grant university different are first of all, typically a connection with place. And so, I think a significant amount of our time and effort is devoted to things related to our state, and to applied issues and applied problems.

> Clearly, the beginning of the land-grant mission was through agriculture. But I really see the land-grant mission going

ideally across the whole university. So I think things that we would see in public-policy areas or other kinds of activities are just as relevant for the land-grant mission and are just as effective.

Fred Beier's view focuses on social responsibility:

The land-grant mission means that you have open access as far as students are concerned. And as far as the university is concerned, it means that you have some kind of agricultural mission, some kind of extension that goes out and serves the community. That may mean the classic definition of agricultural extension agents and that sort of thing, but also at the University of Minnesota it means that you have evening programs for nontraditional students. A lot of us participate or have participated in those kinds of programs. And generally it means that you have a social responsibility to the state.

Dick Broeker's eloquent response to our question about the connection between the land-grant mission and the ERC provides evidence of just how powerful the land-grant mission is to provide meaning and authority for public scholarship efforts. We include his complete and rather lengthy response below because it strikes us as being full of insight and wisdom:

That's what it's all about. It strikes me that this is a value decision that an institution makes about its role in the larger community. Like a lot of value decisions, it's a difficult one. There is no economic sense in doing this compared to the other things you could be doing at the university.

It's no different than parents raising a child. There's no economic sense in raising a child these days. It costs you a lot of money, and it's a lot of grief and a lot of lost sleep. But you do it because you value that.

That's not unlike the kind of decision that has to be made with the university about its relationship to smaller interests throughout the state, based on the priorities of those interests, not the priorities of the university. The land-grant mission cannot be logically justified in economic terms. It can't be justified in world ranking terms. It's got to be justified on something of softer value something about the sense of community and the role the university plays that has got to be accepted for what it is. If you don't buy that, this is a foolish exercise. There just isn't enough there from any of the other standards that tend to motivate institutions similar to the university.

We seem to have moved into a culture where the judgments that we use are based on different criteria. Just pick up the paper. Everybody wants to be world-class. Everybody says, "We have to be a world-class institution. We have to have a winning baseball team. We have to have a world-class stadium. We have to be ranked in the top five of schools of business. We have to have one of the best 100 corporations in America." To achieve those payoffs, you have to give up a lot of important things that get in the way.

So in some respects, if you take the world-class race that universities are wound up in, rural interests are a millstone because they just slow you down. Working with two small greenhouses in southeast Minnesota isn't going to get you a world-class ranking. It's that simple. And therefore, why do you do it?

You've got to make a value decision about what's important. If the race to grab the golden ring is most important, you're going to cut off some things that are getting in your way or slowing you down. I think that's where this issue has to be dealt with.

How important are rural communities? How important is the way we raise food, not just how cheap that food is? How important is the connection between communities and faculty and students throughout this state?

I will assure you, all of those things will slow down the attempt to grab the golden ring, as it is often described by university people who are in a different race than I am. And that's a choice that the university makes as an institution. It's the choice that's made in the athletic program at the university. Do you want the #1 ranked football team? Or do you want a group of athletes who are also in there for the education? It's a very clear tradeoff. You can have them both in some cases. But by and large, you either have a mediocre football program or you have a high-powered football program with a low graduation rate.

It's that same kind of trade-off here. How do you take these interests that often drain each other? How can you be world-class and yet have the community relationships that seem to deplete the money you have available for doing big league research that has nothing to do with those small producers in rural Minnesota?

The argument is made, "They'll be helped by this. We'll go off and do this world-class research, and everybody will be the beneficiary." It's like the father who says, "I'm never going to play with my kids. Instead, I'll make a lot of money. Then when we have a lot of money, we'll all benefit from it." Well, we know it doesn't work that way. But we delude ourselves into believing that that's the way it should work. So that's how the land-grant mission is. It's a value that needs to be clarified and dealt with up front.

A Final Note

A few months after Dick Broeker retired from his position as executive director of the ERC in 2004, he died suddenly of a heart attack. Broeker's death is a tragic loss, not only for his family and friends, but for all those who admired his tenacious organizing and his passionate commitments to rural Minnesota, a sustainable food system, and the land-grant mission. When Broeker left the

ERC, its programs and work were thriving, despite a significant budget cut that had just been imposed on the organization. Both the budget cut and Broeker's retirement and tragic death highlight the fact that the long-term viability of the ERC's effort to establish a partnership with the University of Minnesota is fragile and vulnerable. It depends on line-item funding from the state legislature, the support of people inside and outside the university, and the hard work of those who do the tough, day-to-day organizing of the relationships that must be established and maintained between campus and community.

Of course, the success of the ERC's work so far has not been solely due to the extraordinary quality of Dick Broeker's organizing talents. The talents and abilities of the people in the region have contributed a great deal to the enterprise. Jeff Gorfine wanted to make sure we understood that. In his words, this is what the ERC's success proves:

> People who are farming, people who are involved in natural resources and tourism, folks from the community, can lay out a research agenda and an education agenda and outreach agenda that's pretty damn strong. It doesn't have to be just academically driven. We know what we need, or we feel we know what we need, and where we need the help.

The regional partnerships are proving to be effective vehicles for facilitating public scholarship, and ordinary citizens are proving to have much to offer as active participants in shaping and conducting it. In the end, however, those involved in the partnerships, question whether what they've done will be enough to sustain the work over the long haul. "The worst possible outcome," Dick Broeker told us, "is to get a couple of good community-university partnerships going and assume this means the experiment is successful. Success can only be claimed if the partnerships reflect the full load of citizen leadership and sustainability commitment envisioned by those who conceived of the regional partnerships in the first place."

(Parts of this paper first appeared in Experiment in Rural Cooperation: Engaging University and Community, *by Karen Lehman and Julie Ristau, and* Southeast Minnesota Food and Community: One View of Many, *by Karen Lehman.)*

References

Experiment in Rural Cooperation. 1999. *Resource Mapping Survey.*

Experiment in Rural Cooperation. 1999. *Where Do We Go from Here? Putting the Retreat's Business Statement to Work.*

Guidelines and Operating Principles, University of Minnesota Regional Agricultural and Natural Resources Sustainable Development Partnerships. 1998. Partnership Task Force Report.

Meter, K. and J. Rosales. 2001. *Finding Food in Farm Country: The Economics of Food and Farming in Southeast Minnesota.* Community Design Center.

Minnesota Round Table on Sustainable Development. 1998.

Minnesota Statutes. 2004. "Section 4A.07: Sustainable Development for Local Government." http://www.revisor.leg.state.mn.us/stats/4A/07.html

Partnership Task Force. 1997. "Regional Sustainable Development Partnerships: Guidelines and Operating Principles." Unpublished document.

Regional Sustainable Development Partnerships, University of Minnesota: College of National Resources, College of Agricultural, Food, and Environmental Sciences, and University of Minnesota Extension Service. http://www.regionalpartnerships.umn.edu/about.html.

Southeast Minnesota Partnership. 1998. *Distilling the Current Definitions: Being Clear on Mission and Principles.*

Southeast Minnesota Southeast Foods Work Group. *Maximizing the Regional Food Opportunities in Partnership with the University of Minnesota.* Unpublished document.

Chapter Four:
The North Country Community Food and Economic Security Network

A Profile of David Pelletier, Associate Professor of Nutrition Policy, Division of Nutritional Sciences, Cornell University

Interview conducted by Scott Peters

Profile edited by Margo Hittleman, Scott Peters, and David Pelletier

A Note of Explanation about This Chapter:

This chapter is presented in the form of a practitioner profile rather than a formal case study. Profiles are edited transcripts of recorded interviews. Think of them as oral histories of practice stories. The stories practitioners tell in their profiles serve as revealing windows into their work and experience. They offer intimate glimpses of what practitioners choose to tell us about the most challenging moments of their work. Their accounts help us to see well beyond tidy job descriptions to the messy complexity of "real" work.

In this profile, David Pelletier provides a remarkably candid and reflective account of the evolution of his academic career. The story of public scholarship he tells is equally candid and reflective. We come to see why and how he took on multiple roles as organizer, facilitator, coach, civic educator, and scholar in an action research project in the North Country, an area comprised of six counties that border the Adirondacks in upstate New York. We learn a great deal about the civic and academic promise of public scholarship from Pelletier's profile. But we also learn about its limits and challenges.

As good stories often are, Pelletier's practice story is both inspiring and troubling. Far from answering all our questions about the practice of public scholarship, it raises new ones by illuminating areas of work and experience that are typically hidden from view. We include it in this collection with the conviction that its central lessons and insights are of great value in coming to understand and advance the work of engaging campus and community.

Background

I grew up in and around Lowell, Massachusetts, home of the Industrial Revolution in the United States. I stayed there through my childhood, until I went off to the University of Arizona at the age of 18.

I would characterize my family now as the working poor. My father was a corrections officer in the Massachusetts Department of Corrections. He completed tenth grade and then went into the Navy during World War II. When he came back, he did not complete high school. Like so many others, he settled down and started a family. There were six children: one brother and twin sisters above me and two sisters below me.

In general, it was a very good family life, a very good upbringing. Clearly, we struggled. My father was an authoritarian type. We had to relate to him with circumspection. It was spillover from the stress of being a corrections officer. He never brought work home in an overt way, but he carried big stresses around inside. My mother got her high-school education and became a stay-at-home mom. We had a kennel, and she ran the kennel. So I grew up in a small-town environment, and we made do with very simple things.

There was no ethic about being involved in the community or a sense of public life when I was growing up. And I learned zero about that from my undergraduate experience. I did my graduate work at Penn State, a land-grant university. I was in biological anthropology, but we were studying people from the detached scientific model. I focused on nutrition.

My dissertation was based on classic disengaged, detached field surveys in Western Samoa. I did send a copy of my dissertation back to the health department in Samoa about two years later, but that was the extent of it. My advisor at Penn State actively discouraged us from having even a paragraph at the end of our dissertation on public-health implications. Here we were studying obesity and heart disease and we could not include public-health implications. In his view, that was for public-health people to do, taking into account a wider range of considerations.

I came to Cornell in 1984 as a one-year post-doc to work on nutrition surveillance, which was ostensibly to process survey data and help government agencies use it for better program and policy development. The implicit notion was that we don't have as much action on nutrition as we would like because we lack information—statistical information in particular. We all knew that there were political issues involved, but the program I joined was premised on applying the techniques of nutritional epidemiology to improve the information base for decision making. We tried to advocate for and foster that decision making as much as possible, but always from a technical rationality. At the time, I didn't even realize that that was only one form of rationality.

Transformations

If you were to focus on my work on the North Country Project and what that represents and compare it to my thinking and my work when I first arrived in 1984, I don't think you'd see any similarity at all. I've gone through a series of personal, intellectual, and professional transformations in the 16 years I've been here. Social commitment and values are not what brought me into anthropology. It had more to do with the intellectual challenge. The social dimensions grew as I got into the work.

In retrospect, I was very much underdeveloped in terms of my social and political awareness and critical consciousness until I had been here a couple of years. And then, the turning point was very gradual. It came through struggling with my notion of how to create positive change and defining what positive change meant. It's inevitable that if you work with these issues, you begin seeing their many dimensions. Eventually ideas about moral and social justice emerged, and then I recognized broader and broader links to the way societies are organized and, ultimately, to the way our society is organized.

I went to Malawi for three years, still working for Cornell, but collaborating with UNICEF (and the government and the local university) on nutrition surveillance. That's really where cognitive dissonance entered in. That's when I realized that the theory and principles of nutrition surveillance, as conceived up until that time, were not working, and could not work.

The project I got involved with there was analyzing national survey data. In the pilot area in the north of the country, insects had wiped out the staple crop of cassava. We did survey work to determine the extent of food security and nutritional wasting in adults and children. I did this almost single-handedly, although I worked with a committee at the regional level. We produced reports, and then we pushed for decision making to get relief and development work going in the affected district.

What impressed me the most in reflecting on the experience— and I published this when I came home—was how little the survey data was used, and how symbolically important it was to policy-makers to have done it. But I was most impressed by the local knowledge that was vital for intelligent project planning about the local ecological conditions, economic situation, and cultural factors. That had to be collected qualitatively from the local people.

As the regional committee proposed interventions for consideration by the national government, I realized that the survey data was providing only five percent of the information that was actually feeding into our recommendations. I realized that in the course of doing the survey, I had had a lot of interaction in the communities, and it was input from the extension staff and the other committee members who had broader knowledge about the local context that we were able to make intelligent project plans. The survey itself was almost irrelevant to that planning.

For example, if you think the alternative to cassava is growing maize, you have to know that monkeys exist in the forest in this area that destroy maize. The people had tried growing maize for years. The national government had been telling them, "Grow maize, grow maize," and the monkeys kept destroying it. The soils were too sandy; the rains were too prolonged. They'd all "been there and done that," and you had to have access to that knowledge.

So I began to think about how district-level and regional-level planners might make these reconnaissance visits to local communities, collect that data, come back and draw up their plans, and then implement those plans in a top-down fashion. My big take-home message was that we needed to figure out how to collect local knowledge for project and policy planning. That was one breakthrough.

The next breakthrough was realizing that communities need to be involved in other planning stages, not just providing information. If they're going to support something and it's going to be sustainable, then another reason for involving them is so that they will buy into it, they will understand it, it will be theirs. That's the second major reason for involving the local level. And that's where I was for about four years after returning from Malawi. I did a lot of work with UNICEF at the national level on their strategies for nutrition information and nutrition policy. I wrote articles on how we need to broaden nutrition surveillance to include these other aspects. All of that was very innovative at the time.

I also got involved in New York State in the community-based nutrition monitoring that had been started by another faculty member, following the standard international model of "collect more information and then press to have it used by decision makers." I had seen that that was not going to be enough. The problem was not lack of information about the nutrition situation. It was the lack of demand for that information and the lack of a desire to act upon it. Changing that state of affairs was not going to be triggered by statistics. It could only be triggered by people talking about the issue as they do about most community problems. It had to become a subject of discussion to become real to the decision makers.

The model we had here in New York had the nutritionists talking with each other, collecting data, and then sending fact sheets to decision makers in other agencies and hoping they would be used. That's what had been set up, and the local nutritionists themselves were concerned that no one was using this wonderful information. They asked us to help figure out ways to improve utilization; we turned that around to start with discussion among relevant stakeholders about issues and problems and what might be done about them. This new model basically said that through those discussions, you create demand and awareness and concern about these food and nutrition issues. It might become apparent that you need to know more about exactly how many people are hungry, or why people don't use food stamps when they're available, and so on. Then you collect that particular information and bring it back, and it will be used. You don't have to worry about it. It will be used because those people have asked for it.

I developed that model as a result of some of the interactions with UNICEF, where we were rethinking how to do it internationally. It also came from the literature on knowledge utilization. Throughout the 1980s, there was this growing literature in the social sciences on why good evaluations of the Great Society programs were not used in decision making. We totally ignored that internationally, and we were totally ignoring it in the community-based nutrition monitoring. So I wove that into this new model that basically involved agency people—no citizens yet.

I still had one more transformation or epiphany to make. We pilot-tested that model in four counties. It fell apart because you needed to keep the same group of people coming to monthly meetings for about six months to get them through the various steps of the discussion and problem analysis process. And by the end of six months, you basically had the nutritionists talking to each other again. So we didn't push that model as the way to do it.

About a year after that, I got some money from the Centers for Disease Control to do some more experimentation at the community level on models that might work. It came with very few strings attached. They were still putting it under the nutrition-monitoring rubric, but they appreciated the need to develop demand. So they let me have the freedom to do that.

By that time, as a result of continued reading and reflection, I saw the weaknesses in the agency-driven model. I realized that agency personnel can provide local knowledge; they are the decision makers and they need to be involved. But there's one thing they can't bring, which is the real public values that, in my view at that time, only citizens hold.

So in using the CDC money, I tried to think of a model that would do several things. One, it would not take six months. It had to be time-compressed. Two, it should integrate values and interests, not just knowledge about the local situation. And three, those values and interests should reflect the citizens, not just the agency people.

To complete this part of the story about the evolution of my thinking, there are two more pieces to tell. First, a nutrition student had taken a course with John Forester, a professor in Cornell's Department of City and Regional Planning. This is when I was doing the community-based nutrition monitoring, generation two, with the agency professionals driving the train. The student kept coming back and talking about democracy. And I was saying, "Yeah, come on. Let's not get ideological about it." This was my attitude at that time. I was more interested in gathering local knowledge and involving local stakeholders so that they would act on it. Better nutrition was the objective of it all. Democracy was this other thing out there that didn't concern me at the time. It seemed too "PC." But by the time that project didn't work, and I had continued reading and reflecting, I realized that if you want to make choices among problems and priorities and how to address them, then there is a need to gather authentic public values and democracy comes back into the picture. So I didn't resist democracy anymore, or think of it as overly ideological or PC. I saw that democracy was probably the center of the puzzle.

Second, I participated in a search conference (Emery and Purser 1996) at Cornell. Larry Fisher and others from the Center for the Environment were trying to get people on campus working on community-based initiatives. The search question was How can community-based initiatives thrive at Cornell? I was really impressed by the power of the search conference. So by the time I got involved with people in the North Country that seemed to me to be the most attractive model. I felt it stood a good chance of integrating values and interests. It did seem democratic at the time. It did make claims to propel action afterwards. And it was time-compressed.

So that represented the third generation of thinking on my part, which is now centered in public values. By public values, I mean that the notion of what we ought to do and what our local food system ought to look like can only come from the people themselves. It can't be gained by an opinion poll because people have to interact with each other, deliberate about that, and learn from each other in order to arrive at some notion of what that ought to look like.

The Practice Story

The North Country Project began in 1996. The North Country is comprised of six counties: Jefferson, Lewis, St. Lawrence, Franklin, Clinton, and Essex. They form an upside-down horseshoe around the Adirondacks. The area is very rural, sparsely populated, and very poor. The poverty statistics are as bad as they are in New York City. The area is very badly affected by the decline of the dairy industry and the regional economy in general.

Just in terms of the raw socioeconomic statistics, you could say that the North Country is as deserving as any other poor area in upstate New York. Had they not been the ones that were coming together at the time, I could have done this project in many other places. But as the CDC was finalizing the transfer of grant funds to me, the nutrition educators in extension in all six counties and the community action people responsible for the local food programs had been meeting for about a year in the North Country to regionalize an Expanded Food Nutrition Education Program (EFNEP) and programs related to it.

As they were getting done with regionalizing EFNEP, they said, "Maybe there are other things we should think about doing on a regional basis." At that point David Bruce, who was executive director of Cornell Cooperative Extension in Jefferson County, contacted Jennifer Wilkins (one of my colleagues at Cornell) and me, and asked, "Would you be willing to be on a conference call so we can talk about what we might do regionally and how the campus might help?" Jennifer and I participated in that call.

A month later, they were having a meeting. I can't remember if they invited me or if I said that I'd be happy to go up because I had this CDC grant—we were looking for five to eight counties, which is what the grant proposal said. They said, "Sure, come to our next meeting."

So I went up to St. Lawrence County for a meeting in the basement of the Canton Free Library. At the time, the nutrition educators in the North Country were being assisted by Bill Breidinger, a guy from the Department of State who oversees all the community action programs. He facilitated that meeting; I was just a participant. They did some brainstorming about what they were concerned with at the regional level and what they might like to do. They were concerned about everything, from

NAFTA and the pressures it was going to put on the dairy industry, to welfare reform and the fact that surplus commodities were
drying up. They were already getting more people showing up at
food pantries. They mapped out all their concerns, but it was a
very diffuse picture and too big for them to manage.

I had a suggestion: "What if we do a project where you go
down to your county level and involve more people in each of
your counties in assessing the local issues and coming up with
plans to change what they want to change?" And they said, "That
sounds fine." So it wasn't a matter of my selling them something.
It actually was a match made in heaven.

Once I laid out what was involved with doing a search conference, they said, "This is going to take some of our time. We need
the consent of our executive directors." So too, for the community
action people.

So Bill Breidinger from the Department of State went around
to all the community action directors. I went around to all of the
extension directors, laid out the concept, and asked if they'd like
to participate. One of them said, "Can you give us an estimate of
how much time it will take?" So we literally had to add up how
many hours and days it would take, including the time is would
take for them to attend a conference in Hartford on food security
and find out what people in Hartford were doing. We had some
in-service and professional development built into it.

We were going to use grant funds for all of that, bringing
participants together on a regional basis monthly for all of the
planning as well. So we estimated that it was about 22 days
altogether, and that 11 would come from community action and
11 would come from extension. Actually, the real estimate was
half that, but we doubled it to be generous—and that turned
out to be an underestimate. Then we floated the idea past the
executive directors and they said, "Okay." Some of them were
"gung-ho." Others were tepid but didn't want to be left out.
They were skeptical partly because community food security
was new to them as a concept.

Community food security is a concept that's being pushed
by the Community Food Security Coalition, a national organization. It has two aspects. One is access to safe, nutritious food by
low-income people. That's the traditional aspect. The other is
concern with the structure of the food system and the desire to
relocalize as many functions or activities as possible in the food
system, because of concern about corporate control and environmental impacts. So that was the official definition of community
food security.

The extension directors didn't see how all this really fit into
their existing view of the world or their programs. A search
conference was also new to them, and they probably perceived
some risk to it. But I assured them that there were grants newly
available through CDC and USDA and that this was actually a
good fit with what extension should be doing.

Getting approval from the directors was an important part of
this project, and we explored this a lot. I, of course, wanted all
six to buy in. Others on my staff were telling me that I was crazy,
that I could never get six, and that we shouldn't try for six. I personally thought, "We're probably going to end up with three or
four, but I don't know which three or four they are. So we have
to shoot for six, allow a few dropouts, and we'll have what we
need." But if we could get six, that was fine with me.

I viewed the resistant executive directors, extension staff,
and some others in the community as policy gatekeepers who I
needed to get through or go around—getting just their grudging
consent, if necessary—to give people in the communities a
chance to speak. I had a sense that every one of these counties
was willing to duck, let welfare reform roll off their backs, and
do nothing about it, regardless of the actual situation in the
county. But we went ahead with the project, in contrast to some
practitioners who will not do a search conference unless there's
buy-in from management, because they feel otherwise there will
be no follow through in terms of actions. But I thought it would
deprive the community people of an opportunity to allow these

unelected illegitimate gatekeepers, as I saw them, the power to reject this.

There's a real ethical choice that needs to be made there. Are you going to give agency people that kind of power to deny the voices from residents? This project would allow the community a chance to do some organizing around issues important to them, and put pressure on local organizations to change in the direction that those people wanted.

Several of the extension directors wanted to know whether "we are buying into something for the long run here." My private hope was, "Well, I hope you'll support what comes out. You're supposed to be cooperative extension." What I actually said was, "Well, according to the theory of the search conference, people buy into the follow-up activities as per their level of interest generated in the search conference. Everybody gets a chance to insert their interests and values into the action agenda. So it's kind of automatic that when you get through with this, you're going to want to support it because you've made it yourself." That's what the theory says. So that was a safe response for me to give them.

Some of them were afraid they would be left out and they jumped in, especially since there were rivalries between the community action agencies and extension in a couple of counties. In one county, in particular, I remember telling the executive director, "Don't feel any pressure. I know the community action agency is gung-ho on this, and we can work with them. Don't feel you have to do it all." By the end of that conversation, he was in. I didn't know about the tension. I found out afterwards that there had been an ongoing feud, and then it all made sense.

So that brings us to a whole lot of organizing. After Bill Breidinger and I got the directors' consent, the first thing each county had to do was put together a community advisory group with 8 to 12 people: farmers, consumers, retailers, and residents. That group later identified everybody else who would be invited, and they made all the decisions about the logistics. We gave them guidance on such matters as how to do a peer reference system and a snowballing peer system to identify the right people. (When I say "we," I should clarify that. I had a full-time research assistant, Vivica Kraak, whom I had hired during my community-based nutrition-monitoring project. So I had already worked with her for about three years or so. She was the coordinator for the whole North Country project. Chris McCullum, my graduate student, also worked with us, and I had already recruited Bob Rich, who works with Industrial and Labor Relations Extension at Cornell and is very experienced in search conferences.)

We had a memorable two-hour session in Lake Placid where we brainstormed all possible combinations of a name. They ended up calling themselves, "The North Country Community Food and Economic Security Network." Each one of those words was deliberate, and they made it fit for them.

To step back, I saw this as an integrated research-extension project in which I would help these counties and, in particular, the extension people in these counties, pull off this work. At that point, public issues education was very much on my mind. I was involved with discussions about that on campus. Bill Lacy, the director of Cornell Cooperative Extension at the time, had started a public issues education (PIE) task force a year or two before that. I was on it to try to think about how we could expand PIE within the extension system. So this was a natural linkage. I wanted to use a PIE approach as an extension effort. I was bringing in some expertise in the form of Bob Rich.

At the same time, I saw an important opportunity for me to do research on what happened in the search conferences and as a result of the search conferences. I was very much aware at the time that the claims for all the wonderful things that happen in a search conference, and as a result of a search conference, were totally untested except through practitioner experience. I saw some potential frailties in relying solely on that.

I also wanted to test the meaning and importance of the official concept of community food security as articulated by the Community Food Security Coalition—test it with real people and real communities. Was it just a bunch of "yuppie" food activists who were pushing it because it was meaningful to them? I purposely wanted people in the North Country to play with this concept and find meaning in it themselves and label it for themselves. The Community Food Security Coalition was saying there are problems with the mainstream food system and here are some alternatives. And those alternatives revolve around re-localization. And there's a whole set of values underlying that: environmental, social justice, anti-corporate, all the rest. I could see some virtue in those alternative values, but I wondered how meaningful they were to people on the ground.

Rather than doing an opinion poll or launching some question-naire-based approach, I thought the only way to answer that question was through action, through deliberation and action. And so, in a way, the project was one large attempt to give people an opportunity to reflect on their food system and come up with action plans that better reflected their values and aspirations. And then help them to organize to fulfill those visions to the extent they deem desirable within the resources they have.

What's nice about a search conference is that it allows the participants to discard labels for the moment and just talk about food system issues. The meaning emerges from their shared history, their ideal future, and everything that they talk about. I was very much aware of the politics of problem definition and labeling that the literature talks about, and I was very conscious of ensuring that participants had free play with the idea of community food security locally so that it would mean something personal to them.

I didn't have big teaching responsibilities at that time, so I spent a lot of time in the North Country. I could have spent more. In each county, we would have regional meetings with the community action and extension staff about every two or three weeks. We were helping them with the organizational task— helping them get comfortable with what a search conference is, how you do the peer reference system, how you set up an advisory group, and who should be on it.

We did those regional meetings, as well as county-specific meetings for technical assistance, to help them with those organizational tasks. I would alternate with Vivica and with Bob Rich in doing a lot of that preparatory work. Whoever went to those organizing meetings would take a more active role because the local group was looking to us for advice on some very specific matters. But sometimes it would turn around and they would say, "Okay, let's start brainstorming this list of people we might start the peer reference system with." So we would turn into facilitators at that point, go to the flipchart, and help them make the list of the farmers, the social-welfare people, and so on.

Then all six search conferences took place within a six-month period—one in each county, with an ice storm right in the middle. It was during the winter. People said, "You're crazy. You're not going to get six search conferences done in the North Country." Somehow we did it—between October 1997 and March 1998.

Then we had the multi-county conference in Albany in May or June of 1998. Fifty people from across the region came together from the 34 different working groups that were formed as a result of the search conferences to see what each had come up with. This was the first time they had the chance to see each other's work. Vivica and I also organized people from relevant state agencies that might have money, legislators from the North Country, and about 20 Cornell faculty members in different departments who had relevant subject matter expertise.

I made several trips to Albany to talk with agency people in their offices. I couldn't visit legislators because the extension people, our partners in the North Country, thought that would be too much meddling. Actually I did make a lot of phone calls to legislators' offices inviting them to be there because I couldn't be confident that extension people or others in the counties would do it. So I went out on a limb and did all those invitations myself. I invited about 20 to 30 legislators.

The Search Conferences

I had hired Bob Rich as a consultant to the project to be the search conference manager because I knew he was very good with groups. He managed five of the search conferences. He couldn't go to one of them at the last moment, so Vivica and I stepped in and managed it. We had watched him three times.

For the first five search conferences, Vivica was the co-facilitator with Bob. The two of them would be at the front of the room trying to capture everything that was said. I sat in the background and watched and listened and learned. In a search conference, the group moves back and forth like an accordion from large group to small group. Then you come back out to the large group and give your report, and so on. I would sit in on the small groups, move from one group to another, and just be a fly on the wall. We had other graduate students observing as well.

The basic sequence of the search conference begins with creating a shared history during the first session. The next session you do the ideal future, which answers the question If we could have our ideal future, what would it look like? Then you move on to the probable future: If we take no action, what will the future look like? That creates the contrast that makes the choice to take action obvious.

From that point on, you start moving into the more traditional components of strategic planning, saying, "How can we convert the present into this ideal future?" You break the suggestions into elements, and then you develop tasks and goals around each element. People organize into work groups to deal with the tasks and goals.

Each search conference was different. To start with, the physical setting was different in each case, ranging from the bottom story of a VFW building to a small room in the county fair building in Jefferson County. In some ways, the first search was the most intense. There were about 45 people, with a heavier-than-usual representation from the dairy industry. The small size of the room thrust us together in a way that subsequent meetings

did not, and some of the discussions got very intense, very emotional. There was some tension between the social-welfare and the
dairy lobbies.

Some of the most emotional testimony came from the dairy
farmers. After we had done the shared history—including, of
course, the big farm crisis in the 1980s—people who worked for
the Farm Bureau or were very large dairy farmers and had been
in farming their whole lives gave accounts of what it's like to see
your herd sold off. They would break into tears when they were
telling that. They gave accounts of suicides that had happened in
the county. The people around those people committing suicide
knew what it was all about: it was about struggling to stay in
business. But in the community at large, it didn't even register
that this was what it was all about.

So there were these personal testimonies from the dairy
side. They were very compelling to a lot of people. On the other
hand, in the evaluation that was done—interviewing people
individually—and in the written midpoint and end-of-conference
evaluation, some people expressed the concern that the dairy
people were dominating the discussion. And even though I
guess they could relate to what was being said at some level,
they felt that too much airtime had been either given or taken
by the dairy group.

Midway through the conference, someone made a casual comment about "those welfare people." And then one of "those welfare people" who was at the conference, who happens to work for
the community-action agency, stood up and said, "Wait a minute.
Watch how you talk about us people." And then she went on to
talk about the role of poverty and depression. She gave a little testimony about her personal life. So there were values being kicked
around and challenged all over the place. Another value conflict,
in the second county, was whether people on food stamps should
be forced to use the stamps only for healthful food. As a practical
matter this is not a local decision, but it illustrates the value-laden
nature of these policy questions.

Follow-up Work

In terms of follow-up work after the search conferences, we went back with a post-search conference event in each county to bring people back together. Even though right after the event they had all said, "Yes, yes. We want to get back together," typically only about a third to a half would come back together. Bob Rich facilitated those events. He would say, "Okay, where do we stand? What are you facing? How can we help?" Chris McCullum, our graduate student, focused on Jefferson County in her dissertation, so she stayed on there for about six or seven more months. She was not acting as an organizer and facilitator, but she wanted to take part in, and listen to, what happened in the small working groups that were trying to implement the various action plans. Therefore, they had more communication from us.

We stayed engaged in some fashion in all of the counties. We helped them develop a regional grant proposal for the Kellogg Foundation and one for USDA, neither of which was funded. In addition, the Albany conference was our big effort to put them in touch with faculty from the university and about 20 people that attended from state agencies. People also came from various organizations around the state. New York Farms and other food, farm, and nutrition organizations networked to try to get support for their agendas. At the end, I very explicitly reminded them: "We're on call. If you need something, let us know. Maybe we can help. But from here on out, you're in the driver's seat. What you get out of this will depend on how much you put into it."

Based on our earlier experiences with the community-based nutrition-monitoring project, Vivica and I felt that people would meet only when we went to the county. They were meeting because we were coming. We felt as though we were grabbing them by the hand and pulling them along, instead of playing the supportive role. As soon as we stopped coming, they stopped meeting. We felt that, in an ironic way, the external assistance at some point began to erode the development of a sense of ownership and responsibility for moving forward on their own. So we used the phrase, "on tap, not on top" numerous times. That's the philosophy that we were playing out.

Then, the grant ran out. There was no way we could have sustained field presence on that scale with 34 working groups. Bob Rich was happy to try, but we would have needed another infusion of money from CDC, and CDC wasn't interested.

There were 34 groups formed as a result of the search conferences. In a final search conference session, people sign up to work on different goals that they've created. If certain goals don't have enough people sign up for them, they're put on the back burner. That's how priorities are set. After the search conference, either the extension people, the community-action people, or somebody in the community had to display leadership and support some or all of those working groups.

In one county, for instance, the extension educator, who was an ag educator who had been involved from the beginning, tried to do that. He convened the groups. He helped move them through their meetings. He set up a newsletter. Then his new executive director came in and quickly told him, "Get back to what you're supposed to be doing. What are you doing with these groups? I don't want you spending time on that." The director wanted him to spend his time on the financial management of dairy farms, which included helping them with their tax returns. Very traditional stuff. That guy ended up quitting extension. He had many run-ins with this executive director, and this was only one of them. As a result of the conflict, he ended up leaving.

About a year later, this executive director became one of the biggest supporters of community food security. He got a grant for a half-time person from the health department to promote healthy eating. He talked it up to make it a full-time position, saying that whoever we hire can pick up the pieces with this community food security thing. They ended up hiring a crackerjack community organizer, a Hispanic woman who's still doing unbelievable stuff up there. This is the epilogue in Katherine Asher's thesis, a student of mine who did her master's research up there. She started reconvening the groups and doing exactly the type of work that that county could have done—and each of the other counties could have done—right after the search conference.

Reflections

In reflecting on this project, some strategic things could have been done differently. The timing explains a lot. Had these search conferences come at the normal planning stage of the extension cycle at the county level, things would have been a lot different. As it is, we came in midstream. Their plates were full. They weren't even thinking about adding new things, and that's deadly right there. I think a lot of things could have been different if we had made that single change.

The reality of when the grant comes and when the project starts is an external factor that drives some of this. I viewed extension as potential gatekeepers whose current programs were not necessarily aligned with what other parts of the community might want. I guess the overall experience confirmed and deepened that view, although it deserves a second test, timed to their normal planning cycle. And it's always going to be highly variable from one executive director to another, one staff to another.

I originally saw myself working with the extension staff in the organizing aspect of the search conference. I had hoped that I could work shoulder to shoulder with them in analyzing their community, focusing on who should be there and who should be involved, and thinking about this very strategically if we wanted to have action after the fact. I saw us getting into some power analysis and institutional analysis within the community. We never had time for that.

We could have spent a lot more time doing this kind of community mapping. The extension people and the community action people didn't have time to do that with us. We would meet with them about once or twice a month for two or three hours just to get them up to speed on what a search conference is, how you organize it, what community food security is, and the basic mechanics of getting this thing launched. That took all the time that they could muster away from their normal responsibilities. So I wasn't able to work with them to become really reflective about their communities in the way I had originally envisioned.

I think some of the educators would have taken very naturally to that long-term organizing work. Others would have had to reorient their view of themselves and their practice in order to do that. One of the other disappointments was that I had hoped to whet their appetites for picking up skills about public-issues education approaches. I don't see that that has happened, although I haven't done any follow-up interviews. I sent out e-mails to the whole statewide system inviting any extension educator from any other county to come and watch a search conference so that they could see what the potential might be in their own counties. Only Helen Howard from Tompkins County took me up on that. I was willing to pay the full freight, so that was kind of a litmus test at that time of the level of disinterest.

In terms of the important role of the legislators, I was well aware going into this that local legislators who sit on extension's board of directors have a large say in what kind of programs are undertaken. My aim was to have some of them there at the search conferences to learn from this broad cross-section of the community about what issues are on people's minds so that these concepts would not be foreign to them if extension proposed to move in new directions. It was one of my disappointments that only two legislators ended up attending across the six counties. That one county that I mentioned, the one that went gangbusters a year after the fact, was one of those where the legislator attended. That legislator encouraged extension to pick up the ball again and run in this direction.

I think there was strategic distancing going on by both extension people and the legislators to keep them from participating. Extension didn't want to be seen organizing this big public event about this kind of left-leaning concept of food security. In fact, I was told by a legislator at one of the search conferences that

"There's a reason Cornell's colors are red." And I don't think that the legislators necessarily wanted to be seen at a conference discussing food security. It is very conservative up there. So the goal of getting that kind of learning going so that extension would be supported by their key stakeholders to move in new directions was not met.

During this two-year period of planning and doing, I would say I spent 50 to 60 percent of my time on the project. We put 30,000 miles on Cornell fleet cars. That's the equivalent of going to California and back six times or so. It was huge.

I threw myself into it. It was one of the most rewarding things I ever did to go through those search conferences and see the power just emerge. I think it was a very moving experience for everybody who participated. The satisfaction quotient was very high for people coming out of those search conferences. We would have given it glowing praise—if we hadn't done the research on top of it.

The Research Pieces

One research piece was Chris McCullum's work in Jefferson County. She intensively observed what went on inside the search conference and found that the values and interests of low-income people were not reflected in the action plans. She demonstrated that without question. So despite all appearances of being democratic and fair, despite all satisfaction quotients, what actually emerged was not representative of the values and interests of all the people. That had never before been shown in a search conference.

The second piece was tracking these 34 groups, showing that, after a year, only half of them were still kicking, as defined by themselves. And after two years, when Katherine Asher went up, only four of them were still kicking. That's the bad news.

The good news is that many of those who participated reported bringing what they had learned into their normal jobs, into their normal lives, into their churches, into their community life.

And that, of course, would have been totally missed if we had only focused on the number of groups. So the way work really gets done in communities is not with ad hoc groups. It's much more complex than that, and it's difficult to measure very well exactly what all those ripples may have been. There was a lot of work undertaken while the groups were still active, but they couldn't sustain it because they didn't have staff support, and there's only so much you can expect from volunteers.

The other research piece, totally nonparticipatory, was the Q methodology study that we layered on top of this process, which actually produced some more surprises. In Q methodology (Brown 1980), respondents indicate their level of agreement or disagreement with a set of statements (48 in our case) about the topic under discussion, which in our case was the food system. The results are factor-analyzed to identify and interpret a small number of distinct viewpoints (three in our case) about that topic.

We used the Q methodology as a way to assess what people's most pressing values and concerns were about the food system before and after the search conferences. We found that they had changed in very unexpected directions after the conferences. We expected there would be more coming together, finding common ground, and concern about a broader range of issues. Actually, there was a narrowing of issues, focusing mainly on, "How can we keep the kind of agriculture we currently have in place, even though it's struggling?" There was less concern about the environmental dimensions and the hunger and food and security dimensions. That's pretty troubling if that's real, and if, in fact, the search conference led to that kind of narrowing of values. That never would have been discovered without doing this kind of layered-on-top research, which isn't participatory action research (PAR). It's not even in the spirit of PAR, and it raises questions about mixed methods and mixed paradigms.

Being a fly on the wall at one of the search conferences, I overheard an economist from the community say, "Did you do the Q methodology thing?" to another guy. And the guy said, "Yeah."

And he said, "What did you think of that?" And the guy said, "Oh, it's alright. Took a long time." And the economist said, "You know what I'm afraid of. Now that they've recorded our views, this is going to turn into reality. They're going to say this is the way it is. This is the way it should be."

This conversation reflected some deep misunderstandings about what that methodology was about and some mistrust about how we were going to use it. It's one of the things that made me uncomfortable about simultaneously doing this very nice action research with community people and then layering on top a more traditional methodology. I still think it may have been the only way to get at some of the issues, but there's tension there.

The other thing that we could have brought to the conversation—and I purposely excluded it—was some technical knowledge about the actual state of the food system and related social and political concerns. I felt a need to keep experts out of the search conferences for fear they would dominate the conversation and throw water on values and ideas and aspirations that were percolating up. I wanted to have the agendas set based on values, and then bring in the technical knowledge in the service of those action agendas downstream.

Ideally, those two need to be integrated. Whether the power, politics, and the dynamics when you get experts meeting with lay people would allow that is still an open question. Certainly the National Research Council report on "Understanding Risk" that I often point to holds up this ideal: that it is possible to manage different forms of discourse and knowledge in the same conversation in order to arrive at a robust, well-informed public judgment about what ought to be done. I am still attracted to experimenting with those kinds of models of decision making—citizen juries, for instance. If we can construct adequate models like that, then scholarship (such as that practiced by many people who develop technical, political, and social insights) definitely can be part of that conversation. And the conversation would be so much richer because of it.

The reason I held it back, my own expert knowledge and that of others at Cornell that I could have had present at the search conferences, was because of my concern about the micro-politics, the micro-dynamics that would be set up where people would start expressing their aspirations in the search conferences, the citizens and so on, and articulating their goals for the ideal food system, and too soon in the process and in the wrong way these experts would say, "No, no, no, no that's not possible." Or in one way or another squash it. And I think there is a dialectic about the right time and way in which to try to articulate technical considerations, economic harsh realities, and political harsh realities, with the aspirations that are being expressed. My feeling was if you do that too early you don't even give the values and aspirations a chance. And let's face it, all of the expert knowledge that we have accumulated is predicated on a view of the world that is shaped by a certain set of values and assumptions. So we'll never get ourselves out of the box if we don't give the alternative values space to be articulated and then see how expert knowledge can come in with a different set of assumptions.

The Tenure Track

About the time that I got the CDC grant that provided funding for the North Country Project, I went into a tenure-track position. For the ten years prior to that, I had been in a research track running on soft money, doing my own thing. When I got the CDC grant, the meter started running for my tenure. The idea was that I would have the three-year review and then two to three more years to put the package together.

Interestingly, when I took the tenure-track position, it was defined in terms of nutrition policy, which to most people in the country would imply working at the federal level. So right away, there was this big question, "What are you doing down there in the community when you're supposed to be doing nutrition policy?" In particular, the department felt that what was presently going on in the name of nutrition policy was not very well thought out. There was no guiding intellectual framework. There were a lot of expert prescriptions about what people should eat based on good science, for instance, but my department felt that certainly nutrition policy must mean more than that. So they wanted to see some intellectual development into the field.

That was my license to delve into these broader fields, the literature on public policy, and so on, and to think broadly. When I got this position, I went around to key people (from biochem to people doing policy) and said, "How should I strategize on this?" And they said, "Whatever you do, make sure it's good quality and take the time to learn new things, to think more broadly. That's what we're looking to you for."

So apart from the 60 percent of my time spent working in the North Country, I spent another 20 to 25 percent of my time reading, which I had not done in ten years because I was on all this soft money. You don't have time to read and reflect when you're on soft money. You've got to be writing the next grant proposal, and theory is not well regarded by development agencies internationally.

I threw myself into it and ended up realizing that we were in pretty bad shape in the way we develop policy in this country, not just in nutrition, but across the board. The dysfunction comes not just from the regular political problems that we're aware of, but also from the technocracy problem where we have experts in administrative agencies who are making values-based decisions that often reinforce the political status quo and that are fundamentally undemocratic.

Ironically, this project was funded by the Centers for Disease Control, which, along with the NIH, usually follows a categorical funding model for different diseases and organs of the body. "If breast cancer is your concern, here's a program. Uterine cancer, colon cancer, heart disease, diabetes? We have a program for you." They actually divide up the human body that way, and that's how funding streams usually come down. Though this has changed more recently—usually at the margin—it is still the dominant model.

Reading the literature on the politics of problem definition and looking at the way we're structured—my God, have we messed it up! Any sense of the whole, of what's of real concern to people at the community level, is totally lost by external funding streams and priorities.

Motives

So I had a bunch of motives for doing the North Country Project. One was to test the salience of community food security. The other was this notion that since nutrition issues are generally not salient in the power circles at the local level, could you get more movement for them if they were piggybacked on sister issues like agriculture? I was actually looking for a mixed agenda to emerge from these search conferences. Nutrition, the way we define it, might get a free ride or at least a good ride—on more salient issues.

During this period, I was developing much broader ways of thinking about policy, in particular, thinking about re-democratizing the way it's done and reconnecting it to public values. Some of my colleagues had, at the same time, defined a new field of applied nutrition. They had coined this term *public nutrition*, but it has none of the participatory democratic engagement connotations of *public* that I'm interested in. It means working in the public sector and/or working with populations, rather than individuals. It is not connected to the public sphere and public values at all. It comes from very experienced academic practitioners—some colleagues in my department and others who have worked internationally and seen that what we're doing isn't well represented by calling ourselves "nutritionists" or calling it "nutrition work." It's deeper and bigger and broader than that, and to get respectability, we need a bigger umbrella that groups it all together. So it's kind of a strategic term, and one that they were hoping would have more clout with important stakeholders. But while it was a vast improvement over "nutritionist," it also was a bit underdeveloped from an intellectual point of view.

My own experiences in the North Country allowed me to greatly expand upon that construct, to give more serious consideration to the meaning of *public* and how that relates to us in nutrition. I knew I would have to have some good research to get tenure, not just intellectualizing about policy, and it probably needed to have a strong empirical, and preferably quantitative, aspect to it. Now there were some safer things I could have done. I could have taken national data sets, analyzed them to hell and gotten three times as many papers published. But we already have dozens of people doing that; no value added in that. That was just going to reinforce the technocratic project, as it is discussed in the critical sociology literature.

Part of the attraction of the Q methodology to me, but only a part, was that it would put some numbers on people's values which otherwise would have to be explored only in qualitative ways. Moreover, you couldn't imagine doing qualitative interviews across six counties with all 200 participants. You needed something like Q. And although Q is quantitative, it's fundamentally based on people's subjective views and values on public issues. So it challenges the normal qualitative/quantitative divide where qualitative is all about interpretive epistemology and quantitative is about external, objective knowledge. For my own purposes, and in order for my tenure portfolio to have hard edges to it, I needed to do the kind of research that I did.

When Katherine Asher and I talked with a few nutrition faculty members recently, one senior faculty member confirmed point blank that "If all David had done was the North Country project with search conferences as an extension project, people would have said 'Well, that was an interesting, perhaps innovative, extension project, but it's not going to get you tenure.'" Quite clearly, the thing that got me tenure was having the research layer on top of it. Quite clearly.

I also had some strategic allies in the department who needed to interpret this work for the others in the department who easily could have misinterpreted it. The upshot is that I had ten years of solid track record in respected, hard-edge nutritional epidemiology, so people gave me the benefit of the doubt that might never have been given to a new assistant professor. So I could afford to take a risk. One of my external reviewers apparently was critical and said, "This guy is supposed to be doing nutritional policy. He's mucking around down at the community level." He just tried to blow me away. I didn't see that letter; you don't have a chance to defend yourself in tenure things normally. So my allies had to draw a circle around that and explain how misguided it was. All of the other external reviewers could see the relevance and could see I was pushing this field in an important direction.

Public Scholarship

The way I've told the North Country story, it's a story about facilitating a conversation. It's a process story. That's not scholarship. It's perfectly possible for someone to facilitate search conferences as an extension project without a larger inquiry guiding it. But in my case, there certainly was.

Part of the scholarship was the Q methodology. That was the detached part that may have been necessary from a methodological point of view. But in my view, the most important part of the scholarship was learning about the world by trying to intervene in it. It was through the action research that I wanted to see how things play out through being engaged in them and being in a position to draw out lessons during and after the process. I had hoped that the extension educators could collaborate in that drawing-out process, but it wasn't possible because of time constraints. But I consider that action research as scholarship: a desire to draw lessons from, and learn about, the world by trying to change it.

I think there are at least two brands of scholarship. One is the kind that's created at universities and shared with university academic communities for increased understanding about how the world works and perhaps how we can improve it. Another is the co-creation of knowledge and understanding that results when scholars from the academy interact with people from the community; from that interaction emerges understandings of the world not evolved from either party alone. I'm a little hesitant about putting the label of scholarship on that. It depends on where the understanding is going to be embedded. The under-standings can be put to good practical purposes locally, but I would probably try to find a different label for that than scholar-ship, because of the sort of traditional or historical connotations that I think are attached to scholarship.

What makes something scholarship is the systematic and pro-longed effort to understand some part of the world. What would make something public scholarship is either that it is designed to be applied for public purposes, so the intention is important, or that it is in fact co-created. I think it's possible for people to do work and never leave the campus and it should be called public scholarship if it meets the criterion that it can be put to deeper public purposes. A danger of doing that in isolation from the public, however, is the possibility of straying too far from public values or concerns even though the intention might be to "do good." Genetically modified foods are a case in point.

Did our work in the North Country Project constitute public scholarship? Maybe the way to answer that is to ask, "What does it mean to be human?" For me, being human is about having ideals and aspirations that go beyond one's self. And being human is a continual struggle to try, not for perfection, but always to go beyond one's self. Fundamentally, I think, we're social animals. We evolved as such, and we derive our meaning from living in close social groups. So the human project, as I see it, involves continually striving to further develop the humanness in us.

If we start there, then I think we could define public scholar-ship in terms of inquiry that better move us in that direction:

knowledge about what it would take to help humans become more human. There's a research aspect to that, but it's fundamentally bound with action. You can only study this stuff by doing action research. The North Country Project was grounded in that perspective. We were not interested in how to decrease the fat content of the diet. We were interested in finding out what food in the food system means to people, helping them identify the changes they feel are most salient and helping them move in the direction of their own ideals. Of course, this involves discovering what the various institutional barriers would be, such as market forces, regulations, and politics, and then trying to peel those back and learn what it's going to take to overcome them.

Clearly, one can't define people's aspirations and ideals other than through deliberation. People have to come to it themselves. What kinds of disciplines or scholars need to contribute to that project? It seems to me, we need humanists, social scientists, and, when technical knowledge is required in order to arrive at good judgments, you need technical experts. From a practical point of view, you can't have all that in the same place at the same time all over the country. So we need models, and we need research on ways to help this happen. Having an extension system in 3,000 counties across the land where those conversations can be fostered probably brings us to the ultimate potential of the land-grant system.

The Land-Grant Mission

The mission of the land-grant system is fundamentally about being a public institution. As such, I think we should be doing work that the private sector does not have the incentive to do or addressing issues that might be created in part by the private sector (corporate as well as societal). When problems arise, public institutions are responsible for addressing them in some fashion. I'm a strong believer in the university's three-fold mission of research, education, and extension, although I certainly don't see extension in the dissemination role. I think we should be involved in more community development approaches. We should be facilitators of a development in social improvement.

In nutrition, we are perhaps situated a little differently than people in agriculture because we fundamentally share an interest in nutrition and the consumer. So while we have people doing genomics research, it's motivated by a desire to understand metabolism better so that we can find ways to improve the health or well-being of people. In that regard, we're different from a lot of people in Cornell's College of Agriculture and Life Sciences.

The best contrast is with food science. They're interested in food, and some faculty get their money from companies to develop or improve food products. For them, the bottom line is making it tastier or more attractive, developing a better bottom line for the company. They do all the "pre-dental" stuff. We do the "post-dental" stuff. We're interested in what happens after it goes in the body, as well as some of the pre-dental stuff. But what they would be willing to call a success, in terms of a new product, sometimes raises all sorts of alarms for us.

It's really interesting to see what happens when food science people have a seminar and some nutrition people go over there. We're often the testy ones who are asking different kinds of questions. We introduce tension that otherwise wouldn't exist in those seminars. We have a natural alignment with the consumer and what we might consider the public interest is defined in relation to the biological needs of the consumer. But consumers also value the tasty, inexpensive, and convenient foods that food scientists help develop. So we have value conflicts at the center of this. That's why I think we need better ways to engage with the public, precisely so that neither department misrepresents public values.

In keeping with the role of the university in general, I think we have a responsibility to raise tough issues for debate that political forces would otherwise make sure don't get raised. Land-grant institutions began with a commitment to improving rural life: life in the larger sense, not in the instrumental economic sense of individual families. However, one of the questions I have about those early days is how much was rhetoric versus reality in the way the politics actually played out. Clearly, there may have been pressures on the system coming from farmers who wanted certain kinds of services from the land-grant institutions, and they may have gotten them. I don't know what the portfolio actually looked like in terms of extension people working more broadly on the quality of life versus working on agricultural productivity and efficiency (which in those days was much more closely correlated with quality of life).

When I first came here, the land-grant mission and its meaning was not on the radar screen for me. It didn't matter. In fact, my first choice was to get a position at MIT. That fell through, and it was suggested to me that I come here. I got my degrees at Penn State, which is a land-grant university but I wasn't at all connected to that philosophy. I first became aware of it when I was in Malawi. People there would tell me how much they envied the land-grant system in the U.S. because of the way it links to agricultural extension. In many developing countries, ag extension is done by government ministries, and they have little or no connection to universities. Moreover, our extension is multi-sectoral. It has people working on agriculture, nutrition, and financial management. It is a nice all-purpose community development organization.

As I did more development work in other countries and saw the stovepipe approaches to development, I appreciated how really valuable it is to have a single organization at the local level that can work on all of those issues. Whether they do or not is another question, but conceptually, they could. I often felt myself that if we didn't already have a system like this, we'd probably be saying we need to create one, because it's exactly what you need when you have CDC and all the others coming down with their categorical funding for special issues and there's no sense of the whole.

Now clearly, extension is not exploiting its potential nearly the way it should, but the potential remains. And the way our society is headed, if you play out the trajectory, and if Congress can be discouraged from doing anything rash, I think we're going to rediscover the relevance. By we, I mean not just the people in the system, but also society, which is going to rediscover the relevance of an organization like extension.

I know what I wish extension could do, but I'm afraid it's not possible in the current political climate. I wish the system would raise issues that society should be discussing up and down and across all parts of this land. Issues like the environment, health care, poverty, food insecurity, corporate accounting scandals, gross social disparities in wealth and opportunity, you name it. Clearly, that would be seen as a huge political intervention. But as I said earlier, tenured faculty are tenured, I think, so that they can feel free to raise those issues, and I feel as though we're not fulfilling that responsibility. In fact, most tenured faculty members have fallen into other traps. Imagine the power of the system if it weren't just tenured faculty, but the extension system, that could raise those issues in forms that are meaningful to local people. We could create the kind of movement that I think this country needs.

That's being very idealistic. The obstacles are enormous. However, I think if we can keep Congress from taking rash actions and destroying the system, the current and future generations are going to see the potential in extension and the land-grant system. The system can't do it by itself, though. Society has to wake up.

What depresses me most is the extent to which society doesn't seem to be awake. There's little evidence that they are. All I can take hope in is that things still have to get quite a bit worse before there will be a wake-up call that will activate enough people.

Realistically, we're going to need organizers and activists and leaders from civil society to make a counter-movement happen. But there are so many forces stacked against it. Government agencies, Congress, and the land-grant system are really in the grips of a very powerful corporate machine. There's only one thing that can extricate us, and that's a broad social awakening. I see young people like Katherine Asher coming in with the values that we would want. But can enough of them come into the system and become deans in colleges of agriculture? And even if they did, would they be the same by the time they got there? Not without a broader social change.

I guess there's a part of me that is actually quite pessimistic about it, although I know these things do work like pendulums. And I think there will be a wake-up call. It will be spasmodic. It won't be rational. Who knows how it will begin and actually end up, but it will happen eventually.

But regardless, I guess I have to take solace in the fact that I'm doing my part. That part is increasingly apart from doing real projects like the North Country. I've put a lot more value on my role as an educator these days. That's the only reason I'd be involved with four courses at the same time, which is much more than the norm in my department. I think we're doing something really important and really special in the two graduate courses that all of our students in community and international nutrition take. I see that as the ultimate calling. If you can do nothing else, do something like that. At the same time, I'm pushing my research on better models for policy analysis and policy development to the federal level. The obstacles are enormous there.

If I think about how much I've changed in the last ten years, I wonder how different I'm going to be ten years from now. There's a part of me that can't resist thinking I'm going to be very outspoken and make full use of the protected academic freedom that I have. But I can't just be a critic. I'm going to have to do something clever, as I did at tenure time, to make the reality known to the public. Maybe I can be part of the awakening process.

There's really important research to be done, and I don't know if anyone's doing it. This is when I wish I had a student outside of nutrition to look into this, to pull together the trends and antitrust allegations and settlements and other misbehavior that we know is going on and somehow make all this public knowledge. I suspect some are doing that, but I don't know that literature. I think if more people knew of the extent of it, they'd be quite shocked.

It's interesting that the folk wisdom of the people in the North Country was revealed in these search conferences. One of the comments I heard repeatedly during the informal discussions in the search conferences was, "I had no idea other people felt the way I do." This is vivid testimony of the need to create spaces for public discussion as a prelude to change.

People know fundamentally, instinctively, how bad it is and that there's a lot of monkey business going on and that the political system stinks in the way it currently operates. Even though they can't put a number on it, they can't necessarily give you specific instances, their instincts are right. But I think people don't see how they can make a change right now. There is a collective sense of powerlessness. There's no broadly salient agenda people can rally behind right now. But when there is one, and when there are ways people can engage with it locally, things can move very quickly.

References

Brown, S. 1980. *Political Subjectivity.* New Haven, CT: Yale University Press.

Emery, M. and R. Purser. 1996. *The Search Conference: A Powerful Method for Planning Organizational Change and Community Action.* San Francisco, CA: Jossey-Bass.

(Editors' Note: Pelletier published three refereed journal articles related to his work in the North Country project.)

Pelletier, D., V. Kraak, C. McCullum, U. Uusitalo, and R. Rich. 1999. The Shaping of Collective Values through Deliberative Democracy: An Empirical Study from New York's North Country. *Policy Sciences* 32:103-131.

Pelletier, D., V. Kraak, C. McCullum, U. Uusitalo, and R. Rich. 1999. Community Food Security: Salience and Participation at Community Level. *Agriculture and Human Values* 16: 401-419.

Pelletier, D., V. Kraak, C. McCullum, and U. Uusitalo. 2000. Values, Public Policy, and Community Food Security. *Agriculture and Human Values* 17: 75-93.

For more information about the development and use of practitioner profiles for teaching, research, and organizational and professional development purposes, go to:
http://instruct1.cit.cornell.edu/courses/practicestories/index.htm.

Chapter Five:
Bringing Scholarship to the Orchard
Integrated Pest Management in Massachusetts
by Dan Cooley and Bill Coli

Introduction

On the surface, this is an account of a research and teaching program intended to reduce or even eliminate the use of pesticides in New England apple production, using a general approach called integrated pest management (IPM). IPM involves biology and ecology, as well as economics and politics (a different history of the program might emphasize its technical evolution). This story, however, suggests that scholarship in the arena of a public issue, in this case agricultural pesticides, must be public scholarship if it is to truly succeed. In fact, it shows that the process of building successful IPM programs is largely public scholarship.

It's important to keep in mind that an apple IPM project, unlike a polymer science or computer engineering project, won't make anyone a great deal of money. The research and educational goals of apple IPM have been to improve public welfare, without any ancillary patents that might also benefit the researchers and their university. While apple IPM has gotten its share of grant support, it hasn't and never will generate the funds to build buildings or endow a professor's chair. Neither will it, of itself, solve a major public health problem like AIDS. We hope it has contributed and will continue to contribute to tangible but hard to quantify benefits, such as community well-being, farm-worker health, environmental quality, and food safety. Several things make apple IPM public scholarship. For one, the teaching and research reach well beyond campus. The labs extend beyond the brick and ivy to the orchards of New England, the libraries go beyond journals and papers to include the experience of people who seldom set foot on university grounds, and the lecture halls include cold barns and hotel conference rooms.

The research and teaching practiced in this story are part of a scholarship born in America to serve the needs of a largely agrarian public. The Morrill, Hatch, and Smith-Lever Acts created a system to educate the public, many of whom couldn't get to a campus. This meant working with people, on farms and in their communities, and doing research that answered questions relevant to rural citizens. In recent years, in states like Massachusetts, the public is no longer largely agrarian, but agricultural issues still affect the public and the public scholarship model still provides the most effective way to address them.

These days, programs focused on agricultural issues constantly have to fight the perception that they are a vestigial anachronism in a modern university. On a more fundamental level, programs that involve public scholarship—research and teaching that contribute to local public good using public dollars—must fight for survival in universities that increasingly reward those engaged in "private" scholarship—that is, research and teaching that can obtain major grant support, whether or not it addresses the public needs of local citizens.

Perhaps because public scholarship like IPM engages nonacademics, it is viewed as less scholarly. As will be shown, the truth is that public scholars must produce typically scholarly publications and teach advanced courses and then, unlike many of their colleagues, engage people outside academia in the scholarly process. For example, ecologists and entomologists around the world knew Dr. Ron Prokopy as an innovative researcher in insect behavioral ecology and evolution, while most New England apple growers knew him as "Ron the apple bug guy."

While his students and technicians performed experiments on the insect colonies in the basement lab of Fernald Hall, Prokopy himself might have been knee-deep in dew-covered grass chatting with a grower about the family or the price of apples. Faculty who engage in public scholarship serve two masters—in this case, apple growers and the college personnel committee. For Prokopy to succeed academically, that is, get tenure and be promoted, he had to obtain grants, publish in well-regarded journals, and teach graduate and undergraduate classes on campus. For example, he and a colleague discovered that the apple maggot fly *(Rhagoletis pominella)* had moved from its native American host, the hawthorn *(Crataegus sp.)*, to an imported host, the domestic apple *(Malus domestica)*. They held this up as an exciting example of sympatric speciation (one species diverging into two separate species in one geographic location) by publishing in reputable journals and speaking at academic meetings. For Prokopy to succeed in his public (extension) role, he had to satisfy the apple growers of Massachusetts that he who would help them keep apple maggots out of their fruit.

The entomologist prior to Prokopy had lost his job because apple growers felt he wasn't helping them. Prokopy showed growers that the apple maggot's predilection for round, red objects could be useful, and placed sticky red bocce balls in apple trees to determine whether growers needed to apply an insecticide. The bocce balls soon engaged growers in the same research process that demonstrated sympatric speciation.

As with many who engage in public research, Prokopy viewed this public interaction as an opportunity, not an added burden. He never considered ignoring the growers so that he might focus on less applied aspects of his work. Prokopy loved apples, the people that grow them, the places they grow, the insects that feed on them, all of it. Just as important but less obvious, he knew that application often informs discovery in his more theoretical work. Prokopy also understood that teaching growers how to manage apple pests taught him how to best apply his theories, and made his classroom more relevant and real to his other students. He maintained that combining public engagement with more typical university scholarship creates better research and teaching in both arenas.

Finally, while in many ways this is a success story, it is also a cautionary tale. For all the success of apple IPM and IPM in general, the system of public scholarship so vital to its development appears to be losing ground to more privatized, corporate models of research and teaching. This trend needs to be reversed if scholarly efforts like the UMass apple IPM program are to continue.

The Background

The University of Massachusetts, Amherst started as an agricultural institution, called the Massachusetts Agricultural College, and built the first Agricultural Experiment Station in the country. Like many land-grant universities, it has since morphed into a major research and teaching institution, with myriad programs in arts, humanities, science, and technology. In fact, one could reasonably ask how quality agricultural programs could develop and flourish, even exist, at today's UMass, Amherst. In the urban, high-tech economy of this small New England state, farming may be romanticized at times, but just as often the image of farming is dowdy and unfashionable. The general opinion is that farming in Massachusetts is quaint and nice, but hardly essential, and that real agriculture happens in the corn and soybean acreage, the feedlots, or the endless orchards and vegetable fields of more westerly states.

When it comes to generating support for the University of Massachusetts, the in-state academic competition includes Harvard, MIT, Tufts, Boston College, Amherst College, and a host of other excellent schools. Much public support in the state goes to these private institutions. And while ambitious young scientists may go into cloning cattle or bio-engineering plants, large segments of agricultural research attract little interest, particularly the idea of actually working with farmers on applied projects away from the lab, which has all the status of keeping roads paved or the trashbins empty. In the general public, most people really don't care to know much about agriculture, the state's land-grant institution, or the associated extension programming, as long as the system is working. As columnist Dave Barry put it, "Agriculture is important, but boring."

In Massachusetts, the attitude that agriculture isn't very important arises in part from demographics. The farm population in Massachusetts is 0.015 percent. Massachusetts is the third most densely populated state, behind New Jersey and Rhode Island, and just in front of Connecticut. And while agricultural product sales reached an all time high of $454 million in 1997 (Holm et al., 2000), this is a small fraction of the gross state product of $223 billion in the same year. In terms of demographics and economics, two of the most important drivers of political decisions, agriculture is a nonfactor on Boston's Beacon Hill. Given this setting, it's almost miraculous that the University of Massachusetts built an internationally recognized program in ecologically based pest management in apples.

Agriculture also has been in decline nationally. Agricultural economists have suggested that agriculture in general is no longer relevant to the American economy (e.g. Blank 1998). It's a purely economic argument, dismissing other reasons people may have for farming, food security issues, or the fact that farming may offer benefits beyond profitability. In the purely short-run economic terms of Blank's book, a divestment of agriculture is presented as the culmination of efforts to free Americans from the "drudgery of the farm," allowing them to pursue more lucrative, less laborious careers.

The problem is, from our perspectives in UMass apple IPM, a great many growers are rowing like galley slaves against a flood of red ink precisely because they don't see their farms as drudgery at all. They enjoy growing apples. They don't at all like getting squeezed off their farms. To fight it, commercial producers in the Northeast have started a revolution of sorts. They are ripping trees out of the ground, downsizing, replanting, and refinancing, and trying to extricate themselves from the global commodity business in favor of direct sales or niche markets. Unfortunately, some are simply selling to the developers. Orchard land makes expensive house lots, and it remains to be seen how many hillsides will start sprouting houses instead of trees.

Serious economic problems in the business began some 15 years ago, in 1989, with the explosion of the Alar controversy. At least for a time, apples were transmuted from the symbol of health to Snow White's poisoned fruit. This was followed by an outbreak of disease caused by the bacterial human pathogen, *E. coli* O157:H7, in a batch of contaminated cider that led the U.S. Department of Agriculture (USDA) to decree that all cider would have to be pasteurized, irradiated, or carry a skull and crossbones label. The latest blow has come from overseas, for apples are a labor intensive crop, and labor in places like China and Chile is much cheaper than it is in Massachusetts.

What is the relevance of IPM, one part of the overall business of growing apples, in this globalized economy? To answer that, it is necessary to know something about apple IPM. And to understand apple IPM, one needs to understand a little about the pests that bother apples and how people have attempted to deal with them.

An impressive number of microbes and insects try to take advantage of the nutrients in cultivated apples. Even the short list of pests of apples in Massachusetts encompasses some 15 insects and mites, and another half dozen diseases. Where apple trees have evolved with these pests, and without human intervention, they develop various ways to ward off the insects and microbes, in order to survive and reproduce. However, this usually costs the tree something in terms of its ability to produce fruit and seeds, so wild trees produce fewer, smaller apples than commercially cultivated trees. When we abandon the care and feeding of commercial varieties of apple trees, they generally don't last very long. We humans have taken over the role of protecting the apple in order that the apple will produce more and larger fruit for us.

While this process of providing protection started when people first cultivated apples, it began in earnest with the first broad use of insecticides and fungicides about 100 years ago. By 1948, a guide for Massachusetts apple growers recommended a series of 12 "sprays" a year, the common method for applying pesticides being a water-based solution sprayed on the trees. The land-grant system in general advocated the use of pesticides to improve yield and quality. Pesticides were a cheap, predictable way to eliminate insects, diseases, and weeds in the orchard, the miraculous technological solutions to problems that had plagued apple growers for centuries.

Unfortunately, when we attempt to control nature without fully understanding it, our victories may be short-lived. The euphoric adoption of pesticides in the twentieth century began to be tempered when unintended effects surfaced. In the environmental arena, Rachel Carson's *Silent Spring* ignited public concern over the harmful effects of pesticides on some wildlife. At the same time, the miracle chemicals had begun to fail when insects and microbes developed resistance to them.

It was clear that overuse of some pesticides generated resistance and environmental problems. However, it was not clear what to do about it, and many argued that agriculture should aggressively pursue new and better pesticides, a new generation of miracle technologies. At the same time, during the late 1960s and early 1970s, a few scientists at land-grant universities began to look at an alternative that would reduce pesticide use but still adequately protect crops. The basic idea was that the risk of pest damage in the future could be estimated by keeping track of pest populations, and only when the population became a potential threat would a spray be applied. Another basic idea was that rather than relying exclusively on chemicals, a mix of pest management methods should be used to attack pests on several fronts, decreasing the chance that a pest would become resistant to any one management tool. If the approach were successful, it would save growers money, maintain the efficacy of pesticides, and decrease pesticide pollution. The question was, could IPM actually work in fields and orchards?

Apple IPM in Massachusetts: Beginnings

We certainly don't want to imply that we have been the sole group, or the most important group, in the development of apple IPM. Apple IPM is a large area of research, and excellent programs abound, as indicated by the large number of overviews (e.g. Hull et al. 1983; Whalon & Croft 1984; Bostanian & Coulombe 1986; Kovach & Tette 1988; Gadoury et al. 1989; Bower et al. 1993; Blommers 1994; Gurr et al. 1996; Suckling et al. 1999; Biggs et al. 2000; Solomon et al. 2000). In fact, it is only by participating in this larger research community that the Massachusetts team could have a successful program. Even within UMass, the apple IPM program is part of a more general IPM effort, and support from colleagues working in other commodities and different aspects of IPM have been crucial to any success the apple team has had. In fact, apple IPM demonstrates the importance of the reciprocal relationship between good public scholarship and cooperation between researchers from different institutions.

As IPM concepts emerged in the early 1970s, they particularly captured the imagination of one young entomologist, Ron Prokopy. Prokopy had grown up on his uncle's orchard in Connecticut. From his early life on the farm he recalled going with his uncle to twilight meetings, which are still a staple of extension education programs. Prokopy grew up with the land-grant system, from extension meetings featuring scientists from the Connecticut Experiment Station, to matriculating at Cornell University where he got a Ph.D. in entomology. He inherited the philosophy and methods of public scholarship and learned the new ecological concepts behind IPM. He brought these with him when he came to the University of Massachusetts in 1975.

In a fortunate coincidence, during the next year USDA announced a grant program for IPM research. Prokopy had spent time at the University of Texas and frequently traveled to Texas A & M University, a center of IPM development. He knew the influential scientists and the latest ideas in the ecology of managing agricultural pests and could hardly wait to take advantage of the funds just starting to flow from the federal government.

Prokopy formed a team at UMass with a plant pathologist, a pomologist, and an ag economist to obtain the grant that started the first formal apple IPM project in Massachusetts in 1978. To a large extent, the new team was a marriage of convenience. Like most land-grant universities, UMass is segregated into departments for different disciplines, each having its own culture, teaching, and research agenda. In present-day academic circles, the term *pest* is generally understood to include microbial pathogens, weeds, and vertebrates as well as arthropods, but in 1978, a pest was an insect and pest management belonged to entomology. Yet for the IPM grants, USDA strongly encouraged researchers to work in interdisciplinary teams, a forward-thinking request designed to integrate pest management with the entire crop production system. Hence, Prokopy enlisted the other scientists working in apple research and extension to participate in the grant, though like most arranged marriages, the process of getting to know each other and learning to really work well together would take time.

Prokopy never planned that his IPM research should be done in a small state that produced a moderate amount of apples but in retrospect, Massachusetts had a number of elements that made it a good location for the project. In 1978, the apple business in the state was large enough to be significant, but hardly huge. From 1973 to 1988, Massachusetts consistently ranked twelfth in apple production in the U.S., growing about 100 million pounds a year over most of that period (Stout et al. 2000). The giant in the

Northeast, New York, grew ten times as much and was the Number Two producer nationally. The size of the apple industry and the excellent apple research and extension program in the Cornell system might have made it seem improbable that the first apple IPM efforts in the region should start anywhere else. But when it came to starting up an IPM program, size of industry and university program were not necessarily advantages.

In Massachusetts, driving from orchards in the northeastern Berkshires to orchards near I-495 due west of Boston takes no more than an hour and a half. About 150 growers produced virtually all the apples in Massachusetts. UMass researchers and extension specialists could interact directly with a significant portion of these growers regularly, something that was more difficult to do in New York. Certainly, people at Cornell were interested and working in apple IPM from its early days, but in New York, it would take a huge effort to move IPM onto farms. To do it, IPM specialists would need to change the thinking not only of a significant number of growers, but also some key research and extension people around the state. In Massachusetts, the small team of researchers was already committed, there were three extension specialists, and if 15 or 20 key growers could be convinced to try IPM, that might be enough.

On the surface, Prokopy was not the ideal man to sell IPM to fruit growers. In 1978 he still kept most of his long hair from the 1960s and carried paperwork and field equipment in a woven Guatemalan hand bag. Most Massachusetts apple growers had ignored the 1960s. Prokopy arrived in banged-up state vehicles to hang colored, sticky cardboard and bocce balls in the orchard. And the IPM message ran counter to the pest management dogma of the previous decades, when the university, county extension and pesticide salesmen had all been telling orchardists that they needed to spray chemicals weekly, sometimes more, to prevent pests. Most growers did not care why mites were becoming resistant to miticides, but simply wanted to know which new miticide would work. Yet Prokopy was asking them to hang colored sheets of sticky cardboard and bocce balls in the orchards, count bugs, and keep track of the rain and temperature. Naturally, the pesticide salesmen, who would occasionally shadow the university field teams from orchard to orchard, suggested that this IPM approach threatened disaster and was unproven theory from the ivory tower crowd at the university. The growers, looking at Prokopy and the colored bocce balls, were inclined to agree.

But Prokopy, having grown up on a fruit farm, was not an ivory-tower scientist. He may have been an idealist but he understood growing apples. And after talking with him, a few influential growers recognized that. Perhaps more important, the orchard advisor for the largest apple packer and distributor in Massachusetts, William Pearse of J. P. Sullivan, saw that the promise of better pest management with fewer pesticides could really help growers, and if the promise materialized it would be important that the apple growers of Massachusetts be in the vanguard of those using it. Prokopy was a little different and intense, but Pearse liked him.

In his rounds checking quality in the orchards, Pearse quietly suggested that growers give some of this IPM stuff a try. He traveled with the field personnel of the IPM team, learning firsthand the purpose of the sticky traps and how the research would establish a threshold for treatment for each insect. At the same time, he offered an opinion on what might be acceptable damage to fruit and what management practices the growers might reasonably be expected to change.

Prokopy worked tirelessly and asked the field crews to work just as hard. Technical specialists and students drove the state daily, visiting orchards at least once a week, climbing trees, inspecting thousands of fruit and leaves, and, most important, talking with the growers about what they saw. Prokopy also visited orchards regularly, talking apples, cajoling, and convincing growers to try his way on just a small part of the orchard, just to see how it worked. The other faculty didn't share Prokopy's level of personal involvement in the IPM project. The horticulturist had known most growers in the state for years and regularly visited their orchards, but his Yankee conservatism wouldn't allow him to jump up to his neck into something as speculative as IPM. And while the pathologist quickly began testing and demonstrating IPM approaches for apple diseases, spending 12-hour days driving around the state and bantering with apple growers did not seem to him to be a good use of time. Yet, in retrospect, it was probably Prokopy's unrestrained enthusiasm for IPM, coupled with consistent one-on-one attention that gradually convinced growers to use the new methods.

And they had additional motivation. Growers saw pesticide resistance and increasing pesticide costs as growing problems and they were looking for solutions. IPM offered one. As Rajotte (1993) has pointed out, over its history the adoptive force behind IPM has changed from resistance management and cost reduction to environmental issues and food safety. In 1978, pesticides in the environment played little part in most growers' decisions to cooperate with the IPM program. Pesticide resistance, saving a little money, faith in Bill Pearse's judgment, and Prokopy's traveling IPM road show had the greatest effect.

While the initial conversions were not easy, the adoption rate of IPM soon grew exponentially. Once key growers tried IPM, an extension adage came into play: "What a man hears, he may doubt; what he sees, he may possibly doubt; but what he does himself, he cannot doubt" (Seaman Knapp, one of the founders of cooperative extension). In Massachusetts apple IPM, the early users literally participated in research and teaching by donating their trees and agreeing to spray them using the IPM rules. In 1979, 16 commercial orchards contained trees under IPM management. Meetings were held regularly at these farms where growers could see and talk about the IPM results and learn how it was done.

At the same time, regularly talking with growers usually kept IPM researchers grounded around the realities of what producers were facing on an almost daily basis. The feedback loop, from recommendation to grower to adjusted recommendation, is still critical to IPM. Field experiments can be adjusted quickly to accommodate the differences between research expectations and on-farm reality.

By 1979, the Massachusetts Fruit Growers Association was contributing the equivalent of $13,000 (inflation adjusted) to the apple IPM project, complementing the USDA grant and base funding for research and extension supplied by federal Smith-Lever funds and state funds. In addition, because of the OPEC oil embargo it wasn't always possible to buy gas for the program's big old station wagon and sedan, and one grower gave an apartment for summer field staff in eastern Massachusetts.

Growers were willing to invest because IPM was working. In the second year of the program, apples under IPM averaged 6 spray applications, while conventionally managed blocks averaged 11. Costs for insect and mite sprays were cut by nearly 50 percent, from $106 to $54. At the same time, insect injury was actually lower using IPM—3.7 percent vs. 5.4 percent in conventionally managed apples (Coli et al. 1979). For diseases, the results were less dramatic but in the right direction: an average of 1.4 fewer fungicide applications, costing $22 less in the IPM blocks, with no difference in fruit damage.

In addition to the traditional on-farm demonstrations and other established extension methods, two new ways to get information to growers were developed: the weekly *Pest Message,* and the annual *March Message.* The *Pest Message* delivered time-critical information on the constantly shifting situation in apple orchards during the growing season. The *March Message,* by comparison, took a long-term, sometimes philosophical, look at the latest trends in apple IPM.

The evolution of the *Pest Message* reflects changes in technology and demonstrates the critical importance in IPM of obtaining and distributing information. The struggle to glean and deliver this information before it becomes obsolete has always been stressful. During the growing season, IPM data is collected daily from field staff, growers, and consultants. Once a week, it is analyzed and used to formulate recommendations that are sent out to all apple growers in the state. Originally, the technology and methods involved in the *Pest Message* process were quite simple. After the weekly data had been analyzed and recommendations written up, Prokopy would phone each of the three regional extension fruit specialists in the evening and read the *Message* to them as they madly wrote it down. Transmitting somewhat cryptic but critical information like "Plant bug captures. Granville, 2.7. Bolton 3.1... ." took up an hour or more each Tuesday night. The next day the regional specialists would type the message up and mail it to growers. Gradually, as new technologies became available, recorded phone messages, FAXs, computer networks, and the Internet made compilation and distribution much quicker and more timely, but it remains a deadline-driven process.

Within USDA and extension, many have suggested that modern technology can be used to replace personnel and do the things that extension has traditionally done with farm visits. The *Pest Message* may provide some insight on this. Certainly, Web-based data collection and distribution have been a valuable teaching tool. Growers whose orchards are not being visited by the IPM team can still read about what is going on statewide. The *Pest Message* delivered information when it was most relevant to growers and took advantage of "the teachable moment." Growers consistently list timely information of the sort delivered in the weekly *Pest Message* as one of the most valuable extension products. Yet ever since county extension in Massachusetts was largely dismantled in 1992, growers in many commodities have chronically complained that they need more on-farm consultation. It appears that technology does not replace field specialists in the minds of some growers. Perhaps it will take time for growers and extension to adapt the Web to really work on-farm.

The *Annual March Message to Massachusetts Fruit Growers* also has proven valuable in communicating with producers.

Contrasted with the immediacy of the *Pest Message,* the *March Message* has been a more contemplative, fireside reading for the last days of winter before the hectic growing season starts. It also was a way for Prokopy to collect his own thoughts about the state of the art in apple IPM. Originally, it provided information that did not get into the primary set of pesticide recommendations used in Massachusetts, the *New England Apple Pest Control Guide.*

Prokopy and the team could review and write material in January and February then photocopy the *March Message.* In its way, it brought those growers who chose to read it into the "literature review" aspect of the IPM research project. The *March Message* also provided a place to test ideas that may not have been ready for the mainstream guide, though over the long term the *N. E. Apple Pest Control Guide* has become the *N. E. Apple Pest Management Guide,* a reflection that the ideas of IPM have become more institutionalized in the region. Still, the *March Message* remains the place where innovative apple growers in New England look to see what is in the offing for pest management in the upcoming growing season.

As well as the *Pest Message* and the *March Message,* UMass Extension publishes a quarterly called *Fruit Notes,* a grower-oriented journal that regularly includes apple IPM articles. Information exchange like this, outside more formal research publications, is critical to the public scholarship of IPM. Within the constraints of refereed publications, it is difficult to present applied and somewhat speculative information. Many land-grants support publications like and *Fruit Notes* that allow researchers to write a type of scholarly publication for both growers and other applied researchers. Similarly, annual meetings of growers generally publish proceedings that include research talks.

In addition, apple IPM researchers, educators and consultants in the Northeastern U.S. and Canada regularly gather at the Vermont IPM Conference for informal presentations and discussions. Add this to the formal scientific journals and meetings and the whole is a continuum of knowledge production and use, going from basic research to field application. It is a system somewhat unique to land-grant researchers, extension specialists, and public scholarship. Given the richness of apple pest management expertise in the region, this system has been another key part of the foundation supporting development the Massachusetts apple IPM program (Coli et al. 1983).

In summary, a number of circumstances combined to get the apple IPM program up and running: a modest but still significant number of orchards; an interested faculty and professional staff; regional specialists willing to support the effort; a zealous academic leader and a visionary and supportive industry leader; and a rich network of researchers and educators throughout the Northeastern U.S. and eastern Canada. By the end of the first five years of the program, it appeared that IPM could be used successfully in commercial apple orchards (Coli et al. 1983).

Apple IPM in Massachusetts: Maturation

The ways that you actually catch an apple maggot fly, for example, and how you decide whether it represents a problem can be fascinating, but those details are beyond the scope of this story. Many of these details have been outlined in scientific publications that talk about Massachusetts (Prokopy et al. 1980) or other parts of the world (e. g. Asquith & Hull 1979; Gruys 1982; Whalon & Croft 1984, Tette et al. 1987; Gadoury et al. 1989).

Suffice it to say that, at the end of 1982, the federal IPM grant in Massachusetts ended with the basic components of an apple IPM system in place. The results of the program were encouraging, reducing average insecticide use by about one-third and fungicide use by about one-fifth (Coli et al. 1982; Becker et al. 1982). The first operating manual for this system was developed over the coming two years, a booklet titled *Integrated Pest Management of Apple Pests in Massachusetts and New England* (Coli 1984), put together by the apple IPM team with funding from the USDA's new Office of IPM Programs. People who had worked in the program were ready to take on private consulting as a business, notably New England Fruit Consultants. The original IPM grant had ended, but growers were willing to partially fund a specialist to work in IPM (Coli & Prokopy 1982) and extension funds would be used to keep the *Pest Message* and other information flowing.

But should the university use the few new federal IPM dollars it got to further develop apple IPM, or should it shift funds to develop IPM systems in other crops? Pesticide issues were heating up in the state with the discovery of two agricultural chemicals (ethylene dibromide, a common soil fumigant, and aldicarb, an insecticide applied to soils) in shallow wells in the Connecticut Valley town of Whately. There were resistance issues in potatoes where the Colorado potato beetle ran rampant. Resources were meager, and a good argument could be made to shift them from apples to other crops.

The issue was divisive. Prokopy argued that any agricultural ecosystem is dynamic and that, while the overall direction of decreasing pesticide use was favorable, each year had been different, demanding new approaches. For example, early progress with mites, when growers had reduced miticides by nearly two-thirds (Coli et al. 1982), had faltered. Natural biocontrols were erratic, and if growers increased miticide use to compensate, the old nemesis of pesticide resistance returned. Besides, the ultimate goal of an IPM program should be to use minimal pesticide, perhaps no pesticide, and while there were promising methods that might lead to further reductions, they needed to be developed and tested. The parties haggled and lobbied deans, department heads—anyone in a position to influence disbursal of the funds.

As has often happened, bad news about pesticides is good news for IPM. Apple IPM had shown that an ecological approach offered a potential solution to pesticide problems. In 1983, the Massachusetts Department of Food and Agriculture (DFA) worked with the university and farmers to convince the state legislature to appropriate more dollars for IPM research and education. With new money, UMass could address both apples and new crops.

As the apple IPM program matured, the infusion of new state dollars eased the grant-hunting job. But the steady pesticide reductions of the first five years of the project had stalled. Prokopy declared that "pesticide reduction under first-stage, first-level IPM has reached a plateau over the past five years in Massachusetts" (Prokopy & Cooley 1992). Further reductions would mean moving to what he had termed "second-level IPM," that is, an IPM that relied either on nonpesticide management tools or when pesticides were needed, used environmentally benign chemicals. This would mean major new research.

Prokopy's thinking about IPM evolution had led him to conclude that to reach the goal of sustainable pest management, IPM programs in different crops tended to go through four identifiable levels, based on needs established by monitoring pest populations or weather. (Prokopy 1993):

First-Level IPM	Integrates chemically based and biologically based tactics for a single class of pests. It can include the full continuum of chemically based to biointensive practices (Benbrook 1996).
Second-Level IPM	Integrates multiple management tactics across all classes of pests.
Third-Level IPM	Integration with the entire crop production system on a farm, i.e. the interface of IPM and sustainable agriculture.
Fourth-Level IPM	Integration of the political and social components in which IPM works, including environmentalism, regulatory restrictions, public education, and dialogue with policymakers.

The first level relies on pesticides, but their application is based on needs established by monitoring pest populations or weather. As noted, the second level relies on nonchemical and low-toxicity methods. The third level involves integrating pest management with all other aspects of the production system, including such things as fertilization, variety selection, equipment used, and the host of other elements that go into successful crop production. Finally, the fourth level integrates this production system into society, so that consumers, environmentalists, and all those with an interest in agriculture support IPM. In this case, support means that society is willing to pay for what Prokopy and others anticipated would be increased costs for the more advanced IPM systems.

In the first stage of the UMass apple IPM program, growers generally saved money by spraying less, with a little additional effort to get the information needed to do it. As the program matured, the team considered ways to move into the second and third levels of IPM, all indications were that the costs of implementing advanced pest management methods would be higher and risks would increase. The key question was, would the alliance of growers, state, and university continue to cooperate on the project? Rather than pressing the issue, the team retreated from broad-scale commercial testing of new IPM techniques and slowly began to evaluate a set of possible tools in a few grower orchards and the university research orchard. The rest of the 1980s was devoted to solidifying and broadening the success and adoption of IPM.

Public funds and grants have always fueled apple IPM. Throughout the 20-plus years of the program, team members have spent hours writing hundreds of pages of proposals and reports. Prokopy relentlessly pursued funding, covering the backs of recycled paper in an almost indecipherable script that has led to millions of dollars for apple IPM. Others have spent days in meetings and hours on the phone with the administrators and politicians that control public funds, teaching them about IPM, and the value of the program at UMass, thus bringing in more millions to UMass for IPM. While growers have given critical dollars to apple IPM, the amounts have not been nearly enough to cover expenses, and their largest contribution has been their orchards, time, and knowledge.

Why apple IPM would need millions of dollars, even over a couple of decades, may baffle many. The short answer is that the ecology of apple orchards is very complex, and indiscriminate agricultural chemical use tends to mask that complexity. As chemical use declines, the organisms that would live in a nonsprayed orchard begin to re-establish themselves, sometimes creating unexpected problems.

An example might help illustrate the point. While it has largely faded from public memory, in the 1980s, the apple growth regulator daminozide, or Alar, raised a major ruckus in the press. There was some research on Alar suggesting that unusually high rates might be carcinogenic. On the other side, most scientists agreed that any reasonable analysis of the research showed that realistic exposure rates to daminozide, even conservative ones, presented virtually no risk to people or the environment. In 1986 the first rumbles of a potential Alar problem had hit Massachusetts, where the state Department of Public Health proposed eliminating its use by 1988, and a national public relations effort spearheaded by the Natural Resources Defense Council made the use of Alar untenable by 1989 (Rosenberg 1996).

The issue presented the UMass apple IPM team with a serious problem, because, even though Alar was not a pesticide, it was a chemical that had important, indirect effects on apple pest management. It did this by allowing McIntosh apple trees to tolerate more leaf damage than they could otherwise. McIntosh trees, which made up about 75 percent of the apples grown in Massachusetts at the time, have a nasty habit of dropping fruit just at harvest. These "drop" apples bruise, making them nearly worthless. McIntosh trees drop apples all too readily under the best conditions, but if stressed, apples can rain to the ground well before pickers can get to them. Insects that eat apple leaves in the late summer put a stress on the trees. The more leaf damage, the more stress, the more drop. Alar use was ubiquitous, and so action thresholds telling growers when populations of foliar insects had reached damaging levels were developed on trees that could tolerate some feeding stress without dropping apples. Remove Alar, lose the stress tolerance, and growers would have to spray earlier and more frequently to keep populations of foliar insects at lower levels.

Were there alternatives to increased pesticides? Horticulturists scrambled and suggested that pruning trees lightly in mid-summer might color McIntosh fruit earlier, allowing it to be picked earlier, thus avoiding most of the drop problem. Pathologists and ento-mologists suggested that taking out foliage with this summer pruning might improve the effectiveness of any pesticides that did get applied afterwards. A couple of seasons of intense field studies indicated that summer pruning could, indeed, mitigate the drop problem without increasing the need for pesticides. The point is that finding an answer to the change of just a single chemical in the apple production system required a couple of years of research.

The Alar story also illustrates a point about the type of public scholarship the IPM team was doing at the time. The best way to address the public's concern about Alar was to bring them into the IPM process, a leap to fourth-level IPM. To an extent, the apple IPM team tried to engage the various stakeholders, growers, public health, and consumer groups in meetings and discussions. Inevitably, polarization killed real dialogue and any hope for a reasoned approach. For the public, any suggestion of a risk to health posed by an agricultural chemical was too much. The apple IPM team, quite sympathetic to environmental and food safety goals, tried to point out that while there were prob-lems with some agricultural chemicals, Alar didn't appear to be one of them. The simplistic solution—ban Alar now—meant that IPM researchers had to launch a crash program to keep New England growers in business rather than focusing on more serious pest management problems. The public ignorance of real agrichemical problems and reasonable solutions, and conversely the growers' and academics' ignorance of the public's concerns, convinced the IPM team that getting public involvement in IPM would be crucial to success.

Apple IPM in Massachusetts: The Next Levels

Prokopy launched second-level IPM work in earnest in 1991 (Prokopy & Cooley 1992). The more advanced management program was designed to get adequate pest management with "no spray after May." In fact, the most optimistic cut-off date for pesticide applications was mid-June, but May was more poetic.

Again, detailing how the second-level approach was carried out is beyond the scope of this story, but it is important to reiterate that as pesticides decreased, the complexity of the management problems often increased. Another example: so-called "mite friendly" pesticides could promote biological control of mites. Oil sprays could also promote mite bio-control, smothering the "bad" mites while leaving predator mites healthy. Unfortunately, the mite-friendly approach greatly complicated disease management. A common fungicide, captan, interacts with spray oil to damage apples. To complicate matters further, switching to an alternative fungicide (one of the ethylene-bis-dithiocarbamates or benomyl) can sterilize or kill predator mites. Again, a change in one part of the system quickly demanded changes in other areas.

The second-level system began trying to deal with these complexities. And while results were generally positive, after four years of the second-level IPM project, the results were not as clear as they had been in the first-level work. Initially (1991-1992), insect damage to fruit in standard, first-level IPM orchards was the same as in the second-level orchards. However, in the next two years, fruit damage where second-level methods were used jumped to 4.8 percent, on average, while it was only 1.9 percent in orchards using standard IPM (Prokopy et al. 1996). The second-level approach had reduced those insecticides targeting fruit pests by nearly 40 percent, but at a cost. On the disease side, the second-level approach had reduced fungicide sprays by about 30 percent, with no increase in fruit damage (Prokopy et al. 1994; Cooley & Autio 1997).

However, grower willingness to cooperate in the effort was dropping. For example, in nearly half the cases in which it was recommended that growers delay their first fungicide application in the second-level blocks, they failed to wait, largely because they were unwilling to take the risk. Behind that reluctance lay the fact that a huge increase in global production had caused apple prices to plummet. Growers faced increasing pressure to eliminate as much fruit damage as possible as cheaply as possible. Yet the second-level IPM experiments demanded more time and risk tolerance from them. For some labor-intensive jobs, like placing and cleaning apple maggot traps, the university team and scouts carried the burden, while for other jobs, such as mixing special loads of fungicide and applying them to a small block of trees, the growers were asked to do the work.

The predictions made prior to the start of the second-level work proved correct: it was clear that the new biologically based management methods would take more time and effort than chemically based methods had. This would ultimately cost money, and the global competition in wholesale apples was eating away any chance wholesale growers had to increase their prices to compensate. By the mid 1990s, if crop damage increased from 0.5 percent to 1.5 percent, it might be enough to eat up profit completely.

At this point, many growers had cooperated in the IPM program for nearly ten years. The roster of participants in any given year always changed a bit, for any of several reasons. Sometimes the team would need particular types of trees—trees that would require summer pruning, for instance, and if a grower didn't have those kinds of trees a new orchard would have to be enlisted. Other problems arose when growers, either mistakenly, or due to constraints, failed to follow the experimental protocol. And by the early 1990s, private IPM consultants, some of whom had worked for the UMass IPM program, were in business and apple growers didn't need to cooperate with the university in order to get IPM consulting. Bill Pearse had retired and no longer pushed the J. P. Sullivan growers to try new IPM methods.

It was in this climate that the team decided to invite the grower participants to a winter advisory meeting. We hoped that by engaging them in a more detailed discussion of the research, they would remain enthusiastic about participation. The growers could also tell us, before the growing season started, what they felt were the most pressing problems, what looked to them as though it would work, and what sounded stupid. The grower advisory group proved invaluable in moving the research along. Over the decade, members from retail stores, environmental nonprofits, and other academic institutions were added, helping to move the IPM effort towards the fourth-level community involvement goal. And, in spite of all the reasons they might have used to opt out, each year a group of apple growers committed their time and orchards in order to see if new IPM methods would be even better than the ones they already had.

Public Scholarship and Public Funds

On the positive side, the 1990s began with the UMass apple IPM program exploring new and exciting aspects of what was becoming known as sustainable agriculture. The research efforts had opened up promising options for reducing pesticide use in orchards, new ways to help growers use IPM to market their crops, and in the process, educate the public about this new ecological approach to pest management. The idea of more advanced IPM that integrated biologically based pest management systems with the overall production systems on farms fit into a new USDA emphasis on agricultural sustainability. That is, public scholarship at UMass was well aligned with public needs as expressed by USDA.

On the negative side, it was not clear that the citizens of Massachusetts and their elected representatives on Beacon Hill felt that research and education around agricultural issues warranted hard-to-find tax dollars. By 1992, a series of political and economic storms had combined into a hurricane that threatened to destroy UMass Extension and with it, the apple IPM program.

To appreciate the implications of this event with respect to public scholarship, it's important to realize that the land-grant system in the U.S. is a composite that does research and teaching in a unique way. The fibers in the composite are university faculty and field-based professionals, and the matrix that holds them together is an amalgam of federal, state, and local (county) dollars. This structure allows research to be done at several levels, from basic discovery in university labs to applied development in agricultural businesses and, at the same time, links teaching to the research, from university classrooms to on-farm meetings and demonstrations. If some of the fibers are removed, or the matrix of funding is reduced, the whole structure is weakened.

That's what happened in Massachusetts beginning in 1988, with Michael Dukakis' failed run for the presidency, the consequent transformation of the Massachusetts Miracle into a deep recession, and the dissolution of almost all county government in the Commonwealth. As county governments were dismantled, the state had given funds to the UMass Extension to keep extension offices going around the state. But soon after taking office in 1991, new Governor William Weld, with the support of the legislature, first eliminated state extension funding, then appropriated the bare minimum necessary to receive federal extension funds. Years later a legislator explained that Beacon Hill had lost touch with extension. Extension and the university did not engage legislators in agricultural research and education. In the old system, county commissioners made sure that extension worked on issues relevant to their local legislators and met with them regularly. Without county involvement, the local links were weakened and the political feedback system largely lost.

Interestingly, the budget debacle did not have a big effect on the apple IPM program. For one thing, Prokopy refused to be depressed. Through the crisis, he maintained consistent optimism. "In my experience," he would tell a downcast member of the group, "things happen for the best. We will get new opportunities out of this." For apple IPM new opportunities did come, in part because Prokopy and Coli tried to keep the public and policy-makers involved.

Prokopy insisted that the best research was informed by real-world outreach and teaching. Certainly aspects of the research should contribute to fundamental science, and be favorably reviewed by researchers who had no interest in its application. Still, aspects of the research also needed to interest producers. People doing apple IPM had to work in both the theoretical and applied worlds. For this reason, the apple IPM team had never depended heavily on county specialists, but had worked largely out of the Amherst campus with growers. When two of the three county extension specialists in fruit production were lost to the cuts, it was not a major blow to the program. In fact, in spite of the severe damage to agricultural extension in Massachusetts, IPM actually would flourish thanks to steady state and federal support specifically targeting the program.

If survival is a measure of success, what role did public scholarship play in the relative success of apple IPM during the budget crisis? To answer the question it might be useful to look at another well-regarded program at UMass, the animal biotechnology program. Just as the Departments of Entomology and Plant Pathology hired faculty in IPM during the 1970s and 1980s, the Department of Veterinary and Animal Sciences hired faculty who worked with the new molecular biology and genetics. The animal biotechnology program, among other successes, would produce the first cloned cows, a tremendous scientific and technical achievement. Yet, unlike the IPM program, animal biotechnology would ignore extension. The department in general decided that its research and teaching mission should minimize local efforts and focus on more global issues. So, researchers in animal biotechnology did not consult growers and did not travel to farms around the state to implement applications of their lab work. In fact, dairy and livestock producers complained about the lack of services from the department. Yet this model kept the animal biotechnology program intact and flourishing through the early 1990s budget crisis, while agricultural extension floundered.

Both apple IPM and animal biotechnology produced excellent scholarship from the university's perspective, as indicated by grants and publications in scientific journals. That meant that the university would value these programs. By comparison, extension in general did not produce much in the way of academic scholarship, nor did most staff have credentials typical of academics, in particular Ph.D.'s. The segments of extension that engaged in grant writing, publishing, and other scholarship survived the budget cuts. Those staff who limited themselves to answering questions and passing on information generally did not. Based on that evidence, it appears that good scholarship was critical to survival during the Massachusetts budget crisis.

That is not to say that the university or state legislators could distinguish the public scholarship of apple IPM from the more typical scholarship of animal biotech. Many aspects of the two programs were similar. The animal biotechnology program carried out campus-based research using graduate students and post-docs to augment faculty. So did apple IPM. The apple IPM program did studies to solve basic scientific questions that addressed real-world agricultural issues. So did animal biotechnology. Animal biotechnology worked with biotechnology businesses and public granting agencies, while apple IPM worked with apple production businesses and many of the same agencies.

But the animal biotechnology research never engaged the public nor, apparently, did it ask the big questions about sustainability. Admittedly, the apple IPM program engaged only a small part of the public directly: apple growers and a small group of people interested in agriculture, the environment, and food. But the long-term goals of apple IPM were always to contribute to the economic and environmental sustainability of local agriculture. The program stressed the importance of local agriculture, as opposed to large-scale, global agriculture, because those of us involved in it believed local agriculture to be critical to community viability, even in an urban state like Massachusetts. The contribution of cloned calves to agricultural sustainability is not at all clear. And while the knowledge generated by apple IPM research is available to anyone, the knowledge generated by the animal biotech research has been rapidly privatized. By the standards of this book, the biotech research is not public scholarship and the apple IPM program is. However, when it came to survival during the budget crisis, what mattered was scholarship, period.

The apple IPM program made a unique attempt to engage the general public in IPM during the 1990s through a program called Partners with Nature. Partners with Nature was designed, basically, to market IPM, use IPM in marketing, and in the process, educate consumers. The development of the program started when cooperating farmers wanted to use their cooperation in UMass IPM to market to consumers. At the same time, IPM coordinator Bill Coli (who was also part of the apple IPM team) felt it was critical to generate public support for IPM. Coli felt that the public had to be educated as to what IPM was and how it could benefit the vast majority of the people in Massachusetts who did not live on farms by providing a better environment and safer food. It's essentially IPM at the fourth level. That is, for IPM to be successful, ultimately, communities and their policymakers must realize its value to the public, otherwise, they won't support it.

The first attempts at connecting IPM and marketing came from the farmers' side. This led to the program producing and distributing signs that identified farms as cooperating with IPM. The signs caught on, and soon many farms displayed them, including a potato farm that was cited for pesticide use violations.

Fortunately, the press never made the awkwardly ironic connection, but the IPM program realized that there had to be some assurance that people identified with IPM were actually doing IPM.

Coli decided to tackle this problem by working with the Massachusetts Department of Food and Agriculture to develop a certification program for growers of various crops. Each crop was to be certified separately, using a set of appropriate standards. Each standard in the list for a crop was given a point value. To be recognized as doing IPM, a grower would review his pest management practices with a certification specialist and receive points for each standard met. If a grower accumulated roughly 70 percent or more of the available points, they were certified as IPM growers. The program thereby recognized those growers who met IPM standards, around the marketing theme "Partners with Nature" (Hollingsworth et al. 1992; Van Zee 1992). Growers could identify their products with a logo and associated marketing material. It was hoped that this might educate the public about some of the complexities surrounding pesticide issues, the environment, ecology, and their food.

As Partners with Nature took shape, a number of growers involved with the different IPM programs signed up to participate. However, within some commodities, particularly the apple and cranberry growers, the idea was controversial. A number of growers, including those involved in IPM for years, were concerned that the adoption of a certification program would raise more questions with consumers than were answered. Many of the orchardists selling directly to consumers liked the education and marketing material, while the wholesalers did not see it as useful. A few resented the implication that producing apples without using IPM was somehow unsafe, while others didn't feel that consumers would respond to the IPM label, particularly if it meant paying a premium.

Remarkably, while these are exactly the sort of scholarly research questions that a faculty member in marketing might address, the program never brought in that type of researcher. Rather, it depended on studies generated by IPM specialists— biologists—not economists or marketers. Unfortunately, from 1993 through 1999, out of all the farms that might have participated in the Partners program, at most only 53 did. It wasn't clear to the biologist/marketers why participation was so low. The Department of Food and Agriculture decided that the low participation didn't warrant further funding, and Partners with Nature ended in 1999. While it was never stated, it was also clear that the complaints about IPM certification from apple and cranberry growers also played a role in the Partners' demise.

One can speculate that a more scholarly approach to Partners with Nature might have developed a program that brought in more participants. That is, having a strong research base might have provided more knowledge and built a more successful program and added another connection between the IPM outreach and university research. It may have made the program less dependent on the DFA funding, by providing other sources of grant money.

Alternatively, listening more closely to the needs and concerns of all the growers, and trying to find a way to accommodate their issues in the marketing program might have helped. Perhaps, unlike the biological research, Partners was too "top down," substituting surveys for real communication. Partners with Nature never worked with consumers in an IPM education effort. Rather, it delivered a message from "experts." Working extensively with consumer groups would have developed a dialogue between them and the growers and launched the public education effort that the Alar crisis had suggested was needed. If public scholarship depends on both reciprocal engagement with the public and rigorous academic scholarship, Partners may have come up short on both counts.

Sustainable Apple Production

Aside from the disappointment with the Partners with Nature program, IPM had moved along well in the 1990s. One of the more interesting developments had a few of the Northeastern land-grants entering into a research program with the Rodale Institute, long known for its research and education in organic farming. In the 1970s and early 1980s, the land-grant system viewed organic agriculture as based on crackpot science and, if of any use at all, limited to the home garden. However, by the end of the 1980s, more and more consumers and commercial farmers were becoming interested in organic food. In 1988, USDA created the Sustainable Agriculture Research and Education (SARE) program. While sustainable agriculture is not the same as organic agriculture, the Rodale Institute was a strong booster for the program. Given the UMass apple team's interest in sustainable apple production, our readiness to move into more biologically based pest management, and a chronic need for more dollars, the group prepared a proposal.

There were facets of USDA's SARE program that were compatible with public scholarship. It wanted demonstrated grower participation in the research and demonstrated outreach to growers. In addition, it strongly encouraged participation across state lines, and between non-land-grant and land-grant institutions. For the most part, the UMass apple IPM team felt well positioned; we were already working with growers and researchers in other states. And we had an idea. One of the most intractable aspects of the apple pest management system had always been managing apple scab. Scab required many fungicide applications in a typical season, year in and year out, and in spite of progress, eliminating scab would require a radical change in approach. One such approach would be to junk the standard, scab-susceptible varieties like McIntosh and substitute scab-resistant apple cultivars (SRCs). A few apple-breeding programs had actually developed SRCs that appeared to have commercial potential, but no one had yet tested them in a commercial setting.

Prokopy, as might be expected, had thought of the idea some years earlier and was one of the first to plant a small orchard of SRCs. Soon after settling in at UMass he had purchased an old farm in the hill town of Conway, and in 1977, planted his own small orchard of SRCs. Perhaps the time had come to try some larger plantings in commercial orchards and test the more advanced insect management methods on those blocks.

UMass, in collaboration with researchers at Cornell's Hudson Valley Lab, submitted a proposal to SARE to do the SRC work. We soon learned that another group in the Northeast, consisting of researchers at the University of Vermont, Rutgers, the Rodale Institute, the Geneva Agricultural Experiment Station, and Cornell were preparing a similar grant. We called the coordinator for the Vermont/Rutgers/Cornell/Rodale group, in an attempt to submit a joint proposal. Negotiations failed. The UMass/Hudson Valley group wanted to emphasize biointensive IPM in SRCs, while the other group focused on SRC marketability and horticultural performance. There was no time to develop a compromise proposal and each group submitted its own version of an SRC proposal. The review committee shot back the suggestion that the two groups should join forces or forget funding. The shotgun wedding created a huge project, with several visions of how to run it, and no designated coordinator, but the sense of community among the Northeast apple researchers won out over individual agendas.

If the SARE project proved anything, it was that scab resistance, while potentially eliminating a significant part of the pesticide load from apples, was far from the most important factor when a grower chose what to plant. Changing something as fundamental as the cultivar in the orchard sends waves of change throughout the production and marketing system. The SARE orchards unveiled problem after problem with the SRCs, and while the knowledge gained was invaluable, to date, the commercial production of Liberty apples and other SRCs, except on a very small scale for direct sale growers, remains unprofitable (Penrose 1995; Murphy & Willett 1991; Merwin et al. 1994; Prokopy & Cooley 1992; Prokopy 2003). In IPM, there are no magic bullets. However, the inclusion of the Rodale Institute did bring organic interests to the IPM research table, certainly adding to the public nature of the scholarship.

"When Will You Be Done?"

For years, in our annual requests to the IPM program for funds for the apple project, the review committee has asked, "When will you be done with this project?" The question implies that going from conventional pest management to an IPM system is like changing the assembly line at a Ford plant: you make the changes and crank out better or cheaper cars. People are becoming aware that the industrialization of food production has serious drawbacks, as pointed out in popular books like *Fast Food Nation* (Schlosser 2001). IPM researchers realized this early on and have been attempting to come up with better ways to produce food and fiber ever since. The answer to the question, then, is "as soon as we develop an economically and environmentally sustainable apple orchard," and that looks as though it is still some way off.

Probably people think that IPM can be "done" or completed in a relatively short time because they view it largely as first-level IPM. That is, the goal is to develop a way to measure pest pressure and a threshold for treatment so that a given pesticide can be used at maximum efficiency. We hope that this account has shown that this is just the beginning of a long process that develops through increasingly complex levels, and that real success in IPM is achieved when it is used as part of a sustainable agricultural production system. We hope that shortly the public will come to see that agriculture is an important part of preserving Massachusetts' communities, and that an economically, environmentally, and socially viable agriculture is essential to their long-term security and well-being.

Interestingly, public scholarship like IPM works at several levels. Just as an IPM program may move from a level that involves simply a few growers and an entomologist, to a level that adds pathologists, horticulturists, economists, store managers, consumers, conservationists, politicians, and deans, public scholarship may involve a small slice of the public or attempt to involve whole communities or regions. In apple IPM, the circles of involvement have widened from a fairly small set of growers and researchers in Massachusetts, to programs in virtually every Northeastern state as well as in many other parts of the world. IPM systems have been crafted for many crops, and as more people become engaged in IPM, the possibility of third- and fourth-level IPM approaches reality.

As the Partners with Nature example shows, engaging a larger part of the public in IPM can be difficult. The recent *IPM Roadmap* outlines strategic directions for IPM in the U.S. in the future. Focus areas still include agricultural crops, but they also include natural resources and recreational areas and residential and public areas. Read this as a move to manage pests on soccer fields, in parks, on suburban lawns, or in city apartments. The Alar scare demonstrated that the public cares about apples, but to engage the public on a consistent basis, IPM must address problems most people face year in and year out. Alar and apples have, after all, largely disappeared from the public consciousness. To engage the public in a specific program like apple IPM, it will be necessary to engage people in a broad range of IPM programs and issues. Apple IPM in Massachusetts has and will continue to contribute to the effort of broadening the engagement in IPM. Three "graduates" of the program, people who have worked in the orchards and labs at UMass, illustrate the point.

One is Tom Greene, who earned a Ph.D. while working with Ron Prokopy. But rather than going into academia, he built an IPM supply business. Starting with manufacturing the red sphere traps used for apple maggots, and expanding into other traps and equipment, the business grew and eventually became a part of a larger company that supplies natural resource and agricultural businesses. Greene meanwhile moved on to address the problem of broadening the involvement of the public in IPM, becoming one of the founders of the IPM Institute, a national organization that fosters the development of IPM, and presently is studying issues such as certification and risk management. We hope that the Institute will continue to foster public scholarship in IPM.

Two other graduates, Robin Spitko (Ph.D. in plant pathology from UMass, Amherst) and Glenn Morin (M.S. in entomology from UMass, Amherst) started a crop consulting business, New England Fruit Consultants, that originally supplied IPM information and recommendations to apple growers, but now has grown to do research and provide consulting for government agencies, including EPA and USDA. Spitko has also held leadership roles in the National Alliance of Independent Crop Consultants. She and Morin have been looking at ways that IPM can progress in the face of the economic realities facing much of U.S. agriculture.

In the last 20 years, ripples from the UMass apple program and other IPM efforts have spread to wider portions of the public. As Prokopy pointed out, ultimately, sociological and political factors become as important as biology in determining the success of IPM. For the specific apple IPM program at UMass to succeed, the IPM approach needs to be embraced by a significant part of the general public. Meanwhile, Prokopy worked unrelentingly on his smaller stage, pushing to achieve his goal of ecologically sound apple production, trying to bring the rest of us with him.

Postscript

After this chapter was written, Ron Prokopy quietly and suddenly died in his sleep, on May 14, 2004. His great heart unexpectedly and tragically stopped. That a man so fit and who paid so much attention to health should suddenly die stunned everyone who knew him. The previous three days, he had been traveling around Massachusetts, checking research plots in orchards and speaking with and to growers at twilight meetings. He was 68.

Ron understood life at so many levels it's hard for the rest of us to fully appreciate the breadth of his life's work. He had an almost uncanny understanding of the organisms he studied, designing simple yet elegant experiments that cut to the center of key questions. His ability to communicate his insights in insect behavior to scientific colleagues can be seen in a legacy of over 400 scientific publications and numerous awards, including a Guggenheim Fellowship and a Fulbright grant.

His skill in communicating with apple growers is less generally known to those outside of New England. As one of his close colleagues, Wes Autio, put it, "He understood the constraints imposed on farmers both by the natural world and by society." One example that I will always remember involved Ron at a twilight meeting describing to growers how plum curculios located an apple tree loaded with new fruit. For the better part of 20 minutes, Ron talked while he lay and crawled on the orchard floor, demonstrating a curculio's eye view of the world.

Perhaps more important to the people he worked with, Ron was much more than an expert in pest management and ecology. He was a good friend. The numerous examples of his caring didn't become clear to us until after his death, when people shared their stories. In just one, a private IPM consultant told of a heartbreaking accident in which a son in an orcharding family lost his legs in a tractor roll-over. For months, Ron made many calls both to the son and his father, talking far less about insects than about the future, recommending books, and offering encouragement during the long and difficult healing process. The young man and his father had told the consultant that they might not have gotten through it without Ron.

In his life, Ron showed us that science and the university can be a powerful tool for improving peoples' lives, but only if we take our scholarly work and invite, cajole, and convince people to get involved in it with us. Ron was the best of us, and we will sorely miss him.

References

Asquith, D. & L. A. Hull. 1979. "Integrated Pest Management Systems in Pennsylvania Apple Orchards," In *Pest Management Programs for Deciduous Tree Fruits and Nuts*, pp. 203-222, ed. D. J. Boethel and R. D. Eikenbarry. New York, NY: Plenum Press.

Becker, C., K. G. Pategas, and W. J. Manning. 1982. Apple Disease Management in Massachusetts: 1981 Results and Four Year Summary. *Fruit Notes* 47(2): 12-19.

Benbrook, C. M. 1996. *Pest Management at the Crossroads.* Yonkers, NY: Consumer's Union.

Biggs, A. R., H. H. Hogmire, and A. R. Collins. 2000. Assessment of an Alternative IPM Program for the Production of Apples for Processing. *Plant Disease* 84:1140-1146.

Blank, S. C. 1998. *The End of Agriculture in the American Portfolio.* Westport, CT: Quorum Books.

Blommers, L. H. M. 1994. Integrated Pest Management in European Apple Orchards. *Annual Review of Entomology* 39:213-241.

Bostanian, N. J. and L. J. Coulombe. 1986. An Integrated Pest Management Program for Apple Orchards in Southwestern Quebec. *Canadian Entomologist* 118:1131-1142.

Bower, C. C., L. J. Penrose, and K. Dodds. 1993. A Practical Approach to Pesticide Reduction on Apple Crops Using Supervised Pest and Disease Control: Preliminary Results and Problems. *Plant Protection Quarterly* 8:57-62.

Coli, W., ed. 1984. "Integrated Pest Management of Apple Pests in Massachusetts and New England." Cooperative Extension C-169.

Coli, W., and R. J. Prokopy. 1982. Grower Responses to the Apple IPM Program. *Fruit Notes* 47(3): 11-15.

Coli, W., R. J. Prokopy, and R. Hislop. 1979. Integrated Management of Apple Pests in Massachusetts Commercial Orchards—1979 Results: Insects and Mites. *Fruit Notes* 44(6): 9-14.

Coli, W., R. J. Prokopy, and W. J. Manning. 1983. Future of Tree Fruit IPM in Massachusetts. *Fruit Notes* 48(2): 7-8.

Coli, W., et al. 1982. Integrated Management of Apple Pests in Massachusetts, 1981 Results: Insects. *Fruit Notes* 47(1): 15-25.

Cooley, D. R. and W. R. Autio. 1997. Disease-management Components of Advanced Integrated Pest Management in Apple Orchards. *Agriculture, Ecosystems, and Environment* 66:31-40.

Gadoury, D. M., W. E. MacHardy, and D. A. Rosenberger. 1989. Integration of Pesticide Application Schedules for Disease and Insect Control in the Northeastern United States. *Plant Disease* 73:98-105.

Gruys, P. 1982. Hits and Misses: The Ecological Approach to Pest Control in Orchards. Entomologia. *Experimentalis et applicata* 31:70-87.

Gurr, G. M., et al. 1996. Evolution of Arthropod Pest Management in Apples. *Agricultural Zoology Review* 7:35-69.

Hollingsworth, C., et al. 1992. Massachusetts Integrated Pest Management Guidelines for Apple. *Fruit Notes* 57(4): 12-16.

Holm, D., D. Lass, and R. Rogers. 2000. The Changing Landscape of Massachusetts Agriculture. *Massachusetts Benchmarks* 3(1).

Hull, L. A., K. D. Hickey, and W. W. Kanour. 1983. Pesticide Usage Patterns and Associated Pest Damage in Commercial Apple Orchards in Pennsylvania. *Journal of Economic Entomology* 76:577-583.

Kovach, J. and J. P. Tette. 1988. A Survey of the Use of IPM by New York Apple Producers. *Agriculture, Ecosystems, and Environment* 20:101-108.

Merwin, I. A., et al. 1994. Scab-resistant Apples for the Northeastern USA: New Prospects and Old Problems. *Plant Disease* 78:4-10.

Murphy, C. and L. S. Willett. 1991. *Issues in the Development and Marketing of Reduced Chemical Agricultural Products: A Look at Disease-resistant Apple Cultivars.* Ithaca, NY: Cornell University A. E. Ext. 91-34.

Penrose, L. J. 1995. Fungicide Reduction in Apple Production: Potentials or Pipe Dreams? *Agriculture, Ecosystems, and Environment* 53:231-242.

Prokopy, R. J. 1993. Stepwise Progress toward IPM and Sustainable Agriculture. *The IPM Practitioner* 15(3): 1-4.

————. 2003. Two Decades of Bottom-up, Ecologically-based Apple Pest Management in a Small Commercial Orchard in Massachusetts. *Agriculture, Ecosystems, and Environment* 94:299-310.

Prokopy, R. J. and D. R. Cooley. 1992. *Integrated Apple Pest Management: Past, Present, and Future.* Connecticut Pomological Society.

Prokopy, R. J., et al. 1980. Integrated Management of Insect and Mite Pests in Commercial Apple Orchards in Massachusetts. *Journal of Economic Entomology* 73:529-535.

————. 1994. Second-level Integrated Pest Management in Commercial Apple Orchards. *American Journal of Alternative Agriculture* 9:148-156.

————. 1996. Arthropod Pest and Natural Enemy Abundance under Second-level Versus First-level Integrated Pest Management Practices in Apple Orchards: A Four-year Study. *Agriculture, Ecosystems, and Environment* 57:35-47.

Rajotte, E. G. 1993. From Profitability to Food Safety and the Environment: Shifting the Objectives of IPM. *Plant Disease* 77:296-299.

Rosenberg, B. 1996. The Story of the Alar Ban: Politics and Unforeseen Consequences. *New Solutions* 6(2): 34-50.

Schlosser, E. 2001. *Fast Food Nation.* New York, NY: Houghton Mifflin.

Solomon, M. G. et al. 2000. Biocontrol of Pests of Apples and Pears in Northern and Central Europe: 3 Predators. *Biocontrol Science and Technology* 10:91-128.

Stout, T. T., S. A. Ochida, and R. C. Funt. 2000. Ohio Apple Production: National Market Perspective. Bulletin 1188. Ohio State University and Ohio Agricultural Research and Development Center.

Suckling, D. M., J. T. S. Walker, and C. H. Wearing. 1999. Ecological Impact of Three Pest Management Systems in New Zealand Apple Orchards. *Agriculture, Ecosystems, and Environment* 73:129-140.

Tette, J.P., J. Kovach, M. Schwarz, and D. Bruno. 1987. IPM in New York Apple Orchards: Development, Demonstration, and Adoption. *New York Life Sciences Bulletin* 119:6.

Van Zee, V. 1992. Partners with Nature: A Massachusetts Integrated Pest Management Recognition Program. *Fruit Notes* 57(4): 23-24.

Whalon, M. E. and B. A. Croft. 1984. Apple IPM Implementation in North America. *Annual Review of Entomology* 29:435-470.

Chapter Six:
Building a Knowledge Network for Sustainable Weed Management

An Experiment in Public Scholarship

by Nicholas Jordan, Hana Niemi-Blissett, Steven Simmons,
Susan White, Jeffrey Gunsolus, Roger Becker, and Susan Damme

O ur story is set in the discipline of weed science, a branch of agronomy that aims to better understand the ever-present challenge of weeds—"plants out of place"—and to help farmers and other land managers come to terms with these plants. Our aim is to provide a reflective account of a cooperative inquiry carried out by a diverse group of persons. This group shared an interwoven bundle of concerns: about present concepts of weed control, about the processes of knowledge creation that had given rise to these concepts, and about the broader question of how a land-grant university should work so as to more effectively create knowledge needed for social and ecologically sustainable responses to fundamental challenges of agriculture.

We see our cooperative effort as an instance of *public work:* a concerted and persistent effort, by a diverse group of people, aiming to create lasting improvement in a problematic situation that has public significance (Boyte and Kari 1996). We took on the issue of integrated weed management (IWM)—use of a diversified range of methods and practices to address weed problems. Many farmers perceive environmental, agricultural, economic, and social problems arising from current herbicide-based weed-control methods, but are presently unable to overcome the many barriers that stand in the way of more integrated approaches. Our project has convened an ongoing group—representing a range of professions and ways of knowing—that has exchanged experiences, perspectives, insights, and questions, in the hope of producing coordinated innovations in their various professional practices that might significantly lower the barriers to adoption of integrated weed management.

Why Is Public Scholarship Necessary?

In this chapter, we argue for the necessity of public scholarship to the intellectual and practical priorities of the weed-science discipline. Our aim is to establish that public scholarship is not only important in terms of general values such as participation, collaboration, engagement, or democracy, but also is a necessary and efficient avenue towards the particular goals of an applied science.

Our public-scholarship work is strongly motivated by our commitment to seeking sustainability in weed management—that is, developing approaches that will work for the long haul. Sustainability must of course be assessed along multiple dimensions. We must consider whether a weed-management program helps to create a farm operation that is sustainable in social, economic, environmental, and civic terms. Issues of sustainability are at the heart of an increasing volume of questions about the profitability, long-term efficacy, and environmental safety of the discipline's historical focus: herbicidal management of weeds on farms. There is considerable concern about the current predominance of herbicide use—and other similarly simplified approaches, such as reliance on soil cultivation in organic farming—in many kinds of managed ecosystems, such as farms, forests, and waterways (Cousens and Mortimer 1995; Sheley et al. 1996).

Our own assessment is that these concerns are well founded. Simplified approaches tend to be economically and environmentally costly, inefficient in resource use, and highly vulnerable to adaptive and compensatory responses by the weeds (Radosevich et al. 1997). Moreover, these problems are *public* problems: simplified weed-control approaches are an integral part of high-input "industrial" modes of farming that pervasively pollute ground and surface waters, and the cost of these approaches contributes to economic pressures that are increasing farm size and thus powerfully undermining the viability of rural communities (Morse-Elias et al. 2004).

Sustainable IWM will certainly be informed by one product of scholarship: ecological knowledge about weedy plants. Such knowledge is burgeoning through the efforts of plant ecologists. Yet, the application of ecological understanding to weed management and the integration of this knowledge with other relevant knowledge forms (e.g., the more holistic knowledge of people like farmers, ranchers, and foresters) has as yet been quite limited (Cousens and Mortimer 1995; Forcella 1997).

In our judgment, expanded notions of the very nature and meaning of scholarship are needed to overcome these limitations (Boyer 1990). Indeed, as we describe below, much of the scholarly work that has occurred in our project has been in an integrative mode: we found ourselves working to integrate across a range of forms and sources of knowledge, to create new understanding of a complicated story of collaborative work, told by many voices. Predominant concepts of agricultural science scarcely recognize such scholarship. Most certainly, the proposition that social learning is essential to the broad goals of weed science is a sharp departure from an alternative conceptual model, of "technology transfer" (Rogers 1995, Röling and Jiggins 1998), which emphasizes a linear transfer of knowledge from scientists to farmers as the necessary and sufficient basis to improve weed management.

Our experiences lead us to the conviction that, in order to create sustainable IWM, weed-science scholarship must be linked to "social learning" about IWM, in which individuals possessing diverse sources and forms of knowledge cooperate to create new knowledge. (See Svejcar 1996 for a weed-related example.) In this cooperative learning process, people in a group work together to assess the group's work, draw lessons for practice and policy, and identify key issues and challenges. (Ison and Russell 2000; Daniels and Walter 2001; Poff et al. 2003; and Waltner-Toews et al. 2003 provide examples in environmental management settings.)

Social learning will be needed for sustainable management of weed problems because sustainability almost always requires systemic approaches—in this case, contributions from many academic and practical disciplines and knowledge forms (Mack et al. 2000). Specifically, sustainable IWM will require support from new or improved practices in a multiplicity of relevant sectors, including extension workers, farm advisors, input suppliers, researchers, plant breeders, equipment makers, and commodity companies that influence modes of production (Svejcar 1996; Campbell 1998). Moreover, this breadth of innovation will have to be coordinated. For example, plant breeders cannot contribute to weed management without knowledge of what plant characteristics will contribute to creating weed-resistant crop-production practices. Furthermore, the relevant plant characteristics are unlikely to be universal and generic; rather, they are likely to be idiosyncratic to particular crops and the particular environments and economies in which these crops are grown. Therefore, innovation must be coordinated on a local scale rather than on a universal one.

We find an instructive historical case in the multisector innovation that enabled rapid adoption of synthetic fertilizers in the mid-twentieth century (Engel 1997). Rapid adoption was dependent not only on innovation by farmers, but also on the inter-related innovations of equipment makers, grain marketers, agronomists, extension workers, financial institutions, and many others. Indeed, concerted local-scale innovation across multiple sectors seems generally important to meeting complex sustainability challenges in agriculture, such as management of soil erosion (Rickson, Nowak, and Rickson 1995).

These arguments lead us to a working definition of public scholarship that has helped guide our work (Jordan et al. 2002, 2003). The definition hinges on substantial participation by scholars in a public-work project, as noted above. Public scholarship begins when scholars participate in social learning by bringing their scholarly knowledge to bear in a group, as one knowledge form among others of equal value and relevance (Irwin 1995; Ison and Russell 2000). From this participation, scholars draw direction for their scholarship, carry it out, and return to the group to contribute their findings.

We believe that weed science is well positioned to lead in developing a public scholarship of weed management. Weed science arose from more general agricultural research in land-grant universities, research that has a significant heritage of close engagement between researchers and farmers. This heritage lives on in contemporary weed science—for example, in the form of faculty positions in which scholarship and outreach are intentionally coupled. These professorships have no parallel in other academic departments like botany, plant biology, or ecology and evolution, all of which address weed ecology.

Given these prospects and opportunities for a public scholarship of weed management, how should it be developed? There are several related conceptual frameworks that can provide useful perspectives for practice. The notion of knowledge networks (Engel 1997) as settings for public work and social learning emphasizes co-creation of inter-related practical innovations, and conceptualizes development of such networks through a variety of stages and learning approaches (Jordan et al. 2003).

Public work and social learning can also be conceptualized as creation of a so-called "second-order research and development" system (Ison and Russell 2000). Second-order systems emphasize the embedding of scholarship into a problem-identification process that is driven by a carefully facilitated assessment of a complex problem situation by all or most parties whose lives are strongly affected by the situation. This assessment is designed to

uncover a broad range of perceptions regarding the nature of
the problem and the changes that would improve the situation,
to increase mutual respect and understanding among parties,
and ultimately to arrive at a mutually agreeable definition
of the problem and agreed-upon steps toward its solution.
The fundamental purpose of second-order systems is to create
research and development initiatives that are based on shared
and interdependent "enthusiasms for action" felt by these parties,
or at least among a subset who agree that they have the collective
capability to achieve a meaningful degree of improvement in
the situation.

We drew upon these ideas to create an experimental "knowledge network" or "second-order R&D system" that could couple
social learning and public scholarship. We will briefly sketch the
history and modus operandi of our work, and then assess the
outcomes of the project as seen by its various participants. By
inquiring into the experience and insights of all participants, we
hope to deepen understanding of how to organize and support
public scholarship and public work, since these are intrinsically
cooperative processes. Throughout, we address the fundamental
question posed in this book: How can scholarship serve both to
advance public work and to advance the development of an
academic discipline?

An Experimental Knowledge Network

Our project, begun in 1997 and continuing now in expanded
form (Jordan et al. 2000), is an experiment in social learning that
has enlisted farmers, farm advisors, campus- and field-based
extension faculty, and research weed scientists. One of its aims
is to seek learning opportunities that will inspire us to create
coordinated innovations in our professional practice. We hope
that, by joining together to create such new ways of working, we
can transcend our limitations as individual workers and make
genuine progress on the major public issues that drew us to our

work in the first place. To this end, we have established social learning settings—"learning groups"—that appear to be effective in helping farmers find innovative ways to manage weeds and in guiding extension and research workers as they create new ways of working to support farmers.

Organizing the Network

During the summer of 1998, two learning groups were organized—one to address soybean production and the other, vegetables. Each group had 18 members: 3 research scientists, 2 extension educators, and 13 farmers or farm advisors. On the whole, group membership was stable although a few farmers left the groups or joined them in progress. To form the groups, the part-time project organizer did extensive one-on-one recruiting, emphasizing the groups' collaborative research agenda. Each group met five times at monthly intervals between November and April of both 1998-1999 and 1999-2000, once during the summers of 1999 and 2000, and twice in the winter of 2000-2001. Activities in each group were planned through discussion during the initial meetings of each year.

After the initial planning, the groups turned to the discussion of weed problems facing the farmers, and their current approaches to weed management. The groups then agreed to devote several meetings to the biology and ecology of various weed species and to discuss their experiences with managing thes weeds—successful and otherwise. Weed-science researchers presented relevant research findings, followed by extensive discussion and dialogue among group members. Dialogue generally took the form of probing for insights into how the farm as a whole presented both opportunities for, and challenges to, integrated weed management.

In one meeting, for example, a weed researcher described insights into such sources of risk as reliance on mechanical weed control. This presentation spurred a long discussion about other sources of risk and ways of assessing and reducing risk by "fine-tuning" farm operations. Another meeting was devoted to the subject of systematic record keeping and monitoring in farming, with farmers taking the lead in presenting their approaches.

At the final meeting of each year, farmers identified an on-farm project investigating some aspect of nonchemical weed management on their farms, and presented their plans to the group. These projects involved monitoring, record keeping, and evaluation of some aspect of weed control. During the summer growing season, the groups met for a farm visit, and the project organizer visited each farm. When the groups resumed meeting after each summer, experiences during the past growing season with on-farm projects and with weed management in general were the basis of very rich discussions, in which reflections were offered from many perspectives.

Ongoing Work

Could a large number of learning groups exist? How would these function and be sustained? As of this writing, our previous IWM public-work group has largely disbanded, due to major reduction and reorganization of the University of Minnesota Extension Service (UMES) in response to budget shortfalls. Many of the extension educators involved with our pilot learning groups and subsequently, with a more diverse set of eight learning groups, have chosen to retire or take administrative positions. However, we are now working with a new group of extension educators and campus-based researchers to continue to develop the learning-group approach; seven new groups are underway.

The new learning groups are now devoted to the theme of economic and ecological diversification of Minnesota agriculture by cultivation and economic development of new crops such as hazelnuts, decorative woody florals, native prairie species, and grass-fed meat. Most groups are organized and facilitated by a field-based extension educator, with support and participation from a range of campus-based university research and extension scientists; several are convened by the project organizer, because university field extension faculty have been significantly decreased in number due to recent budget shortfalls. In this phase of the project, we are testing the idea that successful learning groups can be facilitated by local extension educators, who are attentive to fostering social learning and are familiar with some basic concepts of new crops and their economic development. The learning groups are supported by university researchers, but less intensively than they were in the pilot groups. A crucial premise of the new groups is that they must be diversified to a greater degree than were the weed groups, by recruiting from a wider range of relevant professionals. Thus, new groups include lenders who could invest in these new crops, state and federal agency workers who could use existing policy instruments to support new crops, and people working in the post-production supply chain who could create new links between the production of new crops and their consumption. Our goal is to use the new groups to initiate integrated development of new enterprises along the production-consumption continuum.

A Tale Told in Many Voices

Our aim in what follows is to portray our project more richly, through the eyes and words of its participants. We will explore their intentions and interests in the project. We will assess whether there is evidence that our project has enabled them to innovate in their professional practices and triggered increases in their enthusiasm for coordinated innovation, social learning, and public work. To learn each person's story, we (Blissett 2002; Blisset et al. 2004) conducted semi-structured interviews (Charmaz 2002), lasting one to two hours, with most participants during 2001-2002. Interviews were taped and transcribed.

Taken together, interview data show first that a strong majority of participants reported the project has furthered changes in their work that were already underway and has triggered additional developments that were unforeseen at the outset. Second, some participants reported that their individual change efforts were coordinated with change efforts of participants in other sectors. Third, the majority of participants reported a deepened commitment to participating in social learning as a means for developing IWM. We believe that this shared commitment represents a considerable convergence and focusing of participants' professional interests, and we conclude that our case provides a clear example of concerted innovation as a result of a social-learning experience.

The Farmers

Almost all farmers reported that group participation empowered them to become better practitioners of IWM, both by changing their basic understanding of weed management and by affording them new insights into IWM practice. An important theme in the interviews was expression of an increased sense of self-reliance and self-confidence in managing weeds using on-farm resources. Many participants reported an increase in the value they placed on their own role and importance as skilled managers; they felt less dependent on outside inputs.

A member of the vegetable learning group told us that she feels "more like a manager... I used to view myself as almost only a person that did the handwork on the hoe and then helped the kids pick." Moreover, many farmers perceived a link between group participation and their sense of increased empowerment to practice IWM. Specifically, participants noted the influence of the groups on thinking and problem-solving approaches to IWM, and on specific management practices. An organic farmer reported that he "thought differently" after being a part of the learning group. He reported a new ability to "think like a weed." He described this as a way that he could manage weeds more proactively by making better predictions about weed behavior. He thought he "did a much better job handling the situations that the weeds presented" by being better able to cope with variable circumstances, such as the weather. A vegetable farmer explained that she "thinks differently because I remember the talks on the biology of the weeds. I think differently and more than that, I feel differently." Another reported that he "just totally thinks more about weeds. I even look differently at [publications] and notice things I never did before." Consequently, he perceived that his "entire thought process is different."

Several participants noted that, prior to their group experiences, they had felt disempowered by competitiveness and lack of communication among farmers. As one vegetable farmer explained, "Farmers are isolated from each other primarily around competition in the marketplace. You don't want to tilt your hand too much. We hold our cards in tight and we close ourselves in, and it's in that isolation that we cut ourselves off from learning." This feeling of isolation was reported by several group members. They spoke of "loneliness" and how other people have "walls up."

Group participants reported feeling empowered because the groups effectively alleviated these feelings of isolation and competitiveness. One organic farmer stated that he "prioritized those meetings; that's how important they got to me. I think we built camaraderie." He noted that he had formed close relationships with others using different weed-management strategies. Group members reported gaining additional empowerment because they felt that their knowledge was important to the groups' learning process. By contributing to group learning, they felt more confidence in the validity and value of their own knowledge.

One member spoke very emotionally about the group's effect on the way he viewed himself and his fellow farmer participants. "We are starting to honor the collective knowledge that farmers have and to treat that knowledge in a professional way. We are creative people by nature and that was very, very clear to me in this group." Another member explained how such validation created feelings of empowerment for him: "The group was all about acceptance and nonjudgment, support, validation, vulnerability, and humility. It gave me that positive push that I needed to keep being innovative." Still another reported that "[The members] establish a trust level, confidence in ourselves to bare our souls you might say—not only on things that were successful, but failures as well."

Many participants commented on the importance of group diversity to the empowering outcomes of the learning groups. Included in each group were farmers with greatly varying farm sizes, as well as those who farmed using different practices, including both organic and conventional approaches. As the groups went on, learning in a group using diverse management systems became important to the members because it allowed them all the opportunity to think together and come to "some type of common ground." One farmer reported that he had anticipated a "defensive posture on both sides" but found that largely absent. An organic farmer reflected: "Too many like things, you have a dull group. Too many opposite things and all you have is a big argument. So it takes a mix to make the group work."

In addition to a diverse range of farmers, group members included scientists and extension educators. Farmers perceived that this additional diversity was essential to their learning process. One observed that the learning groups contrasted favorably with past experiences in which "Ph.D's were the experts and the farmers were the passive recipients of their knowledge." A farming couple noted their appreciation for the "mix of information and science to back it up and the opportunity for everybody to have dialogue around a particular scientific aspect of the problem." In their view, it was very important to this process that the discussion was not solely based on practitioner knowledge or solely on scientific information.

University Extension and Research Participants

Learning-group experience appears also to have strongly increased a sense of empowerment among extension and research participants. In interviews, they described new understandings of the broad goals of their work and new professional capabilities, which they felt increased their ability to attain these goals. They ascribed these new understandings and capabilities to their participation in the learning groups and in many cases related these outcomes to particular experiences in the groups.

Community-Based Extension Educators

All three educators found that the learning groups empowered them to make progress toward several goals they valued highly. First, each reported that the learning groups were effective vehicles for bringing diverse viewpoints together. One educator emphasized his commitment to creating programming that helped farmers gain skills for managing complex farm challenges. In his view, this goal required that he bring together people who viewed these challenges quite differently, because "they need each other" to make progress in building their skills. For another educator, it was of great importance to develop practical knowledge while also asking how practice guided by that knowledge "plays out in the rest of life, in community, and in the broader world." In his words, such practical knowledge was best created when principles and practices are "shaken through more screens." These "screens" are contrasting viewpoints on an issue.

A second broad outcome reported by the extension educators was a new understanding of the role of expertise—their own or others'. In their previous extension work, each educator had viewed the knowledge of scientific or technical experts as largely sufficient to guide practice. In their experience with the learning groups, the educators found that scientific or technical expertise could function quite differently: as one ingredient in an interactive, interdependent process of knowledge construction. As one educator put it, "I think the best adult learning is where there's enough of a common base of knowledge and a recognition that people can learn a little bit in half an hour to get them learning more through a conversation."

Another educator described his dissatisfaction with the use of expertise to prescribe practice: "If I think that I had 500 people in a room and I taught them some particular concept about dairy nutrition or weed control and that they all went home and made great strides with it, then I'm kidding myself in most cases." This educator was also strongly conscious of the role of farmers' expertise and how to promote and elicit this expertise. He was particularly concerned to protect and sponsor the contributions of farmers who held a minority viewpoint in his group—two soybean farmers who had large-scale farms, making heavy use of pesticide and synthetic fertilizers. Over the course of the meetings, he learned techniques for including the knowledge of these farmers in the group's discussions.

Extension Support Staff

Two extension support staff members played vital roles in our project. One had worked for about ten years in staff development in UMES, having a statewide responsibility to work with educators and a wide variety of other staff members. Throughout our project, she has participated in the design and facilitation of the learning groups as settings for social learning. Through her participation, she has gained increased understanding of learning situations that inspire significant professional innovation despite lack of formal and explicit educational structures, and despite time constraints and barriers of geographic, social, and professional distance. Put another way, she has gained experience and enthusiasm for learning situations that have no formal, explicit curriculum or officially recognized "teachers" (Crombie 1995), and yet she is able to facilitate effective reflective practice among participants.

She spoke of the importance of social learning to professional innovation: "Because you're working in a community of learners, it's not just people who come together for a week or a semester, but they're together for a couple years. And so you can build the trust and the safety so that people can be more vulnerable and can really reflect on this. We really need that. I don't think we can do it without that." In her mind, a crucial outcome of such social learning is a conscious sense of empowerment in creating one's own new knowledge regarding complex professional challenges. In our learning groups, she observed, "Those people are creating knowledge that they feel they've got a part of, and they've got it through reflection. They didn't create it out of the blue, because there was science involved, there was research involved, but there was also their own practice. And then there are the conversations, the dialogues. So they created knowledge, but they didn't create the one and only truth."

The second extension support staff worker played a different and critically important role: that of project organizer. She has worked to organize our project from its outset in 1996, supported by a series of grants. Our initial grant was to develop a farmer-researcher "research cooperative" to develop sustainable weed management. At that time, she and Jordan, the project initiators, were becoming aware of organizing methods for cross-sector public work groups (Michels and Massengale 2004). We began to use these methods in a series of one-on-one conversations with a broad range of potential participants. She took the lead in these conversations, in which our goal was to map out diverse perceptions about the purpose of farmer-researcher cooperation and to identify strong individual or organizational interests in some form of cooperation.

This organizing work led to our key decision to orient our project to farmer learning rather than to traditional agricultural research. In early dialogues with farmer members of the Sustainable Farming Association of Minnesota, these individuals were very direct in stating the need for a learning-based project. She reports: "They said we don't necessarily need more information from you; what we really could use is help in putting things together on our farms." At this point she began to focus on net-working and recruiting participants in the learning groups.

She reflects that her agricultural science background—as opposed to a background in organizing *per se*—has had both limiting and empowering aspects. She thought that she brought sensibilities, insights, and perspectives from her agriculture research background to her organizing: "Not everybody who would work in coordinating something would necessarily have the same motivation that I would." As she looked back on her work, she was able to define her essential role: "… facilitating an assimilation of the weed scientists' knowledge and the farmers' knowledge … so a new way of knowing emerges from that."

A major challenge in her organizing work was having some sense of how to begin our project but much less ability to describe the outcomes we envisioned. She told us that "when I was recruiting the farmers, and I was just cold-calling people, I tried to be really up front with the farmers, saying, you need to under-stand, that we university people don't know exactly what the groups are going to do or how they are going to function." She learned to live with her discomfort about this candor: "I felt it was really important to tell them that, even though it made me feel as though we didn't have a clue about what we were doing."

From her work, she has gotten a far deeper sense of the power of organizing. "I'm always thinking about ways that I can talk to people about it [learning groups and the role of organizing in groups]." She continued: "[A] new educator [was] talking to me about how he could see this kind of a learning-group model or process being used for a lot more things than just weed management. Which is of course exactly what we hoped."

Campus-Based Extension/Research Faculty

Both of the campus-based extension faculty members reported that their learning-group experience helped them to better stimulate and support significant change in how farmers thought and acted about weed management. These faculty members had mixed responsibilities: to create and teach educational programming regarding weed management and to do research in support of these programs. Over their careers, both had experienced major problems with technology-transfer approaches, and each reported that the learning groups provided a setting in which they could develop and refine alternatives to these approaches.

One had shifted from updating farmers on herbicide developments to a much broader focus on integration of multiple methods of weed control. In recent years, he had concentrated on helping farmers gain key insights that they could apply to the ongoing design and management of their farm operations. For example, one emphasis has been on the exponential growth process of weed seedlings, wherein weeds can very quickly grow into and beyond controllable size ranges. His intention is to motivate and enable farmers to begin planning and managing their labor schedules with an eye to the rapid growth phases of weeds. He has found that his pedagogical program of opening eyes to characteristic features of weed growth and other aspects of weed ecology is powerful and well received. He reported that he valued the learning groups as safe settings in which to develop and refine this pedagogy. He could "hone skills" and test his "ideas and suspicions" about what audiences might need, and discover "new possibilities" for programming that create awareness about the interplay of weed management and weed biology.

The other faculty member had an unresolved problem in his extension practice. Over the course of his career, he had found himself faced with expectations to provide detailed weed-management recommendations for an increasingly broad range of managed ecosystems and ecosystem managers, which presently range from horticultural crops to wetlands to pastures to roadside areas. He found these expectations impossible to satisfy: little relevant research had been done, few herbicides were available, and relatively few effective weed-control options of any sort were known. Given this deficiency of knowledge, this faculty member had grown increasingly uncomfortable with acting the role of expert. Moreover, he perceived a deeper problem with functioning as an "answer-provider." When he played that role, he feared that his extension clientele did not develop—or even see a need for—a capacity to "think differently about problems" and therefore to "pull more resources in" to remedy problem situations. Even when relevant weed-management information is available, he has concluded that "handing information to them" is often undesirable, because such information is frequently not used effectively. In contrast, he reported that working in his learning group made it possible to "give farmers tools so that they can approach problems in different ways and are able to deal with the next problems on their own."

Campus-Based Researchers

Both of the campus-based research faculty members reported that the learning groups had empowered them to make significant shifts in the objectives and methodologies of their research programs. Over time, each had become convinced that the challenge of creating a knowledge base for sustainable agriculture (e.g., IWM) was fundamentally different from the corresponding challenge for high-input conventional agriculture. Both perceived that knowledge creation must involve a broader range of knowledge forms and sources. These perceptions motivated significant transformations in their research programs.

Previously, these two researchers had emphasized plant physiology and ecology in agricultural settings. One has, in the past five years, redirected his research effort to test the value of learning theory for understanding and facilitating farmer learning. He had been particularly motivated by a perception that much agronomy research was not accepted or noticed by farmers because of a failure to account for the thinking and learning of farmers. He now focuses on collaborating with colleagues in other disciplines to better understand farmers' learning. In this work, he has noticed that he, as an agronomist, can "hear things" in work with farmers that colleagues in other disciplines cannot.

The second researcher reported that he had experienced a major shift in his scholarship because of his learning-group experience. He reports that his work with the learning groups has led him to work with a new set of colleagues in several disciplines to develop a working model of agricultural science that is more directly engaged with complex problems, such as IWM implementation. At the heart of this model is scientists' participation in multiprofessional groups that engage in ongoing collaborative learning and action to address a complex problem. In this model, the group organizes and structures scientific work. This researcher reported a major outcome of group participation: expansion of his research program into an entirely new domain.

Evaluating Our Project as Public Scholarship

Our working model of public scholarship features a public-work group: a diverse group that engages in collaborative action and social learning to address a public problem. Our scholarship on learning groups has been carried out in the context of such a group, organized around our experimental knowledge network for IWM. As noted, that public-work group was largely disband-ed, due to major reorganization within UMES, and a vigorous new group—the Third Crop Coalition—has taken its place and now provides the setting for our work.

Although the IWM group disbanded while still in the early stages of work on a very sizable problem, we can ask whether our effort at public scholarship created civic value by supporting its initial organization and development. In early 2002, our project was built around a core ensemble of about a dozen extension educators, who were each facilitating a learning group, and five campus-based staff and faculty members, who were providing various forms of support to the network of learning groups. We judged at the time that the project was functioning at an early developmental stage as a public-work group. The group was aware that it functioned to support mutual learning and interdependent action, and made some effort to intentionally and strategically pursue such learning. There was a growing ability to articulate a public purpose with associated goals and objectives. Indeed, an important impetus for sharpening the public purpose and strategy of the group had come from the likelihood of major restructuring in UMES. In response, the group of senior extension educators who were involved in the project had recognized the need for taking strategic steps to protect the distinctive extension approaches that were at the heart of our project.

How then, had scholarship figured in the public-work group's development thus far? What social learning, collective action, or other outcomes of public value had been fueled or provoked? First, we conclude that the feedback loop at the heart of our model—in which scholars contribute their research results to a public-work group and in return receive orientation and support for future scholarly work—had functioned well. In particular, we feel confident that our scholarship on the two weed learning groups has been integrated in the social learning of the larger public-work group.

For example, an evaluative discussion was held at the end of the initial two-year phase of each of the two original learning groups. At this point in the project, some formal scholarship had resulted, including a published case study, using interviews to describe the evaluations of participants in the learning groups, and providing an analysis and assessment of the project as a whole (Jordan et al. 2000). All five authors of that published case study participated in these evaluative discussions as both scholars and social learners. We suggest that the scholarship of the case-study authors—i.e., the case study, and other related scholarly work such as grant proposals and testing of project results in other extension work—quite probably had a substantial effect on the case-study authors' contributions and interactions as social learners during these evaluative discussions. Furthermore, at this time, a second study was being completed assessing the nature of learning experienced by the work-group participants (Blissett 2002). This work involved interviews with each participant, in which they had an opportunity to engage in an open-ended reflective discussion about their experiences.

Blissett's study can be seen as a means for creating civic value by enabling and accelerating the social learning and collective action of the public-work group itself. The study clarified the essential interests and individual perspectives of learning-group participants and identified constraints and concerns that arose in their participation. These clarifications were also essential to the academic value of the Blissett study. This conclusion is supported by reports of a number of participants, who reported that the scholarship *per se* had a valuable role in creating a sense of coherence and accomplishment in the public-work group (Blissett 2002). Specifically, the evaluative research in the case provided participants with recurrent opportunities—individually and collectively—for critical reflection on their actions and experiences in the learning groups.

A third example comes from work to evaluate the two weed learning groups as a means of developing sustainable IWM. In early 2002, as senior extension educators in the group anticipated reorganization of UMES, they were acutely aware that evaluation of the learning groups was urgently needed. In response, campus-based staff and faculty published several evaluative research articles (Jordan et al. 2003; Blissett et al. 2004). In particular, our aim was to provide evaluation data that would be useful in the current discourse regarding the future priorities of the UMES. This scholarship has not served to support ongoing work of the disbanded IWM public-work group, but arguably has played that role for the Third Crop Coalition.

We also discern certain important indirect effects of our public scholarship on the IWM group. Simply put, the group would not have existed in the absence of a commitment to public scholarship. As noted, our notion of public scholarship sees organizing work as integral to such scholarship. Thus, our work began with a phase of proactive, self-conscious creation of a cross-sector public-work group. The group was formed from a prolonged interaction between researchers, extension workers, various sustainable agriculture organizations outside the university, and a broadly based civic group concerned with cross-sector organizing. Through dialogue and discussion among these parties, our conceptual model of learning groups was developed in its initial form.

During this initial phase, most participants from beyond the university were uncertain about what might be gained by joining a public-work project on IWM and thus were not highly motivated to organize such a project. For example, some were mistrustful of university agriculture researchers. Therefore, it is critical to recognize the role of our organizer, who was able to sustain the project through a protracted (three-year) phase of problem definition, fundraising, and negotiation. This phase led to an interactive setting for coordinated innovation, wherein extension workers, and researchers could experiment with new approaches to their work, and farmers were able to participate in innovative learning processes, with organizing serving to minimize the direct transaction costs of interaction.

In the allocation of our financial resources, we gave first priority to supporting an organizer because we regarded such work as entirely essential to public scholarship. Moreover, we supported our organizer through research grants, showing that we successfully argued for the academic value of public scholarship, and were thereby also enabled to create civic value through organizing. Our case demonstrates that public scholarship can create new funding streams to help organize public work across significant lines of difference.

After a 12-month hiatus, during which the UMES reorganization was underway, we have been able to reorganize the project under a different theme (diversification of Minnesota agriculture under the banner of the Third Crop Coalition). We conclude that the public scholarship of our project has also had valuable direct and indirect effects on the public work of the TCC.

First, our scholarship has probably played a significant role in the development and design of the TCC. Specifically, the evaluative research revealed evidence of a number of valuable outcomes. Once published in academic literature, these findings could be used in proposals for subsequent grant support, enabling us to continue our focus on proactive, well-supported organizing.

Second, we again ascribe much of the success of our learning groups to the efforts of our organizer. That effort was credited by several participants as probably essential to the relatively strong sense of cohesion, shared purpose, and sense of mutual capability and accomplishment reported by IWM-learning groups (Blissett 2002). We believe that these perceptions are very important outcomes in civic terms. Moreover, they are the basis of what is arguably the most important ongoing civic outcome: that many of the participants in the learning groups have since given active support to subsequent learning groups, by acting as advocates, facilitators, and participants. This carryover effect has continued to the present time, almost three years after the end of the pilot groups, expressed in the actions and words of sustainable agriculture nonprofit organizations, rural political leaders, farmers assuming leadership positions in rural organizations, and university research and extension workers. In large part because of these efforts, learning groups have been accepted as a primary modus operandi of the TCC. Thus, despite its transient existence, the IWM work group seems to have been an effective incubator of active advocates and practitioners of learning-group approaches. Taken together, the evidence in this case strongly suggests that episodes of public scholarship and public work— even if finite and transient—can create considerable civic value when these episodes are linked by organizing into larger, ongoing projects.

It is important to note, however, that a number of complications and tensions have arisen in the interplay of public scholarship and social learning in our project. For many of us, participation involved behaviors that seemingly conflicted with established roles, norms, and values of professional conduct. For some UMES educators, the idea that their work might include playing a co-equal's role in knowledge creation was somewhat novel. One particular challenge was that the educators often could not find time to function in a critically inquiring mode in relation to the project, thus depriving our project of their insights. We tried to meet this challenge by an organizing tactic: actively soliciting the educators' participation by ongoing informal "check-in" conversations, in which their perceptions of the groups and their role(s) were sought, as well as by conducting more occasional formal evaluation interviews.

An important insight from this effort is that "social" learning rests on a base of diligent and persistent organizing, which can identify topics and issues that a group is willing and able to engage. Doubtless, some educators still felt as though they were the passive subjects of someone else's research rather than active knowledge creators. Certainly, we often proclaimed our commitment to co-equality and co-scholarship in our project. However, such proclamations are likely to ring hollow in the absence of a serious commitment to an organizing approach, and scrupulous attention to factors that support or constrain participation in social learning and scholarship in the professional cultures of all participants.

What can be said regarding the academic value of our project's work? Certainly, the work has met a minimalist, publish-or-perish standard of academic value; peer-reviewed scholarship has been published (Jordan et al. 2000, 2002, 2003, 2004; Blissett et al. 2004), as have an invited opinion column in the leading weed-science journal (Jordan 1997) and three invited symposium papers. This scholarship has been explicitly concerned with reporting the perspectives of the various learning-group participants as well as presenting the broader conceptual justification for learning groups. Moreover, the broader context of learning groups—as an avenue for engaged scholarship—has become a central theme in the scholarship of Jordan and Simmons. A number of academic efforts to apply learning groups to various problems in sustainable agriculture have been undertaken. These involve topics of interest to the TCC as well as other topics such as the challenge of converting from a fossil-fuel based economy to a "carbohydrate economy" that would use products of present photosynthesis for energy sources and industrial feedstock. Hence, it would seem that a fairly broad, generative range of scholarly products has been created. Finally, the project has inspired some scholarship of pedagogy, in the form of a course that focuses on collaborative agroecological innovations that blend social and ecological innovation (Jordan et al. 2002).

Despite these indications of productive outcomes, other complications certainly arose. The interview-based case-study methods we used were unfamiliar to all of us, thus raising questions about our competence to work in ways for which we had no formal training, on questions that were not very visible in the weed-science research agenda. Our purpose was to create knowledge whose ultimate evaluation and publication was uncertain and likely to involve outlets whose relevance and legitimacy were not recognized in our discipline. Our situation called for an inductive and responsive approach to scholarship. We found ourselves working not as principle authors of new knowledge, nor as collaborators working with disciplinary colleagues to explore a sharply-drawn and agreed-upon question, but rather as integrators, working across a broad range of knowledge forms to draw forth a deeper understanding of complex situations by integrating multiple viewpoints. Certainly, current norms of agricultural science scholarship do not explicitly recognize such scholarship.

In practice, we have not encountered serious tensions around this issue of scholarly norms. We suspect that the grant support obtained in the work, the production of publications, the place of this work as part of a broader portfolio of scholarship done by each of the faculty participants, and the flavor of innovation in relation to a widely agreed-upon practical problem may all have contributed to the generally favorable response that our work has received in the peer-evaluation process.

A final problem relates to the very large time demands of participating in the social learning of a public-work group. Presently, there is little recognition of how time-consuming this is. A potential resolution lies in the culture around "service work." At present, such work tends to be viewed contradictorily: there is a norm of support for work in university governance and professional organizations. However, such service work is seen as quite disconnected from the core faculty work of scholarship. There is clearly a need for educational and organizing work that will enable faculty to integrate their service and their scholarly work.

Conclusions

At this stage in the development of our case study, we can offer several broad conclusions. First, we assert strongly that public scholarship is necessary to the future development of weed science (Jordan et al. 2002, 2003). It is clear that weed scientists are very much concerned with developing sustainable approaches to weed management and with broadening the scope of their science to encompass invasive plants in managed ecosystems of all kinds, rather than restricting their work to the traditional focus on field crops. In our view, it is plain that a public-scholarship approach can help weed scientists address these concerns.

Second, we believe that some steps toward the public scholarship we envision can be taken and will receive institutional support, provided that a strong argument can be developed for how this scholarship is relevant to the recognized research priorities of a discipline.

Third, we judge that our work thus far has created a modest amount of public value. As the reflections and evaluations reported above and in Blissett (2002) make clear, nearly all participants report that the project has increased their sense of empowerment to pursue complex public problems and challenges through their professional practice. It is true that the public dimensions and outcomes of our work—in both the IWM and the TCC contexts— have certainly been limited in some respects. Neither group can claim that we span a full range of relevant social and professional diversity, nor has our work proved itself over a long period of time. Yet, our scholarship has been effective in making a successful argument for new streams of public resources devoted to a much more expansive public project: creating a comprehensive, transdisciplinary, and transprofessional knowledge base of an agriculture that can better support the health of ecosystems, rural communities, and the public that depends on our food system. We are moving forward in organizing this project in Southern Minnesota. Thus, arguably, our work has been partially generative of public-work initiatives that have considerable potential to produce major public outcomes.

Fourth, we find abundant evidence that public scholarship is wholly dependent on a capacity for organizing. The social-learning processes that are integral to public scholarship require a conscientious, consistent, and well-supported effort to convene, facilitate, evaluate, and refine these processes. Without organizing capacity, the form of public scholarship that we pursue will not occur. It is very important to recognize that organizing capacity need not be provided solely by scholars. Indeed, the qualitatively greater scope and range of civic issues and civic participation that are being engaged by the TCC are directly attributable to organizing work done by public-sector partners. From this experience, we suggest that the relationship between would-be public scholars and organizing-minded partners in public work is likely to be of the utmost importance in developing public-scholarship projects.

Finally, we point out the obvious necessity of well-organized social learning and collective action within land-grant universities for the purpose of creating capacity for public scholarship.

References

Blissett, H., S. Simmons, N. Jordan, and K. Nelson. 2004. Evaluation of Learning Group Approaches for Fostering Integrated Cropping Systems Management. *Journal of Natural Resources and Life Sciences Education* 33:134-140.

Blissett, H. 2002. *Outcomes of Collaborative Learning Groups in Agriculture.* MS Thesis, University of Minnesota, 92 pp.

Boyer, E. L. 1990. *Scholarship Reconsidered: Priorities of the Professoriate.* Princeton, NJ: The Carnegie Foundation for the Advancement of Teaching.

Boyte, H. C. and E. Hollander. 2000. "Wingspread Declaration on Renewing the Civic Mission of the American Research University." http://www.compact.org/civic/Wingspread.html.

Boyte, H. C. and N. N. Kari. 1996. *Building America: The Democratic Promise of Public Work.* Philadelphia, PA: Temple University Press.

Campbell, A. 1998. "Fomenting Synergy: Experiences with Facilitating Landcare in Australia." In *Facilitating Sustainable Agriculture,* ed. N. Röling and M. Wagemakers, 232-249. Cambridge, UK: Cambridge University Press.

Charmaz, K. 2002. "Qualitative Interviewing and Grounded-theory Analysis." In *Handbook of Interview Research,* ed. J. F. Gubrium and J.A. Holstein, 675-694. Thousand Oaks, CA: Sage Publications.

Cousins, R. and M. Mortimer. 1995. *Dynamics of Weed Populations.* Cambridge, UK: Cambridge University Press.

Crombie, A. 1995. "Adult Learning in Group Environments: The Hidden Curriculum." In *Participative Approaches for Landcare,* ed. S. Chamala and K. Keith, 59-72. Brisbane, AU: Australian Academic Press.

Daniels, S.E. and G.B. Walter. 2001. *Working Through Environmental Conflict: The Collaborative Learning Approach.* Westport, CT: Praeger Press, pp. xxii, 299.

Engel, P. G. H. 1997. *The Social Organization of Innovation.* KIT Press.

Forcella, F. 1997. My View. *Weed Science* 45:327.

Irwin, A. 1995. *Citizen Science.* New York, NY: Routledge.

Ison, R. and D. Russell. 2000. *Agricultural Extension and Rural Development: Breaking Out of Traditions.* Cambridge, UK: Cambridge University Press.

Jordan, N., D. Andow, and K. Mercer. 2005. Ecology of Agricultural Systems: A Service-learning Course in Agroecology. *Journal of Natural Resources and Life Sciences Education.*

Jordan, N., et al. 2000. "Learning Groups Developing Collaborative Learning Methods for Diversified, Site-specific Weed Management: A Case Study from Minnesota, USA." In *Cow up a Tree: Knowing and Learning for Change in Agriculture,* ed. M. Cerf et al., 85-95. Paris: INRA.

———. 2002. Public Scholarship: Linking Weed Science with Public Work. *Weed Science* 50:547-554.

———. 2003. Knowledge Networks: An Avenue to Ecological Management of Weeds. *Weed Science* 51:271-277.

Jordan, N. 1997. New Professional Practice to Diversity Weed Management. *Weed Science* 45:191.

Mack, R. N. et al. 2000. Biotic Invasions: Causes, Epidemiology, Global Consequences, and Control. *Ecological Applications* 10(3): 689-710.

Michels, P. and A. Massengale. 2004. Civic Organizing Framework. http://www.activecitizen.org/images/civorgframework.html.

Morse-Elias, D. et al. "Green Lands, Blue Waters Initiative." Unpublished technical paper.

Poff, N. L., J. D. Allan, M. A. Palmer, D. D. Hart, B. D. Richter, A. H. Arthington, K. H. Rogers, J. L. Meyer, and J. A. Stanford. 2003. River Flowers and Water Wars: Emerging Science for Environmental Decision Making. *Frontiers of Ecology.* 1:298-306.

Radosevich, S., J. Holt, and C. Ghersa.1997. *Weed Ecology: Implications for Management.* 2nd Ed. New York, NY: John Wiley & Sons, Inc.

Rickson, R., P. Nowak, and S. Rickson. 1995. "Farmer Knowledge and Participation in Sustainable Agriculture: The Dynamics and Significance of Land Care." In *Participative Approaches for Landcare,* ed. S. Chamala and K. Keith, 179-198. Brisbane, AU: Australian Academic Press.

Rogers, E. M. 1995. *The Diffusion of Innovations.* New York, NY: Free Press.

Röling, N. G. and J. Jiggins. 1998. "The Ecological Knowledge System." In *Facilitating Sustainable Agriculture,* ed. N. G. Röling and M. A. E. Wagemakers, 283-311. Cambridge, UK: Cambridge University Press.

Sheley, R. L., T. J. Svejcar, and B. D. Maxwell. 1996. A Theoretical Framework for Developing Successional Weed Management Strategies on Rangeland. *Weed Technology* 10:766-773.

Svejcar, T. J. 1996. What are Working Groups and Why Should Scientists Be Involved? *Weed Technology* 10:451-454.

Waltner-Toews, D., J. Kay, C. Neudoerffer, and T. Gitau.2003. Perspective Changes Everything: Managing Ecosystems from the Inside out. *Frontiers in Ecology* 1:23-30.

Chapter Seven:

Teaching as Public Scholarship

Tribal Perspectives and Democracy in the Classroom

by Frank Clancy and Margaret Adamek

I In early September of 1998, an unusual letter arrived at the office of then-University of Minnesota President Mark Yudof. Printed on the stationery of the Minnesota Chippewa Tribe (the MCT), an umbrella organization that represents six American-Indian bands but has limited governmental authority, the two-page document was by turns diplomatic, conciliatory, threatening, and poetic. It was signed by MCT president Norman Deschampe, a member of the Grand Portage Band from far northeastern Minnesota, who said he was writing about "a matter of great concern and urgency." The MCT, the letter said, had learned that University of Minnesota scientists were "endeavoring to genetically code and manipulate the wild rice stock native to our reservations." Deschampe urged the university to proceed with "the greatest possible level of caution."

The letter subsequently outlined four inter-related objections to research on and manipulation of the wild rice genome:

Economic: Increased development of wild rice in paddies would economically harm tribal members, who generally refer to themselves as *Anishinaabe* (the adjective or singular noun) or the *Anishinaabeg* (plural noun) (Meyer 1994); the tribe is also known as the *Ojibwa*, sometimes spelled *Ojibway* or *Ojibwe*. The Anishinaabeg, Deschampe pointed out, harvest rice for commercial as well as religious purposes and individual use. Wild rice is, he said, "a unique treasure that has been carefully protected by the people of our tribe for centuries.... Should any party be allowed to genetically manipulate the rice and mass produce the rice in paddies, that would result in harm to our reservations and membership just as surely as if the rice were stolen directly from our rice camps."

Legal/Political: The university's research might violate federal law and treaties between the United States government and the Anishinaabe people. In nineteenth-century treaties, the Anishinaabeg ceded vast areas of land to the U.S. but reserved the right to hunt, fish, and gather rice on that land. The treaty of July 29, 1837, for example, says, "The privilege of hunting, fishing, and gathering the wild rice, upon the lands, the rivers and the lakes included in the territory ceded, is guaranteed to the Indians, during the pleasure of the President of the United States" (Treaty with the Chippewa 1837).

Scientific: The letter expressed concern that a genetically altered strain of wild rice might replace naturally occurring strains.

Cultural/Religious: The spiritual health and well-being of the Anishinaabe people are inextricably linked to wild rice, the letter suggested. "We are of the opinion," Deschampe wrote, "that the wild rice rights assured by treaty accrue not only to individual grains of rice, but to the very essence of the resource. We were not promised just any wild rice, that promise could be kept by delivering sacks of grain to our members each year. We were promised the rice that grew in the waters of our people, and all the value that such rice holds. The tribal signers of the treaty surely understood the singular nature of this rice since they fought a war with the Lakota people over this very resource. This rice from these waters holds a sacred and significant place in our culture."

The letter labeled the University of Minnesota research and the technology that might result from it a "direct threat" to a resource protected by federal law. And the Anishinaabe people, the letter added, were "prepared to undertake every legal and lawful measure to protect our interests in this matter."

Deschampe's letter was widely and quickly distributed among Minnesota's close-knit Anishinaabe communities. On the White Earth Reservation in northwestern Minnesota, for example, the tribe's monthly newspaper, *Anishinaabeg Today,* published the entire letter in its September 1998 issue. Not coincidentally, the editors devoted the entire front page of this issue to coverage of university President Yudof's visit to the reservation the previous month, and another trip by more than 50 university administrators and faculty in early September: Yudof's trip and his meetings with tribal educators and government officials had inspired hope that the university might take the Anishinaabeg's concerns seriously, and White Earth members had helped draft the MCT letter.

A copy of this letter was also sent to the offices of Visions for Change (VFC), an innovative project then located within the University of Minnesota's College of Agricultural, Food, and Environmental Sciences (COAFES) that promoted a sustainable food system and innovative approaches to higher education. A key component of their programming emphasized collaboration between land-grant universities and tribal colleges in Minnesota, North Dakota, and South Dakota through the development of numerous community-led joint ventures between the college and native communities. The letter was circulated to interested parties affiliated with Visions for Change, including Karl Lorenz, a student-affairs administrator who runs COAFES's Honors Program.

By coincidence, Lorenz, who is himself an enrolled member of the Lummi nation of northwestern Washington, had already organized an honors colloquium for the fall quarter entitled "Native American Perspectives on Land Issues and the Environment."

Such small-group seminars, which enable students and faculty members to interact informally, are a centerpiece of COAFES's Honors Program, and typically address timely topics that are directly relevant to at least some COAFES students or that touch on broader societal issues. Lorenz shared the letter with course instructors, George Spangler, a professor of fisheries and wildlife, and associate professor of nutrition, Craig Hassel.

What would happen, those three wondered, if they took the Anishinaabe grievances seriously—if they truly tried to understand the Anishinaabe view of wild rice? What questions must they ask? And who might answer them? What type of learning opportunity would this issue present to undergraduate honors students in agriculture? How would engagement with this issue, in the context of the classroom, move dialogue forward on this unusual and important concern? And, how does one teach a class of predominantly European American students how to sensitively and perceptively penetrate an indigenous worldview?

With the students' consent, Spangler, Hassel, and Lorenz decided to focus the entire seminar on examination of this controversy. Eventually they would describe its premise on the course Web site in these terms:

> This course will introduce students to the problem of perceiving and responding to a Native American perspective on the larger society's investigation of a sacred entity, wild rice. Students should be aware of the fact that eurocentric culture is occasionally (or, maybe even frequently) at odds with the interests of other cultures, including those that are embedded within our geographic boundaries. We trust that, by grappling with a very specific case study in our relationship with Native Americans, students will be able to better understand cross-cultural conflicts, and to develop an appreciation for alternative cultural points-of-view.

Wild Rice

The plant commonly known as wild rice is a grass belonging to the genus *Zizania;* the species *Zizania palustris,* one of three that grows naturally in North America, has been harvested and eaten by native peoples for many centuries, and perhaps millennia. An annual, it grows in marshes, shallow lakes, and slow-moving streams (Oelke, Bloom, Porter, & Liu 1999; Huber 1999). It's an extremely nutritious food, high in carbohydrates and low in fat, with ample amounts of B vitamins and antioxidants (Vennum 1988; Hassel 2001).

Wild rice has been a staple of the Anishinaabe diet for centuries, a critical resource for surviving the region's long, harsh winters. Before the arrival of European settlers, who would subsequently destroy much of the plant's habitat with dams, drainage ditches, and other alterations to the natural environment, wild rice grew in abundance across much of what is now Wisconsin and Minnesota, as well as southern Canada. Traveling up the Fox River in 1673, Marquette needed guides to find his way through the wild rice. One historian wrote in 1850 about a lake where the wild rice was "so thick and luxuriant ... that the Indians are often obliged to cut passage ways through it for their bark canoes." Another writer described rice fields that "stretch as far as the eye can see" (Vennum 1988, pp. 19, 31). Still another wrote, "[N]o other section of the North American continent was so characteristically an Indian paradise, so far as a spontaneous vegetal food is concerned, as was this territory in Wisconsin and Minnesota" (Jenks 1900, p. 1036). As late as the 1950s and early 1960s, residents of White Earth recall that some lakes were almost completely covered with rice.

But for the Anishinaabeg, wild rice has always been far more than an ordinary food, no matter how abundant. According to the tribe's oral history and creation stories, their ancestors moved west over a period of centuries, following prophecies that foretold of a place where food grew on the water (Benton-Banai 1988). The food they called *manoomin* (roughly translated, the "good berry" or "good seed") (Vennum 1988) was thus a special gift from the Creator to the Anishinaabe people. It was—and still is—served at feasts and used in cultural and religious ceremonies. When someone dies, friends and family members leave wild rice at the grave.

Anishinaabe stories describe how the cultural hero Nanabozho was shown the food *manoomin*:

> One evening, Nanabozho returned empty-handed from hunting. Tired, hungry, and discouraged, he approached his fire, and noticed a duck sitting on the edge of his kettle of boiling water. So surprised was he by his good fortune that Nanabozho forgot to draw his bow, and the startled duck flew safely away. Looking into the kettle, Nanabozho found wild rice floating upon the water, but he did not know what it was. Still, he ate from the kettle, and it was the best soup he had ever tasted.
>
> Early the next morning, Nanabozho set out in the direction the duck had flown, arriving after many days at a lake filled with a strange water grass that bore the grain Nanabozho had seen floating in his kettle. Flocks of ducks, geese, and other waterfowl nested in the dense grass and fed on the grain. After that, when Nanabozho did not kill a deer, he always knew where to find food to eat (adapted from LaDuke 1999 and Smith & Vogel 1984).

"Wild rice is part of our prophecy, our process of being human, our process of being Anishinaabe," says White Earth historian Andrew Favorite. "It tells us, in those prophecies, that we'll find the food growing out of the water when we reach our homeland. We are here because of the wild rice. We are living prophecy fulfilled."

Outsiders have long recognized, at least in the abstract, the importance of wild rice to Anishinaabe life. Thus the tribe's 1837 treaty with the United States mentions the right to gather wild rice alongside the rights to hunt and fish. In 1898 and again in 1899, Dr. Albert Jenks, then a doctoral student at the University of Wisconsin, traveled extensively throughout Wisconsin and Minnesota to study wild rice. So important was this food to the people he met—the Anishinaabeg/Ojibwa as well as other tribes like the Menominee—that they were called "the wild rice gatherers of the upper lakes" in his widely cited report, written for the Bureau of American Ethnology (Jenks 1900).

Conflict over wild rice between the Anishinaabeg and the dominant society is neither new nor unusual. As long ago as 1849, the Mille Lacs Band complained that a dam built by white lumbermen on Minnesota's Rum River (in territory ceded by the 1837 treaty) interfered with the wild rice harvest. Six years later, the dispute erupted into violence, and federal troops were called in (Minnesota v. Mille Lacs Band 1999).

Less dramatic but far more prevalent—and, in the long run, far-reaching—were conflicts about how the Anishinaabeg used (and didn't use) this bountiful resource. Jenks, for example, writes, "The primitive Indians do not take production very seriously. Indeed, they do not take it seriously enough for their own welfare, for often they are in want in an unnecessarily short time after the harvest. In the case of wild rice, their want was due not to overproduction and underdistribution, but to underproduction.... They could gather more 'if they did not spend so much time feasting and dancing every day and night during the time they are here for the purpose of gathering'" (Jenks 1900, pp 1073-1074, quoting Motzfeldt, letter, Dec. 3, 1898). Jenks's articulation of the ceremony and feasting traditions that accompanied the annual harvesting reveals how poorly he understood the central significance of the rice and of the community celebrations and rituals that accompanied the gathering. Far from being a waste of time, these events were essential to preserving the life of the community, the centrality of rice to the culture, and the ongoing health of the crop from year to year.

Jenks was at times dramatically wrong: "The Indian," he wrote, "by his use of the wild-rice seed, is a great enemy of the plant, for it will be shown that the plant, unless it is artificially sown, is gradually being extinguished in such beds as are continually used." But his European perspective, which exalted "civilized agriculture," provided the intellectual, political, and moral foundation for dismissing Anishinaabe protests (Jenks 1900, p. 1026). And as Vennum (1988) points out, it was part and parcel of a broader justification of Manifest Destiny: "This view [of Anishinaabe 'underproduction'] was but one facet of the land-use argument of Europeans settling the North American continent; because the Indians were not using the land to its full capacity, they must relinquish their rights to those who would make it more productive" (Vennum 1988, p. 217). It was not until much more recently that this definition of *underproduction* was viewed as the indigenous practices of sustainable landscape management. This process of stewardship was based on a worldview that was at root participatory—well outside the scope of a modernist culture that considered itself disassociated from, and dominant over, nature. Taking only what one needed ensured a viable harvest for the following year. Additionally, Anishinaabeg had reseeding practices in place that also ensured wild rice beds would continue to thrive.

Similarly, some Anishinaabeg have vocally criticized the commercial exploitation of wild rice by non-Indians for almost as long as whites have been trying to grow a hybridized version of *Zizania palustris* in paddies, a variety developed at the University of Minnesota. In 1971, for example, when the paddy-rice industry was in its infancy, one Minnesota newspaper reported, "Some Indians, and a few non-Indians, resent anyone meddling with a crop that has been vital for Minnesota and Wisconsin Indians for centuries." The Anishinaabeg's goal, the article said, was "preserving something that is theirs alone." It concluded: "Besides, they want to keep their wild rice wild" (Gebert 1971). Vennum says "many Ojibway view the commercial

exploitation of this resource by non-Indians as an ultimate
desecration" (Vennum 1998, p. 1).

The Anishinaabeg's complaints, however, were no more
successful than their attempts, more than a century earlier, to
curtail the logging, dam-building, draining, and other development that damaged natural rice stands. At its most extreme, their
concerns were mocked. This legacy of neglect and exclusion by
policymakers characterizes both historic and contemporary
attitudes toward, and experiences of, indigenous people and
their traditional lands. It also represents the misunderstanding
of indigenous approaches to sustainable development, which did
not emphasize intensive resource extraction, but a minimal use
for sustenance purposes.

A 1969 report to the Minnesota Legislature, commissioned by
the Minnesota Resources Commission, described wild rice as a
part of Anishinaabe heritage—something "uniquely his"—yet
dismissed the Anishinaabe way of harvesting and marketing wild
rice as "a September Santa Claus," a "good-berry Mardi Gras,"
and "the excuse and provision for a spending spree." This report,
supported by taxpayer resources, suggests the prevailing attitude
of the public and policymakers toward traditions and beliefs of
the region's indigenous people. The trivialization of their central
icon reflected a fundamental misunderstanding by European
American culture about their own epistemological framework
and that of native communities.

In contrast, this report portrayed the development of a paddy
rice industry as a moral imperative: an agricultural expression
of Manifest Destiny. Some may argue that the report reflects
the totality of the quest for domination by European settlers in
North America.

> To take the attitude of some sociologists and welfare agents
> that "the rice should be left to the Indian" is to close the eyes
> to facts. Once the white man tasted the grain it was no longer
> left to him—it became a delight of anyone's diet. So the white

man will eventually domesticate the grain! To curb the trend by stubborn, lethargic, do-nothingness will be to lose the business to another state with vision and the will to prosper its agricultural community.

If the Indian is to be raised to a level of equality, respectability and become a self-supporting part of [the] Minnesota economy, it is criminal neglect to let him waste his heritage and make no effort to better the one natural resource that is uniquely his (Edman 1969, p. vii; Vennum 1988, pp. 295-96).

In fact, this (decidedly European) vision of planting *Zizania palustris* in paddies and harvesting wild rice for profit dates back to at least the mid-1800s, but efforts to grow wild rice commercially did not begin in earnest until the middle of the twentieth century. The University of Minnesota, through its Department of Agronomy and Plant Genetics, literally helped birth the paddy rice industry. According to a recently published history of the department, a conference was held on the university's St. Paul campus in 1951, at which the 23 participants outlined a research and breeding program. Although that program was not funded, University of Minnesota scientists continued to work sporadically on wild-rice research for the next two decades.

In 1971, the Minnesota legislature approved funding for a research and breeding program designed to assist the nascent paddy-rice industry. Agronomist Ervin Oelke, who had experience working on rice production in California, was named the university's coordinator of wild-rice research. A wild-rice breeder joined the faculty in the summer of 1972. Since then, University of Minnesota scientists have been endeavoring systematically to develop strains of *Zizania palustris* that are more suited to commercial agriculture—in particular, ones that uniformly retain their seed until it can be mechanically harvested in a single pass. For a wild plant, however, this tendency for seed to ripen and drop at various times, known as "shattering," is an extremely useful adaptation.

Although Minnesota researchers and other breeders have made some progress towards that goal, dramatically increasing yield, wild rice has stubbornly resisted being turned into a predictable (and more profitable) crop like wheat or ordinary rice, both of which have a far longer history of breeding for commercial agriculture. Beginning in 1987 and accelerating in 1992, when Minnesota's paddy wild-rice industry began providing financial support for the project, university researchers took a new tack: they began to map the wild-rice genome. By enabling breeders to better understand how traits like shattering are inherited and to follow the inheritance of recessive genes, this research held promise of becoming a powerful tool that would, at the very least, dramatically accelerate the domestication process (Oelke 2000, R. Porter, personal communication).

In August of 1998—the month that Mark Yudof visited the White Earth Indian Reservation—the Minnesota Department of Natural Resources (DNR) granted university scientists a special permit to "examine wild rice stands growing in any public waters . . . for the purpose of taking, transporting and possessing leaf and seed samples for research purposes." The permit, which came from the DNR's Division of Fish and Wildlife, allowed researchers to gather leaf samples from no more than 100 plants on each site and to take no more than five pounds of seed from each. It said nothing about the purposes of the scientists' research and stated explicitly that researchers were not authorized to collect "samples or seeds from waters or in stands that may be under the jurisdiction of federally recognized Indian Bands." In fact, these scientists had been collecting samples in this manner for years but this time, news of the application and research on the wild-rice genome traveled to White Earth and other Minnesota reservations, where it fed both fears and resentment of the university's decades-long support for the paddy-rice industry.

To at least some Anishinaabeg, what the University of Minnesota researchers are doing is essentially sacrilegious. To them, human beings cannot possibly "improve" a sacred gift from the Creator. And to change such a gift for financial gain is blasphemous. "We couldn't look at wild rice that way," says Judy Fairbanks, a member of the White Earth band and a fundraiser at White Earth Tribal and Community College. "This is our gift from the Creator. Interfering with it, changing it, is not a good thing. If it cannot grow naturally any more, whether because of interference with its environment or its very essence—its being, the DNA—then we have disrespected our gift." For indigenous people, icons central to their identity are often an important focus for destruction by a colonizing force—whether it be the decimation of the Great Plains buffalo, patenting of Basmati rice by American companies, destruction of linguistic systems, or genetic coding of a plant. These acts contribute significantly to the precipitous slide toward cultural extermination.

This is indeed a terrible fate to face, and one that is difficult to understand for people of European descent. For those who gladly gave up their language and customs to assimilate into the cultural norms of their new homeland as did most European immigrants, it is very difficult to understand what is truly lost by those who resist this assimilation and collectively yearn and struggle to maintain their traditions.

To the Anishinaabeg, their fate as a people is inextricably linked to the fate of wild rice. "We stand to lose everything," says Joe LaGarde, another White Earth Band member. "That's what's going to happen, if they continue with what they're doing. What happens when this wild rice that's been genetically altered gets in with our wild rice? Will [wild rice] turn into a hybrid? What will happen to wild rice? It will be gone within three years.We're going to lose everything if they continue with this research, what I call messing with our wild rice—with genetically altering it. It's our third prophecy. So we have a duty to protect our future. That's what we're looking at—the future of our people. If we lose our rice, we won't exist as a people for long. We'll be done too."

Important in LaGarde's words is his identification of the Third Prophecy, which outlines an incursion that threatens the stability of wild rice. Thus, Anishinaabeg not only are seeking to protect a longstanding and important commodity, but their religious stories articulate the current situation and dictate what must be done as a response to protect the rice.

The Undergraduate Honors Seminar

Such was the context in which COAFES faculty and staff members planned a seminar called "Native American Perspectives on Land Issues and the Environment." For a century and a half, the dominant society had dismissed and even ridiculed Anishinaabe views about wild rice. For half a century, the State of Minnesota, through its land-grant university, had supported research and an industry that many Anishinaabeg saw as harmful.

As they pondered organizing and teaching this class, Lorenz, Hassel, and Spangler knew they faced an epistemological and pedagogical challenge. Spangler had served as a consultant to the Mille Lacs Band in a treaty rights case that was then at the United States Supreme Court. (In 1999, the Supreme Court ruled that the Anishinaabeg retained hunting, fishing, and rice-gathering rights on lands they had ceded to the U.S.) Hassel had worked with Visions for Change, an experience he credits with radically altering his view of his role as a scientist. In addition to being Native, Lorenz had studied American-Indian history and religions and environmental philosophy, including that of the Anishinaabeg. They wanted to do something different—to go deeper.

How, they wondered, could they avoid the hubris that so often characterized the dominant society's view of Native Americans? Could they do more than describe Anishinaabe views from a Western perspective, and instead help students (and themselves) to understand? How could this course not only address an important local issue, but also respond in a civically accountable way that was in keeping with the land-grant institution's mission of public scholarship?

This challenge required a systematic reassessment of the professor's role in teaching, an important part of teaching as a form of public scholarship. Hassel and Spangler began by showing students the letter from the Minnesota Chippewa Tribe and asking them if they wanted to focus on this issue. After the students chose to examine the issue of wild rice, they were divided into small groups and asked to analyze the MCT letter. What questions should they ask? Who might be able to answer them?

Hassel explains: "I'm a strong advocate of critical thinking. I'm a strong advocate of student-directed learning. I'm a strong advocate of using whatever mechanisms possible to engage students in their own learning, and to have them take responsibility for that. So I made the suggestion that we allow students the opportunity to examine the letter, and then ask, 'What do they get out of it? What are the issues in this letter?' Allow them to unpack this letter and list the issues, based on their reading." This process of student-claimed ownership of the course direction and content provided a purposefully constructed public space, where the key stakeholders set the agenda and outcomes for their own learning. From a public-scholarship standpoint, this democratic approach enabled students to claim and prioritize their individual and collective learning experiences.

From the beginning, students knew, that as a final group project, they would have to make recommendations to President Yudof about how the university should respond to the Anishinaabeg's concerns. In order to do that, the students compiled a list of 13 issues they needed to understand:

1. Legal treaty rights

2. "The University-of-Minnesota side of the story"

3. Economic implications (winners/losers)

4. Research implications (biotechnology)

5. Detachment from general society (general society perspective excludes Native American perspective)

6. Preserving Native American culture

7. Must be players on the political scene (DNR, BIA, legislators ...)

8. Ethical issues and dimensions (equity on use issues—if they can why can't we)

9. "Good intentions" vs. real-life outcomes

10. Environmental issues (preserving the wild stock)

11. Racism

12. Historical perspectives (expropriation)

13. Trust, fear, vulnerability

Even after students had compiled this list, Hassel and Spangler continued to take a fundamentally different approach to teaching. "The stereotypical expectation for a course is that the knowledge exists at the university, and the faculty member represents the source of that knowledge," Hassel says. "In this course, and in other courses I've taught, you have to take the approach that the university is not the source of knowledge but a resource for accessing knowledge. And faculty members are not the experts. They are not the sole source of knowledge, they are not the core of knowledge, but the means by which to access the people who are knowledgeable." This democratized notion of expertise, coupled with the role of professor as facilitator suggests an alternative purpose for the teacher—another key feature of public scholarship.

For assistance, they contacted Joe LaGarde, a White Earth elder who had served on the board of directors of Visions for Change. He, in turn, arranged for a series of speakers, most of them White Earth Anishinaabeg, to visit and address the class. In addition, the instructors invited two of the key scientists working on wild-rice research: Ronald Phillips, the geneticist who was (and still is) leading efforts to map the wild-rice genome; and

Ervin Oelke, an extension and small-grains specialist, who served as coordinator of the university's wild-rice research program from 1972 until his retirement in 2000.

In late October, the class also traveled to the White Earth Reservation, about 250 miles north and west of Minneapolis, where they toured the reservation and heard speakers discuss wild rice as well as an array of other issues, including efforts to restore the band's land base. Established in 1867, the 1300-square mile reservation serves as home to about 5,000 enrolled members. Total enrollment is about 22,000, making White Earth the largest of seven Anishinaabe reservations in Northern Minnesota. But, because of government policies and widespread land swindles early in the twentieth century, individual Anishinaabe people and the tribe actually own only seven percent of the land on the reservation.

The Anishinaabe View

Any attempt to understand the Anishinaabe view of wild rice must begin with the sacred and an appreciation of what wild rice meant and means to them—not in Western terms of history and beliefs, but in terms of their own history and beliefs. White Earth elder Paul Schultz, who helped teach the Honors Course, explains: "From where we come from, the sacred is the absolute essential starting point. And in the case of wild rice even more so, because wild rice is such a sacred sign to us. We were brought to this land where the food grows above the water as a prophecy from our Creator. This is where we were meant to live. The Creator intended for us to always have *manoomin,* wild rice, as a part of our life, as part of our culture, as our reminder of how we got here."

The lives and spiritual well-being of the Anishinaabeg are inextricably tied to wild rice, in a way that science cannot explain or comprehend. Schultz continues:

That rice is not ours. It is a gift given to the people from the Creator. Because of the significance of the rice—it being the symbol to let our people know that we had reached the homeland—it is a continuing reaffirmation for us. That's why we don't want it messed with. As long as that rice is there, the people are in the homeland. As long as the shells [of the rice] are in the lake, and can come to the top of the water any time the Creator wants them to, we are in the homeland.

Our concern is that Western development and Western science, in their quest for doing whatever they have designated is important, would operate with total disregard for that truth. That's what they miss. This isn't about us owning rice. It's about rice and the Creator, being the symbol that we are where we are meant to be. If the rice were to disappear, and the lakes were to be altered so that the shells were no more, and would no longer come to the top of the water, our people would be in great confusion and despair. The whole idea of cause and effect, for the Western mind, cannot come to that truth for us. That's the point of contention.

In the Anishinaabe view of the world, every living thing has a spirit and soul, at least equal and perhaps superior in value to human beings. That perspective is, of course, diametrically opposed to the Judeo-Christian teaching of Genesis, in which God gives mankind dominion over all the plants and animals. Lori Ylitalo, a professor at White Earth Tribal and Community College, explained this principle in a letter to students: "Our creator gave this rice to us. We are no more important spiritually than the plants that the creator gave to us. We are simply the caretakers of this resource. We feel that this is mankind's purpose in life, to be caretakers of the many resources. Because the rice has a spiritual quality, we must treat it with respect."

That is not an easy concept for Westerners, and particularly those trained in the sciences, to accept. It is also a challenge in the context of a public institution, where the secular is purposefully elevated above and separated from the sacred. In *Wild Rice and the Ojibway People,* Vennum says, "Traditional Ojibway life elevates rice above being food simply for consumption or barter. Stories and legend, reinforced by the ceremonial use of *manoomin* and taboos and proscriptions against eating it at certain times, show the centrality of wild rice to Ojibway culture." But these factors, taken together, he concludes, suggest that wild rice was not sacred but instead, "at least in the past, approached the status of a sacred food" (Vennum 1988, p. 58). Vennum's analysis reveals an incomplete understanding of how wild rice is intrinsically sacred to the Anishinaabeg, which forms the cornerstone of this issue historically *and* today. In 1982, a food store unknowingly donated paddy-grown wild rice to the St. Paul American Indian Center for a Thanksgiving meal. According to Charlene Smith and Howard Vogel. American Indians "refused to take the free rice, even though it meant their children might go hungry, because the paddy rice offended their cultural and religious sensibilities. Labeling the paddy rice as wild rice was analogous to misrepresenting non-kosher food as kosher" (Smith & Vogel 1984, p. 794 and Vennum 1988, p. 297 led me to this anecdote).

Others, including some Anishinaabeg, have compared wild rice to bread and wine, which are sometimes sacred in Christian faiths. But unlike those foods, wild rice does not become sacred to the Anishinaabeg through human intervention, when it is blessed. To the Western mind, wild rice presents a kind of tautology: Wild rice is sacred because it is wild rice. In a sense, it's akin to the Hindu view of cows—except that the Anishinaabeg embrace the additional paradox of eating (and selling, on a limited basis) a food they consider sacred. To the indigenous mind, however, all living things possess a soul, a mind, and relationship to all other things. The Anishinaabe worldview is participatory, inter-related, and ensouled, whereas the stance of the Western mind is rational, detached, and objective. Westerners have been trained to reject this view, suggesting scientific illiteracy as the cause for the

Anishinaabeg's concerns. A more complex read of the seemingly incommensurable nature of this epistemology suggests that there exists two relationships to one plant, rather than an archaic and primitive view of something that the rest of us know is inanimate.

For the Anishinaabeg, history likewise plays an important role in their telling of the wild-rice story. This history includes both the broader story of how whites stole their land and deprived them of civil rights, as well as the history of the University of Minnesota's relationship to American Indians. They mention, for example, Albert Jenks, the anthropologist who studied wild rice for the Bureau of American Ethnology and later became a professor at the University of Minnesota.

In 1914 and 1915, a decade and a half after he published "The Wild Rice Gatherers of the Upper Lakes," Jenks visited White Earth and other Minnesota reservations as a consultant for white defendants in a number of land-fraud lawsuits that hinged primarily on the question of whether the individual who originally sold the land was a "mixed-blood" or a "pure-blood" (who by law was not allowed to sell his allotted reservation land). Like many modern scientists who consult in legal cases, Jenks unabashedly used "science" to assist those who had hired him. Jenks measured the heads, faces, and noses of American Indians; he observed eye color, skin tone (his ostensibly scientific method relied on the pinching of arms), hair texture, and teeth.

Quite predictably, his results, which the University of Minnesota published in a monograph, served the defendants' needs. "It was soon discovered that the pure-blood Indian type was noticeable chiefly by its absence" (Jenks 1916, p. 2; Meyer 1994). It should also be noted that Jenks' method of racial science was part of a broader movement at the time, the methodology of which has since been soundly rejected.

Even more pertinent, to the Anishinaabeg, is the history of the university's involvement with cultivated wild rice. Working for decades at the request and on behalf of a couple of dozen white paddy-rice farmers, University of Minnesota scientists helped give birth to, and have supported for decades, an industry that many Anishinaabeg perceive to be economically as well as spiritually harmful. Though the Anishinaabeg never truly controlled their economic interest in wild rice—even before the birth of the paddy-rice industry, whites typically acted as intermediaries and manipulated prices—in real terms, the price of wild rice has plummeted since the 1970s. So there is no history of trust and goodwill between the University of Minnesota and American Indians who live within the state's borders.

In legal terms, the Anishinaabeg make a complicated argument based on the tribe's 1837 treaty with the United States, in which the Anishinaabeg agreed to sell land while the federal government guaranteed them hunting, fishing, and gathering rights on the ceded lands. In its 1999 decision favoring the Anishinaabeg, the United States Supreme Court would write (quoting a landmark 1943 Supreme Court decision) that in order to interpret this treaty, "we look beyond the written words to the larger context that frames the treaty, including 'the history of the treaty, the negotiations, and the practical construction adopted by the parties'" (Minnesota v. Mille Lacs 1999). The Anishinaabeg thus argue that their ancestors' view of wild rice as having a spiritual value and essence worthy of preservation in its natural state, gives them a voice in shaping the plant's future: Norman Deschampe's assertion "that the wild rice rights assured by treaty accrue not only to individual grains of rice, but to the very essence of the resource."

In the honors class and numerous times since, the Anishinaabeg have made it clear that they do not oppose either science or scientific research *per se*. In fact, they argue, indigenous people, because they lived off the land, were forced constantly to observe and learn about the natural world. Scholar Gregory Cajete differentiates between indigenous and Western scientific traditions, suggesting that native science is about circularity, interdependence, and relationship, not about causality, detachment, and objectivity. In order to survive, they had to be scientists. "I don't think we're in conflict with pure science," explains Judy Fairbanks. "It's the value of what to do with [science], or how you use it, how you direct it."

"Not all research is for the good of people," says Joe LaGarde. Clearly, the University of Minnesota's legacy of research in "Indian Country" is not only considered unbeneficial, but extremely harmful.

For the Anishinaabeg who taught this honors class, genetic engineering represents the biggest threat and their greatest fear. They worry that scientists—perhaps relying on a genetic map developed at the University of Minnesota—will eventually do what has already been done to corn, soybeans, potatoes, and many other plants and animals. And that those foreign genes will spread to natural stands of wild rice, much as genetically modified corn has spread beyond its intended boundaries.

What Andrew Favorite objects to, he says, is "When you take the genome, and you take something synthetic, and you alter the natural organic thing, so now you have a hybrid that can affect the natural thing that God created, that's part of our creation and spirituality. That's dangerous, and that's scary, to our worldview. We've already messed with corn. We've got Dolly the sheep."

Vandana Shiva suggests in her pioneering work that indigenous people have experienced colonization in three waves: geographic—in which territories were conquered; development—in which international aid and programs were established to continue resource extraction from former colonies; and genetic research—in which claims are staked on genetic material of traditional plants and the DNA of tribal people by scientists (Shiva 1999, p. 7). Clearly, the Anishinaabeg are not simply rejecting science, but see this research as an ongoing march on a trajectory of colonization that has very nearly eliminated them and all of the things they most cherish.

One Anishinaabe woman puts it this way: "Wild rice was perfect just the way it was made. Why change it?"

Much of what the class learned was knowledge gained from the millennia-old knowledge traditions of the Anishinaabeg that reflects their deep reverence for, connection to, and understanding of the "sacred web of life," not from books and laboratories. On their visit to the White Earth Reservation, for example, students listened to elder Earl Hoagland describe and demonstrate traditional methods of processing wild rice. He also spoke about the sharp decline of once-prolific wild rice stands, and the environmental and cultural factors that have contributed to the deterioration. This experiential element of the class was critical, as it brought students out of the classroom and into the Native community—near the rice and close to the people and their stories. The issue of wild rice for these students was very local— it was unfolding as they learned about it; it was germane to the culture and practices of their institution; and it was sited in their home state. The site-specific nature of this teaching enterprise suggests an important feature of public scholarship—the uplifting of the local over other contexts.

With many different individuals addressing the class, the method of instruction was almost inevitably circuitous and at times repetitious. When asking people to speak, Joe LaGarde made no attempt to coordinate what they planned to say. In some respects, repetition underscored a key point: Students were hearing the voices of a community, from a culture and individuals who value and work for the well-being of the group before the individual. This approach is not haphazard, but an indigenous means of pedagogy. In this tradition, when representatives are invited to speak, they share what they are inspired to share. Thus, certain points were reinforced through repetition, and new perspectives and nuances were added to the overall narrative of wild rice, Anishinaabe people, and scientific research.

Students were asked to reflect and respond to these presentations through assignments that asked for an articulation of a native point of view on an issue. This process enabled them to reflect, synthesize, and articulate what they were hearing, as well as test their own ability to step into a worldview different from their own. And what that group of people wanted and still want from the University of Minnesota continues to be unequivocally clear: they want President Yudof to suspend all research on wild rice until scientists and the Anishinaabeg reach agreement about what direction it should take, and where it should not venture.

To support their claim, the Anishinaabeg point to laws that require scientists to work with tribes before doing research on native graves and anthropological sites and to ethical guidelines that require the informed consent of individuals involved in medical research, as well as the sharing of information. Helen Klassen, Ph.D., the president of White Earth Tribal and Community College, says the Anishinaabeg should have been consulted decades ago. "When you conduct research within a community," she says, "there are guidelines that usually are followed, one of which is to ask permission of the people whom you are going to be studying. Another guideline would be to publish the results and make them available to the community so that they're aware of the study and what benefits will come from it." While this approach is followed when undertaking human-subjects research, plant and animal researchers are neither expected to ask permission of the human community that interacts with these species nor the species themselves. An important civic outcome from this example of teaching-as-public-scholarship is the identification of the need to reform Institutional Review Board and research ethics codes to address indirect risk and harm to vulnerable populations.

University Scientists' Views

Two University of Minnesota scientists visited and described their work on wild rice for the honors class: agronomist Ervin Oelke, who began working with paddy-rice growers soon after he was hired by the university in 1968 and served as the university's coordinator of wild-rice research from 1972 until his retirement in 2000; and geneticist Ronald L. Phillips, whose research on the wild-rice genome is at the center of the current controversy. They believe that the Anishinaabeg and students both misunderstood and misrepresented their work. Oelke even goes so far as to call the class structure a "loaded deck" and its recommendations to President Yudof "a slap in the face" of researchers.

The scientists say emphatically and unequivocally that they will not genetically engineer wild rice or otherwise manipulate the genetics of *Zizania palustris* through any means other than traditional breeding. Phillips's work involves creating a basic map of the wild-rice genome, understanding which genes control which traits and where those genes are located. "From my standpoint," he says, "it's standard genetics. It's standard modern genetics and breeding. We're not introducing new genes. But it is breeding, just like we've done ever since we started agriculture. We're selecting types in order to modify the plant's genetics." It is important to consider Oelke's concern about the nature of the agenda of the course. But when the tables are turned and the viewpoint of a particular substance or approach is exclusively scientific, does this too constitute a loaded deck? This question—one that is critical for our multicultural democracy to grapple with—explores how cultural diversity and epistemology can, should, and do influence pedagogy and curriculum in public institutions.

To the scientists, this research is a logical extension of efforts begun decades ago. *Zizania palustris* is different from other cultivated crop plants in that it has a relatively short breeding history; there's still a tremendous amount of genetic variability even in strains bred for cultivation in paddies (Imle, Phillips & Porter 1999). Compared to crops like wheat, corn, and ordinary rice, *Zizania palustris* is thus unpredictable and, by Western agricultural standards, inefficient. Indigenous cultures might construe this unpredictability as the essential diversity that we need to sustain life on the planet. Eventually, scientists hope, genetic research will allow plant breeders to follow recessive traits closely, improving the efficiency of the breeding process and thus accelerating the pace of domestication. It will, in other words, eliminate much of the trial and error involved in typical plant-breeding efforts.

Phillips began his work on the wild-rice genome in the early 1990s, in response to a request from Raymond Porter, a research associate at the university's North Central Research and Outreach Center in Grand Rapids, Minnesota, who works full time on *Zizania palustris* breeding and genetics. Porter was himself responding to a request by paddy-rice growers that the university conduct basic research on wild-rice genetics. He called Phillips, one of the nation's leading plant geneticists, for advice. To help Phillips get started, paddy-rice growers paid for an initial post-doctoral researcher. Since then, Phillips has obtained funding from a variety of sources, including the Cultivated Wild Rice Council, an industry trade group; the USDA National Research Initiative; and the USDA Agricultural Research Service. Porter's work, which primarily involves the breeding of *Zizania palustris* varieties for cultivation, is funded through the Agricultural Research Service.

This same combination of industry initiative and individual interest prompted initial efforts by University of Minnesota scientists to help develop *Zizania palustris* as a commercial crop, Oelke says: "That's how a lot of things start. We—particularly in agriculture—probably work more closely with the clientele group, so to speak, than engineering and other departments or colleges. So when the clientele comes to us and says, 'Hey, can you help us?'— we listen. And if funding comes, then we do some work. That's just the way that, historically, we've worked in agriculture. If a group comes to us, we'll see what we can do, in terms of helping, if there's someone [on the faculty] interested. If there's no faculty member who has an interest, it doesn't go anywhere either." And, of course, "without any funding, you can't do any work," Oelke adds.

Minnesota's paddy-rice industry is, by economic measures, small. According to the Minnesota Cultivated Wild Rice Council, in the year 2000 approximately two dozen growers raised approximately 6.3 million processed pounds of *Zizania palustris* (worth approximately $9 million wholesale) on 18,000 acres of land in the state of Minnesota. Growers support the council's marketing and research efforts through a check-off program that charges seven cents per processed pound.

By helping agriculture, the scientists believe, they are serving both the public good and the historic mission of the land-grant university. Their work, they say, is especially important to Minnesota growers, who must compete with California farms that typically harvest more than twice as much rice per acre because they enjoy a longer growing season, are hit by fewer storms, and have fewer problems with disease. "As a breeder," Porter says, "my goal is to develop more productive wild rice varieties that will meet the growers' needs. The goal is to develop varieties that are more suited to growers, and particularly Minnesota growers." Clearly, in this equation, indigenous people in Minnesota do not surface as legitimate economic competitors.

Oelke points to the dramatic improvement in yield that has been achieved since 1950, in large part because of plant breeding. Though early paddy-rice farmers harvested just 30 to 40 pounds of finished grain per acre, Minnesota growers today average about 350 pounds per acre. (In California, growers average 1000 pounds per acre.) Ordinary rice produces as much as 9000 pounds of finished grain per acre. "With hybrids, you might be able to get to that range," Oelke says. "It will take a while to get there, because those other plants have been under domestication for thousands of years, and here we're only talking about a 50-year span. [Wild rice] is still too tall; it produces too much green vegetation and not enough seed. Who knows what the potential could possibly be?"

Phillips sees his role as bridging the gap between academic genetics and applied agriculture and acting as a complement to industry scientists who focus almost exclusively on large cash crops like corn and soybeans. "I'm interested in understanding crop plants and trying to bridge that distance between the basic understanding of genetics and how it can be applied to those plants. So I study the genetics of various plants and develop methodologies to make improvement more efficient. I try to think of things that commercial companies won't necessarily do. I've enjoyed working on wild rice, because I think that work is not going to be done by a company. I spend a lot of time on oats, too. All of my work has been to try to complement what goes on in industry.

"I think about what I do as a complement to what others do. And I try to do it in a way that is open to the public and for the public good—try to publish everything, and so on. My goal is definitely to help agriculture in that process." Fascinating in the dialectic surrounding the wild-rice issue is the public aspect inherent in both the course and the historical research agenda. Here is where cultural diversity plays a unique role in rethinking what constitutes public scholarship and how to handle all of the outcomes—anticipated or not—from these inquiries.

From the perspective of paddy-rice growers, the single most important trait is shattering—the tendency of *Zizania palustris* seeds to fall off the plant before they can be harvested. Because *Zizania palustris* is an annual, that's a beneficial adaptation in natural stands of wild rice, since it increases the chance that enough seeds will survive such common obstacles as blackbirds, storms, and human harvesting and thus help the plant to thrive. Corn, wheat, and other domesticated crops all went through a similar breeding process years ago, without, of course, a genetic map. Other traits of interest to scientists include seed dormancy, height, and strength of the plant stem.

A secondary goal of the university's genetic research is to analyze and catalogue the genetic diversity within *Zizania palustris* (Imle, Phillips & Porter 1999). This knowledge, scientists say, may someday help to preserve or restore natural stands of wild rice, which are declining throughout Minnesota. That is, of course, an issue of great importance to the Anishinaabeg.

In addressing fears that traits will migrate from paddies to wild-rice stands, the scientists speak a very different language than do the Anishinaabeg. To them, it's a matter of assessing and minimizing risk. Wild-rice pollen is relatively fragile and does not travel well. If paddies are distant from natural stands of wild rice, there will be little migration of genes, scientists say. In addition, because paddy rice is bred for cultivation, to thrive under narrowly prescribed conditions, scientists say it's highly unlikely that the cultivated traits will make inroads in natural stands since those traits are less well adapted to life in the wild.

"It depends on what you're willing to accept as a threshold [of risk]," Phillips says. "The possibility of a trait coming in from one of the bred varieties that would significantly alter the wild type is probably not very great. But it is possible. So you can't guarantee [that it won't happen]. You can't guarantee that a bird won't pick up a seed and take it 20 miles away. So that's where you have the conflict.... You've got to agree on some threshold, and in our discussions [with the Anishinaabeg], some people said, 'Well one in a million is too great a risk.'" New research, however, demonstrates the drift of wild-rice pollen up to four miles from its original source. Elders are concerned about the distribution of genetically modified seeds through duck populations' ingestion and elimination of modified wild-rice seeds around the state.

Similarly, although Phillips's research on the wild-rice genome might be useful to others who want to genetically engineer *Zizania palustris,* he says this research is tangential to that process. And unnecessary. Scientists have successfully inserted genes into corn, soybeans, and other plants without a genetic map. Oelke says there's simply not enough profit in wild rice to justify the sort of investment that genetic engineering would require.

The Minnesota scientists also see this conflict as an issue of academic freedom. Phillips says:

> There are things that I don't want to do as a person, because I know there is this sensitivity, but I don't want the university telling me I can't do it. There's no way I'm going to start genetically engineering wild rice. I told them [the honors students and the people of White Earth] that. But I don't want to be in an environment where people say, "This is acceptable for you to work on, and this isn't." That's why

we have universities, and why we have people with tenure—
so they can address societal issues, and try to get at the facts,
and then use that information to understand issues better, and
move ahead. It's not uncommon to have social issues that
divide people. And knowledge is probably the best way to
make some kind of progress. So you don't want a university
saying, "You can't do this, you can't do that." But as individuals, you make decisions about what you work on.

The scientists have known for decades about Anishinaabe
objections to paddy-grown wild rice, albeit primarily on economic grounds. Oelke, for example, recalls reading letters to the editor
and hearing complaints as far back as 1968, when he joined the
University of Minnesota faculty. Those objections, however, have
sometimes been obscured by the fact that individual reservations
have occasionally cultivated their own paddies (and at least
one still does). "There was an attempt always to include [the
Anishinaabeg] wherever possible, and help them in the marketing," Oelke says. "Even now, the Wild Rice Council is there to
help them market their grain as well. It seems to me they have an
ideal product to market, and they are marketing it as organic, and
as being from the lakes, so they can get a premium price on it."

The University of Minnesota scientists have also worked
occasionally on projects designed to restore or preserve natural
stands of wild rice, even cooperating with individual Anishinaabe
bands. Porter, the wild-rice breeder in Grand Rapids, Minnesota,
says, "I have worked as much as I could within the bounds of my
position, and my research, to try and find ways that I could do
things which would be of benefit to the reservations." From the
scientists' perspective, this recent conflict has as much to do
with politics as science, since they had been working to map the
wild-rice genome for more than five years when the Minnesota
Chippewa Tribe sent its letter to Mark Yudof. And indeed, the
letter was written while the Anishinaabeg's landmark court case
involving usufructuary rights awaited a hearing at the United

States Supreme Court. (As noted previously, in 1999, the Court upheld the Anishinaabeg's right to hunt, fish, and gather food on lands ceded to the U.S.)

The scientists and the Anishinaabeg nevertheless frame this conflict in radically different terms. Porter, who came to Minnesota from Texas, initially struggled with accusations that the paddy-rice industry harmed American Indians. He says, "I had to work through that, and recognize that this [research program] is happening not for the purpose of harming another group of people, but for the purpose of benefiting growers, and benefiting consumers who want to eat wild rice."

To Ervin Oelke, the conflict ultimately boils down to a single question: Who "owns" wild rice? "Are plants on this earth for all people, or are they just for one group?" he asks. "The issue, I think, boils down to this question of, 'Whose plant is it?' My answer is that I think plants should be used by as many people as possible, for the benefit of humans. Actually, wild rice existed before humans were [in the Upper Midwest]. It just happened to be there at the time of the [Anishinaabe] migration, and they utilized the plant."

And that, say the Anishinaabeg who taught the honors class, is precisely the wrong question. "This is not about ownership," Paul Schultz insists, because that concept implies the right to dispose of or otherwise manipulate "property." And that privilege, he claims, "was never given to science." As a gift, rice was to be preserved, protected, and shared. To the Anishinaabeg, then, *manoomin* exists for its own sake, outside the dominion of humankind. Schultz adds, "Scientists have been granted that right [to manipulate wild rice] for so long that somehow they think 50 to 200 years justifies it for all time. What we're saying is that if you've been making a mistake for 50 to 200 years, that still doesn't make it right today."

The Students' Work and Actions

That two groups of people—each meaning well, and each acting on what it considers principle—could define a conflict in such radically different terms is, in the opinion of the professors who taught this class, exactly the point. "This whole class, I believe, was about an interaction where assumptions are not shared," says Craig Hassel. "There are fundamentally different ways of viewing the world." To George Spangler, part of the course's value stemmed from its location within the College of Agricultural, Food, and Environmental Sciences, which like most land-grant institutions teaches that industrial agriculture is the dominant model of food production and that the purpose of science is to serve that paradigm. Alternative or critical views of commercial agriculture are as rare as classes on Marxism within business schools.

The instructors created a public space where hotly contested perspectives of a local issue were facilitated through a semester-long discourse intended to provoke student learning. As an approach to public scholarship, the instructors simultaneously created public space for discourse on a public issue; democratized the classroom so students were empowered to chart their learning goals; opened a forum for a community who had no access to the institution; and created a process for students to exercise their civic activism within the university community.

As an assignment, students had to write a short paper on the environment from the Anishinaabe perspective. (The White Earth instructors helped grade the papers.) For a final project, Hassel and Spangler asked students to draft a letter to university president Mark Yudof making recommendations about how to address Anishinaabe concerns. In January 1999, they endorsed the Anishinaabe perspective.

"We have learned," the students told Yudof, "that wild rice is important to the Anishinaabe community, not only as an economic resource, *but also is essential to the well-being of the community and rests at the heart of their spirituality and traditions, wholly unlike any other food source*" (italics in original). Although they described the university scientists as "careful researchers with strong professional credentials . . . [who] have obviously served the university well," the students said, "there has been a clear lack of productive communication between the research community at the University of Minnesota and the Native American communities involved. In our opinion, there has also been little evidence of interest on the part of the University to understand issues surrounding wild rice from the perspective of the Anishinaabe."

The class made three related recommendations:

- The university should suspend all research on the wild-rice genome until "there are opportunities for further education, communication and dialogue...."

- Visions for Change should be empowered to convene a symposium "on cross-cultural research issues specific to wild rice," with the Anishinaabeg playing an active role in setting the agenda.

- A standing committee of researchers, the Anishinaabeg, and a representative from Visions for Change should work to resolve the disagreement about wild-rice research and develop closer ties between Native Americans and the University of Minnesota.

Especially in light of the students' letter, the Anishinaabeg who helped organize and teach the honors class saw it as a profound gesture of respect from a powerful institution. They had met as equals. A small group of people within the university, at least, had treated their view of the world with respect. From the Anishinaabe perspective, none of this would have happened without Visions for Change, which for years had worked hard to forge relationships between faculty members and the Anishinaabeg. Similarly, the existence of White Earth Tribal and Community College, a 1994 land-grant institution, provided instructors, organizational assistance, and classroom space when students visited White Earth in the fall of 1998.

But the fate of wild rice remained foremost in the Anishinaabeg's minds. Whether the University of Minnesota would have responded meaningfully to their concerns without this honors class is, of course, impossible to know.

In October 1998, before he even knew about the class, President Yudof wrote Norman Deschampe of the Minnesota Chippewa Tribe, saying that he had asked the interim vice president for agriculture to meet with Deschampe and resolve the situation. Five months later, Yudof wrote to the students in the honors class, telling them, "Rather than terminate support of the cultivated wild rice industry the university and the College [of Agriculture] should broaden its mission to address total natural resource needs including how to assist [in] maintaining wild rice in natural stands." Despite this apparent rejection of their concerns, the Anishinaabeg continued to meet sporadically with university officials and discuss the fate of wild rice, the scientists' research on the wild-rice genome, and other potential research projects of common interest. Though the two sides remained far apart on the fate of wild rice, the Anishinaabeg and the scientists alike remained hopeful that they would be able to reach a compromise acceptable to both. The Anishinaabeg gave credit for this dialogue to the class—and the students' letter—which they believed had amplified Anishinaabe voices and served as a sort of fulcrum.

For a time, many of those involved in teaching the class thought that leverage, however small, might be enough to convince the university to negotiate an agreement acceptable to the Anishinaabeg. In retrospect, says Karl Lorenz, he thinks it was naive to imagine, as he had, that a few faculty members and students could change a vast bureaucratic institution. "In reality, what we managed to do was raise awareness [of Anishinaabe concerns about wild rice]," he adds. "To think that we could effect change was not realistic."

Anishinaabe elder Paul Schultz believes the failure of negotiations exposed a deep-rooted institutional bias at the University of Minnesota towards Western science and agriculture, and against the Anishinaabeg, who do not exalt science above the sacred, and who see as sacred a plant, wild rice, that science wants to change. And that bias, in Schultz's view, prevents the university from fulfilling its historic responsibility, as a land-grant institution, to serve the people of Minnesota—at least the people of Minnesota who are not white. Is the university, he asks, committed to community? And do American Indians qualify as legitimate communities? "If not," Schultz adds, "is it because we are culturally different? In other words, is the ticket to membership in Minnesota still being white, Anglo-Saxon, Protestant, Catholic, or whatever? And if Indians are part of Minnesota's public, does the university carry a moral and ethical responsibility, as a land-grant institution, to sit down and work this matter out in a better way with us?"

Land-grant institutions are typically able to work with communities, Schultz argues, only so long as the community believes in the preeminence of science, and in Western concepts of man's relationship to plants and the environment. But not everyone in Minnesota subscribes to those beliefs. "We are not anti-intellectual," he says. "We are not even opposed to this [Western, science-based] system. But we are railing against this system's self-proclaimed capacity to control us, and to say that we have no contribution to make, even in an argument about something that was a sacred gift to our people." The core of the conflict, in Schultz's view, is the inability of Western science, and thus the University of Minnesota, to respect the sacred.

Even as that effort to negotiate a resolution stalled, the Anishinaabeg began collectively to explore other ways to protect wild rice. Emboldened by his work on the honors class, Joe LaGarde led efforts to form a broad coalition of tribes and sympathetic outsiders, including several University of Minnesota professors, who together tried to figure out how to pressure the university to halt research on the wild-rice genome. "The class," he said, "lit a spark.... What woke me up was to realize that you could take a bunch of young people who had never set foot on the reservation—who had never even been off concrete, really—and get them to understand the problem."

"When the community was asked to share its knowledge," says Karl Lorenz, "it was empowered. And it began to see itself as being empowered." The public-scholarship process was not only effective for the students and faculty, but was an empowering experience for grassroots community members as well. Not only were they the true "experts" around this important issue, but they gained access to the institution and important support from institutional stakeholders.

At White Earth, Helen Klassen and others began planning to prevent similar problems from arising in the future. Again sparked by the honors class, they worked to establish an institutional review board and written guidelines that would govern all research affecting the reservation, the tribe, its members, or its interests, including indigenous knowledge. Once passed, those rules, modeled on guidelines for medical and anthropological research, will require advance approval from the review board, disclosure of the economic and environmental effects of research, and other safeguards. This impact is a direct offshoot from the course and suggests that significant public gains can be made from constructing a course to serve a public good. Usually, Klassen points out, land-grant professors work hand-in-hand with farmers and other communities who are affected by research, in order to ensure that it serves the public good. "In this particular case [wild rice], it was not done that way," she says. "The people within the region were excluded. They were voiceless; they were not seen as important parts of this process. So the economic development and other benefits that might come from that research have never been realized by the native community."

Despite lingering tension over wild rice, Klassen also worked on efforts to build an environmental research and learning center, known as *Nibbi* ("water," in the Anishinaabe language), that will be located on the reservation and operated jointly by the Tribal College and the university.

The University of Minnesota instructors who organized and facilitated the honors course were also affected. It was George

Spangler's first experience in allowing students essentially to steer a course. Although apprehensive, at first, he left impressed by their ability to ask the right questions and to find individuals who could answer them. On an entirely different level, Spangler says, he came to understand that an individual's way of knowing is, to a large degree, culturally defined and, in this case, two ways of understanding wild rice—Anishinaabe and Western— exist in parallel, with each asking different questions, and finding different answers. This realization, in turn, has become an essential ingredient in an interdisciplinary graduate course, called "Ways of Knowing," that Spangler teaches.

For Craig Hassel, that insight was *the* key lesson of the course. Though he had brought outsiders into the classroom before, he says, they had all basically thought like university professors; this was the first time he'd invited speakers who saw the world through a different lens. "Paul Schultz was very eloquent in talking about the spirituality of wild rice and why this was so significant for the Anishinaabe people," Hassel recalls. "The level of student engagement as he was talking was really quite amazing; many were experiencing educational transformation. In fact, I remember telling Karl [Lorenz] on the way back that this is what education is about. It was truly an opportunity for the students to see a fundamentally different way of viewing the world that challenges some of the basic assumptions that we hold but usually do not question. It was very different from any other experience they have had." Hassel learned alongside the students: "I had never experienced such a powerful learning experience—both for me and for a significant number of the students," he says.

Karl Lorenz continues to bring different voices and perspectives into the COAFES honors program. He organized one seminar, for example, that focused on the experience and impact of Hispanic migrant workers in Minnesota. Like the wild-rice course, this seminar brought people on campus to talk about their lives and experiences, which schools of agriculture generally ignore. "What's taught in that college," he says, "is essentially a party line.... The worldview of the dominant culture is echoed without fail in the curriculum." An important part of his job, he believes, is to make sure divergent voices are heard.

For Lorenz, organizing the wild-rice class was also a deeply personal experience. "As someone whose father is American Indian, it allowed me to integrate my worlds, which is something I usually can't do at the university," he says. "There is no place for me to be Indian. In a way, the class gave me a chance to stand by my people.... On a very personal level, I found it healing to see myself included in a world that up to that point had excluded me." But it was more than personal: he also took pride in knowing the class had inspired continuing efforts by the Anishinaabeg to stop genetic research on wild rice.

The nexus of scientific research, economic interests, and cultural diversity have proved to be a fertile ground for learning around the wild rice issue. In this particular case, there are multiple publics—students, researchers, instructors, Native American stakeholders, white commercial producers, industry, and state and federal policymakers. The emphasis on scholarship is focused less on the research in this case study, and more on the public aspects of pedagogy for undergraduate students.

Clearly, the instructors, students, and community-based experts were significantly impacted by their involvement with the course. Multiple, ongoing public outcomes emerged from this course, including development of other courses addressing public issues and using a similar pedagogical format, continued interaction between faculty and native communities, and new policies protecting indigenous concerns in native communities. Students were able to take a local, timely issue and develop a process for their own learning. They asserted their influence as members of a public community by requesting a series of actions by the administration and also learned what it meant to exist in a pluralistic society. Public scholarship in this context is as much about reflecting upon what pluralism means (in this case a pluralism of epistemologies) as it is about addressing a public issue through a democratic, participatory process.

In 2003, this honors course was once again offered, entitled "Native American Perspectives on the Environment." Using the same pedagogical format, professors served as facilitators, students identified learning outcomes, teaching was a collaborative dance between scholars and Native American elders, and experiential learning (including a weekend stay on the reservation parching and winnowing rice, gathering wild fruit and preserving it, making birchbark rice winnowing baskets, and listening to stories about wild-rice traditions, treaty history, native cultural beliefs about landscape and ecological stewardship) were all elements of this course. Once again, students, faculty, and community members alike reported on the deep learning, democratic potential, and power of public scholarship in the form of teaching. While the wild-rice issue has not yet resolved itself, it persists as a rich learning opportunity in which the scholarship of teaching can be practiced around a local civic issue enriching dialogue about ecological values, multicultural collaborations, and the public good.

References

Benton-Banai, E. 1988. *The Mishomis Book: The Voice of the Ojibway.* St. Paul, MN: Red School House.

Edman, F. 1969. *A Study of Wild Rice in Minnesota.* St. Paul, MN: Minnesota Resources Commission.

Gebert, C. 1971. *Modernism Threatens Canoe and Flail.* Fargo-Moorhead Sunday Forum. September 5, 1971.

Hassel, C. 2001. *Personal Communication*, April 25, 2001.

Huber, J. 1999. "Archaeological Implications of Pollen Evidence for Wild Rice (*Zizania Aquatica*) during the Paleoindian, Archaic, and Woodland Periods in Northeast Minnesota." In *Proceedings of the Wild Rice Research & Management Conference,* ed. L. S. Williamson, L.

A. Dlutkowski, and A. P. McCammon Soltis, 40-53. Odanah, WI: Great Lakes Indian Fish and Wildlife Commission.

Imle, P., R. Phillips, and R. Porter. 1999. "Molecular Genetics of Wild Rice." In *Proceedings of the Wild Rice Research & Management Conference,* ed. L. S. Williamson, L. A. Dlutkowski, and A. P. McCammon Soltis, 117-121. Odanah, WI: Great Lakes Indian Fish and Wildlife Commission.

Jenks, A. 1900. "The Wild Rice Gatherers of the Upper Lakes: A Study in American Primitive Economics." In *Nineteenth Annual Report of the Bureau of American Ethnology,* 1897-98, 2:1013-1137. Washington, DC: GPO.

———. 1916. *Indian-white Amalgamation: An Anthropometric Study.* Minneapolis, MN: Bulletin of the University of Minnesota.

LaDuke, W. 1999. The Wild Rice Moon. *Whole Earth* 99 (winter). http://www.wholeearthmag.com/ArticleBin/303.html.

Meyer, M. 1994. *The White Earth Tragedy: Ethnicity and Dispossession at a Minnesota Anishinaabe Reservation, 1889-1920.* Lincoln, NE: University of Nebraska Press.

Minnesota v. Mille Lacs Band of Chippewa Indians, 526 U.S. 172. 1999. http://laws.findlaw.com/us/000/97-1337.html.

Oelke, E., et al. 1999. "Wild Rice Plant Development and Seed Physiology." In *Proceedings of the Wild Rice Research & Management Conference,* ed. L. S. Williamson, L. A. Dlutkowski, and A. P. McCammon Soltis, 54-67. Odanah, WI: Great Lakes Indian Fish and Wildlife Commission.

Oelke, E. 2000. "Wild Rice Breeding and Production." In *Agronomy and Plant Genetics at the University of Minnesota from 1888 to 2000,* 147-152. St. Paul, MN: Minnesota Agricultural Experiment Station, University of Minnesota.

Shiva, V. 1999. *Stolen Harvest: The Hijacking of the Global Food Supply.* Cambridge, MA: South End Press.

Smith, C. and H. Vogel. 1984. The Wild Rice Mystique: Resource Management and American Indians' Rights as a Problem of Law and Culture. *William Mitchell Law Review* 10:743-804.

"Treaty with the Chippewa," July 29, 1837. http://www.fw.umn.edu/Indigenous/TREATY37.HTM.

Vennum, T., Jr. 1988. *Wild Rice and the Ojibway People.* St. Paul, MN: Minnesota Historical Society Press.

Chapter Eight:
Engaging Campus and Community to Improve Science Education

A Down-to-Earth Approach

by Robert Williamson and Ellen Smoak

This chapter tells the story of why and how we collaboratively developed, and implemented an experiential science education curriculum called *Down-to-Earth: Enriching Learning Through Gardening* (DTE) with and for secondary-school students and teachers. The DTE story is a story of public scholarship. We believe that it holds important lessons, not only for historically black land-grant institutions such as our own North Carolina A&T State University (NCA&T), but more broadly for all those who are interested in engaging campus and community in addressing important public issues and challenges.

In the first phase of our story, we describe our motivations for developing DTE and how we went about pursuing it. In this phase, we used focus group interviews, literature reviews, and a field experiment—all typical elements of scholarly research—to inform the curriculum development process. In the second phase, we provide an account of how we tested and refined the curriculum in the context of a community-university partnership with Smithfield Middle School (SMS) in Johnston County, North Carolina. Here, we continued our public scholarship as we implemented and revised DTE with a community that is striving to address challenges related to academic achievement gaps for African-American youth. In the chapter's final sections, we offer reflections on the meaning and significance of our experience in relation to the question of the future of public scholarship in land-grant education.

Background

When the DTE story began, we were at a point in our careers in which we needed to go beyond traditional boundaries in order to grow professionally. Our experience with the development and dissemination of the DTE curriculum gave us an opportunity to bring our academic strengths, research interests, and community outreach efforts into alignment while offering the potential for personal and professional growth. But before we tell the DTE story, we want to provide a brief account of how our formative experiences have shaped and influenced our work.

Robert "Bob" Williamson

Growing up as an African-American in the South during the Jim Crow era, I learned how important access to quality educational opportunities is to the success and empowerment of my community. I had a childhood interest in science that was nurtured by important mentors throughout my secondary, undergraduate, and graduate education. My family heritage was closely tied to agriculture and the land. Contributing to the public good was an important part of my values, upbringing, and professional commitment.

After 15 years working as a research wildlife biologist with the USDA-Forest Service, I became a natural resources specialist with the NCA&T Cooperative Extension Program where I have worked for the last 19 years. My current responsibilities encompass forestry, wildlife management, water quality, and environmental education. My undergraduate and master's degrees were from Howard University; my Ph.D. in wildlife biology was from the University of Massachusetts at Amherst, a land-grant university. Despite that, I learned little about the civic dimensions of the land-grant philosophy of educational outreach while I was student.

Sixteen years of judging student projects, science fairs, and 4-H projects at the local, regional, and state levels continuously reinforced my observation of obvious weaknesses in science projects. Many students, particularly African-Americans, failed to have competitive projects because of an apparent lack of scientific literacy. Having worked as a researcher at two universities and a science educator at four universities, I increasingly felt I should contribute as a scholar to improving this situation. Progress toward scientific literacy should begin with a strong foundation in middle school, but effective resources are lacking to help make this possible. DTE was aimed at addressing this gap.

Ellen Smoak

Most of my career has been spent with the NCA&T Cooperative Extension Program, beginning as a home economics extension agent for six years, working primarily with low-income adults and youth. Formative childhood experiences, like growing up in the South during the integration era and reading *The Grapes of Wrath,* forged a public commitment and interest in making a positive difference in the everyday lives of marginalized people. My parents also demonstrated the ethos of hard work, a commitment to public and higher education, and contributions to the life of the community.

For the last 23 years, I have served as the extension textiles and apparel specialist for NCA&T. I received my bachelor's, master's, and doctoral degrees at the University of North Carolina (Greensboro) in education. As was true of Bob's experience, there was little discussion of the land-grant mission and its civic dimensions during my years of formal education.

In the months before we began our DTE journey, I reviewed a fourth-grade social-studies textbook, focusing on North Carolina.

The book provided a very brief and negative description of agriculture and food and fiber production, focusing primarily on how farmers cause lots of environmental problems. The caption under one picture alluded to the fact that farmers are destroying the earth by using various harmful chemicals. I was very much concerned, as many school systems across the state were using this book. I brought the textbook to the attention of Bob and another colleague, hoping that we could find a way to research, integrate, and apply our collective scholarship and wisdom to help fill a gap in student learning.

Our Common Experience

The primary experience we shared before joining forces on the DTE curriculum was our work in developing educational programs to meet the needs of limited-resource people. As extension faculty members, we provide leadership for statewide programs linked to a variety of issues identified by stakeholders. To accomplish this, we design and use grassroots, not-for-credit educational materials, events, and activities to help improve the quality of life for farmers, homemakers, families, 4-H youth, and communities.

Much of our civic consciousness emerged from a variety of volunteer experiences with numerous social service and community action organizations. Between us, we spent nearly 40 years working with various youth groups, parent-teacher associations, adult church groups, homeless individuals, and in a variety of youth-at-risk venues. We viewed the DTE process—both its development and dissemination—as a way to express our civic responsibility. We saw it as a way to break through the misgivings and mistrust that too often keep communities and universities apart.

With respect to extension at NCA&T, the multidisciplinary approach we took in developing DTE was uncommon. Extension at NCA&T had a more traditional structure that supported and encouraged program development within specialty areas as the primary means of doing business. For years, extension had steadfastly supported a four-way division of roles and responsibilities—4-H, family and consumer education, agriculture, and community and rural development—with little precedent or institutional support for collaboration, either within extension, within the broader institution, or in the community. By adopting a cross-disciplinary public-scholarship approach, we were truly navigating in uncharted waters, which took time for the institution, colleagues, communities, and even ourselves to adjust.

Phase One: Origins and Development

We had several motivations for creating DTE. For some time, we had been trying to come up with ways we might be more effective in contributing to youth education programs. We were looking for ways to become more directly and productively involved in contributing to local communities. We were particularly interested in improving the scientific and agricultural literacy of young people.

The "public problem" we were most concerned with was low scientific and agricultural literacy among young people. Consultation with faculty and community members bore out our intuition that this was an important issue to address. Originally, we wanted to design an effective, science-based curriculum with mutually agreed-upon standards that would use gardening to stimulate learning, critical thinking, and problem solving about science, technology, and food and fiber production. We wanted to provide opportunities that clearly emphasized learning from the familiar to the unfamiliar. We wanted children to become engaged physically, mentally, and emotionally in a variety of hands-on and "minds-on" activities. We wanted students to formulate responsible decision making based on relevant real-world applications that would bring science to life.

In our review of numerous educational materials, we were unable to find a balanced curriculum that used cooperative and individual performance and did not promote one gardening practice over another. We could not find a resource that integrated the use of key science skills like inferring, hypothesizing, measuring, estimating, and experimenting. Therefore, we decided to use a multidisciplinary methodology and combine our skills and talents to develop such a curriculum. Our scholarly work emphasized an interactive, iterative process with relevant community stakeholders—teachers, parents, and youth—that built on our own expertise and community priorities, as well as information derived from focus groups and literature reviews in agricultural and science education, and curriculum and instruction. Subsequently, we authored a well-received student guidebook and published an article in the *Journal of Extension,* both titled, "A Student's Guide to Keeping the Science in Your Science Project" (Williamson and Smoak 1997, 1998). These were intended to help students, parents, and child guardians overcome their fear of science projects.

Knowing that we would inevitably assume accountability for the quality of the DTE curriculum, both of us agreed to contribute equally to researching content, developing experiential activities and authoring various sections. We began by determining what students already knew about food and fiber production through the use of focus groups. We visited Claxton Elementary School in Greensboro to discuss our intentions and ideas with the principal and a few teachers, which led to our recruitment of Karen Marks, a science teacher. Marks was willing to integrate the draft version of the DTE activities into her lesson plans. In a format that stimulated open and honest dialogue, we asked her students what they already knew and what they wanted to know more about. We made time to teach several classes pertaining to health and human safety, environmental management, and horticulture. As a part of this effort, we established our first DTE garden. As the students did most of the planting, nurturing, and harvesting, we focused on how well they used the scientific method to design, collect, and interpret data from three experimental plots.

In the months ahead, a process of replication and validation was carried out at other sites around the state. This helped us determine which approaches and content promoted the best potential for student learning. It also revealed that formal and non-formal youth educators alike were not entirely comfortable teaching science, particularly with respect to plant growth and development. An imperative concern was how to evaluate the usefulness of the curriculum. In order to avoid any personal bias, we hired a team of external evaluators to formulate and pilot test the reliability and validity of the DTE curriculum. They confirmed that DTE could improve science and mathematics skills as well as contribute to social development or life skills. Horton and Hutchinson (1997) indicated that a variety of life skills, creatively embedded in a science curriculum, can help create knowledge as well as communicate and utilize knowledge. In fact, they reported that "there is a greater likelihood that the skills learners apply …will far outlive the usefulness of the knowledge" being promoted in the actual experience. We were pleased to have confirmed that DTE contributed both to life skills and scientific literacy.

As we continued to refine and develop the curriculum, we sought review and counsel from our peers in relevant disciplines. This peer review process yielded several important insights that we were able to integrate into DTE's development. We were advised to develop a comprehensive logic model, diagramming each step, and to prepare alternatives if our first approach failed. DTE was validated for meeting the requirements for middle-school science instruction and correlated with the mandated *Standard Course of Study and Grade Level Competencies* for sixth-through-eighth-grade science education. We were also advised to add activities reflecting the 4-H Experiential Model in order to broaden use by 4-H clubs. Reflecting Kolb's (1984) conception of experiential learning, this theoretical model of learning combines content with experience, reflection, generalization, and application. Following this advice, we produced 18 supplemental experiential activities.

Taking on a project of this scale with the accompanying peer review process, attempting to meet curricular standards of various agencies, and adapting it for various audiences was very time-consuming and often seemed overwhelming. While the experience felt at times as though we were going against the grain in terms of institutional and cultural norms, the entire process added an important layer of rigor to our work that contributed to its quality.

Equally important to the caliber of the end product were the public aspects of developing DTE. The completed curriculum reflects observations from all of our test sites and incorporated recommendations from 25 teachers, youth educators, and over 2,000 young people. This public process enabled us as scholars to ensure that our approach to curriculum development meshed with the interests, realities, and learning needs of the intended audiences. This ongoing testing and dialogue enabled many individuals to contribute to the development of this "public product." DTE was not an expert-driven, detached curriculum. It was, rather, synergistic, integrative scholarship that involved citizens (youth and adult) contributing their ideas and imaginations about what secondary science education should address and how it should be structured.

Down-to-Earth: Enriching Learning Through Gardening thus became a self-contained, user-friendly, instructional resource (Williamson and Smoak 1999, 2002). Led by a youth educator, children use the scientific method to learn about science, botany, gardening, and much more. The curriculum incorporates instructional units that allow youngsters to build new knowledge based on their previous knowledge and experiences. DTE's ten content topics include: understanding the scientific method, growing plants, soil, fertilizer, pests, pest control, sun, safety, water quality, and careers. The instructional methodology makes use of formal and informal teaching methods, presenter background information, concept objectives, and learner competencies. Although many of the activities offer suggestions on how youth educators may connect the gardens to other subjects, DTE is not designed to be an all-inclusive or comprehensive curriculum. The lessons that can be taught at the garden site are limited only by individual creativity.

The scholarly process of information gathering, literature reviews, curriculum development, pilot testing, curricular refinement, and re-testing was followed by implementation in the Johnston County school system. In an extension context, the dimensions of public scholarship are equally important in both the development and implementation phases. Public scholarship must include community engagement, application, and reciprocity as primary features. Implementing DTE in Johnston County proved to be professionally transformative for both of us, teaching us much about how public scholarship can enhance extension work.

Phase Two: Forming a Partnership

Several years ago, the *Smithfield Herald* published an editorial that discussed a variety of educational needs and priorities in Johnston County. Describing a direct link between retaining local, good-paying jobs and the unacceptable achievement gap between African-American and white students, the editorial credited the school board with reducing class size in two of the county's elementary schools, acknowledging that "both black and white students need more one-on-one attention." Even so, the editorial indicated that Smithfield citizens had yet to implement a sustainable, community-based initiative that would enable African-American youngsters to gain marketable skills through education. It suggested that classroom learning can be a launching pad to lift minority students out of economic poverty, rather than a failing system to hold them back. The editorial noted that additional programs to close the achievement gap were "costly and politically unpopular." But the alternative would be an unfortunate continuation of the *status quo*—an unbalanced system in which underachieving African-American high school graduates and dropouts compete for low-paying jobs. This public call challenged the school district to creatively address the academic and economic challenges of its African-American constituents.

The school district was also facing pressure from state policymakers about educational standards for students—again an issue of achievement gaps and district performance. The *North Carolina Education Standards and Accountability Commission Report,* published the year before the editorial appeared, recommended that students be required to meet higher graduation standards. Similarly, the State Board of Education approved the *ABC's of Public Education,* a statewide initiative that holds individual elementary and middle schools accountable for improvements in student performance. Schools showing student test scores well above expectations receive bonus money, while schools scoring poorly are offered intensive assistance. Underachieving schools that refuse such help are targeted for takeover by the state. In order to create successful public schools, as defined by the criteria outlined in this report, parents, educators, politicians, and the general public must be actively and deeply involved. As the editorial indicated, a well-trained workforce improves economic and social outcomes for a community. Therefore, all citizens of Johnston County shared a collective stake in helping to address the student achievement gap or to risk leaving a huge population of children behind.

Nearly 133,200 people live in the largely agricultural setting of Johnston County where the chief agricultural commodities are pork, poultry, and tobacco. The county is situated approximately 115 miles east of North Carolina A&T University, adjacent to Wake County, the location of Raleigh, the state capital. Johnston County ranks among one of the 100 fastest growing counties in the nation (U.S. Census 2000). Many residents of Johnston County are former urbanites who have fled from counties with pervasive crime and high taxes. Unemployment rose from 2.5 percent in 1996 to 4.5 percent in 2002. Between 1996 and 2002, the median family income increased from $38,623 to $54,333. Only 16 percent of the county's population is African-American and 7 percent is

Hispanic/Latino. In 1996, there were 25 elementary and secondary schools scattered throughout the county, serving approximately 21,000 students. Forty percent of Johnston County's high-school students do not graduate in four years.

Just over a week after the editorial appeared in the *Smithfield Herald,* a compassionate and vocal team of 11 Johnston County citizens arrived for a meeting at the NCA&T campus. Several members of the team represented Smithfield Middle School, including the principal, a science teacher, four mathematics teachers, a librarian, and a community activist-school volunteer. A mathematics teacher and a school counselor represented Selma High School. The chairperson of the Johnston County Community College Transfer Program also joined them.

These individuals understood what the editorial had conveyed about the direct relationship between educational achievement and family and community economic status. They also knew that improvement of educational outcomes required more knowledgeable and skillful teachers in mathematics and science. The affluence and prospective civic support available to the Johnston County visitors was evident and impressive. They arrived on campus in a new van supplied by a car dealer who served on the Johnston County Board of Education. They all came ready to play a central role in shaping the social and economic future of their county through educational initiatives directed at the next generation. They sought assistance from this public land-grant institution to help accomplish their vision.

At the center of this matchmaking endeavor was William Clayton, a community activist and school volunteer who was a proud graduate of the NCA&T School of Agriculture. Clayton's idea of establishing a partnership between SMS and NCA&T reflected his understanding of the traditional values and mission of the land-grant system. He presumed that NCA&T would thus be receptive and responsive to the ideas and needs of these citizen advocates. At the meeting's close, Clayton challenged us to become an "engaged institution," reminding us that whatever we embarked on had to be for the good of "all people" and not just one segment of the population.

"It's time to do more than just provide us with lip service or an agreement on paper filled with empty promises. The time is right for us to develop some high-quality learning opportunities, not only for our students but also for everyone who cares to be a part of this historic partnership," Clayton said. He was correct. The legacy of civic engagement that land-grant institutions enjoyed suggested an excellent fit between our extension program and the local school system.

Although key NCA&T administration and faculty were unable to attend, we represented the institution and the extension program on their behalf. As we listened to Clayton, we wondered if the type of public issue presented by Johnston County citizens could be addressed through scholarly service by faculty at a land-grant institution. Was there a proactive service-learning role that research, teaching, and extension faculty might play in finding solutions to help close the achievement gap between the students? From the outset, it was evident that this group had a specific and immediate set of community-based concerns—a situation that called for the reciprocity, scholarly expertise, partnership, and civic focus that exemplifies public scholarship. While their needs and the accompanying request clearly fit within the framework of the land-grant mission and the historical role of cooperative extension, these public expectations were atypical for NCA&T faculty who were accustomed to working primarily with and meeting the needs of their own students.

It would also be a highly unusual and innovative step to take a predominantly European American school district and partner it with a historically black institution. In 17 states, there are both historically white and historically black institutions, more commonly referred to by the years in which they were designated as land-grants by the Morill Acts of 1862 and 1890 respectively. From this point forward, we will use "historically white" and "historically black" in referring to these institutions. There has been ongoing discussion about the audiences, missions, and priorities of the extension system associated with both of these institutional designations. Federal mandates dictate the mission of historically black land-grant extension programs, requiring them to work with limited-resource audiences.

While clearly the cultural understanding, traditional values, ethnic, and racial diversity of the NCA&T extension staff are major contributors to their preparedness to work with limited-resource people, we do not believe that the public cares who provides help and support to have their concerns addressed, as long as they are being addressed. We also believe that the unique mission of extension outreach at historically black institutions is an ideal framework for developing institutional engagement through public scholarship that reflects the values of public inquiry.

In this case, as an institution we were an excellent fit. We had an appropriate curriculum that we had been developing. We shared a commitment to close the achievement gap for African-American youth, we wanted to improve math and science literacy for middle-school children, and we cared about public outcomes for the next generation. Finally, Clayton's longstanding relationship with NCA&T provided a wonderful historical context for the work we were about to undertake.

Before coming to campus, the Johnston County team had drafted a community-university engagement proposal titled, *The Gateway to Success: Math and Science.* The team believed that a solid foundation in mathematics, science, and the use of computer technology would help address the achievement gap between white and African-American students. They also believed that it was essential for students to be qualified for many jobs in a contemporary, information-driven society. Their proposal described how multidisciplinary faculty teams from NCA&T and civic-minded people from Johnston County could join in identifying solutions to the problem. The ultimate goal of the proposal was to help middle-school students improve decision-making and problem-solving skills.

The team's proposal suggested a model for public engagement between grassroots community leaders and the public education system at the secondary and post-secondary levels. Importantly, these community members were not looking for the traditional land-grant outreach model of technology transfer from expert faculty to community beneficiaries. They came in search of partners to help solve a civic problem that mattered to their community. They hoped to identify a broad range of affirmative steps, educational strategies, and solutions to raise student performance with all deliberate speed. The group had identified middle schools as the intervention site, as they were feeder institutions for one of the local high schools, Selma High School.

The Johnston County team hypothesized that better prepared middle-school students would have a greater chance of mastering high-school mathematics and science courses. During middle school, many students begin to think seriously about attending college and preparing for a career. If students plan to pursue education beyond high school to get a technology-driven job in industry, they must have a strong foundation in mathematics and science (Jones & Airola 2002). The visitors knew that mathematics and science courses are difficult for many students and their instructors. They agreed that this might be overcome by integrating more cooperative, hands-on learning opportunities, both formal and non-formal, about "how things work." They also knew that better trained teachers would become a crucial link to nurturing science and mathematics literacy among students through experientially based curriculum materials. This was propitious, since our experience in developing DTE had prepared us to help them advance their agenda.

Immediately following our first meeting with Johnston County citizens, little was done on campus to keep the momentum going. Issues surrounding mandated clientele and competing job responsibilities made people uncertain of what NCA&T could contribute. Meanwhile, the stalwart Clayton met with DeEtte Gray, a Smithfield Middle School science teacher, and Dr. Tom

Houlihan, the superintendent of Johnston County Schools, to review the *Gateway to Success: Math and Science* proposal. Expressing his commitment to the proposed partnership, Dr. Houlihan gave his staff permission to participate. He also suggested that Clayton and Gray meet with the assistant superintendent of curriculum to organize a plan of action.

The assistant superintendent, in turn, sent a letter to teachers and principals at eight Johnston County schools explaining the nature of the partnership. "We have an exciting opportunity available to us ... to join NCA&T and Johnston Community College ... to enhance the delivery of (our) math and science curricula," he wrote. They planned the next face-to-face meeting and invited a team from NCA&T to meet with them in Smithfield.

By the time we made our first visit to Smithfield Middle School, we had a well-developed draft DTE curriculum. But we knew from past experience with similar educational efforts, we had to be prepared for the unexpected. For example, we knew that the urban students were eager to participate. Would rural students respond similarly? Would they recognize the need or value in a gardening curriculum?

We traveled to Johnston County with our dean and a student recruiter to meet with teachers, community leaders, and volunteers. Participants were surprised and pleased to see that their grassroots values and beliefs could be fully integrated into the impending partnership and to understand that their participation would not require additional work on top of what they were already planning for the year. Finally, they were told that mini-grants would be available from a consortium of historically black land-grant institutions working on long-term food-system sustainability to support implementation. Funds could be used to cover expenses (supplies, travel, and equipment) related to implementing DTE at Smithfield Middle School. Of the schools present at this meeting, Smithfield committed itself to being involved, with active encouragement from Clayton throughout the conversation. He agreed to serve as a volunteer at their school and to mentor the new sixth-grade science teacher, Kelly Mance. While Clayton had worked with children as a 4-H agent for 30 years, Mance was a young and inexperienced teacher. More important, however, she was a forward-thinking educator who eagerly accepted the challenge with an open mind. She refocused her lesson plans around DTE and fully integrated the resource into her lesson plans.

Based on our prior experience working with teachers, we knew that very little would happen without the solid support of the principal, Dr. Patricia Harris. Her backing was essential to encourage further involvement from the faculty. Within the next few months, it became clear how passionate Dr. Harris felt about the partnership. She wrote a letter to a member of (then) North Carolina Governor Jim Hunt's Educational Advisory Board and the former Superintendent of Johnston County Schools seeking help to pursue the partnership. "I can see wonderful possibilities ... to use the professors ... and take field trips to the University," she wrote. She also envisioned a "model school," a place rich in resources where students could explore, investigate, conjecture, evaluate, and solve problems. That type of learning environment, along with a civic commitment, would be used to stimulate learning and motivate student performance. "We hope to see an increase in the number of students who think critically and solve problems with a stronger foundation in math and science," wrote Dr. Harris.

The Smithfield Middle School site had enough unused space that Dr. Harris consented to a half-acre plot of land for the DTE garden. A portion of the campus was also made available for the construction of a small greenhouse. Many of the student's transplants were started in the greenhouse as seeds before being placed in the garden.

Clayton further encouraged buy-in from top-level administrators, writing to Dr. Molly Broad, President of the University of North Carolina (UNC) System to request her support. She replied by letting him know that UNC constituent institutions could make a tremendous difference in elementary and secondary education in North Carolina. "By working in partnership with K-12 institutions, our campuses can enhance the depth and breadth of educational opportunities available to pre-collegiate students throughout the state and thereby better enable those students to pursue a college education or other career opportunities," she wrote.

As our relationship with Smithfield deepened, we were able to contribute both to the further development of DTE and to students' learning, the civic issue that had motivated the Johnston County team to forge a partnership with NCA&T. We continued refining DTE as we made regular trips to visit Clayton, Mance, and the Smithfield Middle School students over the course of a year and a half. On each trip, we offered assistance on how to integrate the various DTE activities into other learning opportunities.

The more they learned from us, the more we learned from them. We provided financial support for their participation in professional development workshops focusing on youth education, thus becoming stronger advocates for integrating constructivism and experiential learning activities into the teaching methodology. This synergistic exchange of ideas, refinements to the curriculum, and collaborative leadership in training and implementation required active, intentional commitment and involvement from all of us as partners. Ultimately, the teachers became our strongest ambassadors, often allowing educators from other places to interrupt their busy schedules for tours through the Smithfield Middle School garden and greenhouse.

Mance's sixth graders—nearly 70 in all—were using the scientific method to research different approaches to cultivating hearty potatoes, lettuce, cabbage, beets, tomatoes, radishes, squash, snap beans, field peas, peppers, cucumbers, watermelon, cantaloupe, and various flowers. We were pleased to read in *Smithfield Herald* stories that the partnership and the students' scientific literacy were both flourishing.

Throughout the partnership, Mance discussed the importance of integrating DTE with other subject areas. For instance, she told her fellow teachers how measuring plant growth and yield could be used as models for teaching abstract mathematical concepts. One of the many benefits Mance enjoyed was relating to students outside of her classroom. "It allows me to foster unique relationships with the children that I might not get in class," she said. "The children talk more when we're working in the garden and they tend to freely open up to me." Mance knew that her student's learning experiences and social interactions would be enhanced by racial and ethnic diversity. Her students were asked to use both English and Spanish when speaking about a specific crop. The Hispanic students also told stories about how some plants were connected to their culture. Inspired by Mance, another Smithfield Middle School teacher incorporated DTE into his classroom activities as well.

As word of what was happening at Smithfield Middle School spread, other community leaders and volunteers enthusiastically joined the effort. Local farmers and businesses contributed much of the in-kind support (supplies and materials, labor, equipment, etc.). For instance, a farmer whose property adjoins the school's campus volunteered his time and tractor to till the half-acre garden. Free seeds, transplants, and other supplies were continuously donated by a community feed and seed store. Clayton recognized that volunteers who bring their experience into the classroom help teachers become more effective and dedicated advocates for their students. Hence, Mance said, "the morale and professional support that volunteers like Clayton have shown my sixth-grade science program is invaluable." Clayton says, "When students spend time with their elders, they feel important and special."

Harvested plants were eaten, given away, or sold. Seasonal profits were reinvested in materials and supplies. The gardens were left unattended during the summer, and the gardening cycle began anew in the fall with a different group of students. Parents and school personnel harvested leftover plants at the end of the school year and throughout the early summer months. Teacher and principal reviews about the quality of the harvest helped to increase students' self-esteem. Furthermore, the students became increasingly motivated after receiving moral support and personal visits to their garden site by parents, farmers, and elected state and federal officials and other special guests. School maintenance personnel expressed pride in the garden by regularly mowing the grass around the garden. They also helped the students erect a sign designating the school as a DTE site sponsored by the NCA&T Cooperative Extension Program. After paying a special visit to the garden, the Johnston County school superintendent funded a request to install an underground water line from the school out to the garden. Until that time, the students carried water from the school to the garden in buckets, sometimes using as much as half a class period. Having running water adjacent to the garden inspired the students to try several unique irrigation methods.

Smithfield sixth graders traveled to the NCA&T campus to interact with teaching faculty, research scientists, and extension specialists. While on campus, they were made aware of career opportunities in the food, agricultural, and environmental sciences. And following a visit to Smithfield by numerous land-grant faculty from around the U.S., an Iowa State University visitor, Dr. Eldon Weber, returned home and spoke with colleagues about the DTE program. Dr. Weber was in the process of expanding his "Pizz-A-Thon" program—a competitive event in which student teams develop a marketing portfolio for a fictitious company. Students create an original pizza, researching the pizza's ingredients and tracing them to their origins. Mance and Clayton agreed to host a visit by Dr. Weber and then sponsored their own Pizz-A-Thon. The winning sixth-grade team was invited to compete at Iowa State University (ISU). With the support of the school district and ISU, enough funds were secured to fully sponsor the team and three adults. The students returned with the *Kid's Choice* and the *Adult's Choice* awards for their pizza recipe.

As more teachers from other communities began using DTE, we realized the impracticality of traveling to every community and expending resources to provide training on how to use DTE. We responded to this dilemma by designing and adding a "Presenter's Guide" to the curriculum. The guide includes detailed descriptions on how to most effectively develop, gain support for, implement, and evaluate a DTE learning adventure.

Impacts and Successes

We were very pleased with the success of our partnership with Smithfield Middle School and our DTE curriculum, which was manifested on many levels: public recognition, peer review and acknowledgment, expansion of the program to other sites, news coverage, and other kudos. With respect to the hard-to-quantify impacts of our partnership, success is probably best described by the people involved. A parent and member of the Smithfield Middle School Advisory Council acknowledged the benefits of the partnership after observing how his son, using skills and knowledge gained from DTE activities, planted and helped maintain a garden for an elderly woman. Other parents have expressed their appreciation for how DTE motivates students to learn by "bringing science and other topics to life for children." In 1998, the NCA&T School of Agriculture hosted a national conference on leadership development for land-grant colleges of agriculture. The Smithfield Middle School partnership was selected as a "prime example" to showcase a successful community engagement partnership in progress. One hundred twenty-five conference participants took a tour of Smithfield Middle School and its DTE garden. More newspaper and TV news stories appeared in 2000, 2001, and 2002. The publicity generated numerous visits from farmers, schoolteachers, and administrators from surrounding counties and other states to observe the program, obtain ideas, and duplicate gardening practices.

Outside assessment can also be very helpful in determining if long-term outcomes, such as narrowing the achievement gap, improving job skills, decreasing the dropout rate, or enhancing scientific literacy, are both demonstrable and sustainable. Objective DTE evaluation results show that students increased their knowledge in seven subject areas. The greatest shifts occurred in their knowledge of the scientific method, plants, fertilizer, and pests. Upon completing their participation in DTE activities, students showed a more positive attitude toward science, a greater understanding of the use of pesticides, and a better appreciation for good planning. On an annual basis, children who participated in DTE achieved progressive increases in their science scores from sixth through eleventh grade.

Additional success may occur on a longitudinal basis. Teachers using DTE statewide have reported that students improved a combination of life and science process skills, and academic, attitudinal, and behavioral patterns have also been positively affected. Impact data from county extension agents suggest that DTE helps youth educators develop a positive attitude and enhanced comfort level for teaching science, and develops a cadre of future leaders who have a stronger foundation for making responsible decisions.

We recognize that such evidence does not prove a cause-and-effect relationship. Academic improvements involve a variety of human and personal variables unaccounted for in our work. For instance, perhaps Mance became a more effective teacher because of Clayton's mentorship. The added involvement of parents, community leaders, and volunteers may also have inspired the students to learn.

Down-to-Earth *as Public Scholarship*

As we reflect upon our experience in the DTE story, *participation* and *relationship* emerge as central features of our scholarly work.

These elements characterize the nature, quality, and requirements of well-executed public scholarship and institutional engagement. DTE itself was developed through an iterative, public process involving the citizens and stakeholders who were the ultimate audiences and relevant disciplinary peers. With respect to implementation, the more deeply we moved into a participatory dynamic with our partners at Smithfield Middle School, the clearer our definition of *partnership* became. Mutual responsibility, sharing of knowledge, reciprocity, affection, respect, openness, trust, and commitment were the powerful drivers behind our collective success at implementing DTE at Smithfield. In order to advance the partnership, time as well as human, physical, and financial resources were willingly shared. And the partners were committed to getting the job done.

Unanticipated situations often popped up requiring immediate responses. We tried to remain flexible and responsive. We saw how both sides of the partnership had to be equally prepared to give and take without being disagreeable. This type of partnership was a pioneering effort for all of us. Although we had previous experience working with people in communities, it was mostly through county extension agents. Usually, the contact was based on a one-way sharing of information to meet the needs of a specific audience without the reciprocity so evident in our partnership with Smithfield.

Shared power was a central feature of our partnership, in which all partners had a hand in negotiating strategies that shaped a strong and flexible relationship. There was no designated leader, and each person contributed their strengths in different ways and times. The only member of the partnership whom we considered to be indispensable was William Clayton.

Individuals took care of their responsibilities for the good of the whole. Likewise, we did not establish any formal protocol for communication among partners. Primarily, we made decisions about issues after consultation with those involved at Smithfield Middle School. Most of the communication was handled informally via telephone or in person without the burden of written documentation. At no time did we encounter any unworkable problems. Necessary information flowed freely and equally. If a quick-fix decision was needed, we conferred with each other before a decision was reached.

Collective efficacy refers to a group's shared belief or perception in their capabilities to attain their goals when addressing problems (Bandura 1986). In Roberts' (2000) report, collective efficacy is defined as the belief of each person in the group that there are (1) adequate shared knowledge and skills and (2) effective interactive and synergistic dynamics to expend on a problem. It differs from *self-efficacy*, defined as a person's capabilities to organize and execute the actions required to manage prospective situations (Bandura 1986). Gibson and Dembo (1984) suggest that *teacher efficacy* may influence certain patterns of behavior known to influence achievement gains. Efficacy then, whether on the part of the individual student, groups of students, or teachers, is highly correlated with student achievement.

In the case of DTE at Smithfield, we saw a high degree of collective efficacy as the partnership blossomed and matured, due in large part to the self-efficacy of its members. We saw that investment in teacher efficacy—a large part of our partnership process and of the DTE materials—made a significant difference in student learning and achievement. Early in the partnership, Mance considered terminating her teaching career for a more highly paid job in industry. However, after becoming fully engaged in the partnership, she decided to pursue a master's degree in secondary education to increase her self-efficacy in science and technology. Eventually, the partnership helped her become a very vocal, highly revered role model for her peers.

The term *achievement gap* is used regularly throughout the education literature. Reynolds (2002), however, suggests that when the term is used to denote differences in academic achievement among particular groups of students, it is more accurate to say that there are achievement gaps in the plural form. Moreover, many factors affect student achievement including individual attributes, as well as those of the school, home, and community (Haycock 2001; Reynolds 2002). Nevertheless, Abbott & Joireman (2001) found that socioeconomic status explains a larger percentage of the variance in academic achievement than ethnicity.

To increase the academic achievement of minority and low-income students, Haycock (2001) suggests that high standards, a challenging curriculum, and good teachers are the keys to improvement. Large numbers of low-achieving students are taught by teachers without strong backgrounds in the subject matter they are teaching. Evidence suggests that team motivation and, in particular, collective efficacy are powerful determinants of a team's commitment and action.

The Challenges of Public Scholarship

As is the case with any endeavor, the many challenges we encountered provoked frustration, learning, transformation, and creativity. These challenges emerged at the individual, community, and university levels. They bore different faces and emerged from different tensions.

The process of implementing community partnerships within the university system presented many challenges, not the least of which was effectively communicating the benefits of such partnerships to individuals unfamiliar with the potential rewards. Although the dean sought involvement from other faculty, it was tough for busy faculty to make time in their already busy schedules. In the end, three additional faculty members were able to weave their work with DTE into their responsibilities and were able to contribute on a limited basis. Understanding that engagement is not an "add-on" but can be combined with one's ongoing work is an important paradigm shift for faculty members, one that will take time as institutions become more interested in engagement.

It was truly a challenge to galvanize our colleagues in extension and other divisions of both the historically black and historically white land-grant institutions in North Carolina to commit time, interest, and scholarly focus to this venture. Working in a partnership, conducting public scholarship with an extension program, acting from a multidisciplinary stance, using a collaborative leadership model with no one "in charge," and serving a new audience were all unorthodox dimensions for the school and the individuals. Time constraints and conflicting responsibilities also prevented further involvement from both our colleagues and some Smithfield teachers. Some Smithfield teachers (as well as some from other schools) who considered becoming involved felt it was additional work on top of an already very busy job. Others were accustomed to "flying solo" without the time-intensive, collaborative process that our DTE work engendered.

Professional Recognition and Community Impacts

A number of benefits, both direct and indirect, accrued from this effort. For many citizens, their involvement in the partnership strengthened the sense of community in Johnston County. Smithfield residents developed closer relationships because of their acknowledgement and consideration of concerns that surfaced as a result of their active involvement with the Smithfield partnership. People who had previously been unlikely to find themselves around the same table engaged in healthy discussions on subjects ranging from student discipline to fundraising events. This development of social capital in Johnston County was a positive and unanticipated outcome of our work. Within the local community there were business people, citizens, public officials, and school administrators who had never combined resources or knowledge to work on a common problem until the DTE partnership provided them the mechanism to join forces.

We have also seen a gradual increase in interest on and off the NCA&T campus to secure more human, financial, and technological resources for Smithfield. In response to queries from other departments and individuals on campus about how to develop a model program, we were asked by our dean to prepare, "A Time for Action: Engaging the University with Communities." This paper included a matrix showing how faculty with distinctive expertise in engineering, nursing, technology, business, and education could potentially join the DTE partnership.

The community-university partnership has continued to grow and strengthen. It has now evolved into a strong component of the NCA&T 4-H Youth Development Program. The DTE partnership has also served as a vital means to increase the name recognition and engagement efforts of the university. Prior to our partnership with Johnston County schools, NCA&T was not well known in the county.

The DTE experience also brought citizens an expanded sense of the land-grant mission as one based on civic and democratic involvement—not just in the stewardship of the institution, but in the collaborative development of relevant services, programs, and agendas. This group of citizens came to realize that the staff and resources of a historically black land-grant university were just as meaningful and useful as those at a historically white land-grant institution. And, in fact, historically black institutions could offer a venue for a participatory approach to developing the future social and economic capital of their community. Even small land-grant universities living in the shadows of much larger institutions can play a vital role in reaching various publics. A civic group within the county realized that, although they did not use the traditional method to acquire help (via the county extension office), they were successful in accomplishing their agenda by going directly to the university. Conversely, we found that working directly with communities rather than going through the county-level extension offices could yield dynamic and creative processes and products that were innovative for both the institution and community.

Professional and community recognition also began to pour in, which heightened interest in DTE and encouraged its expansion. We received the first place award for "Innovative Program in Environmental Stewardship" from the Association of Extension Administrators. We were also awarded the L.A. Potts Memorial Success Story Award at the Sixtieth Professional Agricultural Workers Annual Conference. Most notably, we received the first Natural Resources and Environmental Management National Flagship Award given by USDA for development of an exemplary state partnership program. Moreover, we were honored at NCA&T's first recognition of "scientists" who have achieved success through intellectual property, referring to DTE's copyright status. During the dissemination phase, DTE curriculum passed a rigorous review by the National 4-H Jury, which compared the curriculum against a set of validation criteria by an expert panel. Today, DTE is marketed globally by the National 4-H Cooperative Curriculum System, one of only two curricula from an 1890 institution in this prestigious collection.

In addition to this peer recognition, DTE enjoyed a broader impact in the Johnston County schools. Through the diligence of William Clayton and others, including the Johnston County Board of Education and the Johnston County Middle School science coordinator, DTE has become institutionalized within the Johnston County school system. Through a variety of grants and special project funds, we have continued to provide start-up funds for the establishment of new school gardens in Johnston County. Science teachers from every middle school in the county have received in-depth DTE training and have plans to develop a garden program at their respective schools. The DTE program opened the doors for the establishment of a biotechnology partnership between NCA&T research faculty and West Johnston High School, where the former principal of SMS (Dr. Harris), is now serving as the principal.

DTE also began to expand its scope beyond Johnston County. By mid-2002, 300 extension agents and paraprofessionals, teachers, community volunteers, and other youth educators representing 60 of the 100 North Carolina counties had received comprehensive

DTE training. We have also taught youth educators attending national workshops from 37 states how to gain the most from a DTE experience. Youth educators in three foreign countries are also using copies of the curriculum.

Robert Williamson's Reflections

There were positive impacts from the DTE experience, but some persistent challenges as well. Most of all, I felt at ease stepping outside of my traditional role as a natural resource specialist. This transition made it easier to share and learn from others, since I believed that we were spearheading and testing new protocols for extension work. At times, my passion waned because of apathy expressed by administrators and colleagues who were more accustomed to a traditional extension view. To this day, extension practitioners are not considered as academic equals by many of their academic peers. While this could be chalked up to intellectual arrogance and a lack of familiarity with extension work within the academy, extension must also redefine itself beyond the notion of an exclusively service organization. My vision of extension work—beyond the old model of "cows, sows, and plows" in a rural, primarily agrarian America—was embodied by the DTE experience. I believe this type of public scholarship approach is the vanguard for extension. Within extension, however old attitudes are slow to change.

My work in the community reinforced my perception of the need for public scholarship. I observed firsthand how fast the rural landscape is changing from farms to sprawling subdivisions for fleeing urbanites. The partnership helped me to fully appreciate that the state's population is very culturally, racially, and ethnically mixed. I learned how desperately those who still live in cities, as well as suburbs, want help to deal with a subset of urgent problems, such as high dropout rates, achievement gaps, unemployment, and the need for nutritious food.

DTE was a major step toward helping this historically black land-grant institution become an "engaged university." The global success of the DTE curriculum, however, is now paying off in terms of royalties from a national marketing agency. This is a first time event for our university.

Many other immeasurable and intangible impacts emerged as well. The fellowship, friendships, and the glow on people's faces when things came together were priceless. Observing and knowing that the DTE curriculum made a difference in the lives of so many people, young and old, sparked tremendous personal contentment, leading me to develop a stronger desire and commitment to becoming an advocate and practitioner of public scholarship. Finally, the experience made me more determined to be remembered as an extension professional who worked for the good of all people, rather than as a specialist who devoted his credentials to working only with limited-resource people. My affiliation with other authors in this book made this thinking more conceivable.

Ellen Smoak's Reflections

In future years I will look back at the experiences with DTE and SMS with the complete assurance that I was in the right place at the right time. Regardless of any negative feedback we received and discouraging situations we often found ourselves in, there is no doubt in my mind of the value of the work we did. In many ways, the process and all that was involved in the successes we enjoyed defines the ultimate triumph of my 30-year career with extension.

Although I realize that many of our on-campus peers, particularly those in teaching and research, struggle to understand or value the scholarship that extension contributes to the people of the state, I do believe that there is an interest in learning more about us and what we represent. As an organization, extension has been somewhat reticent about sharing its accomplishments. Because of the media attention the DTE project in Johnston County has received, we were thrust into the limelight. If the university is truly interested in engaging itself more fully in communities, there is no doubt that extension will set the pace for others to follow.

The professional awards we received were important to help others—including our on-campus peers—realize the value of DTE. By achieving these honors, our work was acknowledged nationally, but beyond that, I achieved personal satisfaction from rising to a challenge and persevering to the end. I have witnessed firsthand the growth in those who participated in DTE. I have also renewed my faith in the public-education system. Here we had teachers, parents, administrators, and students all anxious to gain the most they could from their experiences in the garden. Not only in Johnston County and Smithfield Middle School, but across the state, we have seen that the community is excited about what happens to the education of children when everyone steps up to the plate and works to achieve a common goal.

The Larger Learning

While the data demonstrated an increase in Smithfield students' learning, it by no means captures the larger learning from the DTE endeavor. We learned a tremendous amount about curriculum development, interdisciplinary collaboration, authentic engagement as a scholarly practice, creating a difference in a community as a democratic act, collaborative leadership, and the development of relationships. The success of this partnership depended on a willingness to be open and receptive to pro-active suggestions rendered by anyone in the partnership. This was seen as more important than trying to jockey for power within the partnership. The partnership involved more than simply asking volunteers to come together as a committee or convening a focus group. It emerged from a sincere desire and commitment to work with a community to find solutions to an array of multidimensional problems that promise long-term public benefits for Johnston County. The public scholarship approach we took to implementing DTE in Johnston County created productive social capital that was beneficial to the community in other ways and contexts long after DTE was first implemented.

A solid entry into the community required a sizeable group of people with a clear commitment to the basic ideals of what the partnership aimed to accomplish. There was an important alchemy of elements that made DTE so successful. Having the right resources, influential leaders, a collective community efficacy, and direct support by interested individuals from a land-grant institution helped fulfill these needs, and, we believe, would be just as effective a combination in another setting or with a different public issue. These resources can be a combination of tangible and intangible incentives, knowledge, skills and expertise, and shared leadership.

Despite reluctance from some colleagues, we realized that an institution of higher education gains greater public credibility as faculty members recognize the importance of collaboration, respect, and trust in interactions with communities. Additionally, when top-level administrators are open to, and supportive of, engagement opportunities, partnerships have a greater likelihood of flourishing. Community activists, parents, teachers, and guidance counselors must be made players in this type of endeavor. Unpleasant experiences for these individuals with a campus faculty member and/or an administrator can lead to a variety of irreversible negative perceptions about the university. A university's positive and visible presence in a community sets the stage for a productive community-university partnership.

Partnering with secondary schools has unlimited potential for closing performance gaps through the participation of concerned faculty at land-grant universities. Many communities are seeking solutions to this and a host of other problems as changes in technology, demographics, competition, and legislative accountability occur. Teaching and research faculty members and university administrators do not always realize what so many extension field faculty members already know: if you effectively address county needs through sustained and active presence, you increase the likelihood of long-term support for your institution. Those who are not sincere about partnership commitments should not get potential community partners excited about possibilities.

As is the case with any scholarly endeavor, there is a need for reflection and analysis on a meta-level. From the development of the DTE curriculum to the creation of the strong partnership that made it such a success at Smithfield Middle School, surfacing and rethinking the many public dimensions of this work have helped us become better scholars. Reviewing the literature on institutional engagement has enabled us to more intentionally think through the public dimensions of our work, the scholarly aspects of DTE, and the implications for our institution, extension, and higher education.

Although the concept of "engaged institutions" entered the higher education vocabulary in 1994 (Holland 2001), the W.K. Kellogg Foundation Report, *Engaging in Youth and Educational Programming* (2001) reports that "engagement—in which institutions and communities form lasting relationships that influence, shape, and promote success in both spheres—is rare." The report points out, however, that "many land-grant universities ... were founded in partnership with communities." This dichotomy between the widely touted public mission and the rare occurrence of genuine engagement aptly describes our own discoveries, experiences, and frustrations.

In our experience, engaging our own institution was not easy. We concur with Norland (1990) and his report that faculty who are "doing extension work" are perceived differently than teaching and research faculty, even though teaching and research is what extension is about. This is a major issue with many ramifications that encompass salary, professional credibility, institutional support, and involvement from faculty outside of extension.

At the initial meeting with Johnston County, few faculty with teaching and research appointments attended. We believe this was due to a remaining perception gap in what constitutes scholarship and how institutional engagement and collaborative, public inquiry can embody the rigor, discovery, and peer-review dimensions of more traditional versions of scholarship. Even though campus faculty and administrators embraced the concept and terminology of the "engaged university" and "public scholarship," few NCA&T faculty took up DTE as a means to embody these ideals. At the outset, initial efforts focused on involving faculty from within the School of Agriculture in DTE. We believe that, if faculty from other departments, such as nursing, engineering or education, for example, had partnered with us, the partnership could have been greatly enhanced. This is an important lesson to learn as we think through future endeavors in creating more engaged institutions as well as specific public scholarship efforts.

Another challenge emerges as the institution seeks to heighten civic engagement. Our emphasis at first was on deepening the partnership between NCA&T and the community. We discovered, however, that building relationships *internally* at land-grant universities significantly raises the visibility and legitimacy of the effort within the institution and is worth paying attention. Many university faculty and administrators are unaware of cooperative extension and may not acknowledge its role in public scholarship. In general, no strong incentives exist for campus colleagues to partner with extension faculty and vice versa. Some departments make direct linkages with communities without involving extension, or conversely they may call on us if they need contacts with specific groups of people. We hope to play a more significant, collaborating role with these non-extension colleagues, beyond serving as a conduit to the public sphere. Interdisciplinary and intercollegiate involvement not only benefits the community in question, but actually impacts the level of credibility and visibility of public scholarship within the institution. Extension services, then, create an ideal platform for influencing how an institution conducts and thinks about scholarship.

Campbell (1991) argues that each of the four types of scholarship described by Boyer (1990)—discovery, application, teaching, and integration—are relevant to those working in extension. Boyer urged individuals to embrace a broader view of scholarship. Extension is an excellent environment for the scholarship of application and integration because of its multidimensional approach to problem solving (Bushaw 1996). Extension practitioners have credentials to conduct research and also frequently have the advantage of sound experience with information dissemination in easily accessible formats. These strengths, combined with the new understanding of the importance of involving many disciplines, will create more dynamic and effective partnerships around public issues. As educators, we all share a responsibility to enhance self-efficacy and that of the public.

Whether inside or outside extension, the key to creating more active and functional relationships within land-grant institutions is enhancing the visibility and definition of public scholarship. Norman (2001) suggests that defining scholarship is not as easy as it appears to be. Many faculty members, unfamiliar with extension scholarship, have difficulty understanding the nature of this type of inquiry. Land-grant faculty with teaching and research appointments may be aware that extension has a rich heritage of providing a unique service to communities through informal activities that help people make connections between theory and practice—largely in support of a productive agricultural system. Patton (1986) reported that "expansion of extension into nonagricultural programming hasn't been universally welcomed, nor is it widely known or understood."

Similarly, Norland (1990) suggests that perpetuating the idea that cooperative extension is the service component of the institution doesn't fully do justice to the land-grant mission and may even harm it by virtue of its incompleteness. Norland encourages *all* faculty to serve communities, because federal land-grant legislation never designated the extension service as the sole provider of the service dimension of the land-grant mission. As we presently consider community engagement through public scholarship, it is more comprehensive and qualitatively different than traditional outreach efforts. The emphasis is now on the total resources of the university-at-large, rather than the individual expertise of the extension staff or the resources of the extension service (Weiser 1996; Schwab 2003).

Patton (1986) identified five central strengths that can become the centerpiece of university outreach, all of which are omnipresent in extension: bottom-up program development; informal education methods; statewide network; applied perspective; and commitment. Thus, the fundamental ideas and practices that can give rise to a fully engaged institution can include the dissemination, expansion, and transfer of these approaches from extension to other venues within the land-grant system. Norland (1990) suggests that one challenge facing extension professionals is changing how they consider the type of work that they do. If they continue to think that extension is just a service, then others will as well. Extension must better assert its unique role within land-grant institutions and for communities, while simultaneously improving its collaborations internally and broadening its services to improve the collective efficacy of communities—a complicated challenge, to be sure.

The invisibility of extension within the institution may explain, to a degree, the rarity of public scholarship in universities. At NCA&T, extension faculty lack tenure-track appointments and scholarly titles and receive lower salary for comparable work. There are no professors or associate professors in extension; we are instead referred to as *subject matter specialists*. This contributes to confusion about the nature of our work and expertise and can encourage intellectual elitism within the research and teaching functions. There are few structured opportunities for collaboration with research and teaching faculty. And, as is always the case, turf issues surface. The "silo" phenomenon among disciplines and between the research, teaching, and engagement functions of the institution—so pervasive and so much a tradition in higher education—occurs at our institution as well.

These tensions constrain broader interest in public scholarship. Key to encouraging and sustaining public scholarship at NCA&T—as is the case across higher education—is the faculty reward system. Within our cooperative extension system, rewards and compensation for building relationships both internally and externally are slight. We have felt frustrated that, no matter how much new publicity or recognition the university received from our partnership, we received no monetary recognition reflecting our work. Fortunately, professional challenge, civic contribution, and the rich experience of the partnership provide intrinsic rewards.

We have seen that the capacity for future grassroots engagement in communities is unlimited. However, if land-grant universities like NCA&T are to serve as catalysts for change or play a significant leadership role, administrators and faculty must recognize that engagement is more than providing knowledge. Faculty and administrators who remain in their academic ivory towers and choose not to engage will find it difficult to resolve community issues. By failing to engage, we tend to increase public mistrust and promote estrangement. Cherished traditions of objectivity, detachment, and expert-driven knowledge production must be broadened to include trust, relationship, involvement, and shared expertise. For those interested in the process of public scholarship and its accompanying emphasis on engagement, a successful shift from a *service* to a *participant* approach depends largely on the ability to adjust to change. We achieved this by stepping outside the framework of our subject-matter boxes. As we found out, few things can be more frustrating than participating in this type of activity without embracing emotional and intellectual flexibility.

Extension, specifically, and public scholarship, generally, confront numerous tensions within the various land-grant institutions to successfully create momentum for public inquiry. Extension systems have their own traditions to build upon and change in moving institutions toward the authentic partnership and scholarly rigor central to public inquiry. Extension staffs must begin to understand with greater depth and complexity how their work does or can have scholarly dimensions. They should also consider how their work can transcend the bounds of extension to other units within land-grant institutions. As long as uninformed publics perceive that we continue to conduct business as usual, we will remain stuck in a time warp and nothing will change. We must stop masking our outreach efforts by pretending to be fully engaged when all we are doing is perpetuating a traditional notion that extension professionals are simply service providers.

In thinking about the role of public scholarship in land-grant institutions, faculty in and outside of extension must begin to think more expansively about the nature of scholarship and how it might engage the public through collaborative partnerships. Extension staff and faculty must begin to consider the work they do as scholarship, making the necessary adjustments to developing programs with the rigor, requirements, and stance of a scholarly approach. For example, our request to have the DTE curriculum reviewed by peer scholars outside of extension aided us both in terms of enhancing the rigor of our work and heightening awareness of the scholarly aspects inherent in this public work among non-extension faculty.

If the Johnston County team had sought our help by going through their local North Carolina State University (NCSU) County Extension Center, our involvement might have been minimal. Because NCA&T and NCSU have different missions and little overlap, there is a traditional sense of which institution serves which clientele. It is routine for NCA&T Extension specialists to gain entrance to a county by first informing the NCSU County Extension director. This holds true even for counties in which NCA&T Extension workers are employed to work with limited-resource people. Although this activity is often looked upon as a courtesy by NCA&T and NCSU administrators, the action can unintentionally perpetuate separatism in a time when "seamless universities" and civic engagement are encouraged by the president and general administration for the UNC System.

Freedom of choice and reciprocal interactions generate synergistic and progressive thinking; encouraging the blurring of boundaries between cooperative extension at our two universities will greatly aid in dismantling some of these roadblocks. Inherent in this challenge is the mainstream community perception that NCSU rather than NCA&T is the "people's university," as they are unaccustomed to thinking of a historically black land-grant as a reputable and inclusive educational resource within the state. This dilemma can drastically affect the formation of partnerships, reducing the level of community engagement by NCA&T specialists. Can the extension program keep such a traditional mode of working and thinking and survive beyond the twentieth century? Does this model of operation make for an equitable partnership between historically white and historically black institutions? We believe that nontraditional models of collaboration between land-grant schools and a variety of communities will assist in dissolving some of the boundary issues that can inhibit productive opportunities for public scholarship and civic engagement.

Sustainability and replicability are important questions when it comes to public scholarship. The type of partnership formed at Smithfield Middle School has not been replicated in other North Carolina communities as proactively as we would like. Although other communities have ongoing DTE projects, a strong university connection has not been nurtured. While the potential for such a connection may exist, we believe that the primary reason that this has not happened is the lack of a strong advocate who is interested and available to facilitate the process. Working more collaboratively with interested county partners to identify knowledgeable and interested volunteers or retired educators may be a viable way to locate such advocates. The issue of organizers and consistent advocates—both within the institution and the community—are key to the success of public-scholarship efforts. That is why the identification of local, public problems and development of locally grounded scholarly responses are critical to the success of any public-scholarship effort. The DTE curriculum will not have the same impact without the partnership that formed to create a vibrant, multidimensional program for the children and the community goodwill generated. Public scholars must understand that central to the success of any public endeavor is effective organizing, consistent presence, local advocacy, and authentic partnership.

Conclusion

Education is a community activity. Any efforts to improve education should start with a sense of collective community efficacy. But working alone, many communities may not be prepared to respond. They often lack adequate scholarship, resources, and expertise.

As we continued to develop a comfortable relationship with Smithfield Middle School and Johnston County citizens through firsthand visits and some nitty-gritty deliberations, we realized that public scholarship was an integral part of a bigger picture. In this process, we not only enhanced our self-efficacy but also improved our scholarship. Hopefully, we also made a difference in the lives of deserving students, teachers, and community leaders through the exchange of knowledge and wisdom related to mathematics, science, and technology.

We have continued to visit Smithfield. Today, as we drive away looking at the reflections in our rearview mirrors, things are definitely different. The first students that participated in the DTE program are now college age. Dr. Harris was promoted to principal at a local high school. Mance left to work on a master's degree at NCSU, turning down an offer to attend Iowa State University. Clayton comes by occasionally to volunteer his skills and talents. He still believes that "a good education cannot be found totally in the classroom. Students need to envision education as a life-long endeavor."

In 1999, a story appeared in the *Smithfield Herald:* "School Lobbies Historically Black Colleges: Smithfield Middle School

Volunteer Calls for Greater Support of School's Down-to-Earth Program." The article was based on an interview with Clayton. He told the reporter that DTE has the potential to become a model for the nation because it shows students practical applications of the science knowledge contained in textbooks. He discussed how the "promising" program needs a greater commitment of resources from NCA&T and similar institutions. "We need some strong university support, and we hope that they will not let us down," Clayton said.

In the fall of 2002, one of Johnston County's newest schools opened with an enrollment of over 800 high-school students. "Thanks to Mr. Clayton, I'm very pleased that our students will also benefit from Down-to-Earth," said Dr. Harris. Clayton has taken to heart a quote by William Jennings Bryan: "Destiny is not a matter of chance; it is a matter of choice. It is not a thing to be waited for; it is a thing to be achieved."

References

Abbott, M. L. and J. Joireman. 2001. *The Relationships among Achievement, Low Income, and Ethnicity across Six Groups of Washington State Students.* Technical Report No. 1. Lynwood, WA: Washington School Research Center.

Bandura, A. 1986. *Social Foundations of Thought and Action: A Social Cognitive Theory.* Englewood Cliffs, NJ: Prentice Hall.

Boyer, E. L. 1990. *Scholarship Reconsidered: Priorities of the Professoriate.* Princeton, NJ: Carnegie Foundation for the Advancement of Teaching.

Bushaw, D. W. 1996. The Scholarship of Extension. *Journal of Extension* 34 (August).

Campbell, G. R. 1991. Scholarship Reconsidered. *Journal of Extension* 29 (winter).

Gibson, S. and M. Dembo. 1984. Teacher Efficacy: A Construct Validation. *Journal of Educational Psychology,* 76:596-582.

Haycock, K. 2001. Closing the Achievement Gap. *Educational Leadership* 58(6): 6-11.

Horton, R. L. and S. Hutchinson. 1997. *Nurturing Scientific Literacy among Youth through Experientially Based Curriculum Materials.* Columbus, OH: Center for 4-H Youth Development, The Ohio State University.

Holland, B. 2001. Exploring the Challenge of Documenting and Measuring Civic Engagement Endeavors of Colleges and Universities. Paper presented at the Campus Compact Advanced Institute on Classifications for Civic Engagement, March 23, 2001. http://www.compact.org/advacedtoolkit/measuring.html.

Jones, A. and D. Airola. 2002. Invited Paper: Closing the Achievement Gap in Math and Science. *Arkansas Educational Research & Policy Studies Journal* (2)1: 85-93.

Kolb, D. A. 1984. *Experiential Learning: Experience as the Source of Learning and Development.* Englewood Cliffs, NJ: Prentice-Hall.

Norman, C. L. 2001. The Challenge of Extension Scholarship. *Journal of Extension* 39 (February).

Norland, E. 1990. Extension is Not Just Service. *Journal of Extension* 28 (winter).

Patton, M. Q. 1986. To Educate a People. *Journal of Extension* 24 (winter).

Reynolds, G. 2002. Identifying and Eliminating the Achievement Gaps: A Research-based Approach. *Bridging the Great Divide: Broadening Perspectives on Closing the Achievement Gaps.* Viewpoints 9:3-12.

Roberts, B. 2000. "Personal Efficacy and Collective Efficacy." http://www.stolaf.edu/people/roberts/psych-121/Efficacy.html.

Schwab, C. 2003. Editor's Corner: The Scholarship of Extension and Engagement: What Does It Mean in the Promotion and Tenure Process? *The Forum for Family and Consumer Issues* 8(2).

U.S. Census Bureau. 2000. United States Census 2000.

Weiser, C. J. 1996. The Value System of a University Rethinking Scholarship. Unpublished paper. Corvallis, OR: Oregon State University. http://www.adec.edu/clemson/paper/weiser.html.

Williamson, R. and E. Smoak. 1997. *A Student's Guide to Keeping the Science in Your Science Project.* NCA&T Extension Publication.

————. 1998. A Student's Guide to Keeping the Science in Your Science Project. *Journal of Extension* 36 (October).

————. 1999. Creating a Down-to-Earth Approach to Teaching Science, Math and Technology. *Journal of Extension* 37 (June).

————. 2002. *Down-to-Earth: Enriching Learning through Gardening.* Saint Paul, MN: 4-H Corporative Curriculum System.

W.K. Kellogg Foundation. 2001. Engaging Youth and Education Programming. Document download from http://wkkf.org/Pubs/YouthEd/Pub665.pdf.

Chapter Nine:
An Exploration of Participatory Methods in a Youth Outreach Program Linked to University Research

by Marianne Krasny

Recently, I received word that the dean of the College of Agriculture and Life Sciences at Cornell was considering mandating that all faculty positions be comprised of at least 50 percent research, with the remaining time allocated to teaching or extension. Stipulating that all positions have at least a 50 per-cent research component could be seen as sending a message that teaching and extension are not as highly valued as research, even though as New York's land-grant school, the College of Agriculture and Life Sciences claims extension as part of its mission.

My position in the Department of Natural Resources at Cornell is 70 percent extension and 30 percent research. The position is unusual in that my 70 percent extension commitment is to young people rather than to adult outreach programs. 4-H is the youth component of extension and my official title is New York State Program Leader for 4-H Natural Resources. Earning the respect of science research colleagues and obtaining tenure and promotions has been especially challenging for 4-H faculty members. In contrast to extension aimed at adult audiences, where faculty members "extend" their own research (i.e., a scientist who conducts research on potatoes shares his/her findings with potato growers), youth extension work generally does not link well to science research. This lack of connection between research and county youth programs is confounded by the fact that most county 4-H programs focus on young children who have limited ability to understand complex science topics. Thus, a 4-H faculty member may find him/herself conducting two unrelated jobs—scientific research and educational programs for younger children. An additional challenge for 4-H faculty in New York State is trying to meet the conflicting demands of county 4-H agents and volunteers in 58 counties, whose populations range from immigrant and minority youth in New York City (NYC) to rural residents in the Adirondack region.

In spite of these challenges, my extension career has been extremely rewarding intellectually and personally, and I hope has allowed me to contribute to both youth development and to our understanding of science education and university outreach. Thus, my first reaction to the dean's suggestion that we consider abolishing positions with such a high commitment to extension was anger: here was another attack on extension that implied that only research is a worthy activity for faculty. Had I been in a 50 percent-research position as an assistant professor, I would never have had the time to delve into extension as an area of scholarship.

At the same time, I find areas of agreement with the dean's suggestion, if it is meant to emphasize the importance of faculty engaging in scholarly work. The problem is the assumption that scholarly activities only apply to research. I feel that they can also be applied to extension. *When a faculty member combines activities fundamental to academia, such as critical and integrative thinking, mentoring students, writing grants, and publishing, with a strong commitment to working with community members, and with the goal of fostering learning and positive social and environmental change, that faculty member is conducting public scholarship.*

How I have attempted to balance the conflicting demands of faculty colleagues, 4-H and other educators, and my own research and scholarly interests are the focus of this chapter. I first explore these themes through a discussion of how our youth program has evolved over the 17 years I have been at Cornell. This is followed by an in-depth discussion of *Garden Mosaics,* a program that uses a participatory approach to engaging youth and community members in research and to engaging educators in designing educational programs. Before embarking on the discussion of these initiatives, I briefly describe some of the influences that helped to formulate my approach to public scholarship.

Personal Background

Unlike many of my extension colleagues, who are from rural backgrounds, I grew up in a suburban neighborhood three miles outside of Washington, D.C. Thus, when I first saw the job announcement for the Cornell position of assistant professor and 4-H Program Leader for Natural Resources, I had no idea what extension or 4-H was. I did have an undergraduate degree in human development and graduate degrees in forest ecology—a combination that seemed to fit the bill as far as the hiring decision was concerned.

In addition to my academic training, several other aspects of my background were influential in the way I formulated the position after I was hired. I grew up in an international community during a time of social upheaval and in a family that was concerned with social causes and that liked to spend time in the outdoors. A number of international families lived on our suburban street, and my friends' parents worked at embassies and at the World Bank. I joined a group at my elementary school called "International Singers," and my parents frequently entertained visiting international scientists. Furthermore, my father is an immigrant, having grown up in Austria and Czechoslovakia. As do many ethnic Jews who immigrated to the U.S. at the time of the Second World War, he values education and did his best to make sure I excelled in school. He also drove my friends and me to play with children at the Junior Village orphanage in Anacostia every other Saturday, thus trying to instill in me a concern for others. The events in Washington, especially the racial struggle and Vietnam War protests, furthered my interest and commitment to social causes.

Furthermore, my parents loved hiking and camping. We spent weekends at Potomac Appalachian Trail Club cabins and summers at the Appalachian Mountain Club's "August Camp." I was also in a girls' explorers club whose activities included competitive whitewater canoeing and kayaking. From these experiences came my love of meeting and learning from people whose cultures differ from my own, a commitment to learning and to helping others, and a love for the outdoors, all of which have contributed to building my career as an extension faculty member in the Department of Natural Resources at Cornell.

When I first came to Cornell as an undergraduate student, I was intimidated by the faculty and felt uncomfortable with the conservative, largely upstate New York student body. I remember standing outside a professor's office for 30 minutes trying to gain the courage to talk to him about how I was afraid to speak up in class. Fortunately, I had a cousin who was an instructor in the adolescent development program in the College of Human Ecology. I gravitated toward her courses, which included field experiences tutoring and house parenting delinquent youth and road trips to observe youth detention facilities around the state. This class embodied some of what today we would call public scholarship.

On graduating from Cornell, I took a month-long mountaineering course in the North Cascades of Washington State. Thus began my outdoor career. I taught mountaineering for the next three summers, obtained a fifth-year degree in botany from the University of Washington, and took a six-month bike trip through Central America. When I returned to Seattle, I couldn't find a job. By default I began graduate school in forest ecology at the University of Washington. I was lucky to have the opportunity to conduct my master's and doctoral research on the Tanana River floodplain in Alaska in cooperation with the U.S. Forest Service. One of the summers I was in Alaska, my high-school-aged cousin helped me with fieldwork and I saw the value of a young person engaging in research.

Our graduate program at the University of Washington was not in any way connected to extension. But I did have a wonderful advisor who worked hard to teach me how to think and write logically and critically. Because these skills are transferable to any research or education program, they have proven invaluable in my academic career, which has involved working across the natural and social science disciplines.

When I learned that I was going to be interviewed for the 4-H Natural Resources Program Leader faculty position at Cornell, I realized I needed to know something about cooperative extension. Living in Berkeley, California, at the time, I called the Alameda County Cooperative Extension office and asked the receptionist if she could explain to me what extension was. This was obviously a question she was not accustomed to being asked! But she did offer to send me their county extension newsletter.

"4-H is the only youth organization with a tie to the research and knowledge of the land-grant university." Although extension faculty and county educators may take the connection between 4-H and the university for granted, this quote from the Alameda County Cooperative Extension newsletter served as the basis for my programming philosophy for 17 years. In short, I feel that 4-H's niche in environmental and natural resources education is in developing science-based programs drawing on the research of the university. Thus, while there are other important approaches to environmental education such as those emphasizing recreation (e.g., 4-H sportfishing programs), and holistic approaches combining spirituality, values clarification, the arts, and science, I feel a faculty member at a major research university is uniquely positioned to provide leadership for a science-based education program.

Evolution toward Public Scholarship

Several years after my arrival at Cornell, the conflict between my commitment to incorporating the results of university scientific research into my outreach work, and responding to the demands of county 4-H programs, became apparent. Meeting the demands of traditional 4-H programs, which focus on younger, rural youth and depend heavily on the interests of local adult volunteers, would not have allowed me to build programs around the scientific research of my university colleagues. Therefore, I decided to expand our audiences to include high-school teachers and other educators who were more interested in science-based programs. In addition to my belief that such programs carry out extension's mission, my decision stemmed from the fact that working in this area was more challenging intellectually and therefore more personally rewarding than developing traditional 4-H programs. Furthermore, as a tenure-track faculty member in a science department, my survival depended on developing programs that were viewed as substantive by my research colleagues. However, choosing this path has meant that I offered less direct support to the county extension offices. In part, I made up for this deficiency by bringing in outside funding to support campus-based extension specialists who worked more closely with the county agents and volunteers.

Another challenge I faced when I first came to Cornell was that my research did not relate to my extension program. My graduate degrees and original 30 percent research commitment were in forest ecology. However, a natural resources youth program focused solely on forest ecology would have failed to meet the needs of most youngsters in New York State, both because it would not have addressed the interests of youth audiences at a time when issues like water quality and waste were receiving broad scale media attention, and because the majority of children in New York live in the New York City and other major metropolitan areas without ready access to forests. Furthermore, the type of forest ecology research I conducted was of very little relevance to children. Thus, for 12 years, I struggled to conduct research and extension programs that were almost completely separate.

More recently, my research interests have merged with my outreach program to focus on developing and evaluating innovative models for university outreach, engaging young people in ecological and participatory research, and participatory program development. Regardless of the discipline, conducting research has allowed me to continue to grow intellectually and to practice critical and integrative thinking in a way that may not have been possible if my responsibilities had been limited to extension. It has only been in the last several years, after changing my research program from forest ecology to evaluating our outreach efforts, that I have been able to more fully engage in public scholarship.

As I have tried to balance my research and scholarship interests with the needs of our stakeholders, my approach to extension has evolved through three phases. I call these the "content," "research," and "learning community" paradigms (Table 1). Whereas the content approach is valuable and of interest to many of our extension audiences, I personally have found the youth research and learning community paradigms present opportunities for more substantive thinking about the way in which universities engage in public scholarship and thus have been more challenging and rewarding. They also have presented numerous opportunities for graduate students to become involved in my research and outreach programs.

Content Approach

During the early years of my work, I did not question the top-down, technology transfer model of extension. The job of

Table 1. *Three Paradigms for Conducting Youth Outreach*

Paradigm: Content

Definition	Faculty deliver science-based content information to county extension agents and other local audiences.
Example Activities	Manuals and brochures developed by faculty. Training for 4-H educators.
Scholarship/ Research Questions	How can recent scientific findings be incorporated into materials for youth and other lay audiences? What are impacts of programs on youth and educators?
Civic Skills and Capacities	Content understanding is important to participating in civic debates. Programs support extension volunteers, who play an important role in mentoring youth.

Paradigm: Research

Definition	Youth and educators conduct authentic research with varying types of collaborations with university scientists.
Example Activities	On-campus research programs for high-school students and teachers. Classrooms and 4-H groups carry out local investigations, focusing on land use, invasive species, water quality, and gardening practices.
Scholarship/ Research Questions	Through participating in research projects, what can youth and other lay audiences learn about the way in which science is conducted? What types of research, (e.g., experimental, monitoring, participatory) can be carried out successfully by youth? What are the impacts of various types of scientist-educator collaborations on participants?
Civic Skills and Capacities	Understanding the nature of scientific research is essential to interpreting science as reported in the media and to participating in civic debates. Investigative skills learned through conducting research can be applied to many aspects of civic life. Community groups and local government may be able to use data collected by youth. Programs support science education reform.

Paradigm: Learning Community

Definition	University scientists, local educators, and community members collaboratively develop and test new programs, together enhancing our understanding of best programming methods.
Example Activities	Educators test innovative educational practice and share their results through the Internet and at workshops and meetings.
Scholarship/ Research Questions	How can university faculty and community educators work together to further our understanding of educational practices? How might such programs build educator skills?
Civic Skills and Capacities	Educators learn investigative and evaluation skills that can be applied in other settings. Educators develop professional networks that can be used in promoting educational change. Educators develop leadership skills.

extension was to transfer scientific findings from the university to the counties. I assumed my role was to develop publications and training programs for 4-H educators and volunteers. When I first arrived at Cornell in 1986, county extension educators expressed the need for more project materials, especially for younger audiences. In response to these demands, I developed 4-H educators' guides that attempted to balance the educators' needs for simple materials with my interest in communicating not only accurate science, but also tidbits of current university research whenever possible. For example, a 4-H forestry project included an activity on forest gaps (then a popular area of research in forest ecology).[1] As part of this content approach, I also arranged for presentations by research scientists at training sessions for 4-H educators.

Youth Research Programs

Origin of Our[2] Programs. Whereas much of the work described in the "content approach" was in response to suggestions by county extension educators, both my interests and the emphasis on engaging students in authentic research from the science education policy and funding[3] community provided the original stimulus for our youth research programs. These programs are guided by a strong belief that, through learning to conduct research, young people will develop a better understanding of science and how research is conducted and thus become more productive members in a democratic society. Research experiences not only allow students to more critically analyze public debates involving science (e.g., global warming), but also provide them with the skills and knowledge to investigate questions that may come up in the future. Developing such research experiences in collaboration with community members can make the research more meaningful to the youth and thus more fully engage them.

Although programs that engage young people in research are not common in 4-H, they are consistent with extension's mission of developing outreach programs drawing from university research. They also are consistent with 4-H's historical tradition and with educational approaches commonly used in 4-H. Extension has a history of teaching farmers and young people to discover new information for themselves. In fact, the earliest 4-H agents engaged farm children in testing new seed varieties in an attempt to show the farmers, who were reluctant to adopt new practices, the productivity of the new varieties. Perhaps unwittingly, the 4-H youngsters and their farmer parents were conducting controlled experiments. Research also fits well with 4-H's emphasis on experiential learning and skill building, and research skills can be viewed as part of a suite of skills important to 4-H, such as leadership and public speaking. Furthermore, conducting research can be an effective means for students to learn about science content (SRI International 2002).

A focus on youth research also allows extension to play a key role in science education reform in this country, which calls for less memorization of words and concepts and more original inquiry (or research) and critical thinking (National Research Council 1996). To quote from the *National Science Education Standards*, "Inquiry into authentic questions generated from student experiences is the central strategy for teaching science…. The school science program must extend beyond the walls of the school to include the resources of the community." Cooperative extension, with its strong community ties and connection to the university, is in a unique position to promote student inquiry.

In spite of these arguments for the involvement of cooperative extension in providing youth research experiences, such programs often are not a good fit with the interests of county extension educators and volunteers, who are more likely to focus on younger children. We have found a few exceptions, such as a 4-H educator who had science research experience, and worked with students in a school enrichment program to raise, release, and monitor the impact of beetles used in the biological control of purple loosestrife. For the most part, however, we have worked directly with teachers and students rather than through the 4-H system.

As our programs have evolved from engaging individual students in research, to developing nationally disseminated inquiry-based curricula, to engaging students in community investigations, we have tried to address several core questions. How can we balance the interests of scientists devoting time to mentor student researchers with the learning needs of the students? How can we provide quality experiences for a large number of students whose teachers may lack research experience themselves and thus find it difficult to facilitate student research? And how might student researchers become engaged in work that is meaningful to their community?

Evolution of Youth Research Programs. It was during our summer high-school student research program that we first addressed the issue of how to define appropriate roles for students and faculty so that both groups would benefit from the research experience. Whereas students may become more engaged when they have the opportunity to conduct the entire research process, including defining the research question, they also benefit from mentoring by experienced scientists and they may not have the ability to define a researchable question on their own. Faculty mentors benefit when students contribute to their research program, which often means they look to students for help in data collection. In our summer research program, we tried to strike a balance between faculty and student interests: the high-school students first collected data alongside graduate students and other scientists who served as mentors and then conducted a small research project addressing a question they defined but related to the overall lab research. The high-school students benefited from these well thought out research experiences, and the scientists generally felt that the time they spent mentoring was about equal to the contributions the students made to their research. Furthermore, the faculty benefited in ways that were not directly related to promoting their own research: They felt that they were "paying back" for similar research experiences they had had when younger; they were able to provide opportunities for their graduate students to mentor younger students; and mentoring younger students brought a more diverse group into their laboratory (the majority of our high-school students were minorities and several had significant disabilities).

The student program eventually grew to include high-school teachers, who not only conducted research in Cornell labs, but also worked with us to adapt their research so that it could be conducted in high-school classrooms. We placed the teachers in labs where the research was logistically simple, involved inexpensive equipment, and addressed issues of concern to the wider public including young people. One summer, for example, teachers worked in labs conducting composting research from the plant pathology, agricultural engineering, and food waste perspectives, and contributed to a teachers' guide designed to engage students in composting research.

Through our NSF-funded program, *Environmental Inquiry: Learning Science as Science Is Practiced,* we expanded these efforts to develop research curricula for high-school classrooms. *Environmental Inquiry* students first learn research protocols (e.g., bioassays, vegetation transects) and then define research projects as a class or in small groups utilizing the protocols they have learned. We feel this progression from mastering skills to conducting original research is consistent with the way a novice graduate student might learn how to conduct research.

In contrast to the on-campus student research program, which depended on substantive engagement of scientists and reached only the most motivated students, curriculum development efforts such as *Environmental Inquiry* may reach thousands of students with only one-time involvement of scientists to help teachers develop the materials. However, science teachers often have had limited or no research experiences themselves, and thus are reluctant to engage their students in research. Our *Cornell Environmental Inquiry Research Partnerships* program provides a middle ground between intensive, on-campus experiences and classroom research directed by teachers. Through this initiative,

Cornell graduate and undergraduate student fellows guide high-school students in research using *Environmental Inquiry* curricula as well as activities that the fellows develop. For example, one fellow introduced the students to various soil tests (e.g., pH, compaction), after which the students used the soils protocols to design and conduct independent research on the impact of earthworms on forest soils. High-school students in this project developed an appreciation of what can go wrong in field research and the problems inherent in interpreting results from a short-term field study. Perhaps more important, teachers who have had Cornell fellows in their classrooms reported that they learned from the fellows how to guide students in research. Prior to our efforts, the teachers had wanted to incorporate more inquiry into their classrooms, but felt they didn't have the skills to do so. The Cornell fellows also have benefited through improving their teaching skills and learning about pedagogy, curriculum development, and educational assessment.

Two of our Cornell teaching fellows developed a project through which high-school students survey insects feeding on phragmites, an invasive species in wetlands and roadside ditches. Knowing the distribution of phragmites insects is important to scientists at Cornell who are developing a biological control program for this species. In an attempt to broaden the involvement of students and the amount of information collected on these insects, graduate student Linda Tompkins and scientist Bernd Blossey developed a Web site through which high-school students can contribute data to the Cornell biological control research project. This project is similar to *Student-Scientist Partnerships* or *Citizen Science* programs, such as those developed by the Cornell Laboratory of Ornithology in which students and adult volunteers collect data about the distribution of bird species (e.g., Project FeederWatch, NestBox Network). Such programs usually originate when scientists have a need for data collection over a broad geographic region, but lack the resources to conduct the field research themselves and thus enlist trained volunteers, including young people, to collect the data. Although such projects may be educational for the participants, they also have been criticized for limiting participation to relatively mundane tasks. In common with other *Student-Scientist Partnerships* and *Citizen Science* programs, we are struggling with how to provide meaningful experiences for young people rather than just using them to collect data.

Through our *Explorations from an Aerial Perspective* program, we experimented with another model for engaging young people in research—one that emphasized community engagement. Through this program, students learned to interpret aerial photographs and topographic maps and then used these tools to investigate land use and environmental problems in their community. Each local program was developed around a question of interest to the educators and students. For example, in Far Rockaway, a run-down community in New York City, students used historic air photos to trace changes in their neighborhood. The community had once been a thriving beach resort with an amusement park and row upon row of cabanas lining the ocean. However, upon completion of the Long Island Expressway, New Yorkers headed to beaches outside the city, and the amusement park and cabanas were torn down to be replaced by vacant lots. City extension educators helped the students to apply what they learned about land use to benefit their community. They became part of a team that conducted a neighborhood conference to develop a plan for the vacant lots, some of which have since been converted to urban farms.

It was through a graduate student's critical analysis of Far Rockaway and similar local *Explorations from an Aerial Perspective* initiatives that I first become aware of the potential for engaging young people in Participatory Action Research (PAR). PAR attempts to break down the distinction between the investigators and those being investigated, by engaging scientists and lay people in the process of inquiry. The approach goes beyond research to encompass education as well as action directed toward social or organizational change (Brown 1985; Gaventa 1991). Because of its emphasis on meaningful engagement of community members and action, PAR has great potential for contributing to public scholarship. At the same time, a pure PAR approach is problematic within academia because it requires that community members be involved in all stages of the research, including defining the research questions. I will come back to PAR in the *Garden Mosaics* case study described below, in which we have incorporated some elements of the PAR approach.

Learning Communities

As we worked to develop ways to actively engage young people in research, we also began asking questions about how to engage educators as active learners and researchers. How might educators contribute to our understanding of outreach education and public scholarship? If they played a significant role in program development, would they develop important skills and would our programs be more likely to address their needs and thus be more effective?

The concept of learning communities was originally developed in the context of sustainable agriculture and natural resources management. Defined as "settings for information exchange and innovation among individuals with varying knowledge," learning communities draw on the expertise of both farmers and scientists to build our understanding of agriculture and resource management (Jordan et al. 2000; Millar and Curtis 1999). Farmers in an agricultural learning community experiment with ways to adapt new practices to the social and environmental conditions on their individual farms, and then share the results of their experiments with other farmers and scientists. The importance of both farmers' and scientists' expertise, along with the need to adapt practices to local environmental conditions and audiences, provide a strong rationale for creating collaborative learning communities in sustainable agriculture and management. Furthermore, such communities can have a positive effect on the adoption of new practices (Ison and Russell 1999; Roling and Wagemakers 1998;

Wuest et al. 1999) and may improve communication among researchers, extension agents, and community members (Gerber 1992). For example, in two different learning communities, one focused on invasive species and the other on maple syrup production, research questions that were of interest to both local and university partners developed out of our collaboration, and county extension agents expressed satisfaction with the local recognition they received as participants in a university-based research project.

We have tried to adapt such social learning concepts developed for farmers to our work with educators. Just as farmers in agricultural learning communities conduct on-farm research to determine best farming practices, county extension agents conduct local educational programs, each of which may be viewed as an informal research project whose goal is to determine best educational practices. Fundamental to creating learning communities in agriculture is the importance of farmer knowledge, in addition to the expertise of university and other scientists. In our outreach work, the value of local educators' knowledge in conducting education programs is self-evident, whereas the technical knowledge of university scientists also is important.

Thus, a third paradigm for our youth outreach work, learning communities, evolved out of our recognition of how educators can contribute toward program development. For example, in the *Explorations from an Aerial Perspective* program described above, we started without a standard curriculum. Rather we trained educators to use the remote sensing and mapping tools (e.g., airphoto interpretation), following which they adapted the tools to fit the needs of their particular audiences and settings. Many of the local initiatives educators developed were included in the program manual. Although, at the time, we were unfamiliar with the social learning literature (e.g., Roling and Wagemakers 1998), we had in essence used their model of collaborative learning communities, in which each educator acted as an innovator building local programs and we all learned from the results of their efforts.

Further development of the learning community paradigm would come later with our *Garden Mosaics* program and would involve educators not only in developing local programs, but also in evaluating and sharing program outcomes, thus adding to our understanding of educational practices. Through *Garden Mosaics*, we have combined the learning community and youth research paradigms.

Scholarship: Evaluating Models for Youth Research and Learning Communities

The discussion thus far has focused on how we tried to balance our interests with those of teachers, extension educators, and students—in short, on the *public* challenge of public scholarship. The other challenge relates to *scholarship* itself. How might we develop a research agenda that focuses on issues of public value, but is also intellectually challenging and satisfies the demands placed on a tenure-track faculty member? The many unanswered questions about the impacts of engaging young people in research and about participatory models of outreach, have become the focus of such a research program.

At Cornell, we have an active group of graduate students and faculty who are addressing research questions related to what motivates educators, youths, and faculty members to become involved in collaborative research and program development and what impact these experiences have on the participants. For example, a graduate student who served as the evaluator on the *Environmental Inquiry* program examined the role of teachers in curriculum development, addressing questions such as whether teachers who are creators (as opposed to simply users) of curricula differ in their implementation of the new materials. Other graduate students are asking questions like: What is the relationship of the student engagement in the inquiry process (i.e., defining their own question) to the quality of research data collected by students? To what degree can inquiry learning be incorporated into science classrooms? Does inquiry science learning lead to the development of citizenship skills? Thus, our programs are creating opportunities for graduate students to conduct research in collaboration with the education community, and they in turn are bringing scholarship to our extension programs.

Garden Mosaics

The name *Garden Mosaics* refers to two beautiful mosaics found in urban community gardens across North America. First are the gardeners, many of whom are immigrants from developing countries or African Americans with roots in rural southern states in the U.S. and thus represent a mosaic of cultures from around the world. Second are the mosaics of plantings that these gardeners create. Many community gardeners grow plants and use cultivation practices that originate from their unique cultural traditions, yet little is known about the diversity of plants and practices in urban gardens. In addition, these practices originated in places where access to commercial fertilizers and pesticides was limited, and thus gardeners often depended on more sustainable ways of adding nutrients (such as composting and intercropping), conserving water (raised beds, mounds and furrows), and controlling pests (use of marigolds to repel nematodes, use of soap solutions in place of commercial pesticides). Young people involved in *Garden Mosaics* use participatory research approaches to document planting practices and the garden's contributions to the social and cultural fabric of the community.[4]

Garden Mosaics is first and foremost a youth education program designed to engage students in conducting research within the context of their local communities. Through conducting research, we hope young people will learn skills that enable them to contribute to a democratic society. They learn how to develop research questions, how to investigate questions in a critical manner, and how to use their research results to define and conduct an action project that benefits their community. Furthermore, through working with elder gardeners, we hope that young people will develop positive relationships with community members and will learn to value the experience and knowledge of elders. Thus, young people are participating in the civic life of their community—seeing and learning from productive adults who create positive public spaces in their neighborhoods. Furthermore, the young people are learning about gardening science from the gardeners and from instructional materials developed by Cornell scientists and educators.

A secondary goal of *Garden Mosaics* is to create a database of ethnic and sustainable gardening practices and of amenities provided by urban gardens. In collaboration with the American Community Gardening Association, we have developed a Web-based community gardening inventory to which *Garden Mosaics* and other groups can contribute. The information collected by the participants can be used by community gardens and community greening organizations seeking to build a case for maintaining these green patches in cities and by social and agricultural scientists conducting research in urban settings *(www.gardenmosaics.org)*.

Garden Mosaics is also an adult education program, designed to address concerns with the top-down, technology-transfer approach of extension, and to build more participatory means of program development. It seeks to create a learning community of educators and university scientists that will further our understanding of how to engage youth as facilitators of participatory research. Through participating in this learning community, the educators develop research and teaching skills, and become regional and national leaders in youth gardening education and research.

Thus, *Garden Mosaics* was chosen as the focus of this chapter because it tackles head on some of the challenges inherent in public scholarship involving faculty members, community educators, young people, and community partners. It combines elements of participatory research, learning communities, and *Citizen Science*. Furthermore, it is a research project that seeks to answer questions like: Under what conditions are students able to conduct research with adult community members? Can students gather information about community gardening practices that is useful to community activists, local government, and researchers? How might we take the interests of young people, gardeners, and other community members into account in designing the research and any actions that result from the research? And how might we create an effective learning community of educators guiding students in research?

The Beginnings

I remember clearly how the idea for *Garden Mosaics* came about. My colleague Nancy Trautmann and I had just completed several years of work on composting education for high-school students. Through this effort, we had developed an interest in engaging students in scientific research and had gained experience working collaboratively with teachers and other educators. We were sitting in my office wondering what our next project should be, in particular how we might focus a new NSF education proposal. We felt composting was too narrow a subject. One of us suggested that we broaden our efforts to include gardening and sustainable agriculture. Because we were committed to working with minority audiences in urban settings, New York City seemed a logical place to start.

We had already visited a community garden in lower Manhattan. The garden was sandwiched between a school we were working with on the composting project and a building serving as a mosque for Bangladeshi immigrants. While visiting the garden, I was impressed by the "mosaic" of different cultures and different gardening practices. The students from the neighboring school, who were mostly African American, had designed a greenhouse that used heat generated by the composting of fruit and vegetable wastes from a local juice bar. They also had built a tiny pond with a stream that used solar power to recycle the water. The Bangladeshis were using raised beds to grow pigeon peas, amaranth, marigolds, and flowering coriander. In essence, they had created a grain-legume intercrop (pigeon peas-amaranth), with marigold to repel soil pests and a flowering plant to attract beneficial insects. Perhaps we could develop an educational program that focused on the sustainable practices of immigrants in community gardens?

Whereas a program teaching young people how to garden in urban settings would have been a possibility, I wanted to pursue my interest in engaging high-school students in scientific research. Thus, a second possibility would have been to have them conduct experiments in the garden, such as measuring the growth of plants under different soil conditions. Neither of these alternatives seemed to build on the uniqueness of urban community gardens, with their intriguing cultural and agricultural mosaics. How might we incorporate our interests in engaging students in authentic research with a program that built on the expertise of community gardeners and the scientific knowledge of Cornell faculty? How might we also take into account the interests of the students, community gardeners, and educators, who would not necessarily want to become involved in a research project, especially one designed by Cornell faculty members?

At the time, we decided to embark on a youth science education program in urban community gardens, I had never heard of participatory research or learning communities. But when I described our project to my colleague John Schelhas, he suggested PAR might provide a useful perspective. He also introduced me to the literature on indigenous knowledge. After reading about PAR and indigenous knowledge, I agreed that *Garden Mosaics* provided a unique opportunity to combine research on community gardening practices using the gardeners as the source of information, with youth education and community empowerment, all of which are fundamental to PAR.

Although I had already served as Principal Investigator (PI) on ten successful NSF education grants, funding for *Garden Mosaics* proved difficult. Whereas NSF is very much committed to serving urban youth, reviewers on panels come largely from a positivist research tradition, and may not be familiar with, or particularly supportive of, participatory research. On the other hand, the USDA Sustainable Agriculture Research and Education (SARE) program supports farmer participation in agricultural research, but does not emphasize youth or urban projects. After several unsuccessful attempts to fund *Garden Mosaics* through NSF and SARE, we finally obtained SARE funding in 1999. The results described below are based on the SARE *Garden Mosaics* program, but the discussion also draws from a larger NSF grant we received in 2001.

During the process of writing the different *Garden Mosaics* grants, numerous educators contributed their ideas about program development. My strongest partnership has been with Gretchen Ferenz and her staff in the New York City office of Cornell Cooperative Extension. Gretchen has served as co-PI on the SARE grant and on the NSF *Garden Mosaics* grant and thus has been intimately involved in program planning, identifying collaborators from different cities, and implementation. She worked with me to set overall direction for the project, which takes into account urban extension program priorities in addition to my interests in youth research, learning communities, environmental science, and sustainable agriculture. On the recent NSF *Garden Mosaics* proposal, Alan Berkowitz, head of education at the Institute of Ecosystem Studies in Millbrook, NY, also has contributed his expertise in K-12 science outreach, engaging various audiences in research, and sustainable agriculture. Currently Keith Tidball of Cornell is the primary intellectual and program partner and has initiated an international component for *Garden Mosaics* in South Africa and elsewhere.

Educator Workshops

Although we did not know of any PAR tools used in U.S. community garden settings, we felt they might be appropriate because of the many similarities between conducting research in developing countries and in American inner cities. Such similarities included potential differences in language, culture, and power between the researchers and community members. Furthermore, we felt that the hands-on techniques would be easy and enjoyable for young people to learn and to implement.

In January 2000, we conducted our first *Garden Mosaics* workshop for educators from six northeastern cities (Allentown, Baltimore, Buffalo, NYC, Philadelphia, and Rochester)[5]. The lead educators were primarily affiliated with cooperative extension, although in Rochester they were volunteers with a food security/ social action nonprofit organization, and in Baltimore they were from a community center. In all of the cities they formed partnerships with community centers or school programs. The lead organization in each city received funds to compensate for staff time and related expenses.

Although participants came away from the first workshop enthusiastic about the project and about working with each other, we were not far enough along in our thinking to give them the specific tools they needed to carry out the projects with students. In fact, at the time of the workshop, I really didn't have a good idea about specific PAR tools that the students could use. I naively assumed that if we introduced the philosophy and meaning of PAR, the educators would be able to figure out how to use these tools to gather the type of information we were seeking about community gardens. This turned out not to be the case. Lacking familiarity with specific PAR tools, the educators felt unable to design their own research projects.

Shortly after the workshop, I came across the excellent *Participatory Rural Appraisal* (PRA)[6] manual produced by the Catholic Relief Organization (Freudenberger 1999). PRA is one type of participatory research. Similar to PAR, it was designed for use in international development, in which traditional research approaches were seen as exploiting local communities and language and literacy barriers prevented the use of standard techniques. Although both PAR and PRA involve collecting information in order to take action to benefit a community or group of stakeholders, PAR is more radical in its focus on community empowerment and on community involvement in setting the research direction. In contrast, in PRA, the development workers or other outsiders determine the research agenda. For example, the PRA practitioners might already have funding from the World Bank to dig wells and they use PRA to obtain information and to work with community members to locate the wells so as to best meet local needs.

PRA methods that we used in *Garden Mosaics* included Venn diagrams of ecosystem (garden) inputs and outputs, historical timelines, seasonal calendars, and participatory mapping (Table 2). We also used quantitative methods, including pH and nutrient tests, to assess soils. In June 2000, we held a second *Garden Mosaics* workshop for educators to learn about the PRA tools and to try them out with gardeners.

Implementing *Garden Mosaics*

During the summer of 2000, teams of educators and volunteers from the six sites worked with a total of 85 young people and 26 adults to conduct the PRA activities at community and home gardens. Youthful participants ranged in age from 9 to 16 years; both the youths and the adults were predominantly African American and Hispanic. At each site, the programs differed significantly, as a result of educators adapting the PRA tools for their specific participants and settings.

At three of the six sites, Allentown, NYC, and Philadelphia, extension educators implemented the program as we had envisioned, i.e., young people carried out the PRA activities with older community gardeners. The young people in Allentown and NYC were participating in summer community center programs and the community centers became critical partners in carrying out *Garden Mosaics*. In Philadelphia, the young people were from a nearby school, but perhaps because of the lack of a structured

Table 2

PRA Activities from Freudenberger (1999) Used in **Garden Mosaics**

Activity	Description
Garden History	Youth ask gardeners to create a visual timeline documenting garden history.
Interview	Youth prepare and conduct interviews of gardeners, focusing on gardening practices.
Mapping	Youth ask gardeners to draw individual plots and entire garden, eliciting comments from gardeners about planting practices. Youth locate garden on larger map of their community.
Seasonal Calendar	Youth ask gardeners to draw a calendar showing plant phenology, garden practices, and events held in the garden (e.g., concerts, weddings) through the season.
Soil Measurements	Youth and gardeners conduct pH and other soil tests and collect soil samples for nutrient analysis. Youth interview gardeners about soil problems.
Venn Diagram	Youth ask gardeners to diagram important factors in the garden and resource flows (e.g., material, human) to and from the garden and broader community.
Action	Based on the results of their PRA research, youth work with gardeners to identify and take action to address needs/problems in the garden.

summer program, it proved more difficult for the *Garden Mosaics* educators to engage them. In Buffalo and Baltimore, the young people also were participants in community center summer programs, but instead of traveling to a community garden to conduct the PRA activities, they planted their own garden at the community center. They then interviewed older gardeners in the community and conducted the other activities apart from the elders in their own garden (i.e., they drew maps of the garden they had created without input from elders). In Rochester, the young people worked at existing school gardens and conducted some of the PRA activities with home gardeners. The youthful Rochester gardeners developed ongoing relationships with some of the elder gardeners, which turned out to be very rewarding for both parties. The program in three of the six cities was not carried out in the way we had envisioned, largely because of difficulties in getting participants to community gardens at times when the gardeners were available, and because many of the participants in the summer community center programs were too young to conduct the PRA activities with gardeners. Through this experience, we became aware of the need to develop several implementation models for *Garden Mosaics* (i.e., separate tracts for younger and older children, community, home, and school gardens) if we wanted to expand participation.

Youth Conducting Participatory Research

Through the work of my graduate student Rebekah Doyle, who spent the summer observing the activities and interviewing educators, youths, and gardeners in the six cities, and who organized a focus group of educators in the fall, we were able to learn from the local *Garden Mosaics* "experiments" about how to engage young people as facilitators of PRA (Table 3). We had expected that the hands-on, visual activities, such as mapping and diagramming, would more readily engage the young people and the gardeners than activities, such as interviewing, that draw heavily on verbal communication skills. Surprisingly, interviewing was the most successful activity both in terms of engaging the young people and the adults and for collecting information about gardening. It is possible that the participants felt more comfortable with an activity that was familiar to them. Whereas asking an adult gardener to draw a map or diagram can be awkward, interviewing was more like talking or teaching.

Table 3
PRA Activities as Adapted by Garden Mosaics Participants

Activity	*Implementation Methods*	*# Sites*
Garden History	HISTORY INTERVIEW. Youth interview gardeners and learn about history of garden.	4*
	TIMELINE. Based upon interview, youth visually depict history through timeline.	3
	SUPPLEMENTAL INFORMATION. Educators use supplemental information (e.g., newspaper articles, photographs) to present garden history.	3
	GARDENER NARRATIVE. Youth listen to gardeners' personal histories.	3
	TOTAL SITES CONDUCTING ACTIVITY	7
Interview	SEMI-STRUCTURED INTERVIEW. Youth pose questions (their own or assigned) to gardeners and record answers.	7
	BRAINSTORMING SESSION. Youth brainstorm their own questions with educator's guidance prior to conducting interview.	6
	PRACTICE INTERVIEW. Youth learn about and practice giving interviews before interviewing gardeners.	4
	SCRIPTED INTERVIEW. Educators provide youth with questions to ask during interview.	2
	TOTAL SITES CONDUCTING ACTIVITY	7
Mapping	OVERALL GARDEN MAP. Youth map the overall garden designating plots and other garden features.	5
	PLOT MAP. Youth map individual garden plots with or without assistance of gardener.	4
	COMMUNITY MAP. Youth map the garden in relation to the community.	2
	PARTICIPATORY MAPPING. Educators ask gardeners to map their plots as youth and educators ask questions about the plants being drawn.	2
	VERTICAL PROFILE. Youth create a vertical profile of the garden.	1
	TOTAL SITES CONDUCTING ACTIVITY	7
Seasonal Calendar	TIMELINE. Youth and gardeners visually depict the growth stages of certain plants using a timeline.	1
	CALENDAR. Youth create annual calendar and note timing of practices, based upon discussion with gardener.	1
	TOTAL SITES CONDUCTING ACTIVITY	2

(Table continued on next page.)

(Continued from previous page.)		
Soil	pH TESTING.	7
Measurements	NUTRIENT TESTING.	7
	DRAINAGE.	2
	TYPE and TEXTURE.	2
	TEMPERATURE.	1
	TOTAL SITES CONDUCTING ACTIVITY	7
Venn	DIAGRAM of INFLUENCES. Educators facilitate discussion with gardeners about influences on the garden and their impact. Based on gardeners' commentary, youth place shapes representing influence on circle representing garden and use arrows to portray direction of influence.	1
Diagram	DIAGRAM of RESOURCES. Youth facilitate discussion with gardeners about the relationship of the garden to the broader community. Youth and gardeners use different shapes to represent the garden and resources and arrows to show the flow of resources in and out of the garden.	1
	DIAGRAM on THREE LEVELS. Educator leads discussion about the garden and influence of surrounding environment (air pollution, etc.) on the garden. The group explores the relationship of the garden on the people within and around the garden and depicts the connections between the garden and the broader city.	1
	TOTAL SITES CONDUCTING ACTIVITY	3
Action	YOUTH ACTION. Youth help organize and give presentations to gardeners and community members at garden event.	3
	Youth present research to community at county fairs.	2
	TOTAL SITES CONDUCTING YOUTH ACTIONS	5
	EDUCATOR ACTION. Educator brainstorms problems/resource needs with gardeners and helps facilitate assistance.	1
	Educators organize dinner for participants and program partners.	1
	TOTAL SITES CONDUCTING EDUCATOR ACTIONS	2

* Several sites used multiple methods to approach an activity. Hence the column totals for each activity may exceed seven.

We were especially pleased that the students successfully facilitated the interviews without the intervention of educators and that the gardeners appreciated the young people showing interest in them. Some quotes from the educators give insight into how the interviews were conducted.

> I would say (to the young people), "Do you want me to go over to the gardener with you? Do you want me to do anything or just be here?" They'd say, "No, just be here," and they'd come back and I'd let them tell me how it went and read me the answers to their questions. The interviews went well, they liked that. *(Philadelphia educator)*

> Until (the young people) were before this person, I for one had no idea how they would just radiate … all of a sudden they were Barbara Walters…. *(Buffalo educator)*

> (The young people) found out as soon as they showed an interest and started asking him things, (the gardener) was willing to volunteer all kinds of information. *(Buffalo educator)*

Additionally, youth were able to develop their own interview questions beforehand and to formulate follow-up questions in response to gardeners' comments during the interview.

> (The young people) had brainstormed their own questions, but then they were able to take it to the next step, to formulate—okay he just answered this, so what does that mean—and then come up with a follow-up question. *(NYC educator)*

In several cases, the educators devised creative ways to engage the young people and the gardeners in the hands-on activities that were more difficult for youths to facilitate. For example, sensing that the gardeners felt awkward when asked to draw a map of their plots, the educator started drawing the map and asked the gardener to help. This approach readily engaged the gardener. In another example, an Allentown educator realized that a PRA activity called a "Venn Diagram" might be threatening or difficult for the children and the adults to understand, and renamed the activity the "Puzzle." She then had the children draw a Puzzle of what was important in the garden and the garden inputs and outputs to the community. Finally, the children facilitated the activity with the gardeners, who readily became engaged and drew a second Puzzle. The gardeners' Puzzles differed in many ways from those of the children, thus demonstrating how the garden meant different things to different participants (Figures 1 & 2). "The children just amazed me with taking it—after I showed them—and they built their own puzzles," the educator said. "They took the senior citizens through the exercise by themselves. I could have left the room."

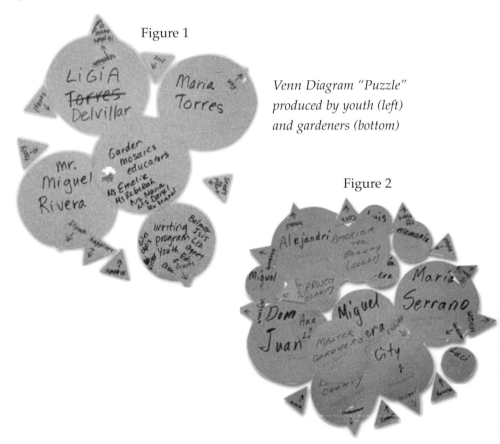

Figure 1

Figure 2

*Venn Diagram "Puzzle"
produced by youth (left)
and gardeners (bottom)*

At a number of sites, the community educators engaged the young people and the gardeners in organizing festivals and educational events at the end of the summer, thus addressing the action component of PRA. However, the PRA activities often took up so much time that there was little time left for action stemming from the research. In addition, we had not yet developed appropriate data forms and Internet reporting systems to enable the young people to contribute to a knowledge base about community gardens that would aid in building support for their protection from developers. As one NYC educator explained:

> The idea was to make the information available for public use also because New York City is in a big community garden crisis. The administration is trying to use that land for other purposes so it's extremely important to have documentation of the benefit of community gardens, where gardeners have been working, often for several years. Indirectly, this would be a tangible outcome—to show through the gardeners' and youth voices how important the community garden is to the community. It would show the cultural aspects as well— vegetables they prefer and practices that are sustainable for the environment (Franz et al. 2001).[7]

Motivating the youths and dealing with behavioral issues were a constant challenge for the educators. The youths wanted to know why they were collecting the data, and sometimes the research questions and activities did not seem relevant. They often preferred hands-on gardening with elder gardeners to conducting the PRA. Seeking ways to more fully engage the young people in conducting participatory research is a challenge we are addressing in the current program.

Gardeners as Participants

The gardeners were more than willing to participate in the interviews, although they often felt awkward about joining in the mapping and diagramming activities. They loved the opportunities to help the children and to talk about their passion for gardening. Some even formed long-term mentoring relationships with youths that have been rewarding to both parties. One NYC community educator put it like this:

> I think that [gardeners are] gaining the knowledge of knowing that there's others that are concerned about what they're doing besides themselves. And that there is people out here that's from maybe a different background, or even different city or borough or state that is looking at what they're doing.... They felt good when we was takin' pictures of them and asking them questions about what are they growing and how they can educate us on things that we don't know. That's a pride that you get from that. It's a difference.

Garden Mosaics *Lessons and Outcomes*

We initially thought a PAR approach and PRA tools would be applicable to the community-garden setting, which has many similarities to the international settings for which these approaches were originally developed. The PRA literature suggests that methods, such as mapping and diagramming, that involve only minimal verbal communication are most successful in international settings. However, the *Garden Mosaics* youths were not able to successfully facilitate the more hands-on activities with gardeners; in contrast both young people and adults became readily engaged in the interviews. The mapping and diagramming turned out to be most successful when used as teaching tools rather than as research tools. For example, diagramming inputs and outputs to the garden allowed the young people and the adults to view the garden from a new perspective, and in one instance resulted in their making plans to recycle organic wastes within the garden rather than rely on "external inputs." Another way in which *Garden Mosaics* differed from PAR was that the young people and the gardeners had almost no involvement in setting the research agenda, and only a few sites completed an action project.

In spite of some of our struggles with finding appropriate methods, the young people were able to gather some information on ethnic crops and planting practices. For example, the youths learned about several plants (e.g., papalo, cilantro, collards, and epazote) being grown by Mexican and other immigrants and by African Americans. They also learned about such planting practices as the use of mounds and furrows to conserve water, and the use of dishwater to deter insects.

The young people benefited from the program in a number of other ways as well. They developed positive relationships and learned from the gardeners, with whom they often shared common cultural and ethnic backgrounds. The young people also developed a sense of responsibility, as well as teamwork, academic, gardening, and research skills. Furthermore, they expressed an interest in and an appreciation for gardening and the role of gardens in their community and the broader environment, and they learned about plants and soils.

However, we are still struggling with the question of how to motivate youthful participants in *Garden Mosaics*. In fact, it seems that *Garden Mosaics* as originally conceived had all the right elements to attract educators (e.g., opportunities for networking with other educators and with university scientists, activism, sustainable agriculture, ethnic diversity, environment), but wasn't nearly so attractive to students. Part of the problem has been our target audience, many of whom have poor academic skills and behavioral problems. Young people in the program who already were highly motivated to learn, and who were in well-structured church, academic, or community-center programs, became very engaged in the activities. In fact, several *Garden Mosaics* participants gave a presentation at the American Community Gardening Association conference in summer 2002. I heard from several sources that this presentation was among the best at the conference. However, we don't want to focus on youths who already have many advantages—thus our efforts to redesign the program.

Garden Mosaics *Redesigned*

We think the key to motivating students lies both in framing the program around the activities that most engage them and in making the research activities relevant by embedding them within an action project for the community. Furthermore, some young-sters may be motivated by the opportunity to participate in a nationwide *Citizen Science* project, collecting data that will be of use to the community-gardening movement.

In the summer of 2002, we found that, in addition to interviewing, young people loved an activity that used aerial photographs, maps, and a neighborhood walk to learn about the community surrounding the garden. Thus, the restructured program includes three research activities that have successfully engaged students in the past, and the results of which will be useful to a larger community gardening and scientific community. First, to help develop a national registry of community gardens and the amenities they provide for the community, young people conduct a "garden hike"—essentially a mobile interview in which they interview gardeners and make observations while walking around the garden. To determine whether amenities provided by the garden are available elsewhere in the neighborhood, youth participants conduct a "neighborhood exploration" using a combination of information collected through maps and aerial photos, neighborhood residents, and a neighborhood walk. Finally, to develop a national database of ethnic and sustainable gardening practices, participants collect oral histories describing how gardeners deal with pests, soils, water, and limited space, and how the practices relate to the gardeners' cultural traditions.[8] The information they collect becomes part of a national database available to community garden stakeholders (e.g., the American Community Gardening Association), scientists, and people interested in learning about community gardens and ethnic gardening practices.

Equally important is the *Garden Mosaics* Action Project, which the students design in collaboration with the gardeners and from which they see immediate results. Through conducting the first three activities in which they become familiar with the garden, the community, and the gardeners, the students have a foundation upon which to define a local action project. Some examples of youth projects come from our 2002 Sacramento site, where youth participants created a landscape design for a new community garden and also developed a list of the English and Hmong names for the garden insects. Other local projects might include surveys of food accessibility and nutrition, experiments on watering, soils, and other management practices, and working with gardeners to define and undertake a garden beautification project (e.g., painting a mural on a wall bordering the garden).

Thus, in the redesigned program, data collection can be used to inform an action project. We feel this approach is not only more motivating for students, but also more closely reflects some of the PAR and PRA goals, which emphasize conducting research in order to take actions that benefit the community.

Learning Community

The first-year program was very successful in building a learning community of educators and university faculty. As one New York City educator said:

> We learn over and over again through our collaborative efforts with faculty and staff on the campus. I think we find that we very much value what each other has to bring to a program and each experience is different.... (Educators) learn from each other as well. We had a workshop in November of 2000 (following one year of project implementation) where we did sharing. A few youth and gardeners came to the workshop, as did the extension educators from all the six cities. That was very enlightening. We learned how things were done differently for different areas—what were the benefits, what were the obstacles. It's just wonderful sharing amongst each other because it helps to enhance our efforts if we're going

to replicate the same program. Often it is also very relevant toward applying what's been learned to another project (Franz et al. 2001).

Thus, the educators valued the collaborations with faculty, other educators, and community members. They also valued the opportunities for professional development and spoke about the project helping them learn to work as a team, reach out to urban audiences, develop partnerships with other organizations, and understand the complex nature of participatory programs. Furthermore, they appreciated the opportunity to expand their gardening skills, to facilitate participatory research, to work with youth, and to learn about ethnic planting practices. In short, the educators seemed to value the opportunities for learning and networking far above the financial or other benefits the program may have offered.

I found these outcomes very encouraging in terms of supporting our ideas about the importance of learning communities. We are building on these opportunities for incorporating significant professional development and empowerment opportunities into the current NSF-funded *Garden Mosaics* project. Rather than using a train-the-trainer approach, we are developing a national "leadership team" of gardening educators from 11 different cities across the U.S. The team members are playing a significant role in defining program direction and implementation and are starting to assume a leadership role for *Garden Mosaics* in their region. We hope that by building such a leadership team, we will not only be able to offer significant professional development opportunities to the educators, but will also create a program that better reflects the needs and interests of participating sites. Furthermore, we hope that the educators will become invested in the program and continue to provide national and regional leadership beyond the period of NSF funding. Finally, we anticipate learning from the educators' experiences with their local programs.

From my perspective as a faculty member, one of the most rewarding aspects of *Garden Mosaics* has been the opportunity to build long-term collaborations with community educators and graduate students focused on learning how to conduct a youth participatory research project in urban settings. At the first *Garden Mosaics* workshop, we knew that we wanted to use a participatory research approach, but had relatively little idea of specific tools and techniques. But by the end of the first year, we had accumulated a wealth of information about how to implement the research activities, much of it gained from the educators and from the graduate students who helped with the workshops and evaluation. We continue to learn from each other and to redesign the program. We have recently incorporated an international component.

Public Scholarship and Garden Mosaics

Garden Mosaics has been our most ambitious and challenging project, and the one through which we have most extensively explored the practice of public scholarship. How have we addressed the public challenges of building partnerships with community members that value the knowledge of and promote learning opportunities for all parties involved, with the ultimate goal of building citizenship skills among young people and other community participants? How have we addressed the second challenge of developing scholarship that is viewed as rigorous by our university colleagues?

Building Partnerships

Central to programs that attempt to embody the principles of public scholarship are issues related to who is initiating the programs and how the interests of all parties are taken into consideration. Greenwood and Levin (2000) claim that, because university faculty set research agendas, social sciences research nearly always focuses on questions that are not relevant to disenfranchised populations. They suggest that only through participatory research in which community members, particularly those who are poor and minorities, are engaged in all stages of a project from defining research questions through interpreting and communicating data, can research truly contribute to the needs of a democratic society. The deliberations of the public scholarship group that meets periodically at the Kettering Foundation in Dayton, Ohio, reflect a less radical view, emphasizing the shared role of community members and academics in defining the problem and controlling the research process.

Earlier, I described how the idea of *Garden Mosaics* came about through a conversation between a Cornell colleague and myself. Thus, this program was not developed in direct response to the demands of our audiences. However, perhaps because it was developed in large part by university faculty, it was able to address some important issues related to civic engagement. For example, it allowed the educators, many of whom were from cooperative extension, to branch out to new, urban minority audiences. Furthermore, because of its emphasis on engaging youth in research, *Garden Mosaics* addresses a key goal of the science education reform movement in the U.S. (National Research Council 1996; American Association for the Advancement of Science 1993). In short, as a faculty member who is somewhat isolated from the demands of local extension stakeholders and who has opportunities to interact with educators and scientists at a national level, I may be able to suggest innovative approaches that meet larger, nationally defined needs.

Furthermore, the fact that *Garden Mosaics* is funded by government agencies may limit our ability to engage educators at the initial stages. Whereas it was necessary to have local collaborators identified before submitting the SARE and NSF proposals, we were reluctant to ask county extension and other community educators to put a lot of upfront time into a proposal that had a high likelihood of not being funded. As a faculty member, I am expected to be entrepreneurial and to take funding risks. However, spending time on proposal development may not help county extension and other educators to succeed in their positions. Additionally, certain aspects of program direction for *Garden Mosaics* were determined by the priorities of the USDA and NSF funding agencies, which in the case of USDA focused on sustainable agriculture and for NSF focused on inquiry-based learning for underserved minority and rural audiences.

Finally, because we have had such significant involvement of educators in the program development stage and because we have conducted in-depth, formative evaluations at all stages of *Garden Mosaics*, I can feel reasonably confident that educators' interests are taken into account as we move forward with this program. In this sense, negotiations related to building partnerships are largely an iterative process, and what is learned from educators at one point in time is incorporated into setting priorities for future efforts.

Partnerships with Educators

In spite of the fact that educators had a limited role in developing the initial program direction, they have been intensively involved in *Garden Mosaics* and plan to continue their involvement in the future. I think much of this interest and commitment stems from the opportunities the program provides for professional development, including a chance to build a national professional network and to connect with university faculty. The program also provides novel ways for nonformal educators, who often have more success with younger children, to substantively engage teenagers. Perhaps most important, the philosophy behind *Garden Mosaics* seems to strike a cord with garden educators. They are excited about a program in which children interact with elders, that addresses multiculturalism in a positive way, and that includes opportunities for young people to learn science through conducting research relevant to their community.

The educators have contributed in many ways to *Garden Mosaics* and have, in turn, learned from their involvement. They have contributed their understanding of working with community members of all ages. They have learned about new ideas and skills that they could incorporate into their programs, and in several cities, they have also learned how to work with new partners, such as urban community-center educators. Although initially they may not have realized how much we were counting on them to teach each other and the project directors about how to implement a pilot participatory research program with young people, they have became very much engaged in experimenting with implementation strategies and in sharing the results of their local efforts. In short, we reached a number of goals of learning communities—educators learned new skills and developed innovative ways to adapt the program to meet local needs, and educators and faculty formed new networks and learned from each other about program implementation. These goals are consistent with public scholarship, which emphasizes the importance of learning on the part of all participants.

Youth Partnerships with Elders

In spite of the fact that many young people did not engage in some of the PRA activities, their interactions with the gardeners were overwhelmingly positive. I find this a very exciting part of the program, especially in light of a concern that minority youths may have limited opportunities to view members of their own community sharing valuable knowledge—many programs bring in experts only from the outside. Another positive outcome was that young people in some instances talked to gardeners from ethnic backgrounds different than their own. For example, in a Philadelphia garden, the African-American kids literally crossed the fence separating the Korean and African-American gardeners and talked to the Koreans about their gardening practices. We hope that *Garden Mosaics* eventually might serve as a model for programs in which young people learn from community elders.

Partnerships with Community Gardeners

In a project related to *Garden Mosaics,* one of my graduate students tried to engage Latino community gardeners in PAR, including defining the research questions and helping her to conduct the research. Her attempts proved unsuccessful, in part because the gardeners had other interests and time constraints. However, once she stopped trying to get them involved as participatory researchers, the gardeners loved the opportunity to share their knowledge and opinions. Similarly, gardeners became very much engaged in interacting with the young *Garden Mosaics* participants in teaching and mentoring roles, though they did not participate as full partners in the research, as envisioned by PAR.

It is unlikely that community members will become deeply interested in setting program direction, except under certain conditions. These might include cases in which their livelihood is dependent on the research outcomes or when they have developed long-term trusting relationships with the researchers. Although initially, the gardeners were most willing to participate as respondents in interviews, some are now beginning to understand the nature of the research and to readily share their knowledge at workshops with new educators. Thus, as we continue to develop ongoing relationships with the community gardeners, and they see what *Garden Mosaics* offers young people and the benefits of collecting information that can be used to help support the gardens, they are becoming more engaged in the research and related outreach efforts. Perhaps eventually they will also contribute to setting research and education agendas.

Partnerships with Nonprofit Organizations

Whereas most *Citizen Science* projects focus on collecting data for scientists, in *Garden Mosaics* we are also working with the American Community Gardening Association to collect information of value to their stakeholders. The information participants gather about the role community gardens play in the community should be useful in building a case for support of these gardens. Through the educators at each site, we have also formed partnerships with numerous local nonprofit community organizations.

Partnerships with University Faculty and Students

Unlike most *Citizen Science* projects, *Garden Mosaics* was not initially defined by the need for scientists to collect data over a broad region. Rather, we are investigating ways to develop more "bottom-up" types of collaborations with scientists. Our strategy is to start with our educational objectives and then look for opportunities for graduate students and faculty to become involved in ways that are mutually beneficial—e.g., through using the data collected by youth, using the community gardening sites for their own research and involving young people and gardeners in their research, or forming research partnerships with the nonprofit groups with whom we have developed collaborations. Our strategy is paying off. Recently, faculty in the Cornell Department of Crop and Soil Sciences have started to develop *Citizen Science* research protocols for *Garden Mosaics* participants and are beginning to provide technical assistance. At our North Carolina site, the educators have connected with scientists at their university who plan to develop a research field station at the community garden and involve young people in their research.

Scientists who are not interested in engaging in the *Garden Mosaics* research but who have a commitment to working with young people on a volunteer basis also have helped out. My experience in *Garden Mosaics* and similar projects is that faculty are generally willing to participate as long as we take care to limit their involvement to areas in which they are most needed and they can easily act on their commitment to enhancing science education (i.e., we handle all logistics and they participate as research mentors, speakers, or technical reviewers).

Cornell students are also active in *Garden Mosaics*, both as researchers and as summer interns at our urban sites. Working with community educators in urban settings has presented some unique learning opportunities for the Cornell students, and through the students' involvement, *Garden Mosaics* has contributed to the teaching and research functions of the university.

Building Democracy

Garden Mosaics and our other youth programs address issues related to science education, immigrants and minorities, and the environment, which have been identified as important to building democracy at the national level. Underlying our focus on engaging young people in research is a belief that understanding the nature of scientific research and scientific communities is fundamental to a citizen's ability to contribute to a modern democracy. Without an understanding that disagreement and uncertainty are part of science, the public easily can be misled by anti-science rhetoric. We have seen this with the global warming issue, where politicians exploit a debate among scientists about the extent of global warming to support anti-environmental policies, often making disparaging remarks about researchers who try to explain the scientific uncertainty surrounding this issue. It is through actually conducting research and engaging in discussions about the nature of scientific research that students and educators can develop an understanding that science is not always able to come up with a definitive answer to a question, that answers change as we accumulate more knowledge, but that at any one point in time scientists work together to develop answers based on the best existing evidence (Fortun and Bernstein 1998). Thus, through engaging young people in research, we hope to better prepare them to function in a democracy.

Another way in which our programs contribute to building democracy is through engaging underserved urban minority and poor rural children. We have some evidence that *Garden Mosaics* helps young people develop communication, teamwork, and academic skills that will allow them to constructively participate in democratic society. Educators in Buffalo initially were dismayed at the attitudes of teenaged participants and in fact, several educators dropped out because of the teens' behavior. However, the educators who stayed with the program noted dramatic improvement. They started with teens who would not look them in the eye. By the end of the program, these same teens were enthusiastically giving presentations about their *Garden Mosaics* projects at the county fair. They had developed communication skills and self-confidence and now considered themselves gardening "experts."

Furthermore, through the engagement in participatory program development, educators gain skills that can be applied to other issues they face in a democratic society. For example, the *Garden Mosaics* educators had opportunities to critically evaluate educational programs, access university resources, network with other educators, and facilitate the youth research and learning. Finally, our outreach programs contribute to a democratic society by focusing on issues that are important to scientists, but that also have significant impacts on young people and their communities—such as urban and sustainable agriculture.

Scholarship

Garden Mosaics represents three aspects of university scholarship that I feel are important: creative and critical thinking, recognition by our peers of the quality of our work, and mentoring university students in research and teaching. In *Garden Mosaics*, creative thinking was involved when we took ideas that had been developed for a particular setting and applied them in an entirely new context. The idea of learning communities originated through work with farmers, but we applied it to our work with extension and other community educators. Similarly, PRA had been developed for use in international development and we adapted it for work with youths in multicultural urban settings. Critical thinking has been inherent in formulating our initial ideas into proposals and to our evaluations and ongoing redefinition of the program. Our creative and critical thinking has been recognized by our USDA and NSF funding agencies and by the acceptance of our publications in refereed journals. Finally, numerous undergraduate interns have developed teaching skills and graduate students have developed research skills through *Garden Mosaics*.

Furthermore, several aspects of our work with *Garden Mosaics* may provide insights about new models for conducting public scholarship. Our work combining the local knowledge of gardeners, with the scientific expertise of university scientists, may contribute to our thinking about how to combine local and expert knowledge as a form of scholarship. Similarly, what we have learned about participatory research may shed light on conducting scholarship within a civic context.

Final Reflections

Each year that I attend meetings of my professional society, the Ecological Society of America, an increasing number of graduate students speak to me about their discomfort with a future career devoted exclusively to research and about their interest in exploring how they might combine education and science. My response is that careers that combine education and science can be challenging yet extremely rewarding, both intellectually and personally.

Intellectually, I have grown through my collaborations with faculty and students, and with participants on the Kettering Public Scholarship project. These individuals have taught me about new approaches to extension, education, and conducting research. For example, I have learned that technology transfer is not the only model for conducting outreach and about the alternatives developed by extension faculty in international settings. I also have learned about my colleagues' research on the nature of science and the challenges of communicating such concepts to students and other lay audiences. Becoming familiar with qualitative research methods and PAR has widened my perspective on how we create new knowledge and think critically, in ways that do not necessarily follow the scientific method that I learned as a doctoral student in forest ecology. Furthermore, through working with scientists in a myriad of environmental disciplines, I have gained insight into research focusing on topics ranging from biological control to environmental toxicology and sustainable agriculture.

Personally, I particularly value my collaborations with extension and community educators and graduate students. Through the educators, I am constantly exposed to new perspectives on science and research and to the challenges and rewards of working with partners in inner city, as well as rural communities. For example, I have seen one of our extension community educators from the Bronx who has worked with us for nine years on the *Explorations from an Aerial Perspective* and *Garden Mosaics* programs, but who has no formal academic training, develop an understanding of much of the science entailed in these programs. I also have seen her uncanny ability to facilitate PRA activities with students and educators, bridging language and cultural differences and resistance on the part of gardeners, to create participatory maps of garden plots and facilitate learning about gardening practices. Additionally, I derive great satisfaction from watching my U.S. and international graduate students gain research and critical thinking skills and from learning about their cultures and perspectives.

Recently, I was speaking to the graduate teaching fellows in our NSF *Cornell Environmental Inquiry Research Partnerships* program about recruiting fellows for next year. One fellow mentioned a graduate student who was interested in applying but had been told by his advisor that participation in the program would not help him get a post-doc or teaching position. Had the advisor known these were NSF teaching fellowships, would he have offered the same advice to his graduate student? Had he known that our fellows have published about their teaching in refereed journals, would he have felt that the fellowship would not enhance his students' chances of getting a teaching position at a university? NSF money and journal publications are academic status symbols—they offer extension programs the same credibility as research. More significantly, I hope they represent our approach to a university youth outreach program, i.e., the fact that we consider these programs as scholarly enterprises, involving creative, integrative, and critical thinking.

At the same time I expect faculty to recognize the value of our outreach scholarship, it is important for extension faculty to value the work of our research colleagues and not expect everyone to be a public scholar. I very much admire my faculty colleagues who conduct basic research and who are superb classroom instructors. These colleagues also are acting on their commitment to the environment and to students and on their love of discovering new information. When engaged in appropriate ways that recognize the unique contributions they can make as well as the pressures they are under, they can be invaluable contributors to university outreach. At the same time, I can offer unique experiences for their students who wish to engage in outreach as an activity and as an area of scholarship.

Engaging in public scholarship is extremely rewarding for individuals such as myself, who are committed to environmental and social causes, yet at the same time thrive on being challenged intellectually in an academic environment. In my case, it also has provided an outlet for a competitive and entrepreneurial nature. Whereas I love integrating ideas to write proposals, in the past I have derived perhaps equal satisfaction from actually being granted an NSF or other competitive award. As I look toward the future, I ask myself whether the ego rewards of getting large grants or publishing journal articles might cloud my vision of the most important societal needs I might address.

As a result of my work with the Kettering Public Scholarship project and *Garden Mosaics*, I am redefining my definition of a university youth outreach program. Rather than defining outreach primarily as drawing from university research, as I did when I first came to Cornell, I also am seeing outreach as contributing significantly to the teaching and research missions of the university.

For example, graduate student fellows in our *Cornell Environmental Inquiry Research Partnerships* felt they learned more about teaching through our program than through working as university teaching assistants; in fact, this program may contribute more to the training of graduate students than to the education of high-school students. Similarly, through providing opportunities for graduate students to evaluate outreach projects, we contribute to the university research mission. I feel that outreach programs that cross the research and teaching functions are more sustainable in the long-term and also contribute to the ideal of a university as a place where knowledge is created and shared.

From a faculty point of view, perhaps public scholarship comes down to valuing and recognizing, and creatively integrating. It involves valuing the knowledge and experience of community partners and faculty colleagues, as well as recognizing their aspirations and the pressures they face. At the same time, it entails recognizing my own research interests and commitment to certain types of outreach and scholarship. Integrating ideas and applying them to new situations is a creative part of all types of scholarship. Public scholarship entails not only creatively integrating ideas, but also integrating the experience, knowledge, and needs of our partners and colleagues.

End Notes

[1] A number of educator manuals and journal articles have come out of the work described in this chapter. Rather than interrupt the text with citations from our work, I have listed these under a separate section at the end entitled "Cornell Publications." The work of other authors cited in the text are listed under "References."

[2] Throughout this chapter, *we* or *our* refers to my close colleagues at Cornell who have been involved in youth environmental sciences outreach. Primary among them has been Nancy Trautmann of the Cornell Center for the Environment, who has initiated many of our youth environmental sciences outreach programs and has been an invaluable contributor to all of them. Other Cornell colleagues who have played a major role in these efforts include Leanne Avery, William Carlsen, and Christine Cunningham, formerly of the Cornell Department of Education, who have been engaged in the efforts with high

schools and curriculum development; Eugenia Barnaba of the Cornell Institute for Resource Information Systems, who was the primary player in our land use outreach efforts; and Rebekah Doyle and Keith Tidball of Cornell along with Gretchen Ferenz of Cornell Cooperative Extension-NYC, who worked on *Garden Mosaics* and other projects.

[3] A number of programs mentioned in this chapter have been funded by the National Science Foundation (NSF), including the high-school student and teacher research programs, Explorations from an Aerial Perspective (ESI 9155290), Environmental Inquiry (ESI-9618142), Cornell Environmental Inquiry Research Partnerships (DUE 9979516), and *Garden Mosaics* (ESI 0125582). NSF guidelines emphasize engaging students in inquiry, including original research. Additional support has come from the U.S. Department of Agriculture (USDA) and from the College of Agriculture and Life Sciences at Cornell University.

[4] In addition to providing fresh food, community gardens serve as open space and as sites for socializing with neighbors, cultural and educational events, relaxation, and recreation. In crowded, urban neighborhoods, these amenities may not be otherwise available.

[5] Because the funding was from Northeast SARE, we were limited to cities in the Northeast. The current NSF program includes 11 cities from throughout the U.S., including Allentown, Baltimore, Boston, Chicago, Greensboro, NC, Ithaca, NY, Minneapolis, NYC, Philadelphia, Sacramento, and San Antonio.

[6] Note the differences between the two acronyms: *PAR* for Participatory Action Research and *PRA* for Participatory Rural Appraisal. I will be using both acronyms in the rest of this chapter.

[7] In addition to quotes from the evaluation conducted by Rebekah Doyle, some statements were recorded by Cornell students in Scott Peters' course, who conducted a series of educator profiles of NYC Cooperative Extension educators engaged in *Garden Mosaics.*

[8] We are also piloting the program with rural youths who will use the gardener profile activity to build a database of traditional gardening practices of elders (*e.g.*, heritage varieties, seed saving). Many of these practices are being lost, hence the importance of collecting this information.

References

American Association for the Advancement of Science (AAAS). 1993. *Benchmarks for Science Literacy.* New York, NY: Oxford University Press.

Brown, L. D. 1985. People-centered Development and Participatory Research. *Harvard Educational Review* 55(1): 69-75.

Fortun, M. and H. J. Bernstein. 1998. *Muddling Through: Pursuing Science and Truths in the Twenty-first Century.* Washington, DC: Counterpoint.

Franz, N., H. Gregoire, and T. V. Savelyeva. 2001. *Garden Mosaics*: A Model Community/Campus Partnership. Unpublished paper. Ithaca, NY: Cornell University.

Freudenberger, K. S. 1999. *Rapid Rural Appraisal (RRA) and Participatory Rural Appraisal (PRA): A Manual for CRS Field Workers and Partners.* Baltimore, MD: Catholic Relief Services.

Gaventa, J. 1991. "Toward a Knowledge Democracy: Viewpoints on Participatory Research in North America." In *Action and Knowledge: Breaking the Monopoly with Participatory Action Research*, ed. O. Fals-Borda and M. A. Rahman. New York, NY: Apex Press.

Gerber, J. M. 1992. Farmer Participation in Research: A Model for Adaptive Research and Education. *American Journal of Alternative Agriculture* 7(3): 118-121.

Greenwood, D. J. and M. Leven. 2000. "Reconstructing the Relationships between Universities and Society through Action Research." In *Handbook of Qualitative Research,* ed. N. K. Denzin and Y. S. Lincoln, 85-106. Thousand Oaks, CA: Sage Publications.

Ison, R. L. and D. Russell. 1999. *Agricultural Extension and Rural Development: Breaking out of Traditions.* Cambridge, UK: Cambridge University Press.

Jordan, N., et al. 2000. "Learning Groups Developing Collaborative Learning Methods for Diversified, Site-Specific Weed Management: A Case Study from Minnesota, USA." In *Cow up a Tree: Knowing and Learning for Change in Agriculture,* ed. M. Cerf et al., 85-95. Paris, France: INRA.

Millar, J. and A. Curtis. 1999. Challenging the Boundaries of Local and Scientific Knowledge in Australia: Opportunities for Social Learning in Managing Temperate Upland Pastures. *Agriculture and Human Values* 16:389-399.

National Research Council (NRC). 1996. *National Science Education Standards.* Washington, DC: National Academy Press.

Roling, N. and A. Wagemakers. 1998. *Facilitating Sustainable Agriculture: Participatory Learning and Adaptive Management in Times of Environmental Uncertainty.* New York, NY: Cambridge University Press.

SRI International. 2002. GLOBE Evaluation. http://www.globe.gov/fsl/html/templ.cgi? evaluation&lang=en&nav=1

Wuest, S. B., et al. 1999. Development of More Effective Conservation Farming Systems through Participatory On-farm Research. *American Journal of Alternative Agriculture* 14(3): 98-102.

Bibliography

Cornell Publications:

Educator Manuals and Web Sites

Barnaba, E. M. et al. 2000. *Explorations from an Aerial Perspective Educator's Manual.* Ithaca, NY: Cornell Media Services.

Bonhotal, J. F. and M. E. Krasny. 1990. *Composting: Wastes to Resources.* Ithaca, NY: Cornell University, Cornell Cooperative Extension.

Carlsen, W. S. et al. 2004. *Watershed Dynamics.* Arlington, VA: National Science Teachers Association.

Edelstein, K. E., N. M. Trautmann, and M. E. Krasny. 1999. *Watershed Monitoring Handbook for Educators.* Ithaca, NY: Cornell Media Services.

Hawkes, J. E. et al. 1988. *Water Worlds.* Ithaca, NY: Cornell Media Services.

Krasny, M. E. 1991. *Trees: Dead or Alive.* Ithaca, NY: Cornell Media Services.

———. 1991. *Wildlife in Today's Landscapes.* Ithaca, NY: Cornell Media Services.

Krasny, M. E. and G. Neal. 1992. *Insects All around Us*. Ithaca, NY: Cornell Media Services.

Krasny, M. E., C. Berger, and A. Welman. 2001. *Long Term Ecological Research Educator's and Student's Manual*. Ithaca, NY: Department of Natural Resources. http://www.dnr.cornell.edu/ext/LTER/lter.asp.

Krasny, M. E., et al. 2002. *Invasion Ecology*. Arlington, VA: National Science Teachers Association.

Krasny, M. E., N. Najarian, and K. Tidball. 2004. *Garden Mosaics* Web site. http://www.gardenmosaics.org.

Krasny, M. E., P. Newton, and L. Tompkins. 2004. *The Value of a Garden*. Washington, DC: American Institute of Biological Sciences. http://www.actionbioscience.org/biodiversity/rinker2.html#educatorresources.

Krasny, M. E., R. Doyle, K. Tidball, and *Garden Mosaics* Leadership Team. 2004. *Garden Mosaics Program Manual*. Ithaca, NY: Cornell University.

Matthews, B. E. and M. E. Krasny. 1989. *Sportfishing and Aquatic Resources Education Program Members' Manual*. Ithaca, NY: Cornell Department of Natural Resources.

Moran, E. C. and M. E. Krasny. 1989. *Water Wise: Lessons in Water Resources*. Ithaca, NY: Cornell Media Services.

Schneider, R., M. E. Krasny, and S. Morreale. 2001. *Hands-on Herpetology: Exploring Ecology and Conservation*. Arlington, VA: National Science Teachers Association.

Silverman, B. G. and M. E. Krasny. 1989. *Bluebirds in New York*. Ithaca, NY: Cornell Department of Natural Resources.

Smallidge, P. J. et al. 2002. Cornell Sugar Maple Web site. http://maple.dnr.cornell.edu.

Trautmann, N. M. and M. E. Krasny. 1998. *Composting in the Classroom*. Dubuque, IA: Kendall Hunt.

———. 2001. *Assessing Toxic Risk*. Arlington, VA: National Science Teachers Association.

———. 2001. Environmental Inquiry Web site. http://ei.cornell.edu.

————. 2003. *Decay and Renewal.* Arlington, VA: National Science Teachers Association.

Journal Articles and Book Chapters

Bartel, A. S., M. E. Krasny, and E. Z. Harrison. 2003. Beyond the Binary: Approaches to Integrating University Outreach with Research and Teaching. *Journal of Higher Education Outreach and Engagement* 8(2): 89-104.

Brown, S. C. et al. 2003. Implementing a 4-H Aquatic Resources Education Program in New York City through Collaborations. *Journal of Extension* 41(2). http://www.joe.org/joe/2003april/iw2.shtml.

DePriest, T. and M. E. Krasny. 2004. Engaging County Educators in Science Education Reform: The New York 4-H Environmental Inquiry Program. *Journal of Extension* 42(2). http://www.joe.org/joe/2004april/rb4.shtml.

Doyle, R. and M. E. Krasny. 2003. Participatory Rural Appraisal as an Approach to Environmental Education in Urban Community Gardens. *Environmental Education Research* 9(1): 91-115.

Gift, N. and M. E. Krasny. 2003. The Great Fossil Fiasco: Teaching about Peer Review. *American Biology Teacher* 65(3): 270-278.

Gurwick, N. P. and M. E. Krasny. 2001. Enhancing Student Understanding of Environmental Research. *American Biology Teacher* 63(4): 236-241.

Kennedy, A. M. and M. E. Krasny. 2005. *Garden Mosaics*: Connecting Science to Community. *Science Teacher* (March).

Koupal, K. and M. E. Krasny. 2003. Effect of a Short-Term Camp Program on Youth Knowledge, Awareness, and Attitudes. *Journal of Extension* 41(1). http://www.joe.org/joe/2003february/rb6.shtml.

Krasny, M. E. 1999. Reflections on Nine Years of Conducting High School Research Programs. *Journal of Natural Resources and Life Sciences Education* 28:1-7.

————. 2005. University K-12 Science Outreach Programs: How Can We Reach a Broad Audience? *BioScience.*

Krasny, M. E. and R. Bonney. 2005. "Environmental Education through Citizen Science and Participatory Action Research: The Cornell Laboratory of Ornithology and *Garden Mosaics* Examples." In *Environmental Education or Advocacy: Perspectives of Ecology and Education in Environmental Education*, ed. M. Mappin and E. A. Johnson, 292-293. Cambridge, UK: Cambridge University Press.

Krasny, M. E. and R. Doyle. 2002. Participatory Approaches to Extension in a Multi-generational, Urban Community Gardening Program. *Journal of Extension* 40(5) http://www.joe.org/joe/2002october/a3.shtml.

Krasny, M. E. and T. C. Marchell. 1993. Expanding the Science Pipeline: The Cornell Natural Resources Experience. *Journal of Forestry* 91:34-38.

Krasny, M. E. et al. 2001. Impacts of Collaborative Research with Extension Agents and Growers: The Sugar Maple Example. *Journal of Forestry* 99:26-32.

Krasny, M. E. and S. K. Lee. 2002. Social Learning as an Approach to Environmental Education: Lessons from a Program Focusing on Non-indigenous, Invasive Species. *Environmental Education Research* 8(2): 101-119.

Mordock, K. and M. E. Krasny. 2001. Participatory Action Research: A Theoretical and Practical Framework for Environmental Education. *Journal of Environmental Education* 32(3): 15-20.

Saldivar-Tanaka, L. and M. E. Krasny. 2004. The Role of NYC Latino Community Gardens in Community Development, Open Space, and Civic Agriculture. *Agriculture and Human Values* 21:399-412.

Schusler, T. M. and M. E. Krasny. (forthcoming) "Youth Participation in Local Environmental Action: Developing Political and Scientific Literacy." In *Critical International Perspectives on Participation in Environmental and Health Education*, ed. B. Jensen and A. Reid. Copenhagen, Denmark: University Press, Danish University of Education.

Trautmann, N. M. et al. 2000. Integrated Inquiry. *Science Teacher* 67:52-55.

Chapter Ten:
Public Scholarship

An Administrator's View

by Victor Bloomfield

I n this chapter I want to reflect on public scholarship from the point of view of a university administrator who has to see this initiative in a broad context and as just one of many competitors for institutional attention and resources. While caution and reserve are required, I nonetheless begin with a clear declaration: I believe that public scholarship and enhanced civic engagement are important for universities—at the core of what we should do. We must work more effectively and closely with our various publics, and we must do a better job of showing how what we do is in the public interest.

I have spent my entire academic career in major public research universities: I received a B.S. from the University of California, Berkeley, a Ph.D. from the University of Wisconsin, Madison, and took a postdoctoral position at the University of California, San Diego, I have held faculty positions at the University of Illinois, Urbana-Champaign and at the University of Minnesota, Twin Cities. Thus I have grown up imbued with the notion that public research universities are among the most important and contributory institutions in our society. They pro-vide high-quality but relatively inexpensive teaching to a broad range of talented students, they produce much of the research and scholarship on which our modern civilization depends, and they translate this teaching and research into direct service to society. Given these essential contributions, it has been puzzling and painful to recognize the steady decline in support for public research universities over the past 20 years. I believe this can be largely attributed to increasing disregard—on the parts of both the university and society—for the real meanings of civic engagement and public scholarship.

I currently serve as vice provost for research and interim dean of the graduate school at the University of Minnesota. I have also maintained active teaching and research activities as a professor in the Department of Biochemistry, Molecular Biology, and Biophysics. This mixture of responsibilities, while demanding, ensures that I keep uppermost in mind the *raison d'etre* of a university—to discover, communicate, and apply knowledge, rather than focus on administrative issues for their own sake. At the same time, my area of research and teaching—molecular biophysics, specifically the polymer physics of DNA—is hardly the sort of stuff that immediately leaps to mind in thinking of civically engaged scholarship. So I have been forced to confront some defining questions that I think are critically important to the proper understanding of public scholarship.

First and foremost, I believe that essentially all research and scholarship carried out at modern research universities is deserving of recognition as public scholarship. Lack of understanding of this point, by both the public and the universities, is at the root of declining support for public research universities.

Public scholarship falls into two main categories that I call "universal" and "local." The distinction between them is important for how universities do their business and for how they are perceived and supported by society. While the value systems of major research universities tend to favor research and scholarship of universal applicability, this book focuses on public scholarship in a specific local context.

My personal involvement with civic engagement and local public scholarship has been on several fronts. My wife Elsa Shapiro, a pediatric neuropsychologist in the Medical School at the University of Minnesota, has been engaged for several years in research on two related research projects in the Phillips neighborhood in Minneapolis, a lower class, ethnic part of the city. One project, the Phillips Lead Poisoning Prevention Project, deals with the incidence and cognitive effects of lead poisoning and its prevention through community education efforts. The other is called DREAMS (Developmental Research on Early Attention and Memory Skills). While my wife has many other research interests, one of her junior colleagues, Cathy Jordan, has devoted her entire career to this effort and is very much concerned that the painstakingly slow process of building trust in the community to enable proper community-based research will affect her professional advancement. Numerous conversations with her have helped me understand practical issues surrounding public scholarship.

On another front, I was invited to serve as chair of the public-scholarship committee of the University of Minnesota's Civic Engagement Task Force, a role I initially rejected because I did not see the connection between my academic experience and the usual definition of civic engagement. I agreed to take on the responsibility only on the condition that my perspective on public scholarship—that virtually everything we do in the modern university falls under that rubric—was acceptable to the chair of the task force, Professor Edward Fogelman. I have since participated in numerous meetings, conferences, and informal discussions, each of which has enlightened me further about the import and ramifications of public scholarship. I am now co-chair of the outcomes and assessment committee in the revised task force structure, now called the Council on Public Engagement.

The specific impetus for this chapter came from participation in the conference on Public Scholarship in the Food System from which this book emerges, a conference organized by Scott Peters of Cornell University and sponsored by the Kettering Foundation of Dayton, Ohio. I was impressed by the deep thought, purposeful energy, and dedication of the conference participants. But I became convinced of the need for a wider university perspective—one that explored the broader importance of public scholarship to the university mission and to public support of universities and that examined some of the complex relationships between public scholarship and traditional academic priorities.

Public Scholarship: Universal and Local

Universal public scholarship is work that benefits humanity, but without a specific local context in mind; the human genome project is a good example. There is little doubt that this project will lead to biomedical insights that will benefit people all over the world, but the specific benefits to people in Minnesota, for example, will be diffused, long-term, and hard to identify. Local public scholarship might involve using the results of the human genome project to identify a gene in the members of a Minnesota family who suffer from a genetic disease.

Local public scholarship has three typical manifestations within universities: (1) traditional agricultural- and continuing education/extension-based work, (2) research on social science and public-policy issues, such as housing, transportation, criminology, or the rural-urban interface, and (3) scholarship that is characterized by reciprocal engagement between the researcher and the community. The latter is featured in the other chapters in this book and is viewed by those who practice it as a vehicle for improving the science and methodology of research in and with communities.

Of course, the distinctions between these two broad categories are not always neat. A new AIDS drug (universal), for example, might need adaptation to local conditions and attitudes before it can become an effective treatment. Conversely, understanding the factors influencing exposure of children to lead poisoning in the Phillips Neighborhood (local) will very likely have broad applications in many other communities.

In my view, both universal and local public scholarship are worthy of the name, but only local public scholarship is commonly recognized as such. We must bolster the understanding of what should be considered public scholarship, and promote agreement by university faculty, staff, and administrators that public scholarship as broadly conceived is a major piece of what major research universities should be doing.

An essential aspect of any scholarship is that it must be recorded and made available for use by subsequent generations—be they other scholars or nonacademic users. Scholarship is not limited to just doing research and gathering data; it involves writing up those data and ideas, subjecting them to rigorous scrutiny, and publishing the results for others to critically assess and use. Subjecting these writings to judgment in the promotion and tenure process is also part of the process. However, an interesting and important issue in peer review of public scholarship is "who are the peers?" Are they just the traditional peer group of academic specialists, or should members of the affected publics—perhaps less expert in the scholarly details but more knowledgeable about the relevance of the research questions and the impact of the answers—also be included as peer reviewers?

Universal Public Scholarship

The public served by a modern public research university is no longer just a local public. Federal granting agencies hope that the research they sponsor will help people throughout the country and the world. There was a rancorous dispute between French and American scientists about who had discovered the HIV virus, but the more important point is that progress in understanding AIDS and other diseases benefits all sufferers around the world; this is truly public scholarship.

Even in the world of agricultural research, the traditional focus of land-grant universities, the focus is changing from local to universal. There is a shift from commodity crops to genetically engineered, high-value-added products. This introduces considerable uncertainty in a global economy with depressed commodity prices and a populace wary of the environmental and health effects of genetically modified organisms. It means, for example, that a lot of the research has moved from the plant breeder and extension agent from the local agricultural college who spend much of their time working directly with local farmers to develop better strains of soybeans for local climate and soil conditions, to plant genome sequencing projects involving international networks of collaborators (including molecular biologists and computer scientists) and to large agrichemical corporations that are exploring not just the genetic basis of disease and pesticide resistance but the potential of soybeans as "nutraceuticals." Both in the private sector and in universities, much more attention is being paid to intellectual property and patenting issues. As a result, the perception that agricultural research serves a public good is diminished.

A modern land-grant university, of course, does much more than agricultural research or research related to rural populations. The faculty and students at these institutions conduct research in molecular biology, condensed matter physics, feminist studies, international relations, management information science, housing policy, and educational psychology, to name just a few currently important areas. This research is supported largely by federal agencies such as the National Institutes of Health (NIH), the National Science Foundation (NSF), the Department of Energy (DOE), the National Endowment for the Arts (NEA), and the Department of Defense (DOD). Much more than half of the external research funding for a modern land-grant university these days comes from these agencies, and relatively little from the U.S. Department of Agriculture (USDA) and state appropriations targeting agricultural commodities.

Note that these agencies are all funded by public money and that they are expected by the taxpayers and the legislators who appropriated the funds to do useful things for the public. Public funds are invested in the hope that diseases will be cured, new magnetic materials invented, cultural insights developed, international conflicts understood, more efficient methods of commerce devised, ways to build affordable housing conceived, and better ways to cope with the diverse educational needs of our children explored. These research projects all constitute public scholarship, but tend not to be recognized as such, chiefly for three reasons:

1. They touch the lives of the public only indirectly after passing through many stages of development, refinement, and (often) commercialization.

2. Their roots are geographically dispersed, depending on interlocking developments from researchers around the world, rather than being focused at the local state university.

3. Faculty themselves, bound up in the specialized arcana of their research, often forget the broader public purpose that motivates and supports their work.

Despite (or perhaps because of) these reasons, I think it is crucial to emphasize the importance of universal, generalizable scholarship to the public—that is, scholarship that is undertaken in the public interest. This, I think, is what higher education and research institutions have traditionally tried to do, in part because scholars are motivated to do good through their research, but perhaps in greater part because research is largely paid for by public funds and therefore more or less represents the areas (such as health and biomedical research) that the public feels are important.

Local Public Scholarship

Local public scholarship, the type emphasized in this book, is involved with particular communities or groups of people. It is important to recognize that there are many publics and that they don't all have the same interests. Many of the researchers who are part of the public scholarship movement tend to be liberals, to want to help poor and oppressed people, and to want to empower others to take better charge of their lives.

They concentrate attention on the working class, recent immigrants, and the poor.

On the other hand, the most commonly thought of purveyors of local public scholarship in land-grant universities—the agricultural experiment stations and extension services—traditionally have served farmers, who are not necessarily poor and are generally not oppressed (although their dependence on banks, international commodity marketing companies, and worldwide factors totally out of their control, may lead many of them to feel oppressed these days). The aim of a traditional extension service is to give them practical advice, but not to liberate and empower them politically.

There are some groups who would like to have help from universities—entrepreneurs who would like engineering or business management help, for example, or mid-career engineers or teachers who would like some continuing education courses—but who may be suspicious of politically liberal activity. There are patient-advocacy groups, coming to the university for help with incurable diseases, such as AIDS, autism, cancer, or Alzheimer's disease, and at the same time joining with others across the country in pressing the NIH to fund more research to quickly find better treatments. There are many interest groups in our society, and each has a reasonable claim to being a "public" worthy of attention by researchers.

Scholarship, too, has multiple and complex meanings. To some in the public scholarship movement, I think, it's the activity of being out among the public, working with people in collaborative research and teaching, in programs formulated by spending time with them discussing their issues and trying to improve their lives—since the publics of interest have usually been needful and disempowered in some way.

An important question is the extent to which the affected publics should be involved in setting the research agenda. Ordinary citizens are sometimes skeptical of academic questions and answers, which may strike them as trivial or confirming the obvious; they may not recognize the need to carefully define questions and methodologies. The Phillips community is always asking, "Why does this research matter to me? Why should I help you by participating in it?" They want to help set the research agenda, to ask questions that they feel will help them rather than promote the academic careers of the university researchers. While populist critiques of science and scholarship can go too far, they are sometimes valid, and it never hurts researchers to be forced to explain why what they're doing could truly be valuable both to scholarship and to society.

If economically deprived, poorly educated inner-city people can play a valuable role in formulating research questions and helping to carry out studies, how about better educated, more middle-class publics? Farmers, such as those who participated in the food system studies presented in this book, already function in many ways as amateur scientists and economists themselves. Many are college educated, computer savvy, and very familiar with the causes and effects in their environment. While they may not have formal scientific knowledge or be particularly interested in engaging in academic research, it appears that they could be enlisted as valuable collaborators.

While urban and suburban issues are gradually replacing the dominant rural emphasis as populations shift, we must not lose sight of the fact that urban/suburban issues are tightly coupled in such areas as food, recreation, transportation, and immigration. As Boyer (1990) has written:

> We are impressed by the service potential of doctorate universities, especially those located in large cities. For years, there has been talk of building a network of "urban grant" institutions, modeled after the land grant tradition. We sup-port such a movement and urge these institutions to apply their resources creatively to problems of the city—to health care, education, municipal government, and the like. What we are suggesting is that many doctoral institutions have not

just a national, but more important perhaps, a regional mission to fulfill, too, and faculty should be rewarded for participating in these more local endeavors.

Public Scholarship for Public Support of Universities

Mark Yudof, former president of the University of Minnesota, is deeply concerned about declining support for public universities. He writes:

> More than a century ago, state governments and public research universities developed an extraordinary compact. In return for financial support from taxpayers, universities agreed to keep tuition low and provide access for students from a broad range of economic backgrounds, train graduate and professional students, promote arts and culture, help solve problems in the community, and perform groundbreaking research. Yet over the past 25 years, that agreement has withered, leaving public research universities in a purgatory of insufficient resources and declining competitiveness (Yudof 2002).

Yudof notes that this decline in state support afflicts nearly all public research universities, and has been a consistent trend over the past 25 years. He attributes the decline mainly to demographic changes, to the decrease in the proportion of families with children, and to an increasingly aging population that is more interested in "health care and public safety than higher education."

I believe that there is another important reason that public research universities are in trouble, both financially and in lost public esteem. We've lost the connection with our publics, who have other priorities—such as care of the aging and corrections—and who no longer understand or trust that the things we do in teaching or research are relevant to their concerns. I am, of course, most familiar with the situation at the University of

Minnesota but I suspect that similar considerations apply to most similar institutions.

At the University of Minnesota, part of this decrease in support is due to inattention to high-quality teaching and student service in the 1970s and 1980s. Although there has been substantial recovery in these areas in the past few years, the perception that the university is the place where the state's good students go and have an experience that shapes the rest of their lives, is only slowly being restored.

More troubling is the lack of understanding that the research we do is relevant to people's lives. When a larger fraction of the population lived on farms or worked in mining or forestry, and the research of the university was concentrated on agriculture or natural resource utilization, the connection could be seen directly. University of Minnesota research developed the taconite industry, led to greatly improved yields and hardiness of soybeans, oats, and other crops, and treated diseases of turkey and swine. Departments of agricultural chemistry, plant science and animal science, agricultural experiment stations, and extension services played direct roles in the lives of many citizens. The medical school educated the state's doctors and dramatically cured the previously incurable by pioneering open-heart surgery and kidney transplants.

Even in the case of agricultural research—the most traditional of public scholarship—and its application through outreach and extension services, not all the outcomes are good. Some farmers in southeast Minnesota feel that the University of Minnesota's advice about soy-corn cropping has created poor landscape health and unsustainable agricultural practices. As a result, they have stopped listening to our experts. Perhaps these poor outcomes and the mistrust they generated could have been averted if there had been a closer two-way partnership between the farmers and university researchers during this work. Some would contend that it is problematic to take agricultural research as a paradigm of public scholarship, since a strong case can be made that its public value has been compromised substantially by negative environmental, social, and public-health impacts.

Currently, our connection with the rural part of the state is weaker, since there are so few people involved in agriculture or forestry or mining, and production agriculture is no longer a reliable moneymaker. The good taconite story is well behind us, and the taconite mines and steel refineries of northern Minnesota are closing. Increasing competition and the cost strictures of the new health-care system have made it difficult for the medical school to be the pioneering leader it used to be. As a consequence, the direct impacts of the University of Minnesota on the economy of the state seem to have diminished.

In fact, by training thousands of students in modern technology, in computing, in communications and design technology, in law and business and the arts, we provide the basis for many jobs and a good share of the state's economy. But the connection is less direct, the experience is more diffused, and the students are perhaps less conscious of what we provide. The same can be said for employers, whose companies and work forces are much more mobile and global than they used to be. The University of Minnesota, and all public research universities, need to do a much better job of making clear how their research, and the educational activities that accompany that research, are crucial to the fabric and function of modern society.

The public should not value the university solely for its role in creating jobs and developing the economy. People sometimes talk of the sciences as abstract and dehumanizing and, too often these days, justify the contributions of research universities purely in terms of economic development. These attitudes, mistaken though they are, point out that in the view of many people both outside and inside the university, the liberal arts and humanities are irrelevant. At the very least, spokespersons for the arts and humanities need to make a more convincing case for their relevance, for the way their presence in the university affects the basic concepts and attitudes of society. As Ellison (2002) writes:

The defining feature of engaged cultural work is a determination to do it all, to undertake complicated projects that join diverse partners, combine the arts and humanities, link teaching with research, bring several generations together, yield new products and relationships, take seriously the past and the future. The driving philosophy is one of both/and, both mind and soul, both local and universal.

Finally, as Harry Boyte, co-director of the Center for Democracy and Citizenship at the university, has observed:

> Public scholarship (and the whole civic engagement enterprise) has real potential to address the erosion of the public world, [to counteract] the rise of consumer/market ways of thinking as the definition of everything. The university has enormous potential to take leadership here.

The challenge to us in universities is to find appropriate ways to connect our scholarship—and our lives as citizens—with the people in the communities we serve and in which we live.

Issues within Universities

Even if one agrees that local public scholarship is important both for universities and for the public, it raises difficult issues of implementation. Faculty worry that they are being asked to add even more work to their busy lives. Or they complain that they are already doing work that serves the public (universal public scholarship); why can't that be recognized so that they're left alone to do their valuable work? Young faculty striving for tenure might wish to direct their research and teaching toward local public scholarship, but feel that doing it properly takes extra time and that such activities are not given much weight in their department's tenure decisions. Communities tend to see a university as a single entity, and previous unhappy experience with an insensitive or exploitative researcher may poison the waters for subsequent scholars who have greater sensitivity or better motives. Balancing the academic freedom of faculty to do the research they wish (within the boundaries set by human-subjects protection), with the possibility that they may damage the prospects of those who follow, is a tricky business.

Despite these difficulties, the promise of public scholarship for universities is great. Not only does it accord with the mission of higher education, benefit the public, and bring greater public support to universities, it can bring internal rewards to universities themselves. Since important public problems are rarely posed or solved within the confines of a single academic discipline, public scholarship can help to build fruitful connections between researchers and teachers from different disciplines. And public scholarship, with its emphasis on connecting the university's research and teaching mission with society at large, can provide additional motivation for the lifelong and distributed learning efforts in which most universities are now engaged.

More Work for Faculty

The mantra of public research universities is "teaching, research, and outreach (or service)." Although we do, in fact, work hard and effectively at all three, most faculty concentrate their efforts on research and teaching. I've argued that much of the research and teaching that faculty do has a strong public service component, and there are departments whose faculty have an explicit outreach mission. Nonetheless, most faculty probably feel that service and outreach is a relatively small part of their responsibility, and that their career advancement both professionally and institutionally depends mainly on their research, secondarily on their teaching, and very little on service.

If more public scholarship and civic engagement is expected, some faculty members fear that it will either add to an already heavy workload, or detract from time available for more valued research and teaching. Given current attitudes and evaluation criteria of professional peers, faculty colleagues, and university administrators, these concerns are grounded in reality. As Paul Sabin (2002) has written about the particular situation of young, untenured faculty, "in the current academic system, assistant professors have to keep quiet and seek tenure before they may safely take on a significant public role." Public scholarship will have to become more recognized and valued by all participants in the academic process, if faculty members are to judge that their own self-interest lies in that direction.

Why Isn't Current Faculty Work Being Recognized?

Much of the quality of life that we enjoy in the modern world is due to research, scholarship, and creative activity coming from universities. Much, if not most, of the work that faculty members do can plausibly be classified as public scholarship in that it directly or indirectly affects the public, is funded by public agencies or foundations whose missions are to create value for society, and is motivated by a desire to help society.

Think of basic and clinical biomedical research funded by NIH or the American Cancer Society; plays, musical performances, and lectures put on by universities and attended by large public audiences; research, consulting, and K-12 partnerships with schools by university psychologists and educators; examination and celebration of the cultural heritage of various ethnic groups by university scholars and students; service of university economists to state and federal government agencies; and research in colleges of engineering and biological science leading to new industries, economic development, and jobs. Public research universities are more deeply involved in the fabric of society than ever before. Why isn't this better recognized and appreciated, either by the public or by the university faculty, students, and staff themselves?

Part of the answer may be the general social trend toward valuing individual recognition and success over broader public purposes. Another part may be the increasing specialization of scholarly work, which makes it difficult to see the bigger picture. I would argue that there are two more explanations: more intermediate stages between research and final outcome, and increasing universality of research and scholarship.

When land-grant universities were formed, and until a few decades ago, most university research was essentially local. This is most obvious in the agricultural area, which performed a much larger fraction of university research than it does now. For example, faculty crop-breeding experts worked directly with state farmers and extension agents to develop varieties that were most productive in local climate, soil, and pest conditions. Although this work persists, farmers get increasing amounts of their advice (and seed stock) from large agribusiness companies. And new faculty hires in agricultural departments are likely to be working on gene sequencing and genome modification projects rather than on conventional plant and animal breeding. The end result of their work will still get to the farm, but the path will be much less direct, perhaps involving patents, licensing to an agribusiness company, review by the FDA, etc. This trend to less direct contact between faculty researcher and farmer client results in less appreciation of the work of university-based agricultural researchers by farmers, politicians, and the general public in rural areas of the state.

Not only is there a more convoluted path between modern agricultural research and its farmer beneficiaries, but the beneficiaries themselves are more widespread and diffused. This is because modern molecular genetics-based research has universal impact. Sequencing the genome of wheat will have implications for improvement of wheat varieties not just in the upper Great Plains, but all over the world where wheat is grown. The researchers who do this sequencing will be recognized primarily by their professional plant genomics peers, rather than by the farmers who grow the wheat. Their research will be funded increasingly by the NSF rather than by appropriations from agricultural experiment stations and state governments.

This growing universality is echoed across the disciplines, with the consequence that the prime audiences for the research are professional peers and federal funding agencies, rather than local populations. The paradox is that the research is likely to be more powerful and more effective in reaching desired goals, but less appreciated by those it is designed to ultimately help. As University of Minnesota professor Nick Jordan points out, the question is "whether the trend towards universality merely makes public value harder for the public to discern, or actually reduces public value"; my own answer is strongly on the side of the former.

Continuous Long-Term Involvement

As noted at the beginning of this chapter, my wife Elsa Shapiro, a professor of pediatric neuropsychology, and Cathy Jordan, one of her junior faculty colleagues, have been working along with several other University of Minnesota faculty members for a number of years on projects in the inner-city Phillips neighborhood in Minneapolis. A major lesson of the Phillips projects is that in order to be most effective researchers must make long-term, personal commitments to working with a community. Month after month, Cathy and Elsa go to community meetings, partly to talk about research, but also to socialize, to share experiences about new babies, to be politically and personally involved. This expenditure of time and personal attention is rewarding for at least some of the University of Minnesota faculty, but it is the sort of thing that the average faculty member would probably have trouble committing to. And yet, it seems persuasive that only by this means can one do high-quality community-based research—learning the right questions to ask; obtaining reliable data; training community informants and technicians who can elicit better responses from their neighbors; persuading parents and their children to show up for testing and interviews and to make some commitments in their difficult and disordered lives to their own health and to research designed to improve the health of their neighborhood.

Working in this way involves an expansion of the tools and mechanisms of scholarship, and a rethinking of the relations between "researchers" and "subjects." To do effective research involving people in communities, requires time, patience, continued long-term involvement, and respect—not just respect for the people as moral beings, but as thinking beings who know things that can help one to do better research. If they feel trust and cooperation, they will offer fuller and more truthful answers. They will be more willing to recruit their family, friends, and neighbors to the study. They will be more likely to stick with a long-term study. They may be able to suggest different or additional questions that the researcher hadn't initially thought of. They may be able to partner with the investigator, providing technical help and perhaps being more effective than a university faculty member in dealing with the personalities and ethnicities in the community. In other words, scholarship can be expanded and made more effective if there is respectful reciprocal engagement between scholars and community partners and if they work together to design and carry out the research.

Issues for Young Faculty

The general difficulties for all faculty members in doing public scholarship that breaks the bounds of traditional scholarly norms are amplified for young faculty without tenure (Sabin 2002). Part of the difficulty is that public scholarship often takes longer. Extra time must be taken to win community trust, establish personal ties, carry out research while working with the community to explain why a given research design is appropriate (and perhaps to change it in response to community suggestions), share the results with the community before submitting it for peer review, and maintain relationships in the community. This extra time is added to the hectic period of starting an academic career with its manifold responsibilities, and often starting a family as well. Burnout is the likely result.

However, as Nick Jordan notes:

> I tend to think that it is too early to conclude that doing public scholarship (in the reciprocal engagement sense) always involves qualitatively more ramp-up time than other forms of scholarship. For example, innovations like the U's regional partnerships for sustainable development can serve as interfaces between publics and faculty, so that public scholarship would not require building relationships from scratch. And of course entering other forms of scholarship also requires ramp-up time. Young faculty reduce this by building on grad school and postdoc research programs. Perhaps engaged public scholarship could be built from a similar base?

Furthermore, public scholarship often deals—as it should—with important and sensitive public issues. These may have a scope that transcends a single academic discipline, making it difficult to apply normal disciplinary standards of scholarship. The high emotional and political charge sometimes carried by these issues may make it more difficult to maintain the objectivity expected of academic research, and to convince academic peers that rigor and critical stance are being upheld. If those peers are senior faculty who will make tenure judgments and who hold a more traditional view of scholarship, untenured assistant professors devoted to public scholarship may feel their career is in extra jeopardy. If the research draws public attention and is mentioned in the local or national news media, feelings of jealousy or fear of controversy among traditional faculty or administrators may compound the problem when the time for tenure decisions comes around.

My own view, based on no systematic investigation but on conversations with several senior faculty, department heads, and higher-level administrators, is that these fears may be overblown.

Many of these academic leaders recognize the need for stronger connections between universities and the publics they serve and will be supportive of faculty efforts to move in that direction. Of course, they expect that standards of academic quality and productivity will be maintained, but they understand and accept that these may be satisfied in a variety of ways.

A Scholarly Approach

Academia values new ideas, and writing about those ideas. As new approaches are formulated, scholarly writing may properly focus more on methodology than on new results. This gives faculty members who are devising new ways of doing public scholarship, both an opportunity and a responsibility to submit their ideas to the scrutiny of their academic peers. Even if research results from extensive community efforts are slow in coming, professional articles about how to do public scholarship properly are necessary and valuable. This should assuage concerns of young faculty who worry that public scholarship will damage their scholarly productivity. It shouldn't, if they write about how to do public scholarship. Such writing should have three audiences: researchers in their discipline who need to be enlightened about new approaches to scholarship; public scholars in other disciplines, with whom comparative approaches can be exchanged; and researchers who might not see the connection between their field and public scholarship or who could use some help developing methods of engaged scholarship.

The breadth of interdisciplinary discussion about public scholarship depends on how it is defined. But there are obvious areas of activity—among them, agriculture and the food system, community medicine, urban youth, affordable housing, and transportation. Each of these has its own publics, history, and current issues. I think that much could be gained by bringing these groups of researchers together, both face-to-face and through journals and books, to share experiences and ideas.

Exchanging ideas about public scholarship should extend into teaching as well as research. The traditional approaches to the academic disciplines tend to emphasize depth, rigor, and highly critical thinking. These should certainly continue to be indispensable, but much discussion and training of students is needed if these standards are to be applied to research problems in which the additional demands and advantages of public scholarship are prominent. Young faculty, who may be developing these methodological ideas as they develop their research, could provide valuable service to their departments, graduate programs, and academic disciplines by incorporating these ideas into the pedagogy of their discipline.

We also need informal discussion, in departments and professional societies, about these new approaches. As Sabin (2002) writes:

> Departments also need to foster more internal dialogue about the relationship between scholarship and public service so that young academics can pursue both responsibly. Core assumptions about the nature of academic scholarship and teaching and how they relate to the world beyond the university need to be aired and discussed. Just by talking candidly and openly about the issue, individual faculty members can support their students and younger colleagues in their efforts to integrate those different aspects of their professional lives.

Poisoning the Well

Universities must cope with difficult criticism, both internal and external, when an insensitive investigator conducts community-based research in a way that antagonizes the community. When other researchers who may have much more sensitivity come along, they are denied permission, or treated badly, because of what the first researcher has done. In effect, all university personnel are identified with the university; if one researcher does badly, it is assumed that all subsequent university researchers will do likewise.

This is not so different from the way the public at large looks at us when there is some other misbehavior by an individual associated with the university—scandalous behavior by a coach or a misuse of research funds by a faculty member. In all of us, there is the tendency to generalize unfairly: we call it prejudice. But when a vulnerable community is treated badly, they have special justification for feeling abused.

The university can claim that it is a neutral party in all of this. If mistakes were made that were not actual malfeasance, then it's just the fault of an inept researcher and not the responsibility of the university. Is that an adequate stance? I think not.

What can be done? The most obvious thing is to try to educate faculty and research assistants how to conduct research in communities, before they go out and do it. There are numerous departmental courses in survey research, many of them excellent. Institutional review boards (IRBs) that oversee human-subjects research also address the problem, and perhaps they're preventing the worst abuses; but an informed consent form needs to be drafted and administered very carefully. The fact seems to be that while the letter of the law is usually followed, a not insignificant number of research projects fail to deal adequately with more intangible human concerns. Human-subjects research, including research in communities, should not only do no harm but should, to the extent possible, benefit the research subjects.

More generally, much potentially valuable community-based research is not survey research, and working effectively with people in communities is not just a matter of getting informed consent. It starts with the process of making a connection with a community and runs deeply through every stage of the process. A university is not just a place to do research, but also a place in which to learn how to do research properly. If new paradigms for the effective conduct of community-based research and public scholarship are needed, universities should develop and teach them. This is a proper aspect of creative scholarship, just as worthy of academic recognition as any other kind of teaching and research activity.

Academic Freedom Issues

What, if anything, should a university do if the maladroit research of one group is poisoning the well for those who may later wish to work in the same community? This question raises significant academic freedom issues. To what extent is it feasible, or desirable, to interfere with the work of a faculty member on the grounds that it is likely to be damaging both to the community and to those who come after?

At least a partial answer is that we don't have unfettered freedom now to do whatever we want in research, if it involves hazardous conditions for human subjects. We insist that all faculty investigators take a short course called Responsible Conduct of Research, which among other things, addresses ethical considerations. If the research involves human subjects, we require the investigator to attend an additional lecture series on that topic. Further, we require all human-subject research proposals to be examined and approved by the IRB.

Beyond such educational and monitoring functions, it is hard to see what further restrictions could or should be placed on community-based research. To prohibit research that has passed the standard tests would indeed violate academic freedom, and we must recognize that nontraditional and unpopular approaches to research are often how progress is made.

What we should do, I think, is improve our institutional training and monitoring mechanisms and confront these difficult issues by using the insights we have gained as we discuss civic engagement and public scholarship more broadly and deeply. Perhaps we should expand our training mechanisms in community-based research, Or perhaps we should include citizen input from the subject community as part of the IRB process. We must make faculty and students more aware that it's to their benefit to do community-based research more sensitively. They'll get much better cooperation from the community and better research results that way.

Building Connections in Universities

Civic engagement activities in the university have the attractive side effect of bringing together faculty and staff who might not otherwise know of each others' existence. For example, participating in the Phillips projects were several pediatric neuropsychologists from the medical school, a scholar specializing in residential technology from the College of Human Ecology, an extension faculty member, an epidemiologist, and a pediatrician. As Boyer (1990) has noted, "Integrative work, by its very definition, cuts across the disciplines. And in the application of knowledge, the complex social and economic and political problems of our time increasingly require a team approach."

This grouping of people in the Phillips projects would have been very unlikely without the nucleating activity of working in a community; and it has led to continued collaborations and friendships. Each such interdisciplinary project can lead to a positive change in the university. The faculty members working on one project learn that there's another group working on something quite different but philosophically aligned. Then somebody gets the idea for a conference to discuss the general issues, and soon there's a whole new energy around the place. It remains to be seen whether this energy will lead to new scholarly productivity—books and journal articles, new journals, and foundation grants for example. Some of this is already happening, as we can see from the very food-system conference sponsored by the Kettering Foundation, from which at least a book will issue, and perhaps a new online journal.

Collaboration among faculty and students from different specialties is not new to universities. Indeed it is at the root of most of the new interdisciplinary areas that are so prominent in modern scholarship. However, the nucleating potential of specialists from different areas working together in a local community or on a local issue seems especially great.

Lifelong Learning

The trend to lifelong learning could help to combat the increasing separation between universities and society. The idea that education is complete after four years of college is defunct. Universities, government, and the public all seem to accept that jobs will change rapidly throughout life, along with the knowledge needed to carry them out. The new knowledge is increasingly sophisticated, and the sort of thing that it would be appropriate for universities to provide. But neither our financial base for providing it, nor a conception of proper faculty work-load, is currently in place. The desired kind of lifelong learning is often expensive, specialized, and hard to deliver to working audiences, especially if it's coupled with distance education with complex and costly computerized delivery mechanisms. And research faculty, who want to discharge their teaching obligations as rapidly and efficiently as possible, are generally not anxious to rearrange their schedules to offer weekend or evening courses to smallish groups of older students. (Business schools seem to be successful in persuading their faculty to teach this audience, largely because it's a relatively well-off audience that can afford high enough tuition to make the deal attractive to faculty members.) Nonetheless, once courses are developed, and faculty teaching loads are rearranged, lifelong learning and distance education could be a useful way of reconnecting with influential adults who are both citizens and learners. As Nick Jordan points out, "This is an attractive idea, that settings for engaged public scholarship can also be settings for ongoing learning by people who address complex situations in their work."

The Broader Scholarly System

A move to a greater recognition of the importance and value of public scholarship will not occur without support from all parts of the scholarly system. As Boyer (1990) puts it, "Moving in this direction requires the support and engagement of university presidents, faculty, faculty governance, professional associations, and accrediting bodies."

NASULGC and CIC Involvement

Many—probably most—public research universities are plagued by declining state support and lack of public appreciation. Some, such as the University of Minnesota, the University of Michigan, Penn State, and Cornell, have developed significant civic-engagement activities. Research on civic engagement has also been taken up by the Kettering Foundation. Valuable as these local and limited efforts are, the issues for the future of public research universities, or land-grant universities (LGUs), might also be addressed more broadly by the National Association of State Universities and Land-Grant Colleges (NASULGC), which is the coordinating body for all LGUs. They would all profit from a coordinated effort: to rethink the purposes, practices, and contributions of LGUs as they concern civic engagement; to involve the public in such rethinking; and to share best practices that would teach researchers how to work with their publics in ways that are useful to both.

Such coordinated efforts are in fact beginning in the Consortium on Institutional Cooperation (CIC), the academic consortium of the Big Ten universities and at the University of Chicago, which represents a large proportion of the leading public research universities. The CIC has established a Committee on Engagement, whose charge is "to provide strategic advice to the CIC members on issues of public engagement. Through periodic discussion and subsequent reporting, the committee should: frame what is meant by engagement; benchmark strategies for public engagement across the CIC; advise the Members (Chief Academic Officers) on collaborative opportunities in this area that might be included in the CIC strategic plan; and identify performance measures."

Another mechanism that could help to forward efforts in public scholarship would be a journal. At present, there are some periodicals that may come close, but there appears to be nothing that focuses directly and explicitly on this area and that draws contributions from a diverse range of public scholarship efforts. Such a journal, which could be print or Web-based, might get foundation sponsorship. It should be a high-class journal, with a nationally and internationally prominent editorial board, that attracts quality contributions. Publication in such a journal should count positively in faculty promotion and tenure deliberations.

What Can Administrators Do?

I declared at the beginning of this essay "that public scholarship and enhanced civic engagement are important for universities—at the core of what we should do." If that's the case, then what can central administrators do to foster public scholarship—both universal and local—and civic engagement while respecting resource constraints, faculty and departmental autonomy, and similar realities? Here, briefly, are some things I believe we can do:

- Provide the "top-down" to complement the bottom-up. Successful civic engagement requires both ideas and commitment from faculty and students and support from key administrators. It's very important that the president is known to be supportive. An administrator a level or two down may have the opportunity to discuss civic engagement ideas with the president, and can also work to enlist other top administrators.

- Help faculty, department heads, and deans recognize ways in which public scholarship can be acknowledged in tenure, promotion, and salary decisions.

- Provide seed resources and small grants and facilitate partnerships with colleges, departments, and other central units to generate larger pools of funds.

- Suggest contacts, note communities of interest, set up meetings, and broker cooperative agreements.

- Use the access that our positions provide to open doors for faculty to talk with community and business leaders, politicians, policymakers, and foundation executives.

- Interact directly with faculty and community leaders who are interested in public scholarship. Actual presence at meetings and conferences, to express support and engage in the sharing of ideas, can provide important encouragement to faculty who are trying to develop programs.

- Articulate the recognition that civic engagement and public scholarship are crucial to the continued support and success of public research universities.

- Foster awareness among the faculty and students involved in universal public scholarship that their research, scholarship, and teaching are largely supported by public funds in response to public needs and that they have significant public impact.

- Encourage university public relations offices to mentor faculty in how to couch their scholarship in terms comprehensible to the lay public in ways that emphasize the personal aspects and consequences of academic work and to place stories about this work in the media. Local public scholarship, with reciprocal engagement at its heart, is particularly suitable for such stories.

- Foster a climate within universities that encourages the articulation—the interaction and mutual support—of local and universal public scholarship, through mechanisms such as education of graduate students in the responsible and ethical conduct of research, as well as through teaching and research collaborations.

Conclusions

Public research universities need to re-engage with the publics that support us, if we are to continue to enjoy their support and trust and to be able to make the contributions to society and civilization that have so distinguished us up to now. The public needs us, and we need the public, but we are in danger of losing this vital connection. On the one hand, we need to clarify and strengthen our message about what we do, to show how the new forms of research and scholarship benefit society at least as much as the old. On the other, we need to partner more with our communities, to look to them as sources of expertise, insight, and stimulation. We need to value public scholarship more in our institutional reward system, in a way that enhances rather than devalues professional contribution. Each university needs to do these things within itself and its surrounding community. But we must also act together, in national scholarly societies and higher education organizations, to reinvigorate our great system of public higher education. Administrators have numerous ways in which they can contribute significantly to the advancement of public scholarship, while maintaining the high standards that both academia and society require.

Acknowledgments

I am grateful to Professor Nick Jordan for his close reading and many insightful comments that helped in major ways to sharpen the arguments in this chapter. I also thank Professor Cathy Jordan and Dr. Harry Boyte for useful comments and suggestions.

References

Boyer, E. L. 1990. *Scholarship Reconsidered: Priorities of the Professoriate.* San Francisco, CA: Jossey-Bass.

Ellison, J. 2002. "The Humanities and the Public Soul." In *Intellectual Workbench,* ed. H. C. Boyte. http://www.publicwork.org/2_4_cmp.html.

Sabin, P. 2002. Academe Subverts Young Scholars' Civic Orientation. *Chronicle of Higher Education* (February 8): B24.

Yudof, M. 2002. Is the Public Research University Dead? *Chronicle of Higher Education* (January 11): B24.

Chapter Eleven:
Findings

by Scott Peters

A century ago, a new type of scholar was envisioned in American higher education. Rejecting the historical stance of "ivory-tower" detachment and isolation, the new scholar was to embrace a stance of close and direct engagement in what University of Georgia's Henry Clay White (1899, p. 37) referred to in 1898 as the "abounding activities of the nation's life." The vision, as Cornell University's Liberty Hyde Bailey (1909, p. 192) articulated it in 1909, was to "put the scholar into the actual work of the world." By becoming engaged in public work—"sustained effort by a mix of people who solve public problems or create goods, material or cultural, of general benefit" (Boyte 2004, p. 5)—the new scholar would find a way to integrate the pursuit of the academy's core teaching and research missions with the pursuit of the public interest or commonwealth.

In state and land-grant institutions, the vision of a new public scholar was put forth as a means of realizing the democratic populist ideal of these institutions as "people's colleges." People's colleges would be characterized, in the words of Ruby Green Smith (1949, p. ix), by their "vigorous reciprocity." They would be "with the people, as well as 'of the people, by the people, and for the people.'"

While the ideal of state and land-grant institutions as people's colleges was never fully realized, a tradition of public scholarship—that is, of scholarly engagement in public work—did, in fact, develop in the state and land-grant system. As the case studies included in this book show, this tradition continues into the present. But as the cases and the interviews

and discussions we conducted with scholars also show, like
the broader people's college ideal, the full promise of public
scholarship remains unrealized. In practice, public scholarship
is *more or less* public and democratic in terms of aims and
methods, *more or less* mutually beneficial for the public and
the academy, *more or less* appreciated, supported, and rewarded.

The contemporary case studies of public scholarship in this
book are situated in the context of widespread concern about the
quality and vitality of our democratic institutions, capacities,
and spirit (e.g., Putnam 2000; Skocpol 2003). They are situated
in the context of concern about the deeply complex and difficult
challenge of facilitating agricultural and food-systems sustainability (e.g., Röling and Wagemakers 1998; Smil 2000). And they
are situated in the context of critical conversations about the
nature and status of higher education's public or civic mission
(e.g., Ehrlich 2000) and of the limitations of prevailing academic
methodologies and practices in pursuing and realizing this
mission (e.g., Greenwood and Levin 2000; Strand et al. 2003).

These issues provide meaning and urgency to the challenge
of learning how the engagement of academic professionals and
students in public work might become *more* public and democratic, *more* beneficial for both the public and the academy, and *more*
appreciated, supported, and rewarded. The collaborative study
that led to the publication of this book was designed as a first
step towards such learning.

In this chapter, I present the main findings from our study,
organized under the three themes we chose to attend to in interpreting our data. These themes include (1) why and how scholars
come to be engaged in public work, (2) the roles they play and
the contributions they seek to make, and (3) the nature of the
challenges and barriers they encounter and how they respond
to them.

In 1990, Ernest Boyer (1990, pp. 13, xii) called on scholars to
"relate the work of the academy more directly to the realities of
contemporary life" by focusing their scholarship on the "social

and environmental challenges beyond the campus." By way of summarizing the essence of our findings, I want to take note of something Dan Cooley told me about how he and his team of University of Massachusetts (UMass) scientists go about addressing the social and environmental challenges involved in growing apples:

> Some people from universities will go into a farm with the idea, "We know it and they don't." I don't think you can do that. The model of "Here comes the knowledge out to you— use it and be free" is not the way we work.

This is an important passage. By naming and rejecting a simplistic model of engagement that is limited to one-way transfers of academic knowledge, Cooley stimulates our interest in learning about the model he and his team of colleagues *do* embrace. What we find when we read about their work in Chapter Five is a complex and time consuming model of engagement that is similar in many ways to the model we find in the rest of the case studies in this book.

Motivated by a combination of academic and civic purposes, interests, and identities, we find Cooley's team and the other scholars in our case studies striving to establish mutually beneficial relationships between campus and community. With respect to scholars, these relationships are characterized by an attitude of reciprocity and humility, by which scholars signal their openness to learning as well as teaching, to listening as well as telling, to advancing public as well as academic interests.

In their accounts of their work, we find our scholars playing both supporting and leadership roles in public-work projects, roles that are tied to their expertise as academics and their interests, ideals, and commitments as citizens. We find them seeking to build relationships and power for the pursuit of public ends, and to mesh their own self-interests with those of the citizens they wish to engage. We find them conducting research and facilitating learning, producing or helping to produce knowledge, theory, ideas, technologies, and material and cultural goods that have academic and/or public value.

In communities, the process of building power and meshing self-interests across diverse groups in order to pursue public ends is called "organizing" (Chambers 2003). In the academy, the process of learning, when it is more than simply acquiring or disseminating skills and information, when it involves creative experimentation and discovery, when it is approached systematically and critically, when its findings are analyzed, written up, communicated, and validated by peers through publications, is called "scholarship." The scholars represented in this book work from a model of engagement that aims to integrate organizing and scholarship. In embracing this model, they are practicing a *public* scholarship that relates the work of the academy directly to the realities of contemporary life.

The cases of public scholarship in this book are both inspiring and instructive. But they should not be romanticized. They provide us with accounts of failure as well as success. While they are in some ways encouraging, they also raise troubling questions about how the ideal of engaging campus and community in mutually beneficial ways plays out in actual practice. Further, they reveal some troubling realities about what scholars who practice public scholarship are up against. Therefore, our cases must be read with a critical eye to their implications and to the issues and questions they raise. Among them, few could be more important to examine and understand than the question of the promise public scholarship might hold for the large and critically important task of renewing and strengthening democracy, in which citizenship is conceived not as voting or "doing good" but as practical public work that is grounded in everyday politics (Boyte 2004).

Choosing Engagement

As noted in Chapter One, James Fairweather's (1996, pp. xii-xiii) analysis of survey data of thousands of faculty from hundreds of colleges and universities led him to the conclusion that "for most faculty public service, including direct involvement in economic development, continues to represent such a small percentage of their job that it hardly registers." Given how apparently rare engagement in public-service-oriented activities is in the American academy, it is by no means a trivial matter to ask why and how some scholars choose to leave the relative comfort of their campuses to actively participate in and contribute to public work—not as off-hours volunteers, but as on-the-clock *scholars*.

As we posed this question during the analysis phase of our study, we began to examine our case and interview data for insight into how scholars understand their professional identities, purposes, and self-interests. In examining these issues, we found three inter-related explanations for why and how our case scholars chose to become engaged in public work. I name and discuss each of these below.

Official Job Responsibilities

Our first finding is that for most of the scholars in our case studies, engagement in the world beyond the campus is structured into their official job responsibilities through what is referred to in the land-grant system as "extension." For these scholars, engagement is not a choice; it is a requirement. The extension or engagement requirement is often expressed in terms of a percentage of effort in scholars' position descriptions. For some scholars, such as the late Ron Prokopy, this requirement is added to their research and/or teaching responsibilities. For others, such as Ellen Smoak and Robert Williamson, it makes up the whole of their appointment.

This is a relatively obvious and superficial finding. It might seem, therefore, that it hardly merits our attention. Yet, it is in fact remarkable—and not to be taken for granted—that engagement is structured into the formal responsibilities of at least some of the academic professionals the land-grant system employs. This is a distinctive characteristic of land-grant institutions that can be traced back nearly a century to the creation of the national Cooperative Extension System (Rasmussen 1989). It is one of the factors that helps explain why the scholars in our case studies became engaged beyond the campus in mutually beneficial ways with the public.

As important as it is not to overlook our first finding, it only goes a short distance in helping us understand why—and especially how—the scholars in our case studies have become engaged in public work. Scholars have a good deal of freedom in interpreting the meaning of their extension responsibilities and how they should be pursued. Mutually beneficial engagement is only one of many possible ways scholars can interpret and pursue these responsibilities. Moreover, not all of our case scholars hold extension appointments. For example, Nick Jordan (Chapter Six) holds a mainstream academic appointment that is evenly split between research and teaching.

Given these observations, we need to look beyond official job responsibilities to discover deeper and more complex explanations. In doing so, we find two additional explanations. The first is tied to scholars' interpretations of the meaning and significance of the land-grant mission. The second is linked to scholars' distinctive commitment to pursue scholarship that interweaves academic and civic purposes and interests.

The Land-Grant Mission

In analyzing our interview data, we find that our case scholars interpret the meaning of the "land-grant mission" in ways that both inform and shape their professional identities, motivating if not compelling them to become engaged as educators and scholars in public work. While the phrase, *land-grant mission*, means nothing to most people, for some scholars inside the land-grant system, including most of those involved in our case studies, it carries deep significance (Bonnen 1998). When these scholars speak of what the land-grant mission means to them, we come to see how they view the public purposes and responsibilities of their institutions, and by implication, their own public purposes and responsibilities.

For these scholars, the land-grant mission signifies a responsibility to share the research knowledge of the university with the people and communities of their respective states. According to the late Ron Prokopy (Chapter Five), "the land-grant mission should be to extend the knowledge base that's developed within the university to the community." When asked about Cornell University's land-grant mission, Marianne Krasny (Chapter Nine) said that, in her view, "our mission is to share our research and science with the people of the state." For Ellen Smoak of North Carolina A&T State University (Chapter Eight) "the land-grant mission is the university reaching out to people in communities, taking the university's research or knowledge base and stepping into the community with that information."

Sharing or extending *already existing knowledge* is not all the land-grant mission means or requires. The scholars in our case studies also interpret the land-grant mission in ways that influence their approach to the production of *new knowledge,* and their views of the purposes the process of knowledge production is supposed to serve. In line with their interpretations, our scholars assign themselves the responsibility of conducting their scholarship in close, face-to-face relation to the people and communities of their states or regions in order to advance public, as well as academic, aims and ends.

Judy Brienza, the University of Minnesota graduate student whose work is discussed in Chapter Three, helps us to see this in her comments about the land-grant mission:

> From my perspective, the land-grant mission is to use education to forward the development of communities, to develop human resources and forward a region's economic position or skills position. It's … why I did my thesis on a practical rather than theoretical issue.

Both my parents went to Rutgers, which is a land-grant university. My dad was on the board of trustees there and … he instilled the land-grant philosophy in me in terms of the responsibilities of the land-grant university towards educating people, and also the responsibility of students who are educated by that system. I'm aware that the taxpayers help subsidize my education. If I'm going to be educated in a subsidized manner, then I have a responsibility to use my education towards something greater than myself.

In Chapter Three, we learn that Brienza does not interpret her self-assigned responsibility to "use" her education for something greater than herself as referring only to the future, after she graduates. Rather, she interprets it in a way that informs her view of how and for what purpose she conducts research for her master's thesis. This explains why she chose to focus her thesis on a "practical rather than theoretical issue."

We learn more from Gail Feenstra and Craig Hassel about how the land-grant mission can shape scholars' sense of identity, responsibility, and purpose in ways that motivate or even compel them to become engaged in public work. Here is Feenstra's answer to the question of what the land-grant mission means to her and how she feels it was embodied in her work with her University of California colleague, David Campbell, in the PlacerGROWN project discussed in Chapter Two:

To me, the mission has to do with involving the local, everyday person in learning, in betterment of their community in some way. And it has to do with taking advantage of the resources at the land-grant institution to make their community a better place, to improve their quality of life, whether economic, cultural, whatever. I think that this project did just that. It allowed us to utilize the resources at this university that helped that community take a step toward becoming more sustainable, which is what they wanted to do. I think that's what the land-grant university is supposed to be doing.

We see here that Feenstra's view of the land-grant mission pushes well beyond the extension of already existing knowledge. It charges her with a responsibility to involve the "everyday person" in learning aimed at improving communities' economic, cultural, and social quality of life.

Here is Hassel's view of the land-grant mission and how he feels it was embodied in the University of Minnesota undergraduate honors class he co-taught on the wild-rice controversy discussed in Chapter Seven:

> The land-grant mission is often characterized in terms of its teaching, research, and outreach functions. I believe that those are important elements, but the land-grant university also serves to create things of public value, of public good. It serves to improve the quality of life for citizens, and it serves to give voice to those sectors of society that are not represented through other avenues. There is also the issue of generating new knowledge, new understanding, and new insight from a mix of worldviews and cross-cultural perspectives. I believe that this class was quite consistent with the land-grant mission in that it brought together students, faculty and knowledgeable citizens around an issue of public concern. We were able to do that in a way that was fairly respectful of diverse perspectives, giving them voice and visibility, and making time for questioning, reflection, critical discussion, and discourse.

Like Brienza and Feenstra, Hassel invests the land-grant mission with a meaning that pushes beyond the extension of knowledge. He articulates a highly collaborative and productive view of the mission as a means for creating or generating "things of public value," including new knowledge and insight. When Hassel says that the mission serves to give voice to unrepresented sectors of society, we see that he invests it with a social responsibility. But it is just as clear from his comments that he views the mission as serving the important academic purpose of advancing learning and scholarship.

In Brienza's, Feenstra's, and Hassel's views, we see a strong connection between the concept of mutually beneficial engagement and the land-grant mission. As they see it, the pursuit of the land-grant mission *requires* mutually beneficial engagement. For them, and for the other scholars featured in this book, such engagement is not a distraction from the core academic missions of advancing teaching and research; rather, *it is a deliberately chosen means for fulfilling them.*

In articulating their views of the land-grant mission, some of our case scholars directly tied the mission to the development of democratic citizenship. According to David Campbell (Chapter Two), the land-grant mission "is about supporting local people, in all their variety, in developing a sense of efficacy, pride, standing, and problem-solving capability that is the heart of the democratic capability of citizens. So the mission is citizenship development." For the late Ron Prokopy (Chapter Five), beyond extending knowledge, the purpose of the land-grant university is "to create a responsible and socially conscious citizenry." For Nick Jordan, (Chapter Six), the land-grant mission

> is to provide a center of learning that is working, above all, to look after the welfare and well-being of the democratic society, supporting decision making on a democratic basis. That means getting everybody who has a stake to participate in decision making with as much of their intelligence and their morality as possible. That's the ultimate purpose of the land-grant university, to support democratic policymaking.

One more view of the land-grant mission helps to bring an important aspect of self-interest into view as a source of motivation for scholars' engagement. Robert Williamson of North Carolina A&T (Chapter Eight) had this to say:

> We can share the resources that we have here at the land-grant. When I say resources, I'm thinking in terms of our faculty as well as money. In turn, communities will be sharing with us their needs and problems. In the long run, they may also be

providing us a pipeline of new students—not only for the school of agriculture, but engineering, nursing, you name it. And those communities need to see your presence in the community. They're the ones that provide the tax dollars that support us. And so we can't turn our back on them, or we can't just isolate ourselves to certain nearby communities and expect to survive. The longevity of these land-grants, I think, depends on them going beyond the traditional extension activity that we've provided in the past by encouraging more program areas or departments from campus to become directly involved in meeting the needs of people out there in the counties.

Here, we come to see engagement both as a means for fulfilling a public obligation and for pursuing scholars' interest in institutional survival. While it would be unfair to say that institutional survival serves as a major motivation behind our scholars' commitment to engagement, we find that it does have some influence. This is not a surprising finding, since we live in a time in which public support for higher education has significantly eroded, raising serious questions about the future (Zusman 2005).

Interweaving Academic and Civic Purposes and Interests

Our case scholars' views of the land-grant mission help us to understand how institutional context and identity shapes their sense of public purpose and their commitment to become engaged as scholars in public work. But we also find a deeper explanation in their distinctive commitment to pursue scholarship that interweaves academic and civic purposes and interests.

In individual interviews, all of our scholars spoke—sometimes quite passionately—of how they developed a sense of civic purpose in the context of their life experiences. Specifically, they spoke of their commitment to the care and protection of the environment and the landscape, community vitality, educational opportunity and equity, economic and social justice, cultural respect, scientific literacy, and democracy. Not surprisingly, given the subject matter of our cases, most also identified an interest in promoting and supporting agricultural sustainability through the development of small-scale community food systems. All spoke of how they have sought to configure or reconfigure their academic careers in ways that enable them to pursue these commitments and interests.

What we find in these accounts is a well-developed sense of civic purpose, identity, and responsibility that is integral to their sense of academic purpose, identity, and responsibility. It should be noted that these particular scholars cannot claim to be completely different from their colleagues in this regard. If asked to do so, most scholars would likely link their work to larger civic purposes. What appears to be distinctive about the scholars in our case studies is the way they conceive of and act on their civic mindedness.

This insight emerged during the first of three group discussions we held with case authors, research project team members, and interested colleagues. At that meeting, David Pelletier—a project team member who is also the central figure in the case study of public scholarship presented in Chapter Four—made the following observation about the first drafts of our case studies:

> What I see in all of this is that for those of us who have developed a civic mindedness, the common denominator that seems immutable is that we all have a conviction or passion or sense of purpose about this kind of work.... We're going to find a way to do it. And some people never develop that, or they're in an environment where they dare not.

We find evidence in our research to support Pelletier's observation. In all our cases, we find expressions of a strong, distinctive civic mindedness that appears to reinforce scholars' "immutable" commitment to "this kind of work"—which we take to mean public scholarship—even in the face of fairly serious challenges that might well deter others. We see scholars whose civic mindedness is of primary rather than secondary importance to their professional identities, motivating them to actively and directly pursue their civic commitments in and through their scholarship. We find that their motivation for becoming engaged in public work as *scholars* is grounded in their judgment that engagement is more than a vehicle for transferring or disseminating the *results* of their scholarship. They see it as offering a means of *informing and conducting* it is well.

Importantly, we find that, for the scholars in our case studies, civic and academic motivations are so closely interconnected that they cannot be separated. Each reinforces and informs the other. In their accounts of their interests and motivations, we find a close and purposeful interweaving of civic and academic purpose. This interweaving is one of the distinctive characteristics of a public scholar.

Consider, for example, how Nick Jordan introduced himself at the beginning of one of our project team discussions held at the Kettering Foundation:

> I'm Nick Jordan from the University of Minnesota. To say a little bit about what I do, I'm an ecologist and evolutionary biologist by training, and I'm interested in what goes on in farms. I'm interested in the question of how ideas from the science of ecology and the study of evolution are relevant to making farms work better.

Here, Jordan introduces himself in terms of his academic identity. But he also makes it clear, virtually in the same breath, that his interests reach beyond his academic field or discipline. He is interested in exploring how he might connect his academic work to a social and environmental challenge beyond the campus: namely, the challenge of making farms work better.

Jordan continues:

> I'm very fascinated by the whole image of farming in partnership with nature as a kind of ideal that is often lifted up, and

which I believe is an essential direction for farming to take. It's where farming has been in the past, and it seems very clear we need to get back to it, to bring it back to life as an ideal.

From these comments, we learn that Jordan's interest in making farms work "better" has to do with the ideal of farming in partnership with nature. We see that he is not just fascinated with this ideal on an intellectual level as a topic of study. He is committed to its advance in the world as an "essential direction for farming to take." He puts himself inside the project of bringing the ideal back to life.

As Jordan continues his introduction, we see that his view of himself as an insider in this project weaves together his academic and civic identities:

It's obvious to me that there are very interesting questions about how farming in partnership with nature is really organized. If you think about it as a question of ecology, how is it that a group of organisms inter-relate in a way that produces the good things that we want farms to produce? I'm also equally interested in the question of how do we organize people to enable that kind of farming. It seems really clear to me that many different ways of knowing are relevant to building the knowledge base that we need to truly farm in partnership with nature.

Here, we see that Jordan does not view himself as having all the answers based on his own "way of knowing" as an academic ecologist and evolutionary biologist. This is significant. It reveals his judgment that in order to make progress on the dual academic and public work of "building the knowledge base that we need to truly farm in partnership with nature," diverse groups of "knowers" must be brought together. This is not an abstract concept for Jordan. It is his work as a public scholar, as we see in the case study he co-authored with his colleagues (Chapter Six).

Finally, Jordan tells us that he sees his public scholarship as reflecting a responsibility that is a distinctive feature of land-grant universities:

> My feeling is that the land-grant university in particular has to take very seriously the question of how different ways of knowing are articulated so as to produce the knowledge base that is needed for complicated systems to work—like farms that are truly partnerships with nature, and lots of other complicated, difficult undertakings that we all know that we should be aspiring to as a society. I feel the land-grant universities really have to lead in figuring out how to do that.

Here we see that in Jordan's view, land-grants must be engaged with a diverse group of "knowers" because this connection offers a means for *producing* knowledge, not simply disseminating and applying it. He tells us that this responsibility is *proactive* rather than responsive, that land-grant universities must *lead* efforts to produce the knowledge society needs to address complex problems.

These paragraphs from Jordan's introduction evoke the "public pledge" William Sullivan (2003, p. 10) calls on civic professionals to make: "to deploy technical expertise and judgment not only skillfully but also for public-regarding ends and in a public-regarding way." We see in Jordan's description of his motivations and purpose a commitment to do exactly that. Looking across our cases and interview data—from Gail Feenstra's and David Campbell's work with PlacerGROWN to Marianne Krasny's work with *Garden Mosaics*—we see academic professionals from the social and natural sciences who express a similar commitment to pursuing the civic professional's public pledge by becoming engaged with their fellow citizens beyond the campus in addressing social and environmental challenges. We see an interwoven blend of academic and civic motivations that compel scholars to become engaged, informed, and reinforced by their official job responsibilities and their interpretations of the meaning and significance of their locations in land-grant universities.

Roles and Contributions

In the case study presented in Chapter Four as a practitioner profile, David Pelletier mentions a negative letter that someone in his academic field of study wrote about his work when he was up for tenure. In the letter, this person criticized Pelletier by writing that "This guy is supposed to be doing nutrition policy. He's mucking around down at the community level."

This is a revealing criticism. It shows what civically engaged scholars are up against in research universities, even in so-called "applied" disciplines such as nutrition policy: namely, a view of scholarship as an elevated and detached activity, something that shouldn't or even can't be practiced by being engaged "down" at the community level.

Our case studies offer strong evidence to counter this view. They show us that scholars can, indeed, engage at the community level in ways that enable them to pursue and advance their scholarship. In fact, they show us that *engagement in public work offers a powerful, and in some ways irreplaceable, means for facilitating learning and producing knowledge.*

Pelletier demonstrated this in his engagement in the North Country of upstate New York. Far from merely "mucking around," what Pelletier did "down at the community level" was to conduct an experiment that was designed to test and advance knowledge and theory in his academic field of nutrition policy. By design, his scholarship *required* him to become engaged in public work. It was productive scholarship, too, as evidenced by three articles Pelletier and his collaborators published from this work in refereed journals, and by the way in which it helped to shape and inform his mentoring and teaching of graduate students and the evolution of his research agenda.

Importantly, Pelletier's engagement in the North Country included more than simply advancing his scholarship, teaching, and research agenda. He did not simply observe, document, and analyze what happened in the public-work initiative that unfolded under the banner of the "North Country Community Food and Economic Security Network." He took on leadership and supporting roles in the initiative in which he sought to make contributions of public as well as academic value.

We learn a great deal about the roles scholars play and contributions they strive to make as active participants in public work from reading Pelletier's case and the rest of this book's case studies. We learn about the different phases a public scholar's work involves. We learn about how scholars as experts try to work out a mutually beneficial relationship with their fellow citizens, one that simultaneously serves as a means for conducting and informing scholarship, for helping citizens and groups to understand and address their interests and problems, and for contributing to the larger task of renewing democracy.

Looking closely at our case studies and interview data, we can discern four different phases in a public-scholar's work:

- Taking the initiative to develop a project idea

- Searching for partners and revising and refining the project idea

- Organizing and implementing the project, producing scholarly and public goods

- Scaling up or moving on

Taking Initiative to Develop a Project Idea

In the academic literature, there is much discussion of the need for scholars and universities to be responsive to the public's requests for help and assistance (e.g., Tierney 1998). But with the exception of Judy Brienza (Chapter Three), the scholars in this book are not working from a responsive stance. Their work does not begin with citizens external to the academy coming to them to ask for help. Rather, it begins when they take the initiative to develop ideas for public-work projects that place them in direct, face-to-face relationships with their fellow citizens.

This is an important finding that has implications for how we theorize what the academy's public-engagement mission is and how it is put into practice. A theory that views the practice of engagement as providing knowledge, technical assistance, and other services in response to the requests of stakeholders misses the *leadership* role we see most of the scholars and academic professionals in our case studies playing.

Bill Coli helps us to see the importance of Ron Prokopy's leadership role in the UMass apple IPM project (Chapter Five). According to Coli,

> While I believe that it's good to respond to needs of stake-holders, while it's appropriate to listen to make sure that we are not just doing ivory tower academic stuff, I think the land-grants have a role to play in terms of providing leadership and vision. Clearly, Ron Prokopy had a vision of why to move tree fruit IPM in a certain direction. After all, 23 years ago, if we had asked the typical apple grower what he or she needed (most of them are he), they would have said, "Give me a new fungicide to control apple scab." They would not have said, "Give me a monitoring device for plum curculio."

Here, Coli is inviting us to view not only Ron Prokopy's engagement work, but the engagement work of the land-grants in general as being about more than responding to the needs of stakeholders. According to Coli, "the land-grants have a role to play in terms of providing leadership and vision." In the specific case of the apple IPM project, we learn from Coli that when Ron Prokopy arrived at UMass more than 20 years ago, he had a vision that was different from that of most Massachusetts apple growers. Growers wanted better fungicides. They were not asking for integrated pest management tools that would help them battle apple pests in a more environmentally friendly way. Why? IPM was a fairly new idea at the time, and had yet to be introduced to apple growers in Massachusetts. Until Ron Prokopy arrived at UMass in 1978, there was no sustained vision or leadership for introducing it.

While the leadership role Prokopy played was quite different from the role of "responding to the needs of stakeholders," there was nevertheless a responsive dimension to it. Prokopy and his team of scientists responded to apple growers' pressing need for assistance in addressing technical problems with pests and diseases. But they did not respond by simply giving growers what they said they wanted. They responded by introducing a new way of addressing technical problems, a way that offered promise not only of meeting growers' interests in managing pests and diseases, but also larger public interests in the protection of the environment and the availability of safe and nutritious food. In other words, they responded by taking the initiative to pursue both growers' self-interests and the larger public interest.

We see this same pattern of responsive leadership in Nick Jordan's development of a knowledge network aimed at helping farmers in Minnesota learn to manage weeds in a more sustainable fashion. And we see it in other cases as well, including Marianne Krasny's development of *Garden Mosaics,* Ellen Smoak's and Robert Williamson's development of their science education curriculum, *Down-to-Earth,* and David Pelletier's development of the North Country initiative. Each of these cases begins with scholars taking leadership to develop an idea for a public-work initiative. But each also involves a degree of responsiveness on the part of scholars to the interests of particular groups and the concerns and interests of the larger or more general public. For example, Ellen Smoak and Robert Williamson independently took leadership in developing an educational resource aimed at addressing large public issues of academic achievement, scientific literacy, and (in their view) misguided conceptions of agriculture.

But as their case also shows, in developing this resource, they were responsive to the specific needs and interests of community members in Johnston County, North Carolina.

David Campbell and Gail Feenstra consciously combined civic initiative and leadership with responsiveness in their case (Chapter Two). Their first step in initiating their community food systems work in California consisted of writing a request for proposals (RFP) for projects aimed at developing community food systems. Campbell describes the challenge he and Feenstra were faced with in writing the RFP:

> The need was to develop some ideas about how people in community settings could develop forms of economic development that had a greater degree of democracy and community control, had a higher environmental sensibility to them, and were more than just passing fancies. They had to have some real tangible on-the-ground value to people, including keeping businesses afloat, keeping people working, and getting the support of community leaders because they were producing some tangible benefits to communities.

In crafting the RFP, Campbell and Feenstra were not only playing an intellectual role through their conceptual development of the idea of community food systems; they were also playing a civic leadership role. The RFP they wrote served as a call for people to engage in the public work of building community food systems. They issued this call on their own initiative. But as we learn in their chapter, their concept of community food systems was not just dreamed up in isolation. It was closely informed by what they called "nascent practical developments" that were already underway in California and elsewhere. Their conceptual work was thus in an important way responsive to practical, on-the-ground experiments.

The blend of initiative and responsiveness in Campbell's and Feenstra's work can be seen in all of our cases. We do not see scholars who are isolated in the proverbial ivory tower, out of touch with the realities of the people they seek to work with, dreaming up "pie-in-the-sky" visions that might not work in the "real" world. Rather, we see scholars who invest themselves in building or joining rich networks of relationships with their fellow citizens. We see them drawing from these networks to inspire, inform, and shape their intellectual and civic work.

Searching for Partners, Revising, and Refining the Project Idea

In most of our case studies, the first step in a public-scholar's work is to propose a public-work project. The second step is to search for partners and revise and refine the concept of the project in conversation with potential partners. This phase of a public-scholar's work is deeply dependent on skilled organizing that is devoted to identifying and meshing the interests of potential partners with scholars' own self-interests. Sometimes scholars play a leading role in the organizing; almost always the role is shared with others.

In his case, Nick Jordan sought assistance with the organizing role from Sue White, a woman who had strengths and skills in organizing farmers that complemented Jordan's skills in organizing his fellow scholars. Together, they set about doing "a lot of one-on-one talking" with faculty, extension educators, and farmers they thought might have an interest in Jordan's idea of forming a research cooperative. This phase of a public-scholar's work takes time. Jordan told me that he and White spent "six months or so" talking with potential partners. The time and effort they invested turned out to be invaluable. They discovered that the scientists they thought might be interested in forming a research cooperative actually weren't sure what, if anything, they wanted to do together. Additionally, they learned that farmers weren't the least bit interested in being part of a research cooperative; they saw that as something that would only benefit scholars. Farmers' real interest, Jordan and White discovered, was in "accelerating" their learning of how to farm using sustainable methods, something they hadn't been able to do to their satisfaction on their own.

Taking what he and White learned from their meetings, Jordan, with the help of a few of his colleagues, revised and refined his original idea. The new project idea he came up with was centered on farmer learning. It connected farmers' interests with Jordan's and his colleagues' reconsidered interests. After revising the project idea, Jordan set about the task of writing grants to fund it.

In this phase of his case, we learn about how Jordan as an academic expert seeks to work out a mutually beneficial relationship with the farmers he eventually ends up collaborating with. The considerable amount of time he and White spend in conversation with farmers enables them to take farmers' interests, experiences, and views seriously. The conversations allow them to identify farmers' interests, as well as common or mutual interests that might serve as the basis of a potential relationship. We see here that Jordan's purpose is not to sell his ideas and interests to farmers, but rather to identify farmers' interests and explore how he might work with them to pursue his own interest in relation to a larger public interest: the pursuit, as Jordan puts it, of "farming in partnership with nature." While he is not deflected from the pursuit of this public interest by his conversations with farmers, we see that, in response to what he learns about farmers' interests, he is open to changing his ideas about how to pursue it.

The work Jordan and White took on requires a basic organizing skill—*listening*—that is more difficult than it might seem. The importance of this skill was repeatedly emphasized in my interviews with the scholars who were involved in our case studies. For example, Gail Feenstra told me that the most important lesson she learned from her engagement work in the PlacerGROWN project was to "seriously listen to what the people in the community are saying." She continued:

> It's so hard. I've watched researchers. They come in with their idea that the people need information. "We will provide information, and that will make a difference." And that is not

what they need half the time. They need political support, or they need money for a processing plant. They don't need information. So much of the time, we think we know what they need, and the thing that we think is what we have. That's what bothers me—the inability to see that, and the tendency to think that what we have is the most important thing. So if you really want to do this kind of supportive, interactive research, outreach or public work, or whatever it is, it's very important to hear what it is that people need and to see what creative ways you can come up with to support that.

Nick Jordan thought he knew what farmers would need and want when he conceptualized his original project idea. But after listening to them carefully, he learned otherwise. Drawing from what he and Sue White learned from their listening, he revised his proposal, shifting the focus from cooperative research to farmer learning. It must not be missed that this revision did not require Jordan to abandon his self-interest as a scholar in producing knowledge. Rather, it enabled him to mesh his self-interest with farmers' interests. This meshing, which was written into the revised proposal, was the result of a process of establishing a "legitimate" relationship between university experts and farmers—legitimate in a democratic sense in that it allowed for the recognition and incorporation of both farmers' and scholars' views, experiences, knowledge, *and* self-interests.

The working out of a legitimate relationship through a process of identifying, discussing, and meshing diverse self-interests in relation to a larger common interest is a crucial component of the practice of public scholarship. What many of the practice stories in this book help us to see is that this process is not one in which scholars function as "selfless" service providers who temporarily abandon their own interests and work in order to "help" the community. Rather, it is a process in which scholars come to integrate their own work and interests with those of their public partners, as both seek together to pursue a larger public interest.

Organizing and Implementing the Project, Producing Scholarly and Public Goods

After they conceptualize and revise their public-work ideas, we see the academic professionals in this book's case studies leading or sharing in the work of organizing and implementing their projects with their community partners. As they move into this stage of their work, we do not see them functioning as activists or volunteer service providers. We see them functioning as scholars who take their roles and responsibilities as researchers and/or teachers seriously. By participating in public work, they aim to produce both scholarly and public goods. They aim to simultaneously contribute to the work of the publics they join and to their academic fields, programs, and literatures.

Every case offers a unique window into a public-scholar's practice with community collaborators. We see Robert Williamson and Ellen Smoak joining with citizens from Johnston County, North Carolina, in the public work of improving the scientific literacy and academic achievement of students from Smithfield Middle School. The product of their collaborative work is a science education curriculum that is both a scholarly and a public good. We see Marianne Krasny, along with colleagues and graduate students, join with community educators to create a public-work initiative designed to engage youth and community members in learning about science and sustainability by acting together to improve their communities. The products of their work include the *Garden Mosaics* program, a Web site, and more than a dozen academic papers, book chapters, and student theses. We see the natural scientists at UMass working with apple growers to learn how to manage pests and diseases. The products of their collaborative work, which has continued over more than two decades, includes timely knowledge and devices and strategies that growers can use to manage pests and diseases in a more sustainable manner, resulting in a cleaner environment, safer food, and hundreds of papers published in academic journals.

A detailed picture of what we see during this stage of a public scholar's work can be constructed from our interview and group discussion data for each of the eight cases in this book. To take just one example, I return to Nick Jordan's and Sue White's work of organizing a knowledge network for sustainable weed management.

After revising their project idea and securing funding, Jordan and White turn to organizing and implementing it. With White taking the lead, this phase begins with the work of identifying and recruiting participants. We learn more here about how Jordan attempts to work out a legitimate relationship with collaborating farmers. He tells us that he took pains to be clear that the learning groups were "experiments," with farmers serving as "co-experimenters." He stresses that the farmers "were not, in any sense, subjects." This signals his intention to work with them in a collegial fashion, as contributing, interested participants with their own stake and say in how the experiments were to be conducted. He makes sure farmers get at least a small stipend for their participation, a sign of his respect for farmers' time and efforts.

Once it is implemented, the project plays out over a two-year period. Jordan tells us that he attended all of the dozen or so meetings of the groups. He views the project as public work and tells us that he tried to be a "full-fledged member" of the public work group. We see here how much of a time commitment public-scholarship can involve, distinguishing it from briefer and more superficial kinds of engagement in which scholars simply offer advice and technical assistance to individuals and groups without maintaining an ongoing, working relationship.

Jordan tells us that his roles included "nurturing" the learning in the project, helping with the ongoing organizing and planning, and serving as the "convener" of group discussions. He also actively contributed to the discussions, drawing from his academic expertise and knowledge. Interestingly, we see that during these discussions, he was pleased to discover that "it only really took a little bit of weed-science knowledge, if it was artfully introduced into the discourse of the group, for us to get very powerful discussions." This "little bit" of knowledge, he says, worked as a "leaven" that stimulated farmers' learning. To illustrate this, he provides an example of how he offered farmers some "ecology knowledge" about soil organisms that he says "opened their eyes to a new view of what was going on in their farms."

Here we see that Jordan's academic knowledge is not simply "transferred" to farmers, but, as he puts it, "artfully introduced into the discourse of the group." This suggests both a special skill and a special sensitivity related to the proper way and time to introduce academic knowledge and theory into the discourse of diverse groups. We also learn that, in Jordan's view, the group discussions were mutually beneficial. Most of the farmers, he says, "really liked these groups." They were "curious and excited" to take some of the things they were learning and try them out, and many of their discussions were "lively and animated." Jordan and his colleagues were also benefiting. According to Jordan, they were "getting a lot of professional energy and ideas from these discussions."

In brief, what we see in Jordan's practice is a scholar taking on organizing, convening, facilitating, and contributing roles in a public-work project that is designed to enable individual participants to pursue their own interests in relation to a broader public interest. The project involves what appears to be free and open discourse, in which different views, perspectives, and "ways of knowing" are drawn upon, shared, and discussed. This discourse serves as a source of learning that is meant to inform and guide action—not just farmers' actions, but scholars' as well. Again, we see that Jordan's engagement doesn't require that he abandon his self-interests in order to "serve" or "help" farmers. Jordan is just as interested in learning as the farmers appear to be. In fact, we see that his whole academic agenda is significantly informed and shaped by what he learns in and through his engagement with farmers.

As Jordan told me, he wanted to ensure that there was a "steady stream of scholarly output" from the farmer-learning project. At the time I interviewed him, these products included five articles and a graduate-student thesis. The focus of this scholarship is on the engagement process itself. The articles and thesis consist, in Jordan's words, of "descriptions of what we've been up to in this whole learning project," placed in relation to a set of "cross-cutting issues" having to do with "this whole issue of how we develop a knowledge base for sustainable kinds of agronomy." Jordan says that he tried to do scholarship that "brings in" farmers' way of knowing and their experience as "resources." The scholarly products thus draw from, assess, and document the learning-groups' potential for constructing a "more promising approach to developing a knowledge base for sustainable agriculture." They are, in essence, reflective reports of the results and significance of public-work experiments.

Jordan's case serves as evidence that engagement can, in fact, be a means for conducting and informing scholarship in serious and highly productive ways. Most of the other cases in this book support this finding. Scholars successfully produced significant academic products that directly drew on what they learned from their interactions and relations with citizens. These products were peer-reviewed and published in reputable academic venues.

I should stress here that our finding that engagement can be a valuable means for the production of scholarly products is not simply about quantity. What is important to recognize is that *the process of engagement can lead to scholarly products of high quality that communicate original, innovative knowledge and theoretical insights that could not have been produced without engagement.* What our cases show are scholars who are creatively, constructively, and productively pushing and expanding the boundaries of their disciplines through the scholarly products they produce in and through their engagement in public work.

I want to return to Jordan's case to raise some important questions about learning and knowledge. What kinds of learning do we see in Jordan's case study? What kinds of knowledge are being constructed? What interests are being served?

In my experience, it is rare that distinctions are made in the academy's public service and engagement work between the different kinds of learning and knowledge such work does or might help to facilitate and produce. Too often, these crucial terms are left as vague, one-dimensional, unproblematic, and atheoretical abstractions. The lack of a theoretical framework prevents us from seeing that there are distinct kinds of learning and knowledge that serve distinct purposes and interests.

Drawing in part from Aristotle, the German philosopher Jürgen Habermas (1972, 1984) has argued that we have three basic cognitive interests. First, we have a *technical* interest in understanding empirically grounded "laws" in order to act "correctly" to control and manage the environment for the purpose of meeting basic needs and wants. Second, we have a *practical* interest in understanding the meaning of a given situation in order to act "rightly" in a moral and political sense. And third, we have an *emancipatory* interest in gaining a critical understanding of the workings of institutions, systems, and societies in order to gain autonomy and freedom from coercion and oppression.

Pursuing these three cognitive interests requires different kinds of learning, linked to different ways of knowing, of generating and organizing knowledge (Carr and Kemmis 1986; Grundy 1987; Mezirow 1995, 2000). The technical interest is pursued through instrumental learning and the development of technical knowledge and skills, drawing especially from the empirical-analytical sciences. The practical interest is pursued through communicative learning that develops judgments about what ought to be done in a moral and political sense, drawing from experience, from ethical, moral, and/or religious frameworks, and from the historical, social, and interpretive disciplines and sciences. The emancipatory interest is pursued through learning that is tied to processes of critical reflection at the individual and collective level, generating both self-knowledge and critical theories that can be used to ground and guide actions aimed at overcoming oppression and injustice and achieving autonomy and freedom.

Using this framework, what we see in Jordan's case study is a combination of instrumental and communicative learning aimed at the pursuit of technical and practical interests. The task of managing weeds in a way that moves toward what Jordan calls "farming in partnership with nature" is both technical and practical. In other words, it is both about acting "correctly" and "rightly." It must be approached through a combination of scientific knowledge about ecology and practical knowledge about the moral and political meanings of farmers' situations and obligations and the social and environmental implications of their actions.

Here we see that the challenge of managing weeds using sustainable methods is not one-dimensional; it is not merely a technical challenge, but also a practical challenge. It is, in other words, a highly complex challenge that cannot be satisfactorily met by applying universal technical knowledge. As Jordan puts it, the task of farming in partnership with nature is "a much more complex and localized proposition than industrial farming." In his view, it requires developing a "parallel understanding of how it is that biologically diverse agri-ecosystems function, and also how it is that they are to be husbanded, or stewarded, or managed." The first understanding links up with the technical cognitive interest, the second links up with a combined technical and practical interest. Jordan's farmer-learning project, localized in the discourse of diverse public-work groups, serves as a means of generating and communicating both. Jordan and his university colleagues take the lead in contributing to the first understanding, drawing from their academic knowledge, and the farmers take the lead in the second, drawing from their localized knowledge of their farms and of farming. Each supports the others' learning. We can see then, in a tangible way, how it is that engagement can indeed be mutually beneficial.

It should be noted that Jordan's case study does not appear to directly involve the emancipatory interest. The point of the farmer-learning groups is not to generate critical theories aimed at understanding and overcoming oppression. It should not be missed, however, that Jordan and (presumably) the farmers, scholars, and extension educators involved in the project are working out of a critical perspective on the industrial agriculture system. But their critical perspective precedes their engagement; it does not emerge from it. In their public and scholarly work, Jordan and the farmers and extension educators are not engaging in critical reflection aimed at generating critical theories about industrial agriculture. Rather, they are engaging in experiments aimed at facilitating and generating learning and knowledge that can be used to inform the technical and practical work of pursuing farming in partnership with nature.

Looking across the other cases in this book, we again find similarities with Jordan's case. In the implementation phase of most of the cases, we see scholars playing organizing, convening, facilitating, and contributing roles in public-work groups. We find scholars seeking to draw out the knowledge and experiences of their partners through discourse, during which they "artfully" introduce their own academic knowledge and perspectives. We find their work to be centered, with varying degrees of emphasis, on the first two cognitive interests—the technical and practical interests—rather than on the emancipatory interest. Yet, we find in all cases that scholars do appear to hold critical perspectives that ground and guide their work.

In terms of what we learn from our case studies about how scholars organize and implement their public-work projects, there is one point that is worth stressing in especially strong terms. The point is that pursuing the academy's engagement mission in mutually beneficial ways is not simply an intellectual project; it is also an *organizing* project that requires skilled organizers. While some of the scholars in our cases have organizing skills that enable them to play key roles in organizing and maintaining relationships and in creating and maintaining a space that is conducive to effective public work, in every case we find people other than the lead scholar also playing key, and often leading, organizing roles.

Scaling Up or Moving On

Upon completing a public-work project, we see our case scholars do one of two things. Some of them, such as David Campbell and Gail Feenstra, David Pelletier, and Craig Hassel, move on to new projects. This is often done in ways that are closely informed by what they learn from their public-work experiences.

For example, David Pelletier's engagement in the North Country initiative was partly aimed at discovering whether the "public values" of ordinary folks at local levels are consistent with the values activists are espousing in the national Community Food Security Coalition. Through his research, he found that they are. But he also reports learning something else that turned out to be key in providing direction for his research agenda, leading him to move on from this project to another. He says that halfway through his work with the North Country communities, it became "crystal clear" to him that

> State, federal, and local regulations as well as harsh economic realities were going to be really powerful constraints on what these communities could themselves do. So I saw myself having to push my focus to regulation and policy at the state and federal levels after this was over in order to try to remove some of those constraints. So I took the public values that I heard and learned about in the North Country, which resonated with the community food security movement, and tried to push that into policy at USDA.

Other scholars, including Ron Prokopy and his colleagues, Nick Jordan, and Marianne Krasny, built on what they learned and the relationships they established by scaling their projects up to a higher level. In the UMass apple IPM case, the first round of public work led Prokopy to envision a four-level model of IPM that served as a map for scaling their work up over a period of

many years. In Marianne Krasny's case, lessons from the first
round of the *Garden Mosaics* initiative led her and her colleagues
to envision a means for deepening its intergenerational learning
and community action dimensions, which were then pursued by
scaling the project up under a second round of funding.

In Nick Jordan's case, the decision to scale up was closely
informed by the scholarship he and his collaborators conducted
in the first round of their project. Upon reflection and analysis,
the experiments in creating a knowledge network were deemed
a success. Jordan and his partners were then able to take what
they learned, leverage the project, and begin a new round
of experiments.

In Jordan's case, we see how two public-work products
became essential resources for additional work. First, the scholarly products they produced provided an intellectual resource that
significantly enhanced their ability to reflect on what they had
done and learned in ways that enabled them to begin to envision
how to scale their project up. Second, what Jordan deemed to be
the most important product of the pilot phase of the farmer-
learning groups—namely, a "diverse and excited group of
participants" that constitute "an organized base of people"—
"provided a resource in the form of social and human capital.

Here we catch a glimpse of one of the contributions public
scholars help to make through their engagement in public work.
That is, the important task of "public making," of forming and
creating publics. A *public,* according to David Mathews (1999,
p. 1), is "a diverse body of citizens joined together in ever-
changing alliances to make choices about how to advance their
common well-being." The organized base of people brought
together in Jordan's farmer-learning groups, if it continues to
develop and mature, holds promise of becoming a public.

We see a public-making contribution—at varying stages of
development and success—in several cases in this book, including
the PlacerGROWN case, the Experiment in Rural Cooperation
case, the North Country case, and the apple IPM case. To take one

as an example, in their work as public scholars in PlacerGROWN and other related projects, David Campbell and Gail Feenstra tell us that they seek to "envision and catalyze food and agricultural publics." Writing in Chapter Two that "publics must be patiently nurtured into being before their civic energy can be tapped," they argue that "scholars working in land-grant universities have a special responsibility to take on this work of creating and engaging democratic publics, since this work is at the heart of the historic land-grant mission."

For Campbell and Feenstra, the land-grant mission is centered on civic engagement as a means for advancing civic learning and development. This helps to explain why in their work with PlacerGROWN they did not limit their roles and contributions to the provision of technical assistance, expertise, and knowledge from their academic disciplines. Their view of the land-grant mission gave them not only the authority, but (in their minds) the responsibility to move beyond these roles and contributions in order to contribute to civic development—including public making—as well.

David Pelletier's work with the North Country Community Food and Economic Security Network provides another example of how public scholars seek to contribute to public making. As a nutrition-policy scholar, Pelletier's self-described goal is to learn how to improve nutrition policy by connecting public values to planning and public-policy development processes. The North Country case shows us one of the ways he pursued this goal. Pelletier deliberately connected his academic work to social and environmental challenges related to community nutrition. He did so in ways that succeeded in advancing both his own academic work—his research and teaching—and the public work of democracy in northern New York State.

We see Pelletier taking on a civic-leadership role by initiating conversations with community agencies in the region about their concerns over food, nutrition, agriculture, and economic security issues. He offered a specific method—a search conference—for engaging citizens in a process of deliberation and action in relation to these issues (Emery and Purser 1996). He and a small group of his colleagues and students then helped to organize and facilitate the search conferences in six different communities in the region.

Based on Pelletier's account of what transpired, the search conferences appear to have been a powerful mechanism for facilitating learning at the level of the practical cognitive interest, helping citizens to make meaning of their situation in order to act "rightly" to shape a better future for their region. Through Pelletier's own insistence, experts (including Pelletier himself) were kept on the sidelines of the search conferences, allowing citizens to name and discuss their own values, ideals, beliefs, interests, perspectives, and experiences, coming to their own judgments about issues relating to community nutrition and economic-security. Thus, the search conferences became a vehicle for connecting public values to the community nutrition and economic security policy process. They also became a vehicle for public making. The process produced 34 diverse working groups of citizens in six counties. While most of these groups stopped meeting after only a short while, a few did continue to meet and evolve into working publics.

Contributing to the Renewal of Democracy

The public-making role that we find in Pelletier's, Campbell and Feenstra's, and Jordan's practice stories reveals one of the ways that engagement offers a means for scholars to contribute to the task of renewing democracy. Before naming our additional findings on this matter, it is useful to review how scholars are commonly understood to contribute to democracy and democratic life. In prevailing views on this issue scholars contribute to democracy in one of two ways: (1) as autonomous, independent intellectuals acting as social critics or (2) as responsive technical experts acting as neutral service providers.

In the first view, articulated in some detail by Amy Gutmann (1999), scholars' central contribution to democracy is to protect against tyranny by acting as social critics. To make this contribution possible, society grants scholars the privileges of professional autonomy and academic freedom. This enables scholars to conduct their work without fear of retribution by the state or other interests, allowing them to independently and critically "assess existing theories, established institutions, and widely held beliefs" in ways that "make it more difficult for public officials, professionals, and ordinary citizens to disregard their own standards when it happens to be convenient" (Gutmann 1999, pp. 175, 188). Scholars functioning in line with this view sometimes act as "public intellectuals" by writing or speaking to public audiences about public issues in ways that are meant to influence the general public's views, opinions, and actions (Jacoby 1987; Fink 1997; Wolfe 1997, 2003; Posner 2003; Melzer 2003).

In the second view, scholars try to meet the needs of specific stakeholders. Acting in a responsive manner, they provide stakeholders with knowledge and a variety of technical and intellectual services. The knowledge and services they provide are developed and delivered from a stance of dispassionate neutrality (e.g., Taylor 1981; Smith 1994; Kellogg Commission 1999).

There is a third view that is not widely held in the academy, but which has gained support and interest over the past few decades (e.g., Fay 1987; Lather 1991; Gitlin 1994; Hammersley 1995; Strand et al. 2003). In this view, scholars contribute to democracy as politically engaged intellectuals. They reject neutrality and openly advocate for particular political goals and ideologies. In doing so, they take on a social-critic role. But they play this role in a collaborative rather than an independent and autonomous way by functioning as action researchers who co-create knowledge and theory with the oppressed and disenfranchised. Scholars' aim, in this view, is to upset power imbalances and transform structural inequalities by producing emancipatory knowledge and theory and by empowering the oppressed.

While it is my view that the scholars in this book's case studies do practice a form of action research in which they function as politically engaged intellectuals (albeit with moderate rather than radical politics), none of these three views of how scholars contribute to democracy fit our cases very well. For example, while Nick Jordan's work is based on a strong critique of industrial agriculture, he does not function as an autonomous social critic who is trying to protect against tyranny. While he uses his technical expertise to help address the needs and problems of farmers, he is not functioning as a responsive technical expert dispensing services from a stance of disinterested, dispassionate neutrality. While he is working in a collaborative fashion with farmers who can, in certain ways, be accurately described as being disenfranchised, he is not openly ideological and he is not directly striving to upset power imbalances and transform structural inequalities.

We find the scholars in our case studies contributing to the renewal of democracy in three different ways:

- First, by configuring their professional identity, responsibility, and practice in civic as well as academic terms, our case scholars contribute to the renewal of democracy by renewing the democratic spirit, purpose, and function of the academic profession. This is not a trivial matter, as the professions can and do play roles in democratic life that erode rather than strengthen citizens' voices, self-interests, and power by blocking opportunities for participation (e.g., Sullivan 1995; Fischer 2000).

- Second, our case scholars contribute to the renewal of democracy by taking leadership in creating opportunities for citizens to engage in public work. As shown above, public work provides a means for public making. It also provides a means for people to answer a key question Boyte and Kari (2000, p. 38) pose: "How do we become a people who see our individual self-interests embedded in the general welfare, who have more faith in each other and in our public institutions, who can act together with poise and boldness?"

- Third, our case scholars contribute to the renewal of democracy by taking on a civic-education role as they engage in public work that addresses social and environmental challenges related to sustainability. This role involves scholars in facilitating learning and constructing knowledge that inform and strengthen citizens' judgments, actions, and capacities.

While our cases offer evidence to support these findings, they also show that the full democratic promise of public scholarship is far from being fulfilled. As stated at the beginning of this chapter, we find that public scholarship in practice is more or less public and democratic, more or less mutually beneficial, and more or less appreciated, supported, and rewarded. With respect to the latter, public scholars encounter many challenges in their work that constrain their abilities to participate in public work in ways that are mutually beneficial for the academy and the public. It is to this finding that I now turn.

Challenges and Barriers

We find in this study that scholars face four main kinds of challenges in pursuing a model of engagement that is expressed through the practice of public scholarship. As will be evident in the following discussion, these challenges are not limited to individual matters related to the development of the intellectual and civic skills and capacities public scholarship requires. There are also challenges arising from cultural, economic, and political trends and dynamics.

Time Commitment

One of the more obvious challenges many of the scholars in our case examples encounter in their engagement work has to do with time. Put simply, it takes a lot of it. Listen to Nick Jordan:

I would say that it's certainly true that to be a full-fledged member of a public-work group is very time consuming in a way that there isn't a lot of support for. It's time consuming particularly if one needs to actually be involved in the organizing of the public work group. I've been key to that organizing, as well as being the scholar who works in relationship to that public work. So just the large time cost of this work obviously has to be mentioned.

As we see from Jordan's comments, it isn't just the amount of time that creates a challenge. It's the way the extra time is spent: namely, in organizing and becoming a "full-fledged member of a public-work group."

For David Campbell, the lack of support for the time commitment that is required to engage with communities in public work in deep and sustained ways is a reflection of the university's "misguided" priorities. He finds that these priorities show up in his own work patterns, as we see in the following excerpt from his reflections about his experience with Gail Feenstra in the PlacerGROWN project:

Apart from whatever else is misguided in terms of our priorities or emphasis out of the university, I think part of what's wrong with how we work—or what could be better—is just how little time we make for that real follow-up connection. There's always the next thing to run on to. So as Gail and I worked on the first case study we did of the PlacerGROWN project, it deepened our sense of responsibility or connection with these people and their project and made us want to have more space and time for clear reflection. I think we're both aware that we haven't done a lot of that.

In the case of PlacerGROWN, why didn't we make it more of our business to insert ourselves into the situation, not to say, "Here's what you're doing wrong; do it right," but to be more part of the ongoing conversation there? That's a tough challenge. I work with county people statewide, and to take the time to do that thoroughly and well within any one place means saying "no" to a lot of other things.

From Campbell's reflection, we can see that part of the difficulty in making a bigger investment of time for "follow-up connection" is that it requires saying "no" to other opportunities and responsibilities. In Campbell's position as director of the statewide California Communities Program, this is hard to do. The impulse to say "no" is, in a real sense, structured into his position by the reality of his statewide responsibilities.

We learn from Campbell's and Feenstra's case, however, that when scholars make a deliberate choice to invest time in relationships, even at a relatively modest level, there is an intellectual and civic payoff. We learn this as Campbell continues his reflection on what happened when he and Feenstra decided to invest time working with people in Placer County to harvest lessons from the PlacerGROWN project by constructing a case study about it (Campbell and Feenstra 2001). The case study involved several visits to Placer County, many interviews, and lots of back-and-forth interaction with the organizers of PlacerGROWN. According to Campbell:

> One of the things that happened when we wrote the case was we learned about the thinness of our relationship with the communities, and how much we didn't know of the local knowledge. For example, our whole lens was how does this thing fit into the bigger scheme of this movement that we're trying to ferment here? And their whole picture was, here's what happened ten years ago in our county with the development of farmers' markets, and then PlacerGROWN came along and now we've got Placer Legacy, which is a new ag conservation program they have in the county. And the people who are involved in these are some of the same people, and some new players are coming in as things go along. So they were really sensitive to the local evolution and history. And you talk about rigor and making meaning out of

something! Digging in to the degree that you value that sense of the local history helps open up a whole new vista on what this means that if we had just done a real quick hit and run we would never have gotten.

Here we see that the rigor of the research process and the quality and trustworthiness of the knowledge Campbell and Feenstra constructed were greatly improved by investing additional time in relationship building. The extra time opened up a "whole new vista" on the meaning of the PlacerGROWN project that Campbell and Feenstra would have missed if they "had just done a real quick hit and run." The experience, as Campbell reflects back on it, serves as an important reminder that when relationships with communities are "thin," scholarship is likely to be thin as well. In this case, Campbell's and Feenstra's thin relationships with the people in Placer County had an effect on their initial understanding of the nature and meaning of the PlacerGROWN story. Their initial understanding was not only thin, it was misleading. Deepening their relationships helped to deepen their scholarship.

Despite the limited success of his work in the PlacerGROWN project, Campbell still feels as though he has not yet dealt with the challenge of time as well as he would like. When the issue came up during one of our project team meetings, Campbell said:

> It's getting clearer and clearer to me how much more time I need to spend on relationships and on the continuity of relationship. And unless I am committed at that level, the fruit of trying to work in the mode that I'm working in isn't going to be there. I'm recognizing that I haven't done that very well up to this point of time. I'm also recognizing that I'm up for promotion right now and I've published three articles since I was last reviewed, so I can say "three" to people and they'd say, "Oh, you're okay. That's all I want to know."

In this reflection, Campbell is telling us two things we should take note of. First, that spending more time with communities in building relationships isn't just a matter of activism or civic duty; it's a crucial ingredient in doing good scholarship. Campbell tells us that unless he spends more time, particularly on building relationships, "the fruit of trying to work in the mode that I'm working in isn't going to be there." The "fruit" is the product of his public scholarship, which includes both academic papers and contributions to civic learning and development. Second, in the last bit of Campbell's reflection, we catch something that might help explain why he hasn't yet made the time commitment he knows he should make. He tells us that he recognizes that as long as he is continuing to publish articles at an acceptable rate, prospects for promotion are good. He doesn't have to invest more time in building relationships to be successful; all he has to do is publish. We might presume that he also recognizes the possibility that if he does invest more time in following up and building deeper relationships with communities, he would have less time for writing articles, jeopardizing his chances for promotion.

While this is indeed a possibility, it need not be a reality. As we learned in our study, persistent follow-up and relationship building does not necessarily involve a sharp tradeoff in scholarly excellence and productivity. In fact, it can be of crucial importance in ensuring scholarly excellence and productivity. David Pelletier's practice story of his intensive work with six counties in northern New York State offers evidence that a scholar can invest a major amount of time in building relationships with communities in a way that is quite productive in academic terms. As we were discussing the issue of time commitment in Pelletier's case at a project team meeting, Victor Bloomfield, Vice Provost for Research and Dean of the Graduate School at the University of Minnesota, offered the following observation:

> I would say that one of the lessons from David Pelletier's story, and a couple of other stories that I'm beginning to learn about, is that time is a part of this kind of scholarship, if it is to be done right. I'm a biophysicist, and so what I have to do is spend a lot of time preparing material and making sure the

instruments are calibrated before I do those five minutes of experiments. Good scholarship always requires preparation. And what I think is true in a lot of areas of research is that people haven't yet owned up to the preparation that needs to be done—working with communities, building trust, building knowledge of context, and a whole variety of concerns that need to be addressed before the work means very much.

This is an important lesson. But it is also a challenge, one that many of our case examples show has not yet been adequately addressed. Bloomfield's way of framing the challenge as simply an expected and necessary component of good scholarship holds a measure of promise in helping public scholars justify and defend the time commitments they make in working with communities.

Skills, Capacities, and Dispositions

A second major challenge is that of developing and practicing the skills, capacities, and dispositions that public scholarship requires. As we discovered in Nick Jordan's case, these include organizing skills such as listening and meshing self-interests, convening and facilitation skills, and both the disposition and capacity to simultaneously pursue civic and academic purposes in ways that are effective, respectful, and productive.

Jordan's reflections on his experience with the farmer learning groups help us to see that one reason why these skills and capacities prove to be challenging is because scholars have not been prepared for them in their academic training. According to Jordan, "To some extent I found it challenging to do this sort of work because it's clearly not anything that I have any official academic training to do. So it's uncharted waters for me. It's an unfamiliar way of working."

As Jordan continues, we learn that what is especially unfamiliar and challenging about public scholarship is that it requires scholars to give up the kind of predictability and control they are used to having in their work. In Jordan's words:

It's unpredictable. It just really challenges you to be very responsive as a scholar to the unfolding of the situation, and to be prepared to make of it what you can. Academics are really challenged in this stuff because you don't have very much control over what really goes on.

So, to the extent that you form a research agenda, it's not at all like doing an experiment where you prepare plots of ground and put out some plants and watch what happens. You have less control over that than you might think, but this, you have radically little control. When people get together in these learning groups, I have no authority to control that conversation. I can only put my two cents in about what direction we ought to be going.

And to the extent that you as a scholar feel that, "OK, I've set up this experiment with learning groups. I have these hypotheses that I want to test out," that's not, I think, a very healthy or realistic way to proceed. It calls for a much more light-on-your-feet M.O. as a scholar. And so, as a person who likes to plan things in advance and have control over situations, I definitely have been challenged by that.

The challenge of dealing with a loss of control is partly that it forces scholars to figure out how to pursue their academic agendas in the context of open-ended, unpredictable processes of public work. The loss of control also raises uncertainties about the academic payoffs of scholars' engagement work. This is a challenge not everyone is willing to face, particularly scholars who are not yet tenured. As Jordan acknowledges in his reflections, "I would certainly be nervous about doing this kind of work if I weren't tenured." He would also be nervous if it was all he was doing. He explains:

I guess, for me, if I didn't have other parts of my scholarly identity that were a little more under my control, like writing review papers, then I would feel pretty darn nervous. It calls for a person to have a diversified portfolio. Even if the farmer learning experiment's a complete disaster, even if the farmer learning groups prove to be not very fruitful, I can always sit back in my office and do computer models and write review papers, both of which I do. So, in other words … I can do stuff that may flop totally.

A passage from David Campbell's reflections on his experience with the PlacerGROWN project adds to our understanding of the challenge of practicing public scholarship under conditions of uncertainty. As noted briefly above, Campbell and Feenstra began their work in the PlacerGROWN project by crafting and promoting a vision of community food systems in a request for proposals (RFP). As Campbell reflects,

It was really surprising to me to put that vision out there and see that people responded, that I'm not just sitting here in isolation thinking these things up. There's a connection out there, and people are going to take this seriously. Actually, as an academic that was kind of frightening; maybe I'm leading people down the wrong path.

In my work as a classroom teacher, which prior to this had been most of my academic work, it was easy to play with ideas and play with visions, to throw a lot of things out and to try to stimulate thinking. You do that seriously and you hope you have an impact on people's lives. This was a different scale. This was directly influencing some real-world projects that were going to involve the investment of time and energy and money—and not knowing where that would go. There was kind of open-endedness to this vision. It wasn't clear that it was going to change the world immediately or if it was even necessarily the right way of thinking about it. So that was my fear: what becomes of this?

It woke me up to my own responsibility. I think I feel that more strongly now than I did on the front end, when it was

"Let's dream something up." It pushes me toward more deliberate connection with the people whose work I'm evaluating, or sponsoring, or whatever. And it makes me want to be really careful to follow up and see what happens, see what's working and what's not working, and to adjust accordingly on my end.

We can see from Campbell's reflections that one of the key challenges he faced in working with the folks in Placer County was to learn how to be responsible for the real-world consequences of his ideas and actions, something he was not so immediately faced with in his classroom teaching. While this is perhaps not so much a skill as it is a disposition or ethic, actually practicing it does require skill.

Importantly, we see here how the experience of engagement can serve as a means for awakening a sense of responsibility, raising it up, for Campbell at least, to levels that he didn't have when most of his academic work was confined to the campus. This responsibility is not just to do excellent academic work that provokes thinking and learning, but also to do careful public work—careful in that it calls on scholars to consciously attend to the way they influence and affect real-world projects that involve the investment of people's time and money.

In Campbell's own judgment, in the PlacerGROWN project he succeeded better with the academic side of his responsibility than the public work side. As he told me, "Part of what's striking is how frequently I have the sense that my academic work has been of high quality, but it doesn't connect with people." He continues:

A lot of the challenge for me was: What is the right theoretical frame to put around this work? And how much of that do you put in terms of the big political/economic clash versus how much do you view it in much more local terms, as just another community endeavor? Part of what I tried to do with the case study is say that those two things ought to link up and that it's the linkage that academic reflection ought to help promote and contribute to. I feel successful in the sense that I wrote something that tries to do that. But I don't think that that's necessarily making much of a difference in how local people think about what they're doing or how anybody more broadly is thinking about it.

Campbell's honest reflections about how he perceives his work as being more successful in academic terms than it is in civic terms are helpful. They remind us that the skills, capacities, and dispositions that are required to do excellent scholarship that is recognized as such by the academy are not necessarily the same—and may even be in conflict with—what it takes to do excellent public work that contributes to civic learning and development in ways that are recognized as being valuable by citizens beyond the academy. There is an important research agenda to open up and pursue here on the question of how scholars manage to successfully develop and put into practice a set of skills, capacities, and dispositions that enable them to be successful in both academic and civic terms.

David Pelletier's reflections on his own development as a scholar provide some preliminary insight into this question. At a project team meeting, much of which was devoted to collective reflection on the meaning and significance of Pelletier's practitioner profile, he said the following:

I did some more thinking last night about my development. I started reflecting about how I moved from a strictly intellectual interest in nutrition problems to a much greater awareness of the social and political world, and then to the political dimensions of what my work clearly should be. These were major transformations that I went through. I asked myself, "How? How did it happen? What made my journey go in the path that it did?"

I came up with three answers. One was exposure to people and experiences. There were people on campus like my immediate supervisor, people off campus, very rich experiences in

Africa, and then deeply rich experiences in communities in upstate New York. So exposure was one.

Second, and probably the biggest, is what I call letting go— the willingness to let go of my prior convictions, my intellectual concepts, my notion about nutrition being really important. We need to get nutritional improvement, but maybe there are some more important things in life. Letting go of that. Letting go of one's beliefs whether they're about political philosophy or whatever. Letting go is critical to being able to see things from other people's perspective. And I had to let go at several points. But each time I came out in what I felt was a better place, so each time it became easier.

And then third, after you let go and you throw yourself into new situations, whether they're in the literature or in the real world, there's a need to reintegrate, to come out in a new place and say, "How is what I'm looking at here, or going through here, how does that relate with what I used to think?" And that requires a lot of work to try to reintegrate that somehow. It's an ongoing process.

And over all of this are these parameters of uncertainty and reviewing and struggling. There's risk and there are easier ways to make a living. I sort of agonized about this. I think there's some sort of a commitment that's coming from deep inside to put you through this. And somehow, I think a lot of people find themselves in a place where it's either too risky or the reasons for doing it are not clear. So they don't let go, they can't let go, and they're deprived of exposure to people and experiences actually helping them through the process.

What we get from Pelletier's reflection is an awareness of the combined importance of mentors, experience, the willingness and disposition to take risks by "letting go" of prior convictions and intellectual concepts, and the ongoing intellectual work of consciously examining one's views in relation to what one learns

both from reading academic literatures and from experience.
All these things, of course, can be viewed as being important in
the development of any scholar's work. What makes Pelletier different, what makes him a *public* scholar rather than just a scholar
in general, is the conscious move he made in his career to situate
and practice at least some of his scholarship in and with publics,
in pursuit of public as well as academic ends.

Pelletier tells us that embracing a disposition to let go,
especially by working with and learning from non-academics
beyond the campus, is both difficult and risky. In part, this is
because there are strong disincentives in the academy for doing
so. I turn now to a discussion of what we learned about these
disincentives from our study.

Disincentives

One of the disincentives that scholars who practice public
scholarship encounter, particularly in research universities, has
to do with the culture of the reward system. We've already heard
Nick Jordan tell us that he would be "nervous about doing this
kind of work" if he weren't already tenured. This fear is linked to
his judgment that public scholarship is slow and unpredictable,
making it risky for scholars who face pressing expectations to
publish their research quickly.

When I interviewed Fred Beir, an emeritus professor of
economics at the University of Minnesota who played a small
role in the Experiment in Rural Cooperation case (Chapter Three),
he told me flatly that for "junior faculty or younger faculty, it's
very difficult to justify involvement in this kind of thing." I asked
him why. "The academic payoffs just may not be there in terms of
ability to publish in a scholarly journal," he told me. "I don't
think it's fair to ask assistant professors who are not tenured to
spend a lot of time on these kind of activities, because it's the
kind of activity that if you fall in love with it, will take a lot
of your time and may detract from you accumulating the kind of

record that's going to be necessary for you to be recognized by your department and promoted."

Reflecting on his work in the PlacerGROWN project at one of our project team meetings, David Campbell said: "The pieces that I thought were the most creative and the most useful at the community level were the ones that I can't get any university credit for. And the piece that I can get university credit for is the piece that, as I look back, was the least useful for the community folks." At the same meeting, Harry Boyte declared that "at this point, there's no way that the reward structure counts all of the time that goes into building relationships." Boyte is a senior fellow at the University of Minnesota's Humphrey Institute of Public Affairs who has spent a considerable amount of time working with faculty and administrators to renew the University of Minnesota's civic mission. As he continued, he pointed to another dimension of the disincentive for public scholarship that is built into the culture of the academic reward system: "Most of the people that are perceived as doing really important scholarship have civic motivations; they just don't admit it. So we're dealing with a culture where you're negatively rewarded for admitting your public motivations. And that's a huge issue to take on."

It's important to point out that disincentives related to the reward structure are not insurmountable. Our case scholars themselves offer evidence of this. When I asked Nick Jordan how his farmer-learning experiments were viewed by colleagues in his department, he said:

> In my department, I think this whole project has been respected because it's seen as something novel, because we've gotten a bunch of grants, and because I think I've been able to explain why it makes sense for me to do it as a scholarly undertaking. My sense is that the peer review committee that we have understands what I'm up to. I certainly haven't gotten any negative feedback in my annual

evaluation. In fact, now that I think about it, they give you little bulleted feedback pointers, and I think several times there's been a comment that they were pleased that I was doing this.

Scholars in other cases have had similar experiences. After their involvement in the case studies described in this book, David Campbell and David Pelletier were both tenured, and Nick Jordan and Marianne Krasny were both promoted to full professor. Other scholars, such as Robert Williamson and Ellen Smoak, were recognized and rewarded in other ways for their public scholarship work.

Still, the disincentives described above appear to have at least a negative psychological effect, judging from the reflections of the scholars I interviewed. And there are additional disincentives related to professional norms and the politics of knowledge in universities. David Pelletier pointed to this when he told me about the dominance in the academy of what he calls the "expert model."

In his own field of nutrition policy, Pelletier argues that scholars believe that their public role is not to engage with communities but to "to dictate public policy" based on their expert knowledge and judgment. This view stands in sharp contrast to Pelletier's commitment to use his scholarly expertise to enable citizens to bring public values into the policy process through deliberative action research initiatives. We saw him pursue this commitment in his work with the North Country project. A key point here is the distinction between doing scholarship *for* the public versus doing it *with* the public. Whether the former is accepted and rewarded or not in academic culture, the latter appears not to be, at least in Pelletier's judgment.

Craig Hassel, an associate professor of nutrition at the University of Minnesota who played a key role in the wild-rice case (Chapter Seven), adds to our understanding of disincentives related to academic culture, professional norms, and the politics of knowledge. When I interviewed him, Hassel told me what his experience has taught him about professional norms in the land-grant system:

> From a practical standpoint, the land-grant system is, by and large, set up to allow faculty to develop their own research interests and to progress in their careers and professions from a perspective of narrow self-interest. The entire system is set up to facilitate that happening. Whether that happens in a manner that's consistent with the public's interest is purely a function of how that faculty member sees her or his own self-interest.

> Since I've been hired here and have come on board, I've heard precious little conversation about the University of Minnesota being a land-grant university, and what does that mean, and what is our public accountability, and what is the public commitment that comes with that. There's been very little, if any, of that kind of conversation, in terms of the implications for my work as a professional scientist or scholar.

> I think it's because as we're schooled and acculturated, we're steered away from those broader, contextual, philosophical kinds of questions or issues. It's much more important as a scientist to become competent with methods, procedures, data analysis, investigative functions, and the process of generating knowledge than it is to ask, "What is our role?" or "Who do we work for?" Those kinds of questions are very minimally attended to.

By themselves, the freedom in academic culture to follow self-interest and the lack of attention to questions of public accountability and roles don't necessarily add up to a disincentive for public scholarship. But when a scholar chooses to do public scholarship with what Hassel calls "nontraditional publics"—in his case, publics in the Native American community in Minnesota —professional norms can provide a strong disincentive. Drawing from his experience, Hassel reflects:

In the subculture of food science and nutrition at the University of Minnesota, it's quite acceptable to work with the dairy industry and do work that benefits the dairy industry, with the underlying assumption that whatever benefits the dairy industry will in fact benefit the people of Minnesota and the citizens of this country. And that is seen as entirely within the cultural norm. But the more you work with nontraditional publics, there is in fact a strong negative reward system that increases the more marginalized that public becomes. Your work becomes actively discouraged.

I've seen faculty who have engaged in public scholarship with more nontraditional audiences being told, basically, "You need to visit a counselor. You really need to talk to somebody. Are you still happy and healthy?" The individual is maybe making the move of her life and she's engaged, she's doing scholarship, she's doing meaningful work, but the reward system is clearly not there to recognize and support that effort. The exact opposite is in effect. You get nothing for it. In fact you're ostracized often times by peers who are threatened by that.

In Hassel's field of food and nutrition sciences, scholars often pursue what he refers to as the "state's public interest"—namely, its interest in pursuing economic productivity and growth—by working with the dairy industry, as Hassel mentioned above, or with corporations like Pillsbury and General Mills. Traditional publics that scholars work with include consumers who want scientific guidance on nutrition issues. While Hassel has worked with corporations and consumers in the past, even securing his own patents for his discoveries, as his career evolved he got more interested in engaging with nontraditional publics. This explains in part why he was asked to co-teach the undergraduate honors course on the wild-rice controversy that is described in Chapter Seven. His experience with that controversy taught him something about the disincentives and barriers for public scholarship that are tied to cultural norms, including the politics of knowledge at the university. In his words,

> The wild rice controversy really highlights the question, "What kind of knowledge making counts?" And one of the things that comes up is, in the established institution, science really does rule. Science rules. So what you get is something like science versus localized knowledge. Science versus wisdom. You get a culture like the Native Americans who can talk and lay out articulately a long history with a great deal of knowledge with a religious connection and an articulated wisdom system. And they can place that out there on the table, and there's no recognition of it. None. There's no way to recognize that within an institution where science equals knowledge.

> What I see as the barriers to public scholarship are our own cultural norms, the implicit understandings about what it means to be a good professor, what the role of a professor is, what the role of the institution is, specifically along the lines of content-expertise. In order to progress in the way that we need to, we need to be able to give up some of our monopolistic thinking, or at least set it aside and broaden our self-interest-rooted perspectives about why we are here. If we are less concerned with our own parochialism around what knowledge we have and learn to be in a place where knowledge in other sectors of society is exchanged through critical discourse, then there are opportunities for a lot of progress to be made that isn't currently being made.

> From my perspective, there are pressing problems out in society that require this kind of approach. The more complex problems of society require a kind of approach that is more collaborative and involves a sharing of power and a greater participation of voices in the process of defining questions and pursuing alternative solutions. To my way of thinking, our

land-grant universities are not dealing with these kinds of pressing problems in an effective manner, directing resources to them or otherwise helping to address them.

I think there's a lot of opportunity for more progress to be made if a slightly different perspective is taken on the role of these institutions. With not much effort, a significant difference could be made. If we recognize that we do not own a monopoly on valid knowledge or valid knowledge production, we may be able to become less defensive and more partner-oriented. If we're not doing something well or not doing it at all, it doesn't take a lot to do it better. So that, alone, gives me hope.

Hassel's reflections open up space for hopefulness about the possibility of overcoming some of the disincentives for public scholarship that come from cultural norms within the academy. Part of what it will take to maintain this sense of hope in the face of existing disincentives is simply a recognition that doing things differently is always going to be difficult. But that recognition won't mean much unless it is coupled with a deliberate effort to organize, to build allies and support for a different way of doing scholarship. Listen to Victor Bloomfield, speaking in response to what he learned from reading David Pelletier's profile:

I'll get back to the basic question you raised: what were some of our reactions to this profile. One of my main reactions is that it displays how difficult it is, how hard you have to work, and how unpredictable the course is of doing creative scholarship, whether its public scholarship or not.

Most of us as scholars sort of follow the herd. There are obvious questions in the field and obvious methodologies for approaching them, and so on. And that's the way that the typical academic career runs. To do it differently, it takes a lot of courage. And it takes building allies. It takes recognizing that, in your academic environment as well as the broader environment, there's going to be gradations of sympathy and understanding. You can't expect that everybody will immediately roll over and play dead. Nor should you expect that everybody is dead set against it. There's going to be a range of responses, because creative scholarship means blazing new paths and upsetting old values. It's going to be difficult; you're going to get picked on, whether it's public or not.

Declining Public Funding

The glimmer of hope Hassel offers combined with Bloomfield's somewhat reassuring reminder about the difficulty of blazing new paths has to be stood up against our finding of a fourth kind of challenge public scholars in the land-grant system encounter. This is the challenge of pursuing public scholarship in a context of declining public funding. Nick Jordan placed this challenge at the top of his list:

> I would say the most important challenge is that there is a rapid decline in public support for what we're doing. It's just very clear that we're not getting an adequate base of financial support for what we do here. There's a certain managed decline in this department and in this college.

The "managed decline" in Jordan's college—officially called the College of Agriculture, Food, and Environmental Sciences—is, in his view, linked to what he refers to as the "obsolescent story" his college tells about agriculture and the college's role in supporting it. As he puts it,

> There's a current major trend of decline in this institution that in my mind is strongly based on this very obsolescent story that we tell about agriculture and ourselves. That worries me a lot. The obsolescent story is that agriculture is about the production of commodities in an industrial mode, and that that's all it's about. That it's not about public health and it's not about environmental quality, and it's not about rural

communities. The obsolescent story about ourselves, meaning the college that I work in and the agricultural capabilities of the university, is that we serve as a research and development group for the industrialized production of agricultural commodities.

As we see in these comments, the obsolescent story about what scholars like Jordan do doesn't fit with a public-scholarship model of engagement. As long as that is the story that is told, it will be difficult to raise public dollars for public scholarship. Jordan goes on to say what he feels must be done to counter the obsolescent story and thereby stop if not reverse the decline in public funding:

I think that it is essential that we get involved in the effort, actively, to tell quite a different story about farming, and why farming matters to the commonwealth, and what we should be doing differently. What are the hopeful possibilities for doing things differently? So I think working in that direction, sounding that general theme on a number of levels, including to undergraduates here on campus, is clearly important. And getting that message across to the state, to the legislature.

I'm hopeful that we're developing what I think is an increasingly powerful and compelling case against current industrialized agriculture. This case is rapidly expanding beyond the traditional sustainability concerns of environmental quality and rural community well-being to issues like public health, children's health, and environmental quality that are compelling to a much larger group of people. I think that we are coming to connect our notions of how we should function differently as an agriculture college to a broader movement about how universities in general should function differently as engaged, civic institutions.

Interestingly, we find the same theme of conflicting stories in David Campbell's reflections on his work in community food systems projects. When I asked Campbell to tell me if there is a metaphor he would use to characterize his role in PlacerGROWN, Campbell said:

> Chronicler comes to mind. Storyteller. That actually covers the front end and the back end of our work. The visioning Gail and I did with the RFP we wrote is a way of telling the story of what's going on in the world. There are lots of ways to tell that story, and I think the way the ag part of the university tells that story is very different from the way we told it. Our work has the emphasis that it has because that story was crafted and interpreted differently.
>
> The university would say, "Advances in technology equals advances in agriculture equals advances in community." In our version, the advances are leaving lots of folks behind. The advances for some are the drawbacks for others. And in particular, there are advances that are placeless that don't respect the value of particular places. If those places are retained—their vitality and their connection to nature and their heritage—they're going to have to organize because the way the thing's going now, it's going in a different direction.

It's not only at the local level that things related to agriculture are going in a different direction, placing at risk the vitality and heritage of particular places. Decisions are also being made about funding priorities at the campus level that are eroding the capacity of land-grant institutions to work with small-scale community-oriented agriculture. Listen to Dan Cooley speak about what has been happening at UMass:

> We have a department of vet and animal sciences that made a decision approximately 10 to 12 years ago that they were going to very much downplay extension and the applied side of what they do in that department in order to focus on molecular biology and biotechnology. And they've successfully done that. All of their new hires to this day are coming in replacing people that might have been milk production

specialists, you know, you name it. Those old guys that could go out on a farm and know what was going on are gone. They've been replaced by people that don't leave the lab. The administration here more or less aided and abetted that by saying that they were not going to put support into a dairy program or a dairy farm because they didn't feel we had an industry that merited that.

With the erosion of public funding and support and the growing interest in expensive, cutting edge research in genomics and biotechnology, financial support from the private sector has grown in importance. While some scholars do not find this to be troublesome, others do. Among them was Ron Prokopy, who had the following rather strong perspective on the negative effect of financial support for land-grant research from industry:

I see the ever closer relationship between university and industry as a very dangerous thing. I don't like to see universities encouraging their faculty members and researchers to establish ever closer ties to businesses and to try to patent their work. I think it not only removes their independence, but it engenders a certain kind of motivation within the researcher to perhaps conduct studies that the person normally wouldn't conduct in order to profit from them, studies that are less directed at helping the general public at large or the environment. It's a profiteering kind of motive, and this is not what a university should be about, in my opinion, whatsoever.

We should be devoting our energies toward educating, in the larger sense of the word, our students to be responsible citizens. And we should be devoting our research energies to the greatest extent possible to do socially responsible research, not research to enhance the well-being of large corporations. You've got so many people in entomology departments across the country working on the products of industry, trying to evaluate those products. Their work is not focused on other things that I think are of more universal, larger benefit. They're getting a lot of money from these companies to do this work, and I think they're compromising a lot of the purpose of the university in doing that.

Prokopy's concerns are shared by others, including Don Wyse, a professor of agronomy and plant genetics from the University of Minnesota who is one of Nick Jordan's close colleagues. Wyse has done more than complain about the loss of public dollars. He led a major organizing effort in Minnesota to reverse the trend through the establishment of the Regional Sustainable Development Partnerships (see Chapter Three). Funded by a bill passed by the Minnesota State Legislature, the regional partnerships have made new public dollars available for public scholarship in Minnesota. Listen to how Wyse describes how the idea for the regional partnerships was presented to the legislature:

> When we developed the regional partnerships, we presented it to the legislature in a way that emphasized the fact that the public doesn't have an awful lot to say about the research that's going on within the institution. And we presented the idea from this standpoint: "Thank you for all of the money you send to the University of Minnesota, the buildings are beautiful, new computers, we thank you very, very, very much. But it's too bad we can't work on your behalf because you don't bring the gas money to run our new pickup trucks." You know, the idea that whoever brings the gas money, whether it's NSF dollars or Monsanto dollars, they get to put the gas in the truck. And off go our graduate students in that direction.

Clearly, the decline in public funding raises grave concerns about the future of public scholarship in the land-grant system. When this challenge is coupled with others public scholars face, the prospects for engaging campus and community in sustained and serious ways appear to be bleak. Yet, in the face of these challenges, we see a remarkable perseverance in continuing to pursue engagement. And we also see in many of this book's case

studies some promising successes in raising substantial amounts
of money to support it.

Concluding Note

I want to conclude this chapter by relating a particularly
revealing moment from our study. Many academic professionals
from the land-grant system that I have met and interviewed
over the past four years have come to believe that the tradition
of public service and engagement that they associate with the
land-grant mission is no longer supported and appreciated, particularly in colleges of agriculture. This view emerged almost as
soon as my co-editors and I began our research. It was a key
theme at a meeting we convened at the project's midpoint in July
of 2002. The agenda for the meeting was to discuss the first drafts
of our case studies. Sitting around the table at the meeting were
the authors of most of the cases, members of the research project
team, and several Kettering Foundation staff.

The discussion began on a positive note. Several people
expressed enthusiasm about the cases, saying that they found
them to be inspiring and encouraging. The democratic commitments and intentions and the academic and civic contributions of
the natural and social scientists, extension specialists, and other
academic professionals featured in the cases were noted and
applauded. But the discussion quickly turned critical.

When it was his turn to speak, Dan Cooley declared that
the kind of community engagement exhibited in the cases is not
appreciated or supported by university administrators. The only
things that are really respected and rewarded within the research
universities of the land-grant system, Cooley claimed, are publications in prestigious journals and highly competitive grants
from sources like the National Institutes of Health (NIH) and the
National Science Foundation (NSF). As far as the university is
concerned, whether or not scholars are engaged in communities
in their home states is irrelevant. While we might value such

engagement, Cooley said, the university doesn't. "We'd love to change the way the university thinks about it," he concluded, "but we're having a hard time figuring out how to do that."

Don Wyse, who grew up on a farm in northwestern Ohio, spoke next. "I find this conversation really interesting and enjoyable," Wyse began. But as he went on, it became clear that he actually found it to be more troubling than enjoyable, particularly with respect to its implication that the university is to blame for the problem of a lack of understanding and support for civic engagement. "You know, we refer to the university and our academic disciplines as if it's removed from us all," he said. "But it's us." He continued:

> What I have found is that we create within our departments, in our academic world, these problems that we're dealing with. We do. In my department over the years, we've voted as to what positions we have. We vote on tenure. It's us. We decide those things, based upon the partnerships that we have created with those individuals and communities that we give credibility to.

Wyse went on to say what he thought the problem was. "Over time," he argued,

> we've given credibility to other entities than those communities that we, as individuals around this table, are interested in serving. And I don't think that many of us have put enough effort into figuring out how to present the case to continue to provide services to those communities, to interact with those communities. We talk about it as a university that doesn't support it. Well, I think that in many cases we have not put the effort into creating those opportunities to stay in contact with those communities and organize those communities, to really build a base of support. I think we've become lazy.

He related his argument to his own field. "I'm a weed scientist," he said.

If you look at the weed scientists across the country, I would argue that the weed scientists have been basically lazy over the years. What did they do, where did they get their resources, what community did they serve? They served Monsanto because it was really easy as that chemical rep came around each year and gave them that $20,000 check. They never took the opportunity to think about their interaction with the farmers, their interaction with the communities that were using those input products. And now we watch how that's all played out over time. I think it was a level of academic laziness.

Reiterating his original point about who is responsible for the apparent lack of support for engagement, Wyse continued:

I'm one that doesn't want to just point at the dean, at the president. I think it comes very much back to the academic community not being in the position to have the guts and the skills to continue to interact with those communities. So I feel a little uncomfortable as we talk about it like it's someone else's problem. We as members of land-grant institutions moved into these positions, and there was a framework as we were hired to continue to provide the opportunity to meet the needs of these communities. And I think that we in many cases have moved away from that as individual scientists and as an academic community.

As I had learned from interviewing him several months before the meeting at the Kettering Foundation, Wyse's own career as a weed scientist has been oriented toward and grounded in Roseau and Lake of the Woods Counties in northern Minnesota. His specific work has been to help farmers in these counties address the problem of managing weeds in a grass-seed production system. Over a period of 30 years, Wyse's work with his colleagues and students and the citizens of the northern Minnesota region they are collaborating with has generated millions of dollars in economic development by creating and introducing new varieties of grasses and by developing more profitable and environmentally sustainable cropping systems. It has also generated over 100 refereed journal articles in some of the top journals in Wyse's field.

According to him, however, the ability to continue such engagement in the land-grant system is threatened. The "framework" that he claims was present when he was hired that encouraged and enabled him and his colleagues to work closely with communities has eroded. As he recalled in his comments during the Kettering Foundation meeting, "When I arrived at the University of Minnesota in 1974, I was given $30,000 out of the experiment station to work with a community in northern Minnesota. With $30,000 in 1974, you could have four graduate students, you could have a technician, you could run a show. You could really work on behalf of that community." But today, Wyse says, the money available for new hires from the experiment station is down to only $2,000. Needless to say, you can't run a show on $2,000. The result is that he and his colleagues have had to go after grants from NSF, USDA, and agribusiness groups to support their work. Because such grants do not typically support community-oriented public scholarship, he says, "we're basically having to bootleg the work back into the community." Wyse concluded his comments by observing that while the ability to work directly with communities has been a core value in the land-grant system, particularly in colleges of agriculture and human ecology, "I think we've had too many people walk away from it and not organize to build the framework and the support to continue to keep the institution connected to communities."

I relate this revealing moment from our study because it turns our attention to an important truth. The framework that keeps scholars and their institutions connected to communities must be continually organized and built and fought for. It is not something that is passively inherited. It is something that is actively carried on and given new shape and meaning by the conscious effort of those who are committed to it.

The case studies we have developed and interpreted in this study help us to see why and how some academic professionals are reconstructing this framework in their work as public scholars, and what they are up against as they seek to engage campus and community in mutually beneficial ways. While we have learned much from these cases, there is much more to learn and explore. Many questions remain unasked and unanswered. We intend to pursue them in future studies. We hope this book will provoke readers to raise and pursue questions of their own.

References

Bailey, L. H. 1909. *The Training of Farmers.* New York, NY: The Century Company.

Bonnen, J. T. 1998. "The Land-Grant Idea and the Evolving Outreach University." In *University-Community Collaborations for the Twenty-First Century: Outreach Scholarship for Youth and Families,* ed. R. M. Lerner and L. A. K. Simon. New York, NY: Garland Publishing, Inc.

Boyer, E. L. 1990. *Scholarship Reconsidered: Priorities of the Professoriate.* San Francisco, CA: Jossey Bass.

Boyte, H. C. 2004. *Everyday Politics: Reconnecting Citizens and Public Life.* Philadelphia, PA: University of Pennsylvania Press.

Boyte, H. C. and N. N. Kari. 2000. "Renewing the Democratic Spirit in American Colleges and Universities: Higher Education as Public Work." In *Civic Responsibility and Higher Education,* ed. T. Ehrlich, 37-59. Westport, CT: Oryx Press.

Campbell, D. and G. Feenstra. 2001. "A Local Partnership for Food and Agriculture: The Case of PlacerGROWN." In *Creating Sustainable Community Programs,* ed. M. R. Daniels. Westport, CT: Praeger Press.

Carr, W. and S. Kemmis. 1986. *Becoming Critical: Education, Knowledge, and Action Research.* New York, NY: RoutledgeFalmer.

Chambers, E. T. 2003. *Roots for Radicals: Organizing for Power, Action, and Justice.* New York, NY: Continuum.

Ehrlich, T., ed. 2000. *Civic Responsibility and Higher Education.* Westport, CT: Oryx Press.

Emery, M. and R. Purser. 1996. *The Search Conference: A Powerful Method for Planning Organizational Change and Community Action.* San Francisco, CA: Jossey-Bass.

Fairweather, J. S. 1996. *Faculty Work and Public Trust: Restoring the Value of Teaching and Public Service in American Academic Life.* Boston, MA: Allyn and Bacon.

Fay, B. 1987. *Critical Social Science.* Ithaca, NY: Cornell University Press.

Fink, L. 1997. *Progressive Intellectuals and the Dilemmas of Democratic Commitment.* Cambridge, MA: Harvard University Press.

Fischer, F. 2000. *Citizens, Experts, and the Environment: The Politics of Local Knowledge.* Durham, NC: Duke University Press.

Gitlin, A., ed. 1994. *Power and Method: Political Activism and Educational Research.* New York, NY: Routledge.

Greenwood, D. J. and M. Levin. 1998. *Introduction to Action Research: Social Research for Social Change.* Thousand Oaks, CA: Sage Publications.

Grundy, S. 1987. *Curriculum: Product or Praxis.* New York, NY: RoutledgeFalmer.

Gutmann, A. 1999. *Democratic Education.* Princeton, NJ: Princeton University Press.

Habermas, J. 1972. *Knowledge and Human Interests.* 2nd ed. London, UK: Heinemann.

Habermas, J. 1984. *The Theory of Communicative Action. Vol. 1: Reason and the Rationalization of Society.* Boston, MA: Beacon Press.

Hammersley, M. 1995. *The Politics of Social Research.* Thousand Oaks, CA: Sage Publications.

Jacoby, R. 1987. *The Last Intellectuals: American Culture in the Age of Academe.* New York, NY: Noonday Press.

Kellogg Commission on the Future of State and Land-Grant Institutions. 1999. *Returning to Our Roots: The Engaged Institution.* Washington, DC: National Association of State Universities and Land-Grant Colleges.

Lather, P. 1991. *Getting Smart: Feminist Research and Pedagogy With/In the Postmodern.* New York, NY: Routledge.

Mathews, D. 1999. *Politics for People: Finding a Responsible Public Voice.* 2nd ed. Urbana, IL: University of Illinois Press.

Melzer, A. M. 2003. "What Is an Intellectual?" In *The Public Intellectual: Between Philosophy and Politics,* ed. A. M. Melzer, J. Weinberger, and M. R. Zinman. Lanham, MD: Rowman and Littlefield.

Mezirow, J. 1995. "Transformation Theory of Adult Learning." In *In Defense of the Lifeworld: Critical Perspectives on Adult Learning,* ed. M. R. Welton. Albany, NY: SUNY Press.

Mezirow, J. et al. 2000. *Learning as Transformation: Critical Perspectives on a Theory in Progress.* San Francisco, CA: Jossey-Bass.

Posner, R. A. 2003. *Public Intellectuals: A Study of Decline.* Cambridge, MA: Harvard University Press.

Putnam, Robert D. 2000. *Bowling Alone: The Collapse and Revival of American Community.* New York, NY: Simon & Schuster.

Rasmussen, W. D. 1989. *Taking the University to the People: Seventy-Five Years of Cooperative Extension.* Ames, IA: Iowa State University Press.

Röling, N. G. and M. A. E. Wagemakers, ed. 1998. *Facilitating Sustainable Agriculture: Participatory Learning and Adaptive Management in Times of Environmental Uncertainty.* Cambridge, UK: Cambridge University Press.

Skocpol, T. 2003. *Diminished Democracy: From Membership to Management in American Civic Life.* Norman, OK: University of Oklahoma Press.

Smil, V. 2000. *Feeding the World: A Challenge for the Twenty-First Century.* Cambridge, MA: The MIT Press.

Smith, M. C. 1994. *Social Science in the Crucible: The American Debate over Objectivity and Purpose, 1918-1941.* Durham, NC: Duke University Press.

Smith, R. G. 1949. *The People's Colleges.* Ithaca, NY: Cornell University Press.

Strand, K. et al. 2003. *Community-based Research and Higher Education: Principles and Practices.* San Francisco, CA: Jossey-Bass.

Sullivan, W. M. 1995. *Work and Integrity: The Crisis and Promise of Professionalism in America.* New York, NY: HarperBusiness.

Sullivan, W. M. 2003. Engaging the Civic Option: A New Academic Professionalism? *Campus Compact Reader,* Summer 2003, pp. 10-17.

Taylor, J. F. A. 1981. *The Public Commission of the University: The Role of the Community of Scholars in an Industrial, Urban, and Corporate Society.* New York, NY: New York University Press.

Tierney, W. G., ed. 1998. *The Responsive University: Restructuring for High Performance.* Baltimore, MD: The Johns Hopkins University Press.

White, H. C. 1899. "President's Address." In *Proceedings of the Twelfth Annual Convention of the Association of American Agricultural Colleges and Experiment Stations.* Washington, DC: USDA.

Wolfe, A. 1997. The Promise and Flaws of Public Scholarship. *Chronicle of Higher Education* (January 10): B4-B5.

Wolfe, A. 2003. *An Intellectual in Public.* Ann Arbor, MI: University of Michigan Press.

Zusman, A. 2005. "Challenges Facing Higher Education in the Twenty-First Century." In *American Higher Education in the Twenty-First Century: Social, Political, and Economic Challenges,* second edition, ed. P. G. Altbach, R. O. Berdahl, and P. J. Gumport. Baltimore, MD: The Johns Hopkins University Press.

Chapter Twelve:
Achieving the Promise of Public Scholarship

by Theodore R. Alter

As I read the chapters of this book, I am struck by the profound idealism of the engagement movement, the great promise of scholarship that simultaneously adds meaningful value in the academy and in the community, and the deeply felt commitment of faculty striving to bridge academic and community cultures. I am also struck by the challenges facing these public scholars. These challenges point to significant institutional and faculty development issues that must be addressed if we are serious about engagement as scholarly work. My purpose in this chapter is to identify the most important of these issues and to suggest actions for addressing them that will enable us to more fully achieve the promise of public scholarship.

The Kellogg Presidents' Commission refers to engagement as returning to our roots in land-grant and public higher education (Kellogg Commission 1999). The Commission speaks of the importance of scholarly engagement as a means for benefiting both universities and communities. Ideally, communities, businesses, and families can benefit by drawing on scholars' knowledge and skills to address important problems and issues. At the same time, universities and faculty can strengthen their teaching programs and enrich student learning by grappling with significant issues in real-life settings. They can also inform and shape their research agendas through engagement initiatives. Society benefits as well from the civic impacts of engagement in strengthening the fabric of our democracy at the community level. As the Commission points out, reciprocity is central to mutually beneficial engagement for communities and universities. Reciprocity means respecting roles, perspectives, needs, and sources of knowledge. It also means sharing information, knowledge, and wisdom, collaboratively defining problems, and jointly finding meaningful solutions to those problems.

Yet, despite the potential benefits of engagement, and despite historical and current rhetoric about its importance, it is clear that the promise of engagement is not being fully realized. There are several reasons why this is so, including philosophical differences about the nature of scholarship and the roles of the university in society, institutional policy and procedural limitations, budget and other resource constraints, faculty and administrator reluctance to become involved in engagement initiatives due to disincentives they face and, not uncommonly, uncertainty about how to proceed in carrying out such initiatives.

At the core of these issues, in my opinion, is the question of scholarship: more precisely, the question of what it means and what it takes to practice legitimate, solid scholarship in the context of engagement. Deeper, more expansive faculty and institutional understanding of this question and its implications would mitigate substantially the challenges associated with the issues noted above. As the cases in this book document, the scholarship that undergirds the engaged university ideal is neither well understood, nor readily accepted in our universities. Consequently, its practice is underdeveloped and undersupported. In such an environment, it is hardly surprising that the full potential of what we in this book call *public scholarship* is not being fully realized.

As defined in Chapter One, *public scholarship* is scholarship that philosophically and operationally reflects the engagement ideal. The cases detailed in this book highlight the promise of such scholarship for communities and universities. At the same time, these cases demonstrate that the practice of public scholarship is hindered by many challenges, including the time commitment it requires; the difficulties involved in acquiring and building requisite skills, capacities, and dispositions; and perceived institutional and disciplinary disincentives. These challenges limit our ability to achieve the potential of public scholarship.

To help faculty and other academic professionals address such challenges, we must develop and implement comprehensive research and faculty and organizational development agendas devoted to significantly strengthening our capacity for public scholarship and engagement.

Personal Perspectives

My perspectives on engagement, public scholarship, and opportunities associated with both are grounded primarily in my 35 years of experience as a graduate student, faculty member, and academic administrator in two major land-grant universities. For 15 of my 30 years as a faculty member, I served in academic administrative assignments, as head of a department of agricultural economics and rural sociology, interim dean and associate dean for a major college of agricultural sciences, regional and statewide director of a large, complex cooperative extension organization, and associate vice-president for university outreach. My undergraduate education at a highly competitive private institution, where scholarly excellence and social responsibility were central to the academic culture, also profoundly influenced my perspectives on the nature of scholarship and its role in society. These experiences, coupled with my role as a member of the project team for this book, have heavily influenced my current thinking about engagement, public scholarship, and their place in our land-grant and public universities.

In Chapter Ten, Vic Bloomfield makes the point that all university scholarship is public scholarship, because in almost every instance it makes a short- or long-term societal contribution.

He emphasizes that one reason public and land-grant higher education is challenged financially and politically today is that we have not done a good job of making that point and explaining the impacts and public contributions of our scholarship to citizens, community leaders, government officials, and decision makers. I agree in general with Bloomfield's arguments, especially the need for telling the story of those contributions better than we have thus far.

I strongly believe that community-situated public scholarship, as discussed and illustrated in this book, in essence Bloomfield's local public scholarship, is substantive, significant, and profound scholarship that adds meaningful value in both academic and community contexts. I believe it is such scholarship that epitomizes the engagement and land-grant ideals, and I believe that it should be an integral, fully legitimized component of the academic portfolio of public and land-grant universities. As Scott Peters notes in Chapter One, the issue is not about defining public scholarship as an alternative to more traditional forms of scholarly activity. The issue is fostering pluralism in our scholarship and recognizing the special contributions different approaches make to the university's core mission of creating, disseminating, and applying knowledge in service to society.

Public scholarship, by its very nature, engages and integrates campus and community. Strengthening public scholarship requires understanding university and community cultures and their intersection, since public scholars require legitimacy in both cultures (Lerner and Simon 1998). Developing a serious faculty and organizational development agenda for advancing public scholarship thus requires insights from both university and community perspectives. To have meaningful and sustained impact, such an agenda must define new frames of reference, new models, and different structures from those typically in place. In the next section, my purpose is to provide perspective on how we might deepen and expand a civic professionalism in our universities that manifests itself in the practice of public scholarship. Based on my professional experiences over the years and the cases in this book, I highlight the changes that strike me as important for strengthening and supporting university and faculty capacity for public scholarship.

Strengthening University Capacity

From my perspective, there are four critical issues that must be addressed in building university capacity for public scholarship. These include institutional leadership, the culture of scholarship and faculty reward systems, graduate education, and the creation of enabling settings for public scholarship.

Institutional Leadership

When striving for large-scale, transformative organizational change, the need for strong leadership is obvious. As a result of the renewed interest in public engagement in recent years, we see many university presidents, provosts, vice presidents, and deans emphasizing its importance, and by implication, the importance of public scholarship. While such leadership is essential, it must go beyond rhetoric. Otherwise, it will be difficult to convince faculty, administrators, and external stakeholders that the university is truly committed to public scholarship. Not only must a vision for public scholarship as central to university values and functions be articulated, but a plan for how to go about achieving that vision must be detailed. Typically, the former is done well and the latter is given short shrift, resulting in major organizational change initiatives that founder and fail to achieve their promise, leaving frustration and cynicism in their wake (Kotter 1996). The pursuit of the latter involves, among other things, addressing issues associated with disciplinary and departmental cultures; building and supporting enabling settings for public scholarship; putting in place new systemic administrative structures and processes; building leadership commitment and capacity supportive of public scholarship among deans, department heads,

faculty and administrative unit leaders; and building the relationships with external constituents and government officials that are
necessary to support the university's engagement mission.

While top-level administrative leadership is critical for
positioning engagement and public scholarship as core university
values and functions, faculty leadership is also essential. In large
measure, the culture of scholarship and the education and research
programs of the university are determined and shaped by faculty.
Those faculty who engage in public scholarship, those who would
like to, and those who have a large vision for scholarship and the
university in society must assume leadership for creating a new
culture that better supports public scholarship, redefining and
broadening the nature of scholarly activities, revising faculty
reward systems, and building supportive, enabling settings for
public scholarship. These actions are essential for deep and
sustained organizational change. Faculty senate leaders and
influential faculty at all levels within the university, must assume
this responsibility. Ideally, faculty and academic administrators
should work in partnership to bring about these changes.

The Culture of Scholarship and Faculty Rewards Systems

If university capacity for public scholarship is to be strengthened, scholarship must come to be viewed and rewarded in a
more expansive perspective than is currently the norm in most
universities. With respect to changing the culture of scholarship,
Jim Bonnen's (1986) notion of academic and scholarly work along
the knowledge continuum—from the creation of disciplinary
knowledge, to its synthesis and interpretation in a subject-matter
context, to its adaptation and use in problem solving—provides
a helpful conceptual tool. From this perspective, scholars, both
individually and collectively, work across this continuum, with
each stage supporting and informing the other. In this model,
scholarship is integral to both problem solving and the creation
of new knowledge.

Another approach to scholarship is detailed in the UniSCOPE 2000 Report, prepared by the UniSCOPE Learning Community, a group of senior faculty at Penn State University (Hyman, et al. 2000; Hyman, et al. 2001/2002; and Gurgevich, et al. 2003). UniSCOPE stands for University Scholarship and Criteria for Outreach and Performance Evaluation. The UniSCOPE model of scholarship is a multidimensional, dynamic model that conceptualizes teaching, research, and service, each of the primary mission areas of the university, as interdependent and as a continuum of scholarship that involves discovery, integration, application, and education. The UniSCOPE model views the "scholarship of engagement" (i.e., public scholarship as defined in this book) as an integral component of teaching, research, and service that is informed by—and which in turn, informs—discovery and integration, within and across each of the three functions.

The essence of both of these views is a vision of scholarship as a dynamic, holistic, interdependent, and iterative endeavor spanning the entire knowledge continuum. Both approaches view scholarship as integral across the teaching, research, and service functions of universities. Scholarship, in these views, is the thoughtful discovery, transmission, and application of knowledge, grounded in disciplines, professions, and interdisciplinary fields, and characterized by creativity and openness to new information, debate, criticism, and the judgment of peers (Hyman, et al. 2000).

Conceptualizing scholarship in this manner takes public scholarship, and other such engagement activities, out of the traditional category of service space and places it in broader scholarship space. This shift provides an integrated, holistic frame for evaluating and documenting the contributions of public scholarship in both the academy and the community. Philosophically, conceptually, and operationally, it positions public scholarship as a manifestation of legitimate university scholarly activity. I see the cases in this book as clearly being in this broader scholarship space.

As the engagement movement has gained momentum in recent years, many universities have created initiatives, task forces, and forums devoted to reflection and discussion on the concept and culture of scholarship that drives their research and education programs (Wise, Retzleff, and Reilly 2002; Provost's Committee on University Outreach 1993; Hyman, et al. 2000; Weiser and Houglum 1998; University Reappointment, Promotion, and Tenure Committee at North Carolina State University 2003). Such efforts have resulted in public statements of commitment to a broader, more philosophically rich concept of university scholarship and initiatives to provide guidance on documenting engaged scholarship (Council on Outreach 1997; Church, et al. 2003; Committee on Evaluating Quality Outreach 2000; Clearinghouse and National Review Board for the Scholarship of Engagement).

These developments are helping to create the necessary conditions for positive institutional change in support of public scholarship. Because of their scope, catalyzing and legitimizing these changes is an essential leadership function that must rest ultimately with top university leadership. It is obvious, but important to emphasize, that while a rhetorical commitment to change is necessary, it is not a sufficient condition for ensuring profound institutional change. Change must also be actively modeled over time and effectuated through moral suasion by faculty and administrative leaders at all levels in the university. Real changes in policies and administrative procedures that affect tenure and promotion, annual performance review, resource allocation, and other administrative matters that affect faculty support and incentives must also be developed and implemented.

What is viewed as appropriate scholarship is shaped by universities, but it is also shaped in important ways by professional societies. These societies influence profoundly what faculty within disciplines view as legitimate scholarly activity. Broadening notions of scholarship within our universities requires that the professional societies broaden their notions, as well. University presidents, provosts, deans, department heads, and faculty all have a critical role in providing leadership for provoking discussion about the meaning and culture of scholarship within their professional societies. This discussion is a critical step in creating an academic culture in which public scholarship can thrive.

Fully enfranchising a broader view of scholarship has implications for universities beyond how faculty think of their work as scholars. Given university resource limitations, it has potentially profound implications for shifting status, power, and resource relationships among various academic units within the university. For example, as public scholarship becomes as legitimate as traditional forms of scholarly activity, it will give rise to new organizational positions and support structures. It will also increase the competition among different groups for scarce organizational funding and resources. Because these kinds of changes threaten entrenched interests, it is important to recognize the potential for considerable opposition to a fully enfranchised public-scholarship model. This matter is central to the success of initiatives to institutionalize and sustain a new, broader model of scholarship within the university. The dynamic competitive forces that such change can unleash are powerful. Dealing with them requires vision, commitment, openness, and leadership. It also requires an understanding that strengthening public scholarship can result in a positive gain for all academic interests in the university, not a gain for some and a loss for others.

Faculty reward systems must align with new institutional values and objectives. Assuming strong institutional commitment to public scholarship, there must be visible and robust incentives for faculty to be involved in this activity. Otherwise, the rhetoric at the institutional level about commitment will ring hollow. If faculty see that there are no meaningful incentives to participate, public scholarship will be undermined as an institutional priority.

Faculty reward strategies are, of course, numerous. Annual performance reviews, resource allocation decisions affecting faculty support, public and peer recognition for outstanding accomplishments, salary structures and increments, and tenure and promotion review are among the most important leverage points affecting faculty incentives. While promotion and tenure review, depending on the stage of one's academic career, is arguably the most important of these strategies, all provide strong signals about what is valued and what is not valued by the institution.

In the promotion and tenure process, the most problematic issue for faculty peers and academic administrators is what constitutes legitimate evidence of scholarly excellence for those involved in public scholarship. As a part of the effort to legitimize public scholarship, this is a question that has received considerable attention in recent years (Clearinghouse and National Review Board; Committee on Evaluating Quality Outreach 2000; Wise, Retzleff, and Reilly 2002). Much of this work has focused on the variables, measurement, and standards for documenting scholarly excellence in outreach programs and engagement initiatives.

Faculty peers and academic administrators often express confusion and frustration about how to evaluate the scholarly legitimacy of public scholarship activities. This points to the need to focus on criteria for documenting the scholarly excellence of such work. At the same time, I find this confusion and frustration curious. We have little trouble in defining the standards for evaluating the scholarship of those who teach and carry out research in the traditional campus context, although this matter too deserves much serious reflection with regard to the value of these standards. To be taken seriously as scholarship, faculty work must successfully pass through the filter of peer review and evaluation. The same process should apply in the case of public scholarship.

What specific evidence of scholarly contribution should we expect to see for faculty involved in public scholarship? Fundamentally, we need to see evidence of scholarly excellence through engagement. I think, by and large, we can look for the same evidence we typically expect: educational initiatives grounded in current and emerging science; innovation and creativity in teaching, specifically educational program development and design, teaching methods, and educational support materials; significant, positive impact on student learning and behavior; coherent, productive research programs that make important contributions along the knowledge continuum, as evidenced by a robust and continuous stream of peer-reviewed, scholarly publications; participation, through attendance and making presentations at professional, technical, and scholarly meetings; regular publication in professional, popular, and non-peer reviewed publications and outlets; acquisition, sustained over time, of external funding to support education and research programs; participation in departmental and university governance; and service contributions to one's profession and the public.

This familiar set of expectations applies, it seems to me, as much to public scholarship as it does to what is perceived as more traditional faculty scholarship. I suggest we not think of faculty public scholarship and engagement initiatives as somehow so different that we don't know how to evaluate them for tenure, promotion, annual performance review, and salary administration. In short, I suggest that we already have the core evaluative framework in place. We simply need to apply it, rather than continuing to wring our hands about how to proceed.

I do believe, however, that public scholarship includes an additional expectation that must be recognized in assessing its quality. As noted in Chapter One, public scholars embrace the civic professional's public pledge to pursue public-regarding ends in public-regarding ways (Sullivan 2003). Excellence in public scholarship must show evidence of the two dimensions of this pledge. This issue needs our attention, however, because our frameworks for evaluating the civic aspects of public scholarship are underdeveloped.

Graduate Education

Graduate education is a central element of the university academic enterprise. The education and training of graduate students in the disciplines is the primary source of the next generation of scholars, as well as administrative leaders such as department heads, deans, provosts, and presidents. The graduate education process helps stimulate and advance faculty teaching and research and contributes to the process of creating knowledge.

At the same time, it is important to recognize that graduate education is also the primary socialization process for the next generation of faculty and administrative leaders (Austin 2002). The graduate experience not only develops disciplinary expertise and values, but it also inculcates broader academic cultural values, such as what kind of scholarship is valued and why, what evidence is most appropriate for documenting scholarship, the relative scholarly importance of teaching and research, the relative status of different disciplines, the most appropriate ways of knowing, and what it means to be a university professor. These are cultural values that stay with faculty throughout their careers and fundamentally shape their scholarly work and attitudes.

Viewed from this perspective, graduate education is a critical and essential vehicle for leveraging long-term, sustainable change in the scholarly and organizational culture of our universities. Consequently, if we are truly committed to public scholarship as part of our university academic portfolio, the graduate education experience must build the disciplinary expertise, the skill sets, attitudes and values, and the leadership that will nurture public scholarship as central university work and allow it to flourish in the future. The issue here is not having every faculty member practice public scholarship as defined in this book. The issue is creating and fostering a campus culture that understands, supports, and invests in public scholarship in the future.

If we are truly committed to university communities that respect and value public scholarship, we must recognize the fundamental impact of graduate education on our future campus cultures and suggest how graduate education should be changed to reflect this commitment. One possibility is to provide internally funded and endowed land-grant graduate fellowships and assistantships that would enable students both to develop their disciplinary expertise and to be substantively involved in public scholarship and engagement initiatives with a faculty mentor. To be meaningful, such graduate education experiences would be situated in the context of established public scholarship initiatives and fully integrated with students' coursework and research. Of course, not every student will choose this route. The important point is that such an opportunity would be institutionalized formally in graduate education programs. At present, this is not typically the case in our universities.

The Creation of Enabling Settings

Finally, building university capacity for public scholarship requires focused attention to systematically building and sustaining institutional platforms and a climate that supports and nurtures faculty involvement in that work. The challenge is to create enabling settings within which public scholars can achieve their full potential. The creation of enabling settings involves the provision of new resources, or the reallocation of existing resources for targeted purposes. It also requires the restructuring of individual and group incentives, the establishment of new policies and procedures, the development of new initiatives, and a fundamental reorientation of an organization's vision and mission (Korten 1984). In sum, creating and sustaining enabling settings means taking actions that aggregate and focus institutional arrangements and resources in support of particular purposes and initiatives.

The creation of enabling settings that support public scholarship is relatively underdeveloped in our universities, despite the visibility and rhetoric of the engagement movement in recent years and our long and distinguished history of land-grant and public higher education in the United States. My suggestions concerning the importance of faculty and administrative leadership, broadening and enriching our notion of university scholarship, aligning faculty reward systems and institutional values, and reforming graduate education are all issues that should be addressed. But, there are other important issues that also must be addressed.

First, as has been made clear throughout this book, effective public scholarship requires a substantial time commitment. It takes time to build community networks and partnerships, and it takes time to work with and through these networks and partnerships in pursuit of public and academic purposes. Conceptually, this is not unlike the time necessary to establish and scale up a new basic research initiative or research involving field and clinical trials. Providing encouragement, significant funding, and other resources to create and sustain community engagement over the long run would greatly enhance the effectiveness of public scholarship. The story of the Experiment in Rural Cooperation, detailed in Chapter Three, reveals the critical role and importance of community-university partnerships as vehicles for public scholarship.

Another institutional mechanism for enabling public scholarship is the creation and funding of interdisciplinary, issue-focused teams of faculty from across the university, charged with conducting public scholarship that engages community and university in mutually beneficial ways (Lerner and Simon 1998). These teams could be formalized as university-wide consortia. To be effective and respected, they should be legitimized by the university, empowered with administrative responsibility and authority, provided with sufficient resources, and given wide visibility, inside and outside the university. Faculty associated with these consortia become faculty of the consortia as well as faculty of their disciplinary departments and colleges. The aggregation of faculty in consortia not only gives visibility to the consortia and their subject matter, but also to the nature of the work. The consortia also become mechanisms for the diffusion of knowledge among faculty regarding theories of engagement and the practice of public scholarship, areas of faculty expertise that are currently underdeveloped. My personal preference is to have public scholarship embedded within consortia responsible for the full breadth of education and research reflected in a broad and expansive culture of scholarship. This would reinforce the interdependence and integration of all scholarship.

There are numerous challenges in creating and sustaining such consortia. The following are among the most important: articulating a clear scholarly vision and charge; establishing credibility and saliency in the eyes of faculty; ensuring a strong leadership and administrative structure and presence; establishing a welcoming environment and climate for cross-cultural conversation and bridging among disciplines, the research and education missions of our universities, and faculty with diverse interests and perspectives; and providing a strong core funding and re- source base. Progressive, visionary faculty and administrative leadership is necessary to meaningfully address these challenges. Possible strategies for ensuring the viability of consortia include: leadership from presidents and provosts to initiate consortia; situating distinguished senior faculty who are well-respected across the university in intellectual and administrative leadership roles; providing seed funding to draw faculty together to define important issues to address and to do the preliminary planning, data gathering, and analysis necessary to compete successfully for major extramural support; and, funding university faculty positions with teaching, research, and public scholarship responsibilities through the consortia.

External groups often level the criticism that universities are not good listeners or partners. Public scholarship is philosophically and operationally grounded in respectful, mutually beneficial community-university partnerships. While these partnerships are necessarily built around specific issues, there is a pressing need for broader community-university relationships. By establishing more open and effective lines of communication, we create a more receptive external environment for enabling public scholarship initiatives. The day-to-day responsibility for positively representing the university and building and nurturing genuinely respectful, reciprocal external relationships rests, in my opinion, with all university faculty and administrative leaders.

An important aspect of creating positive enabling settings for public scholarship is creating substantive faculty development programs. Such programs should incorporate a rich and diverse portfolio of academic and experiential learning opportunities that focus on matters, such as organizational philosophy, effective practice, and university enabling mechanisms. Learning from faculty peers should be emphasized. Listening to the perspectives of current and potential community partners is essential. Spending time in community settings with citizens and community leaders is invaluable.

The endowment of land-grant professorships is another initiative that would make a major contribution to public scholarship in our universities. These professorships could be the academic and scholarly leadership for the land-grant graduate fellowship program described above. The work of these professorships should reflect the land-grant ideal, thus furthering public scholarship in our institutions.

Clearly, an essential aspect of creating and nurturing enabling settings supportive of public scholarship is the allocation of funds to build and sustain these settings. In the clamor and competition for scarce university resources, tradeoffs among legitimate uses of funds are a day-to-day fact of life. But failure to allocate reasonably adequate funding and other resources to the creation and nurturing of enabling settings for public scholarship sends a clear message about university priorities, despite rhetoric indicating support for such settings. More generally, it is not enough to simply create enabling settings for public scholarship. To make these settings a credible, viable reality it also requires concerted leadership to operationalize administrative strategies and tactics, including the allocation of funds and resources.

Strengthening Faculty Capacity

A central element in strengthening university capacity to support public scholarship is creating and supporting a faculty development program. Universities invest in such programs to strengthen faculty teaching and research capacity. Faculty development programs are legitimate institutional investments, and their existence, scope, content, and funding deserve serious attention as elements central to continuing improvement and excellence in the scholarly work of all faculty. If there is indeed commitment behind our engagement rhetoric, we should certainly invest in faculty development programs that build the capacity of faculty to practice it.

As noted above, graduate education is one of the key factors, if not the key factor, in faculty development. We should view graduate education not just as a disciplinary training ground, but as the first critically important faculty development program, in which students learn about the scope and complexity of the values and missions of the university in society; the approaches to scholarship conducted across the university; and what it means to be a university professor, as opposed to being merely a scientist working at a university.

The key question that must be addressed concerns the types of activities that should be central to faculty development programs designed to support public scholarship. Ideally, the elements of a faculty public scholarship development program should be ground ed in the perspectives of both faculty and non-university partners.

One essential issue that must be addressed is what it means for faculty to operate in "public regarding ways." Effective public scholarship is grounded in a deep understanding of, and sensitivity to, this matter; hence it requires considerable exploration and discussion in faculty development programs, from both community and university perspectives. Key issues inherent in the matter of operating in public regarding ways include the relative roles and relationships among experts and citizens in public work (Alter 1987; Fischer 2000; and Schön 1983), cultural bridging (Lerner and Simon 1998), and effective collaboration. Too often, faculty come to public settings as experts with solutions to problems without carefully listening to the opinions and perspectives of citizens. Consequently, the experience, expertise, and wisdom of local people, who indeed are also experts in the context of their own situation and experience, are often lost in the discussion, along with other possible problem solutions. What also can be lost is citizen and community ownership of the solution, and positive community-university relations, which makes work by other university faculty in that particular community setting more difficult in the future. The dynamic of the interaction between experts and non-experts must be better and more broadly understood if the practice of public scholarship is to result in respectful, mutually beneficial relationships.

Faculty involved in public scholarship also face the challenge of developing the ability to work in multi- and cross-cultural settings. This challenge manifests itself in at least three important ways. One is the commonly referenced matter of working sensitively, harmoniously, and effectively in a world that is culturally diverse with respect to race, ethnicity, gender, national origin, sexual orientation, age, disability, and other such attributes of human existence. Cultural diversity is increasingly the norm in most community settings, and is thus a reality of public scholarship work.

A second challenge of multiculturalism associated with public scholarship is the matter of working from the multidisciplinary perspective needed to effectively address most public issues (Lerner and Simon 1998). A third and central challenge is the necessity of bridging the cultures of university and community. Public scholars must operate and carry legitimacy in both cultures (Lerner and Simon 1998). For those who are committed to addressing public-regarding ends, but find the cultural crosswalk difficult to negotiate, partnering with colleagues proficient in that that skill may be a productive solution. Fundamentally, though, if we are serious about public scholarship, we must hire faculty and professional staff who are comfortable and proficient working in both community and university cultures. In sum, public scholars must understand the multicultural contexts that frame and shape their work; learn to be comfortable working within the dynamic set of complexities, pressures, and ambiguities these contexts create; and develop the communication, networking, and other cultural bridging skills essential to operating in that environment.

From a street-level perspective, in most communities the networking and partnership skills of universities and faculty are typically not well regarded. If we hope to overcome this perception, we must develop more effective partnering and collaboration skills. Collaborations grounded in mutual respect, trust, openness, co-learning, mutual advantage, and reciprocity require time, effort, skill, and humility to develop and nurture. The keys to effective partnerships lie in connecting a project's purpose with the personal interests of the people involved; clarity of purpose; congruency of missions, values, and strategy among collaborators; creation of value for all collaborators; regular, frank, and open communication among collaborators; continual learning for all partners; and commitment by all partners to the collaboration (Austin 2000). Developing the perspectives, dispositions, and skills for building and sustaining effective collaborations is important for faculty if they are to operate in public regarding ways.

A second essential issue for a faculty public scholarship development program is to help faculty understand philosophies, theories, and methods of public scholarship. In this context, some of the more important issues that could be fruitfully explored include: faculty as technical experts or public scholars; universities, civic engagement, and democracy; theories of community and community power; methods of community organizing; community development theory and practice; organizational development and leadership; and, organizational and social change. One beneficial outcome of exploring these topics would be the insights we might gain about how to build platforms that support public scholarship initiatives in community settings. Such platforms are as important as the creation of enabling settings within the university. In effect, the purpose of exploring topics such as these would be to assist faculty in developing their own conceptual approaches and operational methods for working in community settings. I believe strongly that these topics must be addressed through more than simply academic study. Community-based experience coupled with academic study is essential for developing the deep understandings of, and operational facility with, these matters. As part of a faculty development program, rich, deep community-based experience can provide invaluable insights, develop and hone skills, nurture values, and ignite passions associated with public scholarship.

A third essential issue for faculty development is handling controversial public issues in public settings. Public scholarship centers typically on important issues that affect multiple interests or publics, each with differing, sometimes diametrically opposed perspectives on the issue at hand. The challenge for public scholars is to create a context that encourages respectful, informed, meaningful exploration of the issue, one in which all parties are genuinely heard and in which their ideas are thoughtfully considered. This environment is an uncomfortable one for many faculty members because values, beliefs, perceptions, and myths (as opposed to science) often drive the discussion in significant ways. But this can also be a valuable learning experience as faculty members gain knowledge, information, and wisdom that is developed through ways of knowing that are different from those that hold sway in universities. Many scholars are uncomfortable in this context because their way of knowing and expert information is often challenged. They can inform and strengthen their practice as public scholars through exploring the experience and methods of others who are seasoned and effective in this milieu.

For the purposes of this discussion, one other issue strikes me as very important for faculty development. That is the connection between public scholarship and our democratic society. On one level, public scholarship necessarily focuses on a specific issue such as apple IPM, food safety, youth development, or ecologically sound farming. On another level, however, public scholarship is about building and fostering the fabric and practices of our democratic society. Effective public scholarship pursues this end by virtue of the way it is conducted, both by its respectful engagement of multiple publics and the due processes used to engage these publics around a particular issue or situation, and by the way public scholars work with others to create the contexts and processes for engaging multiple publics. In doing so, public scholarship models democratic values and processes. It is important for public scholars to understand the implications of their initiatives for building the democratic fabric of our society, so they can consciously incorporate this perspective into their thinking and work.

A Public Scholarship Research Agenda

Developing a robust research agenda focused on the theory and practice of public scholarship is also an essential element in strengthening university and faculty capacity for public scholarship. There is a pressing need to enhance our understanding of issues such as optimal institutional arrangements to support serious and effective engagement initiatives; community perspectives on university engagement and how it might be strengthened; faculty perspectives and needs regarding public scholarship; the implications of public scholarship for the university academic enterprise and university political positioning; and, the impact of public scholarship on public issues resolution and the practice of democracy in communities and society more generally. There is a paucity of systematic research on issues such as these. Such research is necessary to provide evidenced-based understanding of the nature and significance of public scholarship, and to strengthen university and faculty capacity for supporting and undertaking it.

A robust public scholarship research agenda would include the following four components:

1. *An investigation of the actual practice of public scholarship.*
   Conducting research on the practice of public scholarship is

an essential starting point, and should be, at least initially, the primary focus of this research agenda. We have relatively little evidence-based understanding of the ways in which public scholars conduct their work. There is a great need for more extensive research on what works under what circumstances and why. For example, we need to explore how academic professionals as experts establish respectful and productive working relationships with citizens, how and why they pursue public-regarding ends in public-regarding ways, and how they deal with issues of power and self-interest in the context of public problem setting and solving. Research on topics such as these, especially research that utilizes practitioner inquiry as a key methodology, can help to illuminate best practices and generate other insights invaluable for shaping university and faculty capacity-building initiatives.

2. *An investigation of the civic and academic products of public scholarship.* The key question that underlies much of the debate about public scholarship concerns exactly how it contributes to both the public good and the advancement of the academy's core teaching and research missions. Public scholarship, as defined in this book, is scholarly work that makes significant, substantive contributions to the university, academic disciplines, and our collective public life. Thus far, there is limited systematic evidence to support this conceptualization. Longitudinal evaluation research on the academic and community impacts of public scholarship could help clarify the various contributions it makes to community and academic life. Such research holds the potential for underscoring the benefits that would be lost if public scholarship is not properly supported and strengthened.

Ideally, public scholarship also makes an important contribution to the practice of democracy and the development of civil society. In light of the many threats to democracy, research that explores this relationship would be especially valuable. The local community is an appropriate starting place for such a research agenda, precisely because the community is potentially the most important setting for the civil conversation upon which democracy depends. We need to understand how the practice of public scholarship can best model democracy, and we need to use what we learn about this matter to inform faculty development programs in a way that builds the capacity of faculty to contribute to the democratic process.

3. *Research on the factors that affect faculty and administrator socialization, particularly in relation to the understanding and practice of public scholarship.* One way to approach this issue is through developing a better understanding of the possibilities and implications of undergraduate education as a vehicle for public scholarship and university engagement. Service learning is an obvious possibility for moving this line of inquiry forward. There are now many service-learning offerings that provide students with real-life learning opportunities while simultaneously addressing community problems. Systematic evaluations of these courses and their long-term impacts on students, communities, faculty research and teaching, and university engagement structures and activities are needed. We also need to better understand how undergraduate involvement in applied research can support and further the public scholarship agenda. More important, though, we need to conceptualize new undergraduate education programs that bring students, faculty, and administrators together for activities that reach beyond the university. Research should focus on identifying the ways in which undergraduate education can contribute to the practice of public scholarship and how it can help to build university and faculty capacity.

Because graduate school is where future faculty and administrators become socialized to academic cultures and develop an understanding of appropriate roles and behavior, research that focuses on the relationship between public scholarship and graduate education is essential. Graduate education is arguably the major lever for long-term change in academic, disciplinary, and scholarly cultures. Understanding how the values and practice of public scholarship are being addressed (or not) in graduate programs across disciplines and universities can help in making graduate program adjustments that will influence disciplinary and campus cultures in the future.

4. *Institutional research on university structure and function as it relates to public scholarship.* Structure and function are very much interdependent, in that effective practice is grounded in strong institutional supports. A comprehensive view of university practices—both those that support public scholarship and those that hinder it—is a crucial step in identifying necessary innovations in organizational structures and processes, policies and procedures, resource allocation, administrative leadership, and community-university partnerships.

Concluding Remarks

In my view, public scholarship holds great promise for our universities and our communities. It can build strong community-university partnerships that serve to address pressing issues while positively positioning the university in society. Effective public scholarship, grounded in respectful, reciprocal, mutually beneficial relationships with communities, can also make significant contributions to resolving public issues, advancing the scholarly education and research mission of universities, and nurturing democracy in society. The promise of public scholarship will not be realized, however, without ensuring alignment of the rhetoric of the engagement movement and the reality of university commitment. Ensuring this alignment requires that we move toward a more pluralistic vision and culture of disciplinary and university scholarship, and make a significant investment in university and faculty capacity-building grounded in a substantive, long-term public scholarship research initiative.

References

Alter, T. 1987. "Increasing Our Effectiveness as Public Policy Educators." In *Increasing Understanding of Public Problems and Policies-1987*, 236-240. Oak Brook, IL: Farm Foundation.

Austin, A. E. 2002. Preparing the Next Generation of Faculty: Graduate School as Socialization to the Academic Career. *Journal of Higher Education* 73(1): 94-123.

Austin, J. E. 2000. *The Collaboration Challenge: How Nonprofits and Businesses Succeed through Strategic Alliances.* San Francisco, CA: Jossey-Bass.

Bonnen, J. T. 1986. A Century of Science in Agriculture: Lessons for Science Policy. *American Journal of Agricultural Economics* 68(5): 1065-1080.

Church, R. L. et al. 2003. Measuring Scholarly Outreach at Michigan State University: Definition, Challenges, and Tools. *Journal of Higher Education Outreach and Engagement* 8(1): 141-152.

Clearinghouse and National Review Board for the Scholarship of Engagement. "Evaluation Criteria for the Scholarship of Engagement." http://schoe.coe.uga.edu/evaluation/evaluation_criteria.html.

Committee on Evaluating Quality Outreach. 2000. Points of Distinction: A Guidebook for Planning and Evaluating Quality Outreach. East Lansing, MI: Michigan State University.

Council on Outreach. 1997. *Commitment to the Wisconsin Idea: A Guide to Documenting and Evaluating Excellence in Outreach Scholarship.* Madison, WI: University of Wisconsin-Madison.

Gurgevich, E., D. Hyman, and T. Alter. 2003. Creation of UniSCOPE: A Model for Rewarding All Forms of Scholarship. *Journal of Asynchronous Learning Networks* 7(2): 1-7.

Hyman, D. et al. 2000. UniSCOPE: A Multidimensional Model of Scholarship for the 21st Century. University Park, PA: The UniSCOPE Learning Community.

Hyman, D. et al. 2001/2002. Beyond Boyer: The UniSCOPE Model of Scholarship in the 21st Century. *Journal of Higher Education Outreach and Engagement* 7(1 and 2): 41-65.

Fischer, F. 2000. *Citizens, Experts, and the Environment: The Politics of Local Knowledge.* Durham, NC: Duke University Press.

Kellogg Commission on the Future of State and Land-grant Institutions. 1999. *Returning to Our Roots: The Engaged Institution.* Washington, DC: National Association of State and Land-grant Colleges.

Korten, D. C. 1984. "People-centered Development: Toward a Framework." In *People-centered Development: Contributions toward Theory and Planning Frameworks,* ed. D. C. Korten and R. Klauss, 299-333. West Hartford, CT: Kumarian Press.

Kotter, J. P. 1996. *Leading Change.* Boston, MA: Harvard Business School Press.

Lerner, R. M. and L. K. Simon. 1998. "Directions for the American Outreach University in the Twenty-first Century." In *University-community Collaborations for the Twenty-first Century: Outreach Scholarship for Youth and Families,* ed. R. M. Lerner and L. K. Simon, 463-481. New York, NY: Garland Publishing.

Provost's Committee on University Outreach. 1993. "University Outreach at Michigan State University." East Lansing, MI: Michigan State University. http://www.msu.edu/unit/outreach/missioncontents.html.

Schon, D. A. 1983. *The Reflective Practitioner: How Professionals Think in Action.* New York, NY: Basic Books.

Sullivan, W. M. 2003. Engaging the Civic Option: A New Academic Professionalism? *Campus Compact Reader* (summer): 10-17.

University Reappointment, Promotion, and Tenure Committee at North Carolina State University. 2003. "Recommendations to Provost and Executive Vice-chancellor for Academic Affairs and the North Carolina State University Senate." http://www.ncsu.edu/provost/governance/other_committees/URPTC/2002-2003/reports/index.html.

Weiser, C. J. and L. Houglum. 1998. Scholarship Unbound for the 21st Century. *Journal of Extension* 36(4). http://www.joe.org/joe/1998august/a1.html.

Wise, G., D. Retzleff, and K. Reilly. 2002. Adapting Scholarship Reconsidered and Scholarship Assessed to Evaluate University of Wisconsin-Extension Outreach Faculty for Tenure and Promotion. *Journal of Higher Education Outreach and Engagement* 7(3): 5-18.

Contributors

Margaret Adamek *currently serves as the special projects director at the Center for Urban and Regional Affairs, University of Minnesota. She is the founder and director of the Sugar Project, a research and practice collaborative that explores the linkages between brain biochemistry, mood and behavior disorders, and the contemporary American diet. For the last four years, she co-directed the Northern Lights Leadership for Institutional Change initiative and a national research initiative on higher education reform in the land-grant university system. Her interests include systems and social change, integration of multicultural philosophies as the basis for institutional transformation, and linkages between food, behavior, and the environment. For the last three years, she served as the chair and director of the national Food Systems Professions Education initiative. This Kellogg Foundation-sponsored institutional reform project involved over 120 institutions of higher education and focused on the reinvigoration of the civic, community, and agricultural dimensions of the land-grant university. She has worked for many years with traditional Native American communities on a variety of issues, including tribal government reform, protection of sacred resources, and cultural education for non-Indian people. Adamek is currently pursuing a doctorate in community development at the University of Minnesota. She holds a baccalaureate degree from Carleton College in African/African American Studies and French Civilization and Literature. She can be reached by e-mail at madamek@umn.edu.*

Theodore R. Alter *is professor of agricultural, environmental, and regional economics at Penn State University. He served as associate vice-president for outreach, director of Penn State Cooperative Extension, and associate dean in the College of Agricultural Sciences* *from July 1997 through July 2004. His research and education programs have focused on leadership and organizational change, the scholarship of engagement in higher education, institutional and behavioral economics, public sector economics, development economics, and comparative rural development policy. He can be reached by e-mail at talter@psu.edu.*

Roger Becker *is an extension agronomist-weed scientist in the Department of Agronomy and Plant Genetics at the University of Minnesota. Prior to joining the University of Minnesota in 1987, he was with Monsanto as a product development associate, and prior to that, an extension associate at Iowa State University. His home discipline is agronomy and plant physiology. His project goals broadly include weed management in annual and perennial systems in disturbed and undisturbed habitats. Current projects include management of purple loosestrife in wetlands, garlic mustard and buckthorn in woodlands, weed management in wild rice, processing vegetables, and the environmental impacts of herbicide and non-herbicide weed management systems. He is actively engaged in a broad array of educational efforts to improve the knowledge base in these areas. He can be reached by e-mail at becke003@umn.edu.*

Victor Bloomfield *is Vice Provost for Research and Interim Dean of the Graduate School at the University of Minnesota, where he is a member of the Department of Biochemistry, Molecular Biology, and Biophysics and the Department of Chemistry. He was head of the Biochemistry Department from 1979-91, and founding director of the Biotechnology Institute from 1983-85. His research area is physical biochemistry and molecular biophysics. He is the author or co-author of more than 200 scientific papers and three books on nucleic acids and biophysical chemistry and is a Fellow of the American Association for the Advancement of Science. Bloomfield is the University of Minnesota's representative to the Committee on Institutional Cooperation's Committee on Civic Engagement and is a member of the Steering Committee of the university's Council on Public Engagement. He can be reached by e-mail at victor@umn.edu.*

David Campbell *is a political scientist at the University of California, Davis who studies community governance by focusing on how government, private, and nonprofit organizations collaborate in local workforce, social service, and food systems networks. He serves as a cooperative extension specialist in community studies and as director of the California Communities Program (CCP) in the Human and Community Development Department. His recent research examines community planning processes occasioned by federal and state policy initiatives including welfare reform, the Workforce Investment Act, California's Proposition 10 (First Five), and the California Community and Faith-based Initiative. Campbell has conducted evaluations of state, local, and foundation-funded community development and civic engagement initiatives in over 25 California counties. A native of east Tennessee, he received his Ph.D. from the University of Oregon in 1984. Since 1989, he has lived in Davis with his wife, a Presbyterian pastor, and his teenage son. He can be reached at dave.c.campbell@ucdavis.edu or at (530) 754-4328.*

Frank Clancy *has more than 20 years of experience working as a freelance journalist, writer, and editor. His articles have appeared in numerous newspapers and magazines, including the* New York Times, *the* Los Angeles Times Magazine, Mother Jones, Health, *and the* Columbia Journalism Review. *He has written about subjects as diverse as the death penalty and basketball, race relations and golf. He's written about American Indians for* National Geographic, USA Weekend, *and other publications. He lives and works in Minneapolis and can be reached by e-mail at fclancy@reporters.net.*

William (Bill) M. Coli *is a veteran of over 25 years employment with University of Massachusetts (UMass) Extension where he is the overall coordinator of the Integrated Pest Management (IPM) Program. In addition to having over 30 years of experience in the field of IPM, Bill holds a B.S. degree from Holy Cross College and an M.S. and Ph.D. in plant science from UMass. He is academically affiliated with the Division of Entomology in the Department of Plant, Soil, and Insect*

Sciences at UMass, Amherst, where he is an adjunct lecturer. He has published numerous papers and given many talks on IPM-related research and education, regionally, nationally, and internationally. His major research interests are in the behavioral ecology of arthropod pests and their natural enemies and in developing effective monitoring devices. His most recent research focused on better understanding the role, and potential use of, naturally occurring plant defensive compounds against key apple pests. Coli is also interested in the development of Aeco-labels@, a means for farmers to be recognized in the marketplace for use of environmentally sustainable farming practices. He can be reached by e-mail at wcoli@umext.umass.edu.

Dan Cooley *spent his early years in Vermont, including several years on the family's dairy farm in Randolph Center. He attended Harvard, graduating in 1974 with a vague idea that he would like to work with plants and move back to Vermont. After getting a master's degree from the University of Vermont (UVM) working with the cold-hardiness of apples, he began working in plant pathology labs at UVM and later, at the University of Massachusetts, Amherst. The UMass, Amherst job gave him the opportunity to work on the apple IPM project and eventually get a Ph.D. in plant pathology in 1986. He continued to work with UMass Extension in apple IPM and developed a nationally-recognized program in strawberry IPM. In 1991, he joined the faculty at UMass, Amherst, and consequently became director of the Agriculture and Landscape Program in UMass Extension and the first director of the Center for Agriculture. His research and teaching interests continue in the ecology of diseases and the development of sustainable methods for plant disease management, focused largely on fruit crops. He can be reached by e-mail at dcooley@microbio.umass.edu.*

Susan Damme *is an assistant professor in the Department of Education, University of Minnesota, Duluth. She teaches in an online graduate program in education that emphasizes critical pedagogy and learning communities. She has extensive experience developing and facilitating learning communities in several content areas and settings, including* extension and community education. Her background is in psychology (B.A. and M.A. from the University of North Dakota), organizational development, and adult education (Ph.D. from the University of Minnesota). She can be reached by e-mail at sdamme@d.umn.edu.

Gail Feenstra is the food systems analyst at the University of California Sustainable Agriculture Research and Education Program (SAREP), based in Davis, California. She coordinates SAREP's Food Systems Program, which encourages sustainable community development that links farmers, consumers, and communities. Her research and education efforts include direct marketing, farm-to-school programs, urban agriculture, food security, food policy, and food system assessments. Feenstra's professional training is in nutrition. She has a doctorate in nutrition education from Teachers College, Columbia University. She is also a registered dietitian. She is past president of the Agriculture, Food, and Human Values Society and associate editor of Renewable Agriculture and Food Systems (formerly the American Journal of Alternative Agriculture). In her spare time she loves to garden and cook using foods from her local foodshed. She may be contacted at UC SAREP at (530) 752-8408, or by e-mail at gwfeenstra@ucdavis.edu. For more information about SAREP's Food Systems Program, see www.sarep.ucdavis.edu.

Jeffrey Gunsolus is a professor and extension agronomist specializing in weed science in the Department of Agronomy and Plant Genetics at the University of Minnesota. The primary objective of his extension program is to develop a more sustainable corn and soybean production system using the principles of safe, effective, and cost-efficient weed management. His weed management research program is designed to be applicable to corn and soybean growers' needs and the primary objective is to help growers diversify their weed management program. He is currently investigating how economic risk-efficiency can be used to improve weed management decision making for producers with differing attitudes toward economic risk and with differing time management constraints. Gunsolus received his B.S. and M.S. degrees in animal *ecology and agronomy from Iowa State University and his Ph.D. degree in crop science from North Carolina State University. He can be reached at gunso001@umn.edu. For more information about his applied weed science research and extension program, see http://appliedweeds.coafes.umn.edu/.*

Margo Hittleman *has worked for more than two decades as an adult educator, community organizer, and professional writer, and for the last five years, as an action researcher as well. Through her own consulting company, she facilitates workshops related to participatory program planning and evaluation, community and organizational development, grassroots leadership development, personal empowerment, alliance building, and organizing for systemic social change. In addition, she has served as a development associate for the Center for Religion, Ethics and Social Policy, an information specialist for the Family Life Development Center, and director of the Community Self-Reliance Center, all based in Ithaca, New York. She also co-founded and edited a monthly newspaper,* Community Ink. *She has a B.A. in Biology and Society and an M.A. in Adult and Extension Education, both from Cornell University. She is currently completing her Ph.D. in Adult and Extension Education at Cornell. Her academic work focuses on organizing processes of collective reflection and the dynamic interaction between individual, organizational, and communitywide processes of learning and change. She may be reached by e-mail at mjh18@cornell.edu.*

Nicholas Jordan *is a professor in the Department of Agronomy and Plant Genetics at the University of Minnesota, and director of Graduate Studies for the Sustainable Agricultural Systems Graduate Minor Program. His background is in plant ecology and evolutionary biology. He is interested in the development of more biologically, socially, and economically diversified and sustainable forms of agriculture. Relevant to this broad interest, his research program addresses ecological questions focusing on fostering the symbiotic relationship between plants and beneficial soil organisms as an essential foundation of sustainable farming. He is also interested in the crucial challenge of* *combining scientific rationalities with other rationalities in order to create an adequate knowledge base for sustainable agriculture. Currently, he is working to help organize and conduct participatory action research on local coalitions of social groups in support of multifunctional agriculture production systems. Jordan received his B.A. degree in biology from Harvard College, and his Ph.D. in botany and genetics from Duke University. He can be reached by e-mail at jorda020@umn.edu.*

Marianne Krasny *is professor and director of graduate studies in the Department of Natural Resources at Cornell University. In cooperation with her colleagues and graduate students, she is developing ways to integrate science learning with intergenerational mentoring, multicultural understanding, and community action. She is currently working with U.S. and South African colleagues to create educational programs that combine the indigenous knowledge of community gardeners and small-scale farmers with the knowledge of research scientists. Her programs provide opportunities for U.S. and international graduate students to teach and assess student learning in schools and community settings. Dr. Krasny received her B.A. degree in human development from Cornell University, B.S. in botany from the University of Washington, and M.S. and Ph.D. in forest ecology from the University of Washington. She can be reached by e-mail at mek2@cornell.edu. For more information about* Garden Mosaics, *see www.gardenmosaics.cornell.edu.*

Karen Lehman *has worked on food systems for more than two decades. Beginning with an award-winning documentary on women in farm movements for the PBS series* Matters of Life and Death, *she expanded her work to encompass policy and practice in local, national, and international arenas. She held the Endowed Chair in Agricultural Systems at the University of Minnesota, through which she did the work represented in this book. She has consulted for the Ford and Communitas Foundations on peasant agricultural development in Mexico and Central America and has developed recommendations for national and global agriculture policy for the Institute for Agriculture* *and Trade Policy. She is the co-founder and current board member of the Youth Farm and Market Project, an urban youth-based food system program supported by the U.S. Department of Agriculture's Community Food Projects grants. Lehman was awarded a Bush Leadership Fellowship in 2001 to focus on local food system development. She has a B.A. in third-world studies from Macalester College, a master's degree in public administration from the John F. Kennedy School of Government at Harvard University, and has done advanced course work in public health. She may be reached by e-mail at Karen_Lehman@post.harvard.edu.*

***Hana Niemi-Blissett** is currently working as a farm educator at Gale Woods Farm in Minnetrista, Minnesota. She works to develop and deliver educational programs to all ages that demonstrate the practices and culture of contemporary small-scale production farming and promote land stewardship through agriculture education. She received her M.S. from the University of Minnesota in applied plants sciences/ agroecology and her B.S. from Northland College. Her thesis work focused on outcomes of learning collaboratively in agriculture. She can be reached by e-mail at hana_blissett@hotmail.com.*

***David Pelletier** is a biological anthropologist with a B.S. and B.A. from The University of Arizona in 1977 and an M.A./Ph.D. from The Pennsylvania State University in 1979/1984. He joined the Division of Nutritional Sciences at Cornell University as a post-doctoral associate in 1984 where he conducted nutrition research and policy/program work in developing countries until 1994, through collaborations with UNICEF, USAID, WHO, the World Bank, and other organizations. In 1994 he began a tenure-track faculty position at Cornell and expanded his focus to include nutrition policy issues in the U.S. as well as developing countries, with responsibilities for research, teaching, and outreach. His primary interests relate to developing, applying, and evaluating improved methods for policy analysis and development at community and national levels, with a special focus on the integration of scientific/technical information and social/normative considerations* *through methods for direct public involvement. Current policy concerns include genetically engineered foods, iron overload in the U.S. (arising from a gene-nutrient interaction), soy sauce fortification in China, and child malnutrition in developing countries. He can be reached by e-mail at dlp5@cornell.edu or on the web at http://nutrition.cornell.edu/.*

Scott Peters *is an assistant professor in the Department of Education at Cornell University. He received a B.S. in education (1983) from the University of Illinois at Urbana-Champaign, an M.A. in public policy (1995) from the University of Minnesota's Humphrey Institute of Public Affairs, and a Ph.D. in educational policy and administration (1998), also from the University of Minnesota. Before his graduate study, Peters served for nearly ten years (1984-1993) as program director of the University YMCA at the University of Illinois. His work there was focused on civic education and community development, pursued through a variety of community-university partnerships. His 1998 book,* The Promise of Association, *chronicles the history of the University YMCA for its 125th anniversary. Peters' current research program combines the study of the history of American higher education's civic mission and work with a study of the contemporary civic education and community development practices of academic professionals. His work has been published in several journals, including* Agricultural History, *the* Michigan Journal of Community Service Learning, *the* Journal of Higher Education Outreach and Engagement, Higher Education Exchange, *and the* Journal of Extension. *He can be reached by e-mail at sp236@cornell.edu.*

Steve R. Simmons *is a Morse-Alumni Teaching Professor of Agronomy and Plant Genetics at the University of Minnesota where he has served since 1977. His home discipline is plant physiology and ecology, but he is best known for the use of qualitative research approaches to address agronomically—and agroecologically—relevant questions. He maintains a strong interest in education in which he has led initiatives that utilize pedagogies that foster student-centered, reflective learning, such as decision cases, problem-based learning, and experiential learning. He teaches* *agroecology courses that are suited for students from a very broad array of academic backgrounds. He also has advanced the use of memoir writing as an approach to help foster deeper reflection for faculty regarding their lives as teachers. He can be reached by e-mail at ssimmons@umn.edu.*

Ellen Smoak *was born in Asheboro, North Carolina, a small textiles town. Her parents instilled in her at an early age the importance of service to the community. After enrolling at the University of North Carolina, Greensboro (UNCG), she completed her bachelor's degree in 1974 and her master's degree in 1978. Her doctoral degree, also from UNCG was completed in 1994. She has been part of the Cooperative Extension Program at North Carolina A&T State University since 1975. The majority of her work has focused on educational program development, training, and evaluation. Special interests include protective clothing and equipment for farmers and farm workers, special needs clothing, water quality issues, human health and safety with emphasis on pesticide poisoning prevention, and children's environmental health issues. Currently she is involved with community/ school gardens with an emphasis on introducing youth and adults to the myriad of opportunities found in a garden. Scholarship interests focus on educational programming for youth and adults with low literacy skills, with an emphasis on learning-style preferences. She is particularly interested in facilitating processes that provide underserved audiences an opportunity to realize options and potentials, allowing them to improve and enhance the quality of their lives. She can be reached by e-mail at smoak@ncat.edu. For more information about* Down-to-Earth, *the science education curriculum she developed with her colleague Bob Williamson, see www.ag.ncat.edu/extension/ programs/dte/index2.html.*

Susan White *is a research fellow in the Department of Agronomy and Plant Genetics at the University of Minnesota. She is an organizer of learning groups and is particularly interested in working with farmers, regional citizen groups, and her colleagues at the University of Minnesota and the Minnesota Extension Service to facilitate the development of site-specific farm management strategies that provide environmental and economic benefits, as well as benefits to society. White received her B.S. degree in agricultural education and M.S. degree in agronomy from the University of Minnesota. She can be reached by e-mail at white009@umn.edu.*

Robert "Bob" Williamson *was born a "New Year's Baby" in southern Virginia to parents who encouraged him to escape the destructive atmosphere that surrounded him in the public housing neighborhood in which they lived. As a youth, he developed an interest in science and community service. In 1967, he moved to Washington, D.C., where he received his bachelor's degree in 1971 and a master's degree in 1973 from Howard University. He earned a doctoral degree from the University of Massachusetts at Amherst in 1978. All three degrees are in science. He has taught various science courses at several universities, most recently at Tuskegee University. He also spent more than 14 years working as a research wildlife biologist and forester for the USDA-Forest Service. Since 1984, he has worked as a natural resources specialist for the Cooperative Extension Program at North Carolina A&T State University. Williamson remains an educator as well as an advocate for the rights of brokenhearted, neglected, and abused children. He can be reached by e-mail at robertw@ncat.edu. For more information about* Down-to-Earth, *the science education curriculum he developed with his colleague Ellen Smoak, see www.ag.ncat.edu/Extension/programs/dte/index2.html.*